PRAYER
IN THE
HEBREW BIBLE

OVERTURES TO BIBLICAL THEOLOGY

Editors

WALTER BRUEGGEMANN, Professor of Old Testament at Columbia Theological Seminary, Decatur, Georgia

JOHN R. DONAHUE, S.J., Professor of New Testament at the Jesuit School of Theology, Berkeley, California

SHARYN DOWD, Professor of New Testament at Lexington Theological Seminary, Lexington, Kentucky

CHRISTOPHER R. SEITZ, Associate Professor of Old Testament, Yale Divinity School, New Haven, Connecticut

The Drama
of
Divine-Human
Dialogue

PRAYER IN THE HEBREW BIBLE

Samuel E. Balentine

FORTRESS PRESS   Minneapolis

PRAYER IN THE HEBREW BIBLE
The Drama of Divine-Human Dialogue

Library of Congress Cataloging-in-Publication Data

Balentine, Samuel E. (Samuel Eugene), 1950–
    Prayer in the Hebrew Bible : the drama of divine-human dialogue / Samuel E. Balentine
        p. cm.—(Overtures to biblical theology)
    Includes bibliographical references.
    ISBN 0-8006-2615-X (alk. paper):
    1. Bible. O.T.—Prayers. 2. Prayer—Biblical teaching.
3. Worship in the Bible. I. Title. II. Series.
BS1199.P68B35   1993
248.3'2'0901—dc20   92-20553
                                                          CIP

The paper used in this publication meets the minimum requirements of American National Standard for Information Sciences—Permanence of Paper for Printed Library Materials, ANSI Z329.48-1984.   ∞™

Manufactured in the U.S.A.   AF 1-2615
97   96   95   94   93   1   2   3   4   5   6   7   8   9   10

To
Betty, Graham, and Lauren

.

Contents

Editor's Foreword

When the Overtures series was initiated in 1977, Scripture studies were in a state of great methodological confusion. Since that time, the methodological confusion has considerably abated. Now literary-rhetorical and sociological analyses have clearly emerged as especially useful tools for reading the text, even though they were scarcely in purview in the late seventies. The acceptance and articulation of these methods have both permitted and required the study of texts to be done in a way that would not previously have been possible—or accepted.

The present study by Samuel Balentine is a fine example of these recent methodological developments. Balentine shows himself to be an effective practitioner of these methods, and we are treated to a thoughtful, suggestive reading of the texts.

Balentine has employed literary methods to show that the texts are not simply ways of voicing communication but ways of presenting, portraying, and making present the characters who are involved in prayer. Literary understanding of texts as the *articulation of character* helps us see that prayer texts are not only reportage of what was said but ways in which the tradition constitutes Israel's long memory of communication with God, as a resource for each succeeding generation. Thus Abraham, Elijah, or Hezekiah at prayer are different personalities than they would have been prior to that prayer or without that prayer. Moreover, the prayer texts not only sketch out human personality but also provide a fresh characterization of God. We can conclude that, in a dramatic dimension, the God of Israel would not be this particular God in this particular way without the utterance of this prayer. Balentine's literary analysis thus helps us see that in the biblical text, prayer is a constitutive activity. While prayer serves the constitutive traditioning process of the Deuteronomist (or the Chronicler or some other traditionist), we are prepared to push beyond the traditioning process to say that prayer is constitutive theological activity in a more foundational way for Israel.

In parallel fashion, Balentine makes effective use of emerging sociological method in two ways. First, he pays particular attention to the social location of the scholar (and this particular scholar, Balentine) in the context of the church and of the guild. This initial reflection in the book helps us understand why this kind of scholarly study of prayer is possible and appropriate just now, after such a long time when the subject seemed not to be available for scholarly consideration. The changed sociological situation of scholarship has legitimated a new enterprise of study.

Second, Balentine has used sociological awareness to notice that justice is a major theme of Israelite prayer, and that prayer in Israel is indeed a vehicle for theodicy. That is, prayer is an arena for the adjudication of the incongruity between divine promise and purpose, and human experience and prospect. Israel prays not only in characteristic ways but about characteristic concerns. This awareness excludes any excessive spiritualizing or privatizing of Israel's prayer, or rendering anemic Israel's practice of prayer. Rather, prayer is held very close to the crises and possibilities of social reality.

The results of literary analysis—that prayer is a mode of constitutive characterization, and the results of sociological analyses— that prayer has as its concern social crisis and social reality—are crucial for Balentine's argument. These methods permit the raising of specific issues and the insistence on particular convictions.

These two gains however—prayer as *characterization* and prayer as *theodic vehicle*—only prepare us for Balentine's primary concern, which is properly theological. This is not a study of literary or sociological matters. Rather, it is a bold and provocative theological study. Balentine is clear that prayer is reflective of and derived from the reality of faith. Thus his chapter entitled "In the Beginning God" makes clear that questions of prayer definitely refer to the particular God addressed in prayer. Prayer is possible only because from the outset Israel stands in relation to this particular God who is available for and amenable to such communication. Thus Israel's prayer can never be studied as *how to*, can never be subsumed as spiritual exercise or as religious discipline, without at the same moment acknowledging the *who* of Yahweh, the *what* of covenant, and the *wherefore* of Israel's faith.

Conversely, Balentine also sees that prayer is not only an echo of faith but a constitutive, imaginative practice of faith that itself generates and yields theology. Thus prayer is "two-way traffic between heaven and earth" (p. 48), serious traffic that impinges upon both partners. Israel prays this way because it has this faith; but Israel also is able to embrace such faith because it persists in this particular practice of prayer.

In the end, Balentine has established two points that will be crucial for subsequent discussion. First the practice of prayer, the claims of theology and the power of faith are integrally related. This may not be the case generally or phenomenologically, but it is so in the Hebrew Bible. It follows, on the one hand, that theology cannot be a cerebral, propositional activity but is always the particular characterization of those (divine and human) who people faith. It follows, on the other hand, that prayer is never a detached, pious activity subject to trivialization but an action whereby the claims of the gospel are voiced and over which there is a life-and-death struggle. The propensity to divide theory and practice, proposition and piety, is overcome when one sees that everything of faith is at issue in this activity; everything is unsettled and everything has the chance of settlement.

Second, Balentine has made a convincing case for the interrelatedness of critical and theological activity. To be sure, the prayer texts are embedded in intentional traditions. Thus the prayer of Jacob serves a pentateuchal tradition, and the prayer of Hezekiah is a vehicle for the *Tendenz* of the Deuteronomist. That much we have long known, and we have often stopped there in our thinking. This book shows why and how we must not stop there. Even though the prayer text is always embedded in a traditioning context and intent, it is at the same time—and through the embeddedness—the very way Israel does theology. There is no unembedded theology in Israel. Thus the prayer text is at the same time the historical voice of Hezekiah, the traditioning voice of the Deuteronomist, and the believing voice of canonical Israel, which "holds to God against God." This outcome of Balentine's argument warns us against both a theology that is not embedded in tradition and prayer that is not embedded in a traditioning environment. Neither Israel's faith nor Israel's prayer can happen in a vacuum, without rootage in text and membership in a traditioning process.

In my judgment, Balentine has made a major gain for us in overcoming a long-standing and embarrassing bifurcation. Scholars have not wanted to study prayer and have often stopped with the more general theological program of the Deuteronomist. Pious believers have treated prayer without reference to critical study, because such critical study did not let prayer be prayer but made it a lesser, more calculated activity. Now we can see that a prayer text is a vehicle for a *Tendenz* of the tradition, a vehicle for theological argument, and a vehicle for fresh construals of God and human characters. Prayer is all of these; we may not and need not choose from among them.

This gain past the old categories has in part been made possible, as Balentine indicates, by the changed climate of scholarship, which also reflects the changed needs of our society. That change, however, is only part of the reason for such a fresh argument. The other part is Balentine's passion, erudition, and courage in honoring and taking seriously both his roles as a scholar and as a believer.

Balentine has forged new categories of analysis beyond our old critical pigeonholes. In the end, he has shown that prayer is neither a marginal activity undertaken after intellectual analysis nor an act of piety to fend off critical study. Rather, prayer is an action and a matrix in which every dimension of trust and obedience is at work: at work in the text for the character who prays, at work in the traditions that have embedded and transmitted the prayer to us, at work in the reading community of which we are a part. These prayer texts have required and permitted much hard, disciplined work in the long traditioning process. Now they offer to us an act of communication and a special world that refuses the voicelessness of technical society. In this world of Israel's faithful prayer and prayerful faith, the heavens are not empty, and the earth need not be mute.

Walter Brueggemann

Preface

The journey toward the completion of this book has been long and eventful. Without the support and encouragement of a host of friends I could not have stayed the course. The bulk of the first draft of the manuscript was written during a sabbatical leave at the Georg-August-Universität in Göttingen. I am deeply grateful to the Alexander von Humboldt Foundation for the research fellowship they awarded me, and to Professor Rudolf Smend for his kind and attentive assistance as my "host professor" during my stay in Göttingen.

Walter Brueggemann invited me to contribute a book on "prayer" to the OBT series several years ago. Although I have taken far longer to complete the work than I wanted, Walter has remained always patient, always supportive. I cannot thank him enough for his help.

Several persons read the manuscript as it was developing and offered helpful suggestions for its improvement. I am especially grateful to James Barr, Terry Fretheim, and James Crenshaw. My colleagues Glenn Miller and Keat Wiles also provided valuable critiques and editorial suggestions. Many of the deficiencies that remain in the book can likely be attributed to my failure to follow good counsel when it was offered.

I wish also to express a special word of appreciation to Mary Lou Stephens, Judy Durham, and Evelyn Carter, who typed the manuscript and worked with me so patiently through seemingly endless revisions and retypings. Without their help the project could not have been completed.

Most of all I thank my family, Betty, Graham, and Lauren, to whom this book is dedicated. During the course of my work on this book there has been much turmoil in our lives. On more than one occasion it has been their prayers that have sustained me. I know of no better witness than they to the Hebraic commitment to prayer that binds heaven and earth together in unyielding relationship.

Samuel E. Balentine

Abbreviations

AB	Anchor Bible
BHH	Biblisch-Historisches Handwörterbuch
BHS	*Biblia hebraica stuttgartensia*
BZ	*Biblische Zeitschrift*
BZAW	Beihefte zur *Zeitschrift für die alttestamentliche Wissenschaft*
BZNW	Beihefte zur *Zeitschrift für die neutestamentliche Wissenschaft*
CBQ	*Catholic Biblical Quarterly*
ErIs	*Eretz-Israel*
EvT	*Evangelische Theologie*
FOTL	Forms of the Old Testament Literature
GKC	*Gesenius' Hebrew Grammar*, ed. E. Kautsch, trans. A. Cowley
HAR	*Hebrew Annual Review*
HBT	*Horizons in Biblical Theology*
HTR	*Harvard Theological Review*
HUCA	Hebrew Union College Annual
ICC	International Critical Commentary
IDBS	*Interpreter's Dictionary of the Bible Supplement*
Int	*Interpretation*
IRT	Issues in Religion and Theology
JAAR	*Journal of the American Academy of Religion*
JB	Jerusalem Bible
JBL	*Journal of Biblical Literature*
JQR	*Jewish Quarterly Review*

JSOT	*Journal for the Study of the Old Testament*
JSS	*Journal of Semitic Studies*
JTS	*Journal of Theological Studies*
LXX	Septuagint
MDOG	*Mitteilungen der deutschen Orient-Gesellschaft*
MT	Masoretic Text
NJPS	New Jewish Publication Society Translation
NRSV	New Revised Standard Version
OBT	Overtures to Biblical Theology
OLZ	*Orientalische Literaturzeitung*
OTL	Old Testament Library
OTS	*Oudtestamentische Studiën*
PEQ	*Palestine Exploration Quarterly*
REB	Revised English Bible
RevExp	*The Review and Expositor*
RGG	*Die Religion in Geschichte und Gegenwart*
RHPR	*Revue d'histoire et de philosophie religieuses*
RSV	Revised Standard Version
SBT	Studies in Biblical Theology
TDOT	*Theological Dictionary of the Old Testament*
THAT	*Theologisches Handwörterbuch zum Alten Testament*
TQ	*Theologische Quartalschrift*
USQR	*Union Seminary Quarterly Review*
VT	*Vetus Testamentum*
VTSup	*Vetus Testamentum* Supplements
WBC	Word Biblical Commentary
ZAW	*Zeitschrift für die alttestamentliche Wissenschaft*
ZDMG	*Zeitschrift der deutschen morgenländischen Gesellschaft*
ZKT	*Zeitschrift für katholische Theologie*
ZTK	*Zeitschrift für Theologie und Kirche*

CHAPTER 1

The Subject
and the Interpreter

> It is a difficult and even formidable thing to write on prayer,
> and one fears to touch the Ark.
>
> P. T. Forsyth, *The Soul of Prayer*

As the research for this book progressed, this observation by P. T. Forsyth has taken on an ever-increasing significance. While I cannot be certain of all that led Forsyth to this judgment, I do share his sense of intimidation before this particular subject. On the one hand, to address the subject of prayer in a scholarly publication, even when restricted to the relatively narrow confines of Hebrew Bible study, is to approach an area that historically has not been accorded much attention. It has certainly not occupied the passions and interests of Hebrew Bible scholars in the same way as other themes. Although several recent publications may suggest a change in this situation, one has the impression that this subject has been considered more suited to other forums of discussion, for example, devotional tracts or other spiritual self-help resources, where a steady interest in prayer remains. On the other hand, one may understand the *practice* of prayer as so pervasive in most communities of faith, so commonly—even routinely—the habit of most believers, that a study of prayer seems unnecessary. Indeed, some quarters may view such a study as an academic undermining of what is at heart a fundamentally personal act of piety.

My sense of the pull of these two contrasting perspectives—the one subtly implying that prayer is unworthy of scholarly scrutiny, the other that it inherently resists such investigation—has hovered over the production of these words like an unpredictable cloud. Can a study of prayer find a place in the serious reflections of both the academy and the church? Or will both, for different reasons, deem it unnecessary, perhaps even unwarranted? It is a difficult and formidable challenge indeed.

Why then this book? Why this particular subject from this particular interpreter?

Several years ago Walter Brueggemann surveyed contemporary trends in Hebrew Bible theology and ventured some "provisional wonderments" about the cultural contexts that have provided and shaped our scholarly paradigms.[1] Whether or not he was right in his identification of the forces that shaped the specific theologies on which he focused, Brueggemann was on target with his wonderment about the influence of cultural context on biblical scholarship. Economic and political circumstances shape not only us and our worldview; they shape also our commitments, our passions pursued as scholarly interests, and our presuppositions in marshalling the resource material in support of the claims we think it ought to make. Whether we are members of a confessing community or scholars within an academic context (or both), to a significant degree our work will be an extension of who we are. It is prudent, therefore, to heed Brueggemann's counsel and to "practice enough self-knowledge and self-criticism to be aware of what we are doing."[2]

When I first read Brueggemann's article I was already involved in the early stages of research into the prayers of the Hebrew Bible. I was preoccupied, and contentedly so, with the usual questions: identifying the Hebraic vocabulary of prayer, isolating prayer texts, reaching for a workable definition of prayer. I had not thought to ask why I was working on this particular subject, or what had interested me in prayer and was already likely influencing the work I had begun. It was simply enough to recognize that here was a subject that deserved more attention, a subject that in my reading and thinking I had simply stumbled onto. But Brueggemann's probes set me to thinking not about the subject of prayer per se but about myself and my relation to this subject. I began to think about my social location (to use an expression currently in vogue), and about what might be pushing me toward this subject. I continued to wonder about these factors as the research progressed; now that I am prepared to place my ideas before the reader, it may be useful to preface them with a statement about the influences that are important in shaping my commitments.

---

1. W. Brueggemann, "A Convergence in Recent Old Testament Theologies," *JSOT* 18 (1980): 2–18.

2. Ibid., 15.

Although I have pondered these matters for some time now, I must hasten to acknowledge the unscientific character of my thinking. I am not trained as a sociologist, nor do I possess the tools to assess critically the economic and political influences that are at work shaping my worldview. My reflections are admittedly more restricted to and more guided by personal experience. Yet I have reflected quite a lot on two dimensions of my world that seem to have been influential in shaping the presentation of Hebrew Bible prayer offered here. First, I write as a member of the church as one for whom prayer is an act of faith and belief. Second, I write as a member of the academic community as one for whom faith commitments are neither resistant to nor unaffected by new discoveries and changing demands.

THE CONTEXT OF THE CHURCH

Within the context of the church I have been introduced both to the vitality of prayer within the Christian faith and to its lifelessness, at least as it has often been practiced in my experience. On the one hand I learned from both family devotions and from corporate worship that prayer is an integral part of those occasions when people consciously seek to communicate with God. In my home Bible reading was always followed by prayer; in my church Bible reading, singing, and preaching were always accompanied by prayer. In my Protestant tradition prayers were offered by the pastor and also by laypersons who were called on to pray. As spontaneous as these prayers appeared—we did not generally use set or printed prayers—I began to notice a certain sameness in what was offered. From pastor to participants, stereotypical invocations and conclusions embraced prayers that God would bless, heal, forgive, direct, in accordance with the divine will. These were primarily prayers of submission, acknowledging clearly the sovereignty of God and human dependence. As a young boy I had no cause or need to think that prayer should be anything else.

On the other hand in this same context I first began to realize how woefully irrelevant such prayer could sometimes be. Not coincidentally, it seems to me now, the first shaking of my foundations came as a result of social and political upheavals that intruded into my small, secure world. To be specific, the war in Vietnam thrust me, and a whole generation of idealistic youth, into a world of questions for which no one had prepared us. The issues were quite complicated, and individuals confronted and articulated them in a variety of ways. For me the situation ultimately developed into a struggle to find some equilibrium between Jesus' command to love one's enemies—a message whose meaning was interpreted for me by the various voices of passive or nonviolent resistance of the day—and the civil obligation to comply with the laws of the land—a summons that the church interpreted for me, with the aid of select New Testament texts, as a divine mandate to render to Caesar the duty that was required. Caught between my own immature sense of commitment to both these summons, I began to question many of my former certainties. Stripped of all its intellectual and spiritual veneer, the simple question for me became, Should I fight *in* this war or *against* it? Once I began to decide for one option and against the other, I found myself paralyzed by an even more daunting question—Why?

I naturally turned to the church for guidance in this situation. In a conversation with my minister I shared the questions I had been mulling over and the rather radical options I had been considering. He was a warm and sensitive person, educated and theologically trained, and I am sure what he said contained much wisdom that I cannot now recall. But one comment set me on my heels and remains carved in my memory: "Sam, you must not question God; you must simply obey." It was a comment I suppose I should have anticipated, given the nature of the worship, including the prayers, in which I had been nurtured since my childhood. I had never heard anyone question God, so far as I could remember. Certainly no one had ever been encouraged to question God. As long as my life was relatively stable, it had never occurred to me to do so either. But with stability swept away, the situation was quite different, and somehow, although I did not know why, I knew that minister had to be wrong.

I must beg the reader's indulgence for this foray into a simple and embarrassingly personal episode. I have taken the liberty of reporting it, because it has turned out to be a seminal experience in explaining my commitment to both church and academy. The church taught me how to pray and, more subtly, how not to pray. One was to praise God, but not protest; to petition God, but not interrogate; and in all things to accept and submit to the sometimes incomprehensible will of God, never challenge or rebel. Yet when life's circumstances would not permit either such passivity or such piety, this advocacy of a rather monotonic relation to God seemed destined to silence if not exclude me and, I suspected, other struggling questioners from the ranks of the truly committed, the genuinely faithful. "You must not question God." If one cannot question God, then to whom does one direct the questions? If God is a God whom we cannot question, then what kind of God is this to whom we are committing ourselves?

I realize that I began to see these questions through the very narrow window of personal experience. Given the same historical and social circumstances, a different minister in a different church may have responded to my pleas for help with counsel that could have spared me much of the struggle that followed. Yet I suspect that my experience has not been atypical. As a seminary professor I have had the privilege to participate with churches within my denomination in a variety of roles: as Bible teacher, guest lecturer, supply or interim preacher. My consistent experience has been that most people are well acquainted with the difficulties of life in relationship with God. Few have escaped the personal and social upheavals that pummel us with questions which press faith commitments to the limit of endurance, and often beyond. When people are invited to articulate such experiences *within* the context of faith, the typical reaction is first one of hesitance, accompanied by guilt, and then, at least on occasion, a sense of relief and embrace. "Why have I never heard this before?" I am often asked. Why indeed?

I am persuaded that at least the church of my experience has engaged in a conspiracy of silence—a tacit agreement among those responsible for steering the worship and educational emphases of the church to be optimistic in their outlook of the world, sometimes to the extent of denying radical evil; to be hopeful in expectation of redemption and deliverance, often to the point of denying the possibility of the tragic; and to embrace and encourage probes, wonderments, and questions about life's purpose, and about God, only within contexts carefully calculated not to leave the answer in doubt. Douglas Hall has observed that given this incapacity for the negative, Christianity is reduced to promoting the "official religion of the officially optimistic society. . . . What is offensive to the sensitive is Christian naïvety—not about science, but about evil."[3]

How has it come to be this way? I do not think one can argue that the social situations of the post–World War II generation have provided more insulation than before against experiences of negation. This generation surely has known sufficient disappointment and disillusionment to arouse anxiety and doubt. But somehow the

---

3. D. Hall, *Lighten Our Darkness: Toward an Indigenous Theology of the Cross* (Philadelphia: Westminster, 1976), 112.

church has managed, at great cost, to maintain a level of non-engagement with hurt and doubt that threatens to rob life in relation to God of its vitality and its honesty.

Upon what biblical basis have we been able to get the consent of our minds to mount and to maintain such emphases? That was the question my minister's remarks posed for me years ago. The Bible clearly does not support the portrait of a God before whom one cannot question, doubt, petition, and sometimes demand clarification, even modification or reversal, of divine intentions. At first these questions were only instinctive, not carefully or critically raised. I had no way of knowing for certain whether I could find answers or whether, if I uncovered them, I would agree with them. But with these kinds of motivations—and yes, preconditioned hopes and concerns—I found myself on the beginning of a journey whose next stop was the critical inquiry of biblical scholarship.

THE CONTEXT OF THE ACADEMY

If the church has been slow to embrace models of the human response to God other than obedience and pious submission, one can hardly argue that the academic emphases of biblical scholarship have provided much encouragement to do otherwise. With respect to the broad area of Hebrew Bible theology, for example, Brueggemann's analysis of the contemporary situation makes clear that contemporary scholarship has been slow to incorporate themes from the Psalms and the wisdom materials into the total picture.[4] To put the edge on this point one needs only to recognize that it is in the Psalms, with their witness to the legitimacy of lament within the context of faith, and in the sapiential literature, with its probes into

---

4. Brueggemann's specific focus is on three publications of 1978 (C. Westermann, *Theologie des Alten Testaments in Grundzügen;* S. Terrien, *The Elusive Presence;* and P. Hanson, *Dynamic Transcendence*) in which he detects a common dialectical approach to Hebrew Bible theology. For Westermann the governing dialectic may be described as "deliverance/blessing," for Terrien "ethical/aesthetic," for Hanson "teleological/cosmic." Correlating the first members of each of these pairs, Brueggemann observes that each author, in his own way, has chosen a similar means of categorizing the emphases that constitute the theology of the Hebrew Bible. The "deliverance/ethical/teleological" pole of the dialectic provides the means for addressing the historical-covenantal traditions, upon which an earlier generation of scholars had focused (notably G. von Rad and W. Eichrodt). The second half of each pair, "blessing/aesthetic/cosmic," allows for the inclusion of psalmic and sapiential materials that, in the judgment of each of these authors, previous theologies have neglected.

righteous suffering, the order and disorder of the cosmos, and the justice of divine retribution, that these darker dimensions of the life of faith have their opportunity for center-stage discussion in the Hebrew Bible. The academy's tendency to slight or ignore these materials leaves the impression that the majority voice of Israelite faith and piety speaks in tones of praise and thankfulness for divine order and providential care, with only minor interruptions of dissent or disquiet. Given this emphasis in the academy, in the divinity schools and seminaries whose task is to provide theological and practical instruction for the ministers of the church, my pastor's remarks may be understood as but a small witness to the effectiveness of his theological education.

Perhaps one can now discern a change in the academy's orientation that will address biblical themes heretofore too neglected. Brueggemann himself has recently pointed the way forward with a new proposal that insists on securing a place for those traditions voicing the struggle to "embrace the pain" that inevitably accompanied the Israelite experience with God.[5]

Whether the academy's orientation has indeed shifted and, if so, to what extent the academy will support such a shift remains to be seen. My concern here is Brueggemann's suggestion that one's participation in pursuing certain biblical themes, at whatever level, will be influenced by one's position in relation to two broad sociological settings: the confessing community and the academy. I want to acknowledge that this has been the case in my own work. Indeed, whereas Brueggemann's analysis might suggest that these two contexts support rather fixed lines of inquiry and commitment that perhaps seldom engage one another, or if so only with some loss of commitment on both sides, for me and for many others the challenge is to participate responsibly and effectively in both church and classroom. Hence I judge it important for those who invest themselves in the discussion of prayer that follows to attempt a description of how my own academic pursuits, when coupled with faith commitments, have directed me to this particular study.

Although I did not realize it at the time, I took the first steps toward the making of this book some years ago during my doctoral research. The substance of that work has been published as *The Hidden God,* a title that perhaps is sufficient to indicate something

---

5. W. Brueggemann, "A Shape for Old Testament Theology, I: Structure Legitimation," *CBQ* 47 (1985): 28–46; "A Shape for Old Testament Theology, II: Embrace of Pain," *CBQ* 47 (1985): 395–415.

of my controlling interests at the time.[6] In that work I isolated and analyzed Hebrew vocabulary carrying the theme of the hiddenness of God, as perceived and articulated by the Israelites at numerous critical junctures of their experience. I arrived at rather predictable, though at the time largely unexplored, conclusions: it is simply the nature of Israel's God to be both present and absent, both near and at times seemingly quite distant and uninvolved. The Hebrew Bible candidly acknowledges that the requirements of faith in such a God are exacting. Sometimes the unrelenting questions "Why?" and "How long?" could be addressed convincingly by a recognition of sinfulness. By offering appropriate confessions of guilt and petitions for forgiveness, one could channel the disruptive potential of the experience into renewed commitments of faith. This recommendation is the standard prophetic response to the crisis of faith raised by the specter of exile. Yet other texts report many occasions when such explanations carried little weight, and if pushed in the face of the believer's protest of innocence, they could be branded as a lie or as a cover-up in the defense of a God vulnerable to the charge of injustice. The classic example here is the Book of Job.

In retrospect, two impressions gained from this earlier work have continued to command my attention, the one in more general ways, the other more specifically related to the project at hand. First, with respect to the broad topic of the hiddenness of God, I was surprised to find that scholars have had so little interest in this theme. This neglect is made all the more obvious by the attention given to exploiting the countertheme of the presence of God. I cannot at this point account satisfactorily for the academy's tilt toward presence rather than absence. Since the 1979 publication of S. Terrien's *The Elusive Presence,*[7] however, an increasing number of studies suggest that the academy is moving toward a more holistic portrait of the God of the Hebrew Bible.[8]

A second impression contributes more directly to the present

6. S. E. Balentine, *The Hidden God: The Hiding of the Face of God in the Old Testament* (Oxford: Oxford Univ. Press, 1983).

7. S. Terrien, *The Elusive Presence: Toward a New Biblical Theology* (New York: Harper and Row, 1979).

8. E.g., J. Crenshaw, *A Whirlpool of Torment: Israelite Traditions of God as an Oppressive Presence* (OBT; Philadelphia: Fortress, 1984); R. Davidson, *The Courage to Doubt: Exploring an Old Testament Theme* (London: SCM, 1983); T. Fretheim, *The Suffering of God* (OBT; Philadelphia: Fortress, 1984); W. Lee Humphreys, *The Tragic Vision and the Hebrew Tradition* (OBT; Philadelphia: Fortress, 1985); M. Marty, *A Cry of Absence* (New York: Harper and Row, 1983); B. Vawter, *Job and Jonah: Questioning the Hidden God* (New York: Paulist, 1983).

investigation. Once one begins to credit more fully the Hebrew Bible's candid presentation of God as both predictably near and ever responsive and unpredictably distant, or at least silent, and seemingly in need of arousal, then the role of prayer within the life of faith should assume new importance.

In my previous study I had already begun to probe in this direction. I suggested that prayer can function for the believer as both a means of *articulating* the dilemma posed by God's hiddenness, including the doubt, protest, and anger that often accompany such experiences, and a means of *coping* with these experiences.[9] To the extent that one addresses these matters to God in prayer, one shifts the burden of responsibility for dealing with them away from self and toward God, who alone has the power to provide ultimate solutions. Although such an action seldom insures either concrete or simple resolutions, it does offer a means of maintaining dialogue between God and people, even in the midst of chaos. Without this dialogue the believer is reduced to monologue that threatens a skepticism with the potential to overwhelm faith. One indication of how this possibility may become reality is found in the Book of Ecclesiastes. Here prayer is no longer held out as an effective means of achieving stability in a world dictated by an impenetrable fate (Eccl 5:2; cf. 3:19; 9:2).

I understand this study of prayer to be a logical follow-up to my earlier investigation. It is in essence a continuation of the probe into how the Hebrew Bible portrays and encourages relating to a God who is both present and hidden. Further, the reader will discern in what follows a decided sympathy for prayers that make bold to challenge the hidden God. This sympathy will be most evident in my discussion of the prayers for divine justice and the lament tradition. It has also clearly been influential in shaping my understanding of the relation between lament and praise as it is worked out in the context of both ancient and contemporary worship. These particular emphases, and others less specifically focused throughout the book, reflect my persuasion that prayer in the Hebrew Bible is dominated primarily by the never-ending need of believers to maintain some divine-human dialogue in the face of the imbalance between expectation and experience.[10] I believe the text supports this particular emphasis, as I will try to make clear. Yet I am also aware

---

9. Balentine, *Hidden God,* 164–76.

10. Cf. Hall's discussion of human life as "a dialogue between expectation and experience" (*Lighten Our Darkness,* 19–35).

that this perceived emphasis is happily consistent with my own interest in such a message. While I cannot account for why others have perhaps valued this perspective less, I can recognize at least some factors that have made it important for me. In this respect I have no doubt that I am still driven to secure this particular message as legitimate rebuttal to my minister's counsel of many years ago.

If I admit to both professional and personal motivations for pursuing the subject of prayer and for understanding it in certain ways, I am confident that numerous others go before me who could have, or perhaps better, should have, made similar confessions. In the following chapter I focus in more detail on some previous work on this subject. Here I wish to comment only on one particular part of the history of this research that relates directly to my concern with a scholar's dual commitment to both church and academy.

Quite a number of studies on prayer tend to attribute both previous neglect and previous misunderstanding to something generally referred to as "Protestant bias." One of the earliest references belongs to J. Hempel. In a 1921 lecture entitled "Aus dem Gebetsleben des Alten Testaments," Hempel attributed the neglect of prayer both in biblical theology in general and among evangelical scholars in particular to two interrelated causes: (1) the emphasis on "intellectualism" inherited from the Reformation and the Enlightenment; and (2) in keeping with this intellectual orientation, the Protestant preference for investigation of doctrine or theory rather than issues associated with living piety.[11] Affirming the evaluation of his contemporary F. Heiler, Hempel lamented that the evangelical church was in danger of falling behind the Catholics in the intensity of their prayer life.[12]

Three years prior to Hempel's lecture, Heiler had published the first edition of his monumental study *Das Gebet*.[13] In this work he sought to distinguish genuine prayer (i.e., the simple, spontaneous

---

11. This lecture was published, along with a second address ("Die Bedeutung des Exils für die israelitische Frömmigkeit") under the title *Gebet und Frömmigkeit im Alten Testament* (Göttingen: Vandenhoeck und Ruprecht, 1922). My reference is to Hempel's opening comments, which appear on p. 3.

12. Ibid.

13. F. Heiler, *Das Gebet: Eine Religionsgeschichtliche und Religionspsychologische Untersuchung* (Munich: Verlag von Ernst Reinhardt, 1918). Heiler's work was reissued through five editions in German, and published in English as *Prayer: A Study in the History and Psychology of Religion* (London, New York, Toronto: Oxford Univ. Press, 1932). Unfortunately I did not have access to the first edition. Although Heiler did make modifications in subsequent editions, the substance of his thinking as I have represented it here did not change. Throughout this work I have relied on the English translation.

outpourings of the heart) from formal, literary prayers. In Heiler's judgment, the latter were artificial compositions intended for education and instruction, and as such represented little more than weak reflections of true prayer. He linked genuine prayer, with its heartfelt petition at the center, to Protestant emphases and the more formal prayers to the Catholic preference for mysticism. M. Greenberg has described this linkage as indicative of a "romantic Protestant predilection for the free spirit of the individual."[14]

Greenberg's recognition of the "Protestant predilection" that often influences scholarly assessments of Hebrew Bible prayer is by no means a lone voice of criticism. Such criticism also played a significant role in S. Mowinckel's critique of H. Gunkel's treatment of the individual Lament Psalms. Recognizing the strong note of individualism in these psalms, not to mention their candid and graphic protests and complaints, Gunkel concluded that these prayers were ultimately considered inappropriate for cultic worship. They functioned instead as the private, spiritualized prayers of individuals who prayed outside the ritual of temple worship. Mowinckel charged that this tendency to see personal expressions of faith as separated from the more formal occasions of public worship was merely the result of Gunkel's own "Protestant lack of understanding of the importance of cult and of its real essence."[15]

Subsequent work on the Psalms has repeatedly raised the same criticism. E. Gerstenberger, who has sought to sharpen the understanding of cult in accordance with modern sociological insights, has criticized Gunkel's neoromantic, Protestant preoccupation with private religion.[16] More recently H. G. Reventlow's criticism of the Protestant tilt in the study of prayer has extended this argument even farther. He criticizes repeatedly what he refers to as the *"neuprotestantische"* opposition between cultic and private piety that, in his judgment, has resulted in the effort to impose modern

14. M. Greenberg, *Biblical Prose Prayer As a Window to the Popular Religion of Ancient Israel* (Berkeley, Los Angeles, London: Univ. of California Press, 1983), 39.

15. S. Mowinckel, *The Psalms in Israel's Worship* (2 vols. repr. in 1; Nashville: Abingdon, 1962), 1.12–22. The quotation is from p. 14.

16. E. Gerstenberger, *Der bittende Mensch* (Neukirchen: Neukirchener Verlag, 1980). Gerstenberger has emphasized the importance of the family as the "primary group" in which personal piety has its *Sitz im Leben.* This primary group is seen to function as the small social unit that bridges the gap between individual and community, retaining its identity as a forum for personal piety without giving up its cultic commitments and connections. In this sense it is both individual and cultic in its orientation. For Gerstenberger's criticism of Gunkel, see pp. 154–55.

sociological and anthropological assumptions on ancient litera-ture.[17]

Whether or not one may credit (or charge, as the case may be) the Protestant orientation of some scholars with influencing (or mis-influencing) the study of prayer to the extent some would claim, the criticism has been raised enough for one to take note. My own sense is that the comingling of academic and religious influences in bibli-cal scholarship is more often the rule, not the exception, regardless of the particular subject of focus. Perhaps the subject of prayer only makes more apparent the connections between faith commitments and academic commitments. Unlike some subjects that one may more easily restrict theoretically to the desk or the classroom, prayer is inherently both an idea and an act. Those who are drawn to analyze the idea are very often, perhaps inevitably, influenced by habits acquired in practicing the act. In any case I am compelled to remember the counsel to "practice enough self-knowledge and self-criticism to be aware of what we are doing."

I am well aware that the kind of introspection I have engaged in here is not common in scholarly works. I can anticipate the criti-cism that such an introduction undermines any claim to objectivity in the presentation that follows. I am in fact focusing on a canon within the canon, one particular part of the Hebrew Bible's witness to which I am drawn for personal as well as professional reasons. My presentation of the meaning of this material and of the claims I understand it to make are certainly products of both these per-spectives. While I am trained to approach a text critically, my own life's circumstances have prepared me to hear its message in par-ticular ways. It is appropriate, therefore, to acknowledge that my understanding of Hebraic prayer is offered, self-consciously, as the product of a vigorous "wrestling with the angel"[18] in the ebb and flow of life lived in relation to God.

---

17. H. G. Reventlow, *Gebet im Alten Testament* (Stuttgart: Kohlhammer, 1986), 174, 176, 297, 299, 301, 304, 312, 315.

18. The reference is to the Jacob narrative in Gen 32:22-32. For its use as a description for the scholar's engagement with literary records, though in a different perspective than the one I adopt here, see Daniel J. Boorstin, "The Historian: 'A Wrestler with the Angel,'" *New York Times Book Review,* Sept. 20, 1987, 1.

CHAPTER 2

The Method

Once interpreter and subject are joined, a third element must be stirred into the mix before a written product can take shape: method. By choosing certain methodologies or approaches rather than others, the researcher shapes the resource material in intentional ways. With respect to previous studies of prayer, it is hard to overlook the fact that one methodology in particular—form criticism—has been the primary avenue of investigation. The form-critical approach has coincided with the decision to locate the primary examples of Hebraic prayer in one particular genre of literature: poetry, more specifically, the Psalms. Indeed, with the foundational studies of Gunkel, Mowinckel, and C. Westermann, as well as a host of recent commentators, most notably Reventlow, discussion of the form and function of psalm prayers has attained a level of sophistication and depth heretofore unparalleled.

The present study differs from most previous studies of prayer by focusing primarily on prose and nonpsalmic prayers. For the analysis of these prayer texts, I suggest that form criticism is less useful. In this chapter I seek to develop this argument by surveying some influential previous studies. First, I look at studies that have taken the form-critical route, and then at three works in particular that have attempted to move beyond form criticism. Next I describe the major contours of the approach I follow here.

PREVIOUS STUDIES:
COMPARATIVE RELIGION AND FORM CRITICISM

In the early decades of this century scholars had considerable interest in prayer as a general religious phenomenon, particularly as a device for the comparative study of religion. Several studies of note fall into this category, for example, those of E. B. Tylor, W. James, and G. van der Leeuw.[1] But perhaps the most extensive and certainly the most influential work with respect to the Hebrew Bible is that of F. Heiler, *Prayer: A Study in the History and Psychology of Religion.*[2]

As the subtitle suggests, Heiler's interest is decidedly psychological in orientation. He seeks to identify and to describe the religious genius (in his words, the "naive" piety) that issues forth in devotional communion between a person and God. These "outpourings of the heart," wholly free, informal, and unpremeditated, represent the "spontaneous utterings of the soul" that are worthy of the label "genuine prayer." From the occasions of their first ("primitive") emotional discharge, such prayers in the course of time achieve written form. Through frequent repetition in association with occasions of formalized ritual, Heiler argues, the *form* of the prayer comes to be regarded as more important than the *content.*[3]

In the opening pages of his study Heiler states the thesis that shapes his presentation of all that follows:

> Genuine, personal prayer conceals itself in delicate modesty from the eyes and ears of the profane. . . . The personal devotional life of men of religious genius is lived in secret. . . . To be sure, we know thousands and thousands of prayers which have come down to us chiselled on stone or printed in letters, prayers from ancient temple libraries, and prayers in modern books of devotion. . . . But all these are not the genuine, spontaneous prayers that break forth from the deepest need and innermost yearning of the human heart. . . . Formal, literary prayers are merely the weak reflection of the original, simple prayer of the heart.[4]

Heiler goes on to find an echo of the truly genuine prayer in prophetic prayer.[5] With this as the Hebraic model, he proceeds to

---

1. E. B. Tylor, *Primitive Culture: Researches into the Development of Mythology, Philosophy, Religion, Language, Art, and Custom* (3d ed.; 2 vols.; London: John Murray, 1891). See, e.g., 2.362–74. W. James, *The Varieties of Religious Experience: A Study in Human Nature* (New York: Collier Books, Macmillan, 1961, 1985), 359–71. G. van der Leeuw, *Religion in Essence and Manifestation* (2d ed.; 2 vols.; New York: Harper and Row, 1963), 2.422–34, 519–26.

2. F. Heiler, *Prayer: A Study in the History and Psychology of Religion* (Oxford: Oxford Univ. Press, 1932).

3. Ibid., 71.

4. Ibid., xvii–xviii.

5. Ibid., 228–85. By "prophetic" Heiler refers not just to the Hebrew Bible prophets but to a broad range of biblical and post-biblical personalities (e.g., Jesus, Luther, Zwingli, Calvin, Kierkegaard) who, "while retaining their own spontaneity, independence, and individuality, have been inspired by these biblical characters" (227).

describe the shortcomings of prayer practice in other traditions. He is especially critical of traditions with philosophical or mystical orientations, emphases that in his judgment push genuine prayer to the periphery of religion.

Heiler's insistence on treating only the spontaneous, nonliterary expressions of piety as genuine prayer leaves him with a serious problem. In his view the very act of writing brings with it the transformation of once authentic words into the artificial product of literary form.[6] Since these formal, literary prayers are only "faint reflections" of the genuine article, Heiler is forced to acknowledge that "most sources of prayer are, therefore, only indirect evidences."[7] S. Gill has assessed the consequences of Heiler's orientation in sharp terms:

> Heiler's study of prayer, therefore, was a failed effort from the outset in the respect that he denigrated his primary source of data for his study of prayer, leaving him wistfully awaiting the rare occasion to eavesdrop on one pouring out his or her heart to God.[8]

As Gill suggests, most if not all of one's knowledge for understanding ancient traditions of prayer comes from texts.[9] Whatever the original, spontaneous utterings were, one no longer has the luxury of hearing them directly. Only through texts does one have the opportunity to peer back into the proximity of the experience. As Gill goes on to observe, "Prayer texts almost without exception and to a degree as part of their nature, are formulaic, repetitive, and static in character, much in contrast with the expected free and spontaneous character of prayer."[10] When Heiler's psychological orientation to the subject is joined with the fact of the literary nature of the resource material, a dilemma results. At the very least there is an incongruity that places Heiler's considerations in a "nonproductive position."[11]

The advent of form criticism as a tool of biblical exegesis launched a new era that provided a different orientation to ancient

---

6. Ibid., xix.

7. Ibid., xviii.

8. S. Gill, "Prayer," *Encyclopedia of Religion,* ed. M. Eliade (16 vols.; New York: Macmillan; London: Collier Macmillan, 1987), 11.490.

9. Cf. Gill's helpful distinctions between prayer as *text* (collection of words), *act* (the human act of communicating, including the elements of performance that constitute the act), and *subject* (e.g., in doctrine, instruction, philosophy, theology) (ibid., 489–93).

10. Ibid., 489.

11. Ibid., 490.

texts. Especially as pioneered by Gunkel and Mowinckel, this tool focused serious attention on the form of biblical literature and the formulaic language that gave it its particular shapes. As applied specifically to the Psalms, form criticism began to play the lead methodological role in the study of biblical prayer.

Gunkel and Mowinckel's delineation of the basic types of psalms and their supposed settings in the life experiences of ancient Israel are sufficiently well known as to require no review here.[12] Suffice it to say that so influential has their work been that in the ensuing years Psalms research has been preoccupied with efforts at refining their proposals in two major areas: form and setting. With respect to particular forms of psalms, attention has focused primarily on psalms of lament and psalms of praise. Westermann's distinction between "descriptive" and "narrative" praise, as well as his call for reevaluating the theological importance of the form of lament, has been particularly influential.[13] Concerning the so-called cultic *Sitz im Leben* of the Psalms, considerable attention has focused on providing some clarity as to what should be understood by the term "cultic." The most stimulating and provocative suggestions have come from Gerstenberger and Albertz. On sociological grounds, Gerstenberger has argued for appreciation of the family as the social unit that binds individual to larger cult.[14] Albertz has attempted to capitalize on this idea by contrasting the personal piety emerging out of this primary religious group with the official religion of institutionalized piety.[15]

My interest is not in detailing the history of Psalms research, the scope and complexity of which this brief survey hardly conveys. I want only to suggest that with respect to the Psalms, which, allowing for some nuancing of the term, may be understood as the most concentrated resource for biblical prayer, discussion has seldom moved beyond the fundamental questions of form and setting. Notable exceptions are particularly the studies of Westermann and

---

12. The seminal works are H. Gunkel and J. Begrich, *Einleitung in die Psalmen* (3d ed.; Göttingen: Vandenhoeck und Ruprecht, 1966); S. Mowinckel, *Psalmenstudien* (6 vols.; Kristiania: J. Dybwad, 1921–24); cf. idem, *The Psalms in Israel's Worship* (2 vols. repr. in 1; Nashville: Abingdon, 1962).

13. Westermann, *The Praise of God in the Psalms* (Richmond: John Knox, 1965); idem, *Praise and Lament in the Psalms* (Atlanta: John Knox, 1981).

14. E. Gerstenberger, *Der bittende Mensch* (Neukirchen: Neukirchener Verlag, 1980), 113–68.

15. R. Albertz, *Personliche Frömmigkeit und offizielle Religion* (Stuttgart: Calwer, 1978), 23–96.

Brueggemann.[16] In the main, however, a comprehensive presentation of the *function* of the Psalms within the living worship of ancient Israel has not yet been done.

Still more relevant for the present discussion is the carryover of Psalms research and the methodology of form criticism to the study of prayer. The enduring influence of the form-critical approach on biblical prayer is evident in what are arguably the three most important books on prayer in the Hebrew Bible published since Heiler. The works of A. Wendel, L. Krinetzki, and H. G. Reventlow define and interpret biblical prayer primarily in relation to the Psalms.[17] Both Krinetzki and Reventlow employ form-critical designations to identify and isolate prayers of praise and prayers of lament, and both draw their examples almost exclusively from the Psalter.[18]

Wendel concentrates on the prose prayers of Genesis—2 Kings, prayers he determines to be free from the cultic sphere of institutionalized worship. Even so, the prose prayers he isolates are defined in accordance with the form-critical designations of Psalms' *Gattungen* (e.g., "the praise prayer," "the lament prayer," "the prayer of penitence"). Wendel's procedure is to address to these prayers the typical form-critical concerns of form, time, place, and cause or occasion. Finally, he offers theological observations that are almost always extrapolated from within the individual forms

---

16. Particularly helpful have been Westermann's discussions of the theological importance of blessing (*Blessing in the Bible and the Life of the Church* [OBT; Philadelphia: Fortress, 1978]) and lament ("The Role of the Lament in the Theology of the Old Testament," *Int* 28 [1974]: 20–38; repr. in *Praise and Lament*, 259–80). For an idea of how such themes contribute to the larger picture of Old Testament theology see his *Elements of Old Testament Theology* (Atlanta: John Knox, 1982), 153–216. For Brueggemann note esp. "Psalms and the Life of Faith: A Suggested Typology of Function," *JSOT* 17 (1980): 3–32; *The Message of the Psalms* (Minneapolis: Augsburg, 1984).

17. A. Wendel, *Das freie Laiengebet im vorexilischen Israel* (Leipzig: Eduard Pfeiffer, 1931); L. Krinetzki, *Israels Gebet im Alten Testament* (Aschaffenburg: Paul Pattloch, 1965); H. G. Reventlow, *Gebet im Alten Testament* (Stuttgart: Kohlhammer, 1986).

18. For example, Reventlow addresses the prose prayers that occur outside the Psalter, esp. the intercessory prayers of the prophets (*Gebet*, 229–64) and the prayers of penitence in Ezra 9, Nehemiah 9, and Daniel 9 (ibid., 275–86). But in his judgment such prayers derive from and remain dependent on the cultic tradition of prayer represented in the Psalms.

Reventlow's thesis concerning the cultic background of prayer is important and forcefully presented, and I have not done it justice here. For a more detailed response see my review in *JBL* 107 (1988): 299–301. My concern here, however, is with methodology, and on this point Reventlow does not break with the form-critical approach of his predecessors.

themselves, not from their function within the narrative contexts in which they are located. In essence he treats these narrative prayers like the Psalms, as if their literary context was nonexistent, or as if such a context did not seriously affect their meaning.

One comes away from these form-critical approaches to biblical prayer with two impressions. First, beginning with Gunkel and Mowinckel the study of biblical prayer has been hardly distinguishable from the study of the Psalms. As a result scholars have progressed to firm ground in understanding various prayer forms and the settings from which they derive. One should not undervalue this solid achievement. Yet, second, scholars have come to a position in which a significant body of prayer texts—namely those in prose narratives—receive little attention on their own. The form-critical methodology, with its inherent tendency to standardize and to categorize, essentially strips these prayers of significant contact with the one element of their literary setting that is decidedly different from the Psalms—their narrative context.

THE PRESENT APPROACH:
LITERARY AND THEOLOGICAL FUNCTIONS

Perhaps a new approach is in order. In this study I place the emphasis squarely on just these narrative prayers. I do so partly in response to the prevailing neglect in the academy to which I have just alluded. But more importantly, prayers embedded in narrative contexts often provide insight into the literary and theological functions of prayer not afforded in the Psalms. My work on these prayers has benefited from three particular studies that seek in different ways to move beyond form criticism. Unfortunately two of these remain in the form of unpublished theses, hence their availability is rather restricted. Because I refer frequently to these, as well as to M. Greenberg's short monograph, a summary of their emphases is in order here.

Recognizing the limitations of form criticism, J. Corvin sets out to add a new element to the consideration of prose prayers. By applying what he refers to as "functional criticism," he divides prose prayers into two broad categories with respect to their relation to a literary context. He assigns the largest number of prayers to the category "contextual prayers."[19] In Corvin's judgment, the

19. J. Corvin, "A Stylistic and Functional Study of the Prose Prayers in the Historical Narratives of the Old Testament" (Ph.D. diss., Emory University, 1972), 156.

content of such prayers is so integrally related to the narrative context in which they appear that they have little or no meaning outside this context.

One of the most interesting and revealing characteristics of these prayers is their conversational orientation.[20] Pray-ers and God dialogue with one another, converse with one another, as if nothing more were involved than the casual interchange customary between peers. The language of these conversational prayers is in this regard strikingly simple. Most are introduced by the expression *"X* said *['āmar]* [to God]."* In a number of cases a simple request of a pragmatic nature follows (e.g., for water, Exod 17:4; for healing, Num 12:13-14; for guidance in choosing a leader, Num 27:15). The request anticipates and usually receives a concrete and immediate divine response. These prayers are neither profound nor complex. They do not typically raise issues of theological or philosophical importance. Because of the nature of their request, they do not require extended dialogue on the part of either suppliant or God. Prayers of this description Corvin labels "single-response prayers."[21]

The conversational framework may nevertheless take up issues of fundamental gravity. Corvin identifies two of the most frequent problems addressed by the suppliant in these cases as "innocent suffering" and "proof of God's presence."[22] In these instances, because of what is at stake—nothing less than the fundamental issue of God's presence—one finds a rather extended question-centered dialogue initiated by the suppliant. What is portrayed is a mutual effort between God and suppliant to arrive at some resolution or understanding of the problem.

A second category of prose prayer, labeled "formal prayer," is much less dependent on the immediate narrative context.[23] In fact, given their liturgical tone and their focus on issues not fundamental

20. Ibid., 159.

21. For the full discussion of these prayers see ibid., 180–91. Prayers designated as "single-response" are listed in appendix I (257–58) as follows: Gen 17:18; 24:12-14; Exod 5:22-23; 6:12, 30; 17:4; 32:11-13; 34:8-9; Num 12:13-14; 16:15; 27:15-17; Deut 3:23-25; 9:25-29; Josh 7:7-9; Judg 6:36-39; 13:8; 15:18; 16:28; 1 Sam 12:10; 2 Sam 15:31; 24:10, 17; 1 Kgs 17:20-21; 18:36-37; 2 Kgs 6:17, 18, 20; 20:2-3; 1 Chr 4:10; 21:17; 2 Chr. 14:11; 30:18-20; Neh 4:4-5; 6:9, 14.

22. Ibid., 169–73.

23. Ibid., 203–14. The list of such prayers appears in appendix I (261) as follows: Gen 32:9-12; Num 14:10-19; Deut 21:7-8; 26:5-10; 26:13-15; 2 Sam 7:18-29; 1 Kgs 8:22-61; 2 Kgs 19:15-19; 1 Chr 17:16-17; 29:10-19; 2 Chr 6:14-42; 20:6-12; Ezra 9:6-15; Neh 1:4-11; 9:6-38.

to the immediate context, these prayers usually appear to interrupt the logical sequence of the narrative. When lifted out and taken as individual, self-contained literary units, neither they nor the narratives from which they are removed suffer any perceptible loss of meaning. With respect to both style and vocabulary, Corvin suggests that formal prayers give the impression of having been consciously composed for oral delivery during ceremonial or ritual occasions.[24]

Based on his delineation and analysis of these two types of prose prayers, Corvin offers certain historical and theological observations.[25] In the evolution of prayer forms he proposes a gradual shift away from the conversational prayer, which dominates in the Tetrateuch, particularly in the J narrative, toward an increasing formality. Although formal prayers are by no means frequent—Corvin lists just fifteen total in the whole Hebrew Bible—they do begin to appear with a relatively higher frequency in monarchical and postmonarchical contexts.

This shift in form he identifies with changing theological perceptions. Early sources (for Corvin J is the key witness) picture God as more immanently involved in the affairs of humanity, a perception that is carried by the tendency to portray God in intimate, often casual, conversation with human partners. Beginning with the monarchy Corvin finds a shift away from this anthropomorphic style. The court prophet becomes the spokesperson for God. The direct divine-human encounter characteristic of earlier traditions begins to diminish. As the distance increases between God and humanity in this process of communication, prayers become more elaborate and formalized, espousing for didactic purposes a perception of God's sovereignty decidedly more transcendent in character. To summarize, Corvin proposes an evolution from conversational to formal prayers in keeping with a shift in theological perception from God's immanence to God's transcendence.

E. Staudt's focus is restricted to prayers that occur in the Deuteronomistic literature (Deuteronomy—2 Kings). He suggests three specific criteria for isolating prayers within these texts: prayer is

---

24. Ibid., 206. Corvin observes that formal prayers are distinguished by five rather consistent features. Although individual prayers may lack some of these features, all five are present in the prayer recorded in Ezra 9: (1) the use of the technical prayer terminology *pālal,* "to pray" (cf. Ezra 10:1); (2) reference to a primary audience, "before the Lord" (9:5); (3) reference to a secondary audience, "before the assembly" (9:4: 10:1); (4) the use of the conjunction *'attāh,* "now," to mark an important transitional juncture (9:10); and (5) invocation of God (9:6).

25. Ibid., 79–87, 118–21.

explicit communication; it is initiated by the individual or the community as a whole; and it is effective, that is, it secures response from God.[26] With this definition he identifies seventeen stated prayers in the Deuteronomistic narratives that, taken together, share similar form-critical elements: (1) *description* of the situation that causes the prayer; (2) *introduction,* which precedes the prayer, calling the reader's attention to the actual words of the communication; (3) *invocation;* (4) *declaration,* which serves either to praise God or to justify the petition that follows; (5) *petition;* (6) *recognition,* that is, God's response to the prayer.[27]

Of these six elements Staudt argues that the petition is the stylistic and theological key to the function of prayer in Deuteronomistic literature. With regard to style, these prayers of petition occur at strategic places in a narrative. Placed between a report of some crisis in the divine-human relationship and the ultimate resolution of this crisis at a subsequent point in the narrative, these prayers have the literary effect of shaping a narrative situation. They occur in what Staudt refers to as the "hiatus" between the announcement of God's word and the event of its fulfillment.[28] God speaks or acts; people respond by questioning, challenging, or otherwise petitioning for clarification; and the outcome, from a literary perspective, is understood to be effected thereby. Staudt contends that at this point in people's engagement with God's announced intentions, prayer functions as a theological instrument in the hands of the writer. For the Deuteronomists prayer provides an opportunity both to report and to promote the role of people as coparticipants with God in the shaping of the divine will.

> Relationship does not just happen to Israel; the people play an active part both in developing and maintaining relationship to God. The place where their participation is most evident is in communication with God through prayer. That prayer presents this role of the people in this positive manner is no accident; the Deuteronomist explicitly presents prayer as the instrument for the participation of the people with their God in the unfolding history of Israel's covenantal relationship.[29]

26. E. Staudt, "Prayer and the People in the Deuteronomist" (Ph.D. diss., Vanderbilt University, 1980), 58.

27. Ibid., 71–72. The texts treated are: Deut 3:23-25; 9:26-29; 21:7-8; Josh 7:7-9; Judg 6:22; 10:10-15; 13:8-9; 15:18; 16:28-30a; 2 Sam 7:18-29; 24:10, 17; 1 Kgs 8:22-53; 17:20-21; 18:36-37; 19:4; 2 Kgs 6:17, 18, 20; 19:15-19; 20:2-3.

28. Ibid., 338.

29. Ibid., 339.

One further comment is in order here concerning the methodologies of both Corvin and Staudt. Both begin their studies by calling attention to the need to distinguish between prose prayers and Psalms.[30] Both observe in this regard that (1) prose prayers do not occur in a cultic *Sitz im Leben,* as is generally the case with the Psalms, but solely within the narrative context in which they occur; (2) prose prayers are characteristically specific in nature, not general, as with the Psalms; and (3) prose prayers are usually created for, fused into, and appropriate for only one context, unlike the Psalms, which, by virtue of their formulaic language are appropriate for many different contexts.

Precisely this attention to narrative context distinguishes these two studies from previous ones. Although they obviously differ in the details of their presentation and in the interpretation of individual prayer texts, both operate with the premise that prose prayers function both literarily and theologically in the shaping of narrative. These prayers as a rule do not function independently of narrative contexts. To miss this connection is to make the methodological error of blurring the distinction between psalm and prayer.

M. Greenberg gives pride of place to prose prayer.[31] Although his study is not lengthy, his ultimate focus is quite comprehensive in intent. He proposes that nonpsalmic prayers provide a resource for understanding the "unmediated, direct forms of popular piety" that is not equalled in any other part of the biblical witness, including the Psalms (p. 7).

Before substantiating this claim, Greenberg addresses the current neglect of these prose prayers in the description of biblical religion. If indeed they have great value "as a window to the popular religion of ancient Israel," why have they thus far been neglected? Greenberg suggests one reason may be the very "embeddedness" in literary contexts that is their distinctive characteristic (p. 8). Because prose prayers are so often part of a literary situation, scholars have tended to treat them as mere literary productions, as literary artifacts that do not provide direct or immediate witness to what actually happened. In one sense, Greenberg acknowledges, this char-

---

30. Corvin, "Stylistic and Functional Study," 46–52; Staudt, "Prayer and the People," 38–46.
31. M. Greenberg, *Biblical Prose Prayer As a Window to the Popular Religion of Ancient Israel* (Berkeley, Los Angeles, London: Univ. of California Press, 1983).

acterization is true. All prayer texts have been literarily shaped by authors and narrators. A prayer recorded in a story represents a deliberate choice of the narrator to place it in a particular position and to formulate its content in specific ways. But this shaping should not automatically consign it to the ranks of the inauthentic. As Greenberg argues, "even if it is granted that the prayers are not veridical, that does not foreclose their being verisimilar" (p. 8).

Greenberg lists some ninety-seven prose texts that record the verbal formulation of the prayer.[32] These are scattered throughout the historical books from Genesis to Chronicles, and in the prophets. The most frequently occurring type is the prayer of petition, to which he devotes primary attention.

From a form-critical perspective petitionary prayers follow a set pattern with three principal elements: address, petition, and motivation (p. 11). The form itself is understood to be quite natural, deriving logically from the circumstances of the pray-er. The pray-er needs something that only God can give. An appeal is made to God on the basis of this perceived need and in keeping with the common values shared by pray-er and God. In order to substantiate or justify the petition, the pray-er appropriates carefully chosen words in the hope of motivating God to respond favorably to the request. As important as the recognition of this set pattern is, Greenberg has a more important question: Is this pattern merely a literary creation by the author or narrator, or does it reflect the actual practice of the times? (p. 18).

To answer this question Greenberg probes social situations of interhuman communication for analogies to this divine-human petitionary pattern. He finds such patterns not only for petitionary prayer, which is directly related to petitionary address to a king, but also for prayers of confession and thanksgiving, which have similar social analogies.[33] He concludes that when biblical persons prayed they naturally employed the language of interhuman discourse because this was the only model for interpersonal communication available to them.

Further, words addressed to God follow patterns similar to those common in comparable interhuman situations (p. 20). This ob-

---

32. Ibid., 7. For the listing of texts see p. 59 n. 3.
33. Ibid., 21, 24–26, 30–37. See further R. N. Boyce's suggestion that the social situation underlying the cry *(z'q/s'q)* to God in the Hebrew Bible is the petition of the "legally marginal" to the king *(The Cry to God in the Old Testament,* Society of Biblical Literature Dissertation Series [Atlanta: Scholars Press, 1988], 27–40).

servation does not deny that biblical narrators exercised considerable literary influence over the final shaping and use of prose patterns of prayer. Yet it does warn against supposing that the narrator's presentation is entirely fanciful. Greenberg finds in these prayer texts "as faithful a correspondence as we might wish to the form and practice of everyday, nonprofessional, extemporized verbal worship in ancient Israel" (p. 37).

The failure to reckon with the importance of these prose prayers as sources for understanding biblical religion is linked, in Greenberg's opinion, to a tendency in the academy to dichotomize prayer into either free and spontaneous "outpourings of the heart" (e.g., Heiler) or prescribed and formal prayers such as those represented by the Psalms (e.g., Mowinckel, Gerstenberger; pp. 39–42). Greenberg argues that such a view does not correspond with the biblical data. The spontaneous and the prescribed in social behavior were always mixed. In interhuman as well as divine-human communication the patterned speech form, the conventional openings and closings, the traditional articulations in set situations, made spontaneity truly possible (p. 44). Such "patterned prayer-speech" would be available at all times as an option open to all people for communication with God.[34] A visit to a temple would certainly require the use of the carefully prepared texts of the temple poet. But outside a temple, and sometimes even within such a sacred setting, the Israelite might pray on impulse, without the use of prepared texts. In Greenberg's view,

> Such praying is spontaneous in that it springs from an occasion and its content is freely tailored to circumstances. At the same time it conforms to a conventional pattern of more or less fixed components (topics) appearing in a more or less fixed order. (p. 45)

Appreciation of the patterned prayer speech should illumine one's understanding of biblical prayer in two important areas. On the one hand, if these prose prayers reflect the custom of traditional interhuman discourse, then they ought correspondingly to be recognized as authentic witnesses to the everyday religious piety of the

---

34. In a study of the lament prayer, A. Aejmelaeus has called attention to the underlying pattern of "traditional prayer," which represents one of the basic modes of Hebrew speech. Like Greenberg she argues that such patterned speech, though clearly utilized in the cult, grew out of the living practice of ancient prayers. They were not cultic inventions that the people had to adjust themselves to (*The Traditional Prayer in the Psalms* [Berlin and New York: de Gruyter, 1986], 88–91).

ancient Israelite.[35] On the other hand, Greenberg is aware that, as literary compositions, prose prayers afford biblical narrators the opportunity not only to describe popular piety but also to influence it. These texts are more than just sources for understanding biblical religion; they are also a window through which to view the literary art of the Bible (p. 9; cf. pp. 46–47). One manifestation of such artfulness is the use of prayer as a means of characterization. For example, the choice of a particular motivating sentence in petitionary prayer reveals both the pray-er and his or her conception of God, because "one is persuaded to do what is shown to be most consonant with one's attributes and one's interests" (p. 13).

Although he does not particularly press the observation in this direction, one could logically extend Greenberg's comments on characterization to include the possibility that prayers serve also as literary vehicles for portraying God. Divine attributes such as mercy and compassion, judgment and wrath—or, on a larger scale, even divine presence or absence—may be highlighted by the manner of divine response to prayer. Having God grant a request or deny it, hear a petition or refuse it, may be important literary as well as theological signals for shaping a narrative sequence in accordance with particular claims about God's character.

Set against the prevailing preoccupation with the Psalms, these studies by Corvin, Staudt, and Greenberg represent a fresh approach to understanding the prayers of the Hebrew Bible. Although each retains an appreciation for the *forms* in which biblical prayers are presented, their focus on prose rather than psalmic texts has resulted in a heightened sensitivity to the *literary* and *theological functions* that these forms often serve within narrative contexts. Such concerns are predictably frustrated in the Psalms, where the context of religious address is inherently ambiguous, but they are exceedingly important for prose prayers. Here Corvin, Staudt, and Greenberg have helped to demonstrate that more often than not one's interpretation of prose prayer should depend on the context in which it is placed. Even when one can determine with a measure of confidence that a prayer is not original to a literary context, as in the case of Corvin's so-called formal prayers, one must still interpret the prayer with reference to the literary sequence that it may be interrupting. If indeed one may judge the prayer as a literary com-

---

35. For Greenberg's assessment of the religious implications which may be derived from a focus on Israel's "everyday" piety, see *Prose Prayer*, 51–57.

position, it is not thereby any less revealing of important perceptions about both God and pray-er. Staudt and Greenberg have taken important steps in describing the possibilities in this regard.

In the pages that follow I hope to capitalize upon the suggestions of Corvin, Staudt, and Greenberg concerning the literary and theological functions of biblical prayer. To this end the primary focus is on prose rather than on psalmodic texts. I am indebted to the form-critical investigations that have been so instrumental in defining types and settings of prayers, but in this connection I hope to push beyond the approach as it has traditionally been applied to the Psalms and even, in Wendel's case, to prose prayers. This approach has several methodological manifestations.

First, one may broadly describe this study as synchronic rather than diachronic. When one approaches narrative texts, especially those in Genesis–2 Kings, historical questions such as authorship, date, and redaction inevitably pose serious obstacles to exegesis. Although Corvin rather confidently assigns the majority of his contextual prayers to J,[36] one would have to consult only a few commentaries to realize that scholars disagree about the source of many of his examples. Further, the current unease in the academy concerning the historical provenance of J, whatever the texts that may be so assigned, does little to promote or to encourage certainty in such matters.

Staudt's treatment of Deuteronomistic prayers is similarly open to challenge on several fronts. The probability of multiple editions or redactions of this historical perspective means that the Deuteronomist that M. Noth so confidently assumed was responsible for much of Deuteronomy–2 Kings has become increasingly difficult to locate. Even if one can posit something like a Deuteronomistic theory or tradition of prayer, how far may one credit its influence? The Deuteronomistic shaping of traditions in Jeremiah has long been debated. R. Carroll, for example, argues forcefully that the presentation of Jeremiah as a pray-er par excellence among prophetic figures is the creation of the Deuteronomistic editors, who have shaped the portrait of the prophet to express the experiences, thoughts, and feelings of the exilic situation.[37] Beyond Jeremiah, Reventlow has noted the influence of the Deuteronomistic

---

36. Corvin, "Stylistic and Functional Study," 81.

37. R. Carroll, *From Chaos to Covenant: Prophecy in the Book of Jeremiah* (London: SCM, 1981), 114–15. For a fuller treatment of this issue see Carroll's commentary *Jeremiah* (OTL; Philadelphia: Westminster, 1987).

theory of prayer on postexilic piety, particularly in the late narrative prayers of Neh 1:5-11, Nehemiah 9, and Daniel 9.[38]

The Deuteronomistic tradition seems to become more and more comprehensive in the range of texts that scholars say fall under its influence. With respect to prayer one could mount a defensible argument that almost all the major persons to whom significant prayers are attributed—Abraham, Elijah, Moses, Samuel, Solomon, Hezekiah, Jeremiah, Ezra, Nehemiah, Daniel—are the constructs of the Deuteronomistic editors. Such a theory tends to be self-perpetuating. With theory in hand, one may duly categorize every account of recorded prayer. One cannot fail to notice growing signs of discontent with respect to the whole idea of *the* Deuteronomistic History.[39]

The uncertainty that prevails concerning the historical origins of narrative texts is enough to make one cautious. I am persuaded that Greenberg's basic premise is correct: "Every prayer text is part of a literary artifact."[40] In some cases it is appropriate to suggest that the prayer and the narrative in which it occurs show no observable seams. In other instances it seems clear that a prayer has been inserted into a literary context with the result that the narrative sequence is shaped in a way that would not be true if the prayer were removed. In some of these cases I will venture to cite a consensus opinion as to the source of the insertion. But I do so with the awareness that "consensus" opinion is directly related to a subjective decision to credit some opinions as authoritative and others as not.

In general, however, I choose not to let these questions of historical origin determine the shape of the discussion. Instead, as I have already indicated, I emphasize the function of prayer texts within narrative contexts. This emphasis no doubt means that on occasion prayers which might derive from disparate historical origins are treated together under a common theme. In this regard I am aware of the potential for distorting the original meaning of a text. In spite of this risk, I am persuaded that probing the narrative

---

38. Reventlow, *Gebet,* 277, 280, 284. Cf. O. Plöger, "Reden und Gebete im deuteronomistischen und chronistischen Geschichtswerk," *Festschrift für Günther Dehn,* ed. W. Schneemelcher (Neukirchen: Kreis Moers, 1957), 35–49.

39. For example, D. Gunn has predicted that new directions in the literary study of Hebrew narrative will lead to the "demise of the Deuteronomistic History and the adoption of Genesis to 2 Kings as a standard unit" ("New Directions in the Study of Biblical Hebrew Narrative," *JSOT* 39 [1987]: 72).

40. Greenberg, *Prose Prayer,* 8.

context of prayer has value as a legitimate witness to at least one level of a prayer's meaning.

Second, in accordance with this synchronic orientation, I do not attempt to provide here a history of prayer. Westermann has proposed a plausible historical development, from early prayers whose address is described in simple terms as calling, pleading, asking, and so forth, to later, more extensive prose prayers, whose form and content are more stylized (e.g., 1 Kings 8, Ezra 9, Nehemiah 9). In this evaluation the Psalms are representative of the midpoint in the historical development of prayer.[41]

Westermann has also noted historical development within certain forms of prayer. Particularly relevant for my emphasis here is his discussion of the prayer of lament.[42] In psalms of lament, particularly individual lamentations, the element of protest and complaint is quite strong. Confession or acknowledgment of sin seldom occur; complaint is more often accompanied by a protest of innocence. In postexilic prayers the element of complaint disappears almost completely. In its place one finds rather elaborate confessions of sin and petitions for forgiveness. This shift in emphasis is from the interrogative to the imperative, more specifically, from the protesting question "Why?" to the penitent petition "Forgive," "Have mercy." The move from protest to penitence is in keeping with the historical trauma of the exile, in the aftermath of which any protest of innocence would seem to have lost its foundation.

The broad outlines of Westermann's historical overview are quite helpful, and I suspect that he has offered as clear an understanding of prayer's development as the sources will allow. Yet within this general view of movement from simple forms of prayer to more complex and from certain emphases in prayers to others that take their place, some assumptions have gradually accrued to the larger picture that have not been productive. I include here the seemingly endless debates concerning supposed shifts from corporate to individual or from cultic to spiritualized forms of piety. Often the lines of demarcation in these particular areas, along with the values assigned to them, seem to have been too much influenced by a scholar's own sociological or religious predilections.

One other area deserves mention. A prevailing assumption among scholars has been that the prayer of lament, with its strong note of protest and its implicit charge against the justice of God, is

41. Westermann, *Elements*, 154–56.
42. Westermann, *Praise and Lament*, 165–213.

more or less a product of the exilic period. While the horror and shock of the Babylonian exile sharpened Israel's prayers and gave a heightened sense of urgency, even desperation, to their questions, one must not assume that laments of this type surfaced only in the time of the exile. Such an assumption has resulted in a tendency to portray lament as only a minor response in Israel's dialogue with God, a historical footnote to an otherwise generally optimistic and confident faith.[43] In subsequent chapters I try to show that even though one must be cautious in assigning dates to prayer texts, the significant number of lament-oriented prayers, in both prose and poetic texts, makes plausible that such a response was the norm, not the exception.

In my own presentation I do not, however, enter much into these areas of debate. I am not concerned here to secure individual texts or themes to a set place within a linear development of prayer. Greenberg has proposed that three levels of praying were coeval throughout the period of biblical literature: the patterned prayer speech, the ritual prayer, and the "totally unconventional and art-less" (e.g. 2 Sam 15:31).[44] Any person could pray at any level, sometimes at two or more levels simultaneously, at any time. Given these three levels, perhaps one should suppose that pray-ers could also logically articulate a variety of concerns at any time, in accordance with their changing life circumstances.

Third, although I am concerned to delineate the form and content of prayer texts as precisely as possible, I have chosen not to organize the discussion around these forms. In this respect I depart from the format of previous studies, whose form-critical orientation resulted in a focus on individual types of prayer: lament, praise, petition, thanksgiving, and so forth. Such studies have done much to clarify the various forms of biblical prayer, and I feel confident in directing the reader to them for the details of the discussion. Here I focus more on function than form. Thus I concentrate on prayer as a literary vehicle for providing characterization (of both pray-er and God), for addressing certain themes (e.g., divine justice), and for conveying and promoting certain postures or attitudes (e.g., penitence and contrition).

I am also concerned to attend to the use of prayer as a means of conveying ideological and theological perspectives, again in relation to both God and human partner. In this sense one may see

---

43. See further Balentine, *Hidden God,* 157–63, 171–76.
44. Greenberg, *Prose Prayer,* 46.

prayer not only as a gesture of worship, securing for the pray-er a link to the transcendent, but also as an act of engagement that seeks to secure God's active involvement in both religious and social concerns. Probes in these areas involve an effort to provide a theology of prayer, and from this basis to understand how such a theology might be incorporated into the discussion of the theology of the Hebrew Bible, and more importantly, into the faith and practice of the contemporary believer.

I must address one other issue before turning to the task at hand. How does one define prayer? Before examining the form and function of prayer texts, one must first have some working definition, some reasonable criteria, by which one can isolate particular texts for discussion. The question of definition is especially difficult, and despite several years' investment in this study, I remain somewhat frustrated that precision in this matter seems so elusive.[45] Those who have previously addressed this issue tend understandably to be content with a broad definition. For example, Corvin suggests that all communication addressed to God in the second person may be labeled "prayer."[46] Similarly, Reventlow settles for the "simplest" definition of prayer as the speech of a person or community of persons that brings before God their fundamental or current situation.[47]

Although the breadth of these definitions does permit the inclusion of a wide range of texts for consideration, it has also a number of limitations. On the one hand it leads Corvin to include a number of texts as "conversational prayers" that simply do not seem much like prayer. Would most think of the conversation with God in the garden (Gen 3:9-13) or the dialogue between God and Cain (Gen 4:9-15) as prayer? On the other hand, Reventlow includes the vow and the request for an oracle by lot as forms of prayer. While these are clearly channels of divine-human correspondence, perhaps it is wise to follow Staudt's suggestion that they are related to but not identical with prayer.[48]

Staudt has proposed one criterion that I have found especially helpful. He suggests that prayer is "explicit" communication with God,[49] by which I understand him to mean that prayer has an

45. For a preliminary attempt at definition see S. E. Balentine, "Prayer in the Wilderness Traditions: In Pursuit of Divine Justice," *HAR* 9 (1985): 53-56.

46. Corvin, "Stylistic and Functional Study," 23.

47. Reventlow, *Gebet,* 89.

48. For Staudt's distinctions between prayer and vow, see "Prayer and the People," 61-63.

49. Ibid., 58.

element of *intentionality* about it that makes it distinguishable from other, more general forms of communication. In many cases, particularly in narrative contexts, the communication that passes between God and people seems entirely casual and often dispassionate, as if nothing crucial were at stake. In other cases the communication seems to engage the participants at a different level. In these instances the human speech partner initiates the approach not casually but purposefully, intentionally. The subject of that which is communicated to God is not peripheral or insignificant. It is a subject of deep concern to the one who brings it; a subject that requires divine attention; a subject that, if left unaddressed, leaves one at best with insufficient understanding, at worst in a state of uncertainty that threatens to undermine trust in God. This is most obviously the case in prayers from the lament tradition. In such prayers what is at stake is the pray-er's sense of the trustworthiness of God in the face of defeat and loss and pain that seem unjustified.

In my own research I attempt to locate intentionality in texts in two ways, one specific, concrete, and easily verifiable, the other less specific, more a matter of interpretation and judgment, and therefore less verifiable. First, one may readily identify prayer by the presence of particular key Hebrew words and phrases like *hitpallēl,* "pray," or *qārā' běšēm,* "call on the name," which constitute part of the vocabulary of prayer, or by specific introductory expressions such as "and *X* prayed saying." Second, in addition to these clearly defined prayers, I also count as prayers texts that lack specific prayer language or clear introductions but nevertheless, in my judgment, convey intentional and weighty address to God. For example, some texts begin with the simple statement "and *X* said *['āmar]* to God," which introduces a dialogue that one may understand along the lines of Corvin's "conversational prayers." These conversations, frequent in prose narratives that address crisis situations, usually contain questions about some facet of the divine-human relationship that has gone awry or at least requires some clarification. Petition is an integral accompaniment to these questions as the pray-er seeks to move God to respond by word or deed or both.

Within these guidelines I focus primarily on recorded prayers, texts that preserve the actual words of a prayer. In addition to these texts, however, information on prayer is provided in two other ways. First, a number of texts may suggest or state that prayer has been offered, even though the words spoken are not provided (e.g., Gen 25:21; Num 11:2). In a similar fashion one finds frequent references to God's willingness to "hear" or refuse to hear prayer (e.g., Isa 30:19; cf. Isa 1:15; 16:12; Mic 3:4; Jer 7:16; 11:14), and these too shed some light on both the character of God and those who would engage in prayer. Second, although the purpose of prayer is nowhere explicitly the subject of reflection in the Hebrew Bible, it is possible on occasion to probe behind indirect references in the hope of locating prevailing assumptions. One such place that I examine is the dialogue between Job and his friends. In their counsel and in Job's rebuttal one may discern fundamentally different understandings of the purpose of prayer. Both unrecorded prayers and indirect references to prayers serve as supplementary data in the task at hand.

Having made these comments about subject and interpreter and methodology, I now turn to the Hebrew Bible's understanding of prayer, for which all that has preceded has been only preliminary. My focus is on prayer, inherently a human activity. Yet these prayers are always directed explicitly to God. Before I examine the words addressed to God, it is appropriate, therefore, to reflect on the nature of this God who both summons forth and enables such daring engagement.

CHAPTER 3

In the Beginning God

With these words the Hebrew Bible presents a confessional perspective that shapes all that follows: In the beginning God. Whatever criteria one uses to define prayer, prayer is also, perhaps especially, shaped by this same confession. All prayer is directed to God. In broad terms both the certainty of divine presence and the uncertainty of this presence most often determine the human response to God. These two responses are articulated generally as praise and lament, the one full of confidence, the other of fear. As Heiler observes, such emotions may often alternate for a long time, yet ultimately, for the one who can subscribe to the Genesis confession, trust prevails and prayer results: "Fear, therefore, may be described as the impelling, and hope as the releasing motive of prayer."[1] In this sense, whatever Israel's perception of God, whether unquestionably present or only "elusively" present,[2] it is the fact of God's presence that calls forth prayer in both its sum and substance.

Before examining the content of Israel's prayers, therefore, I pause to reflect on the Hebrew Bible's lead into these faith responses. I begin with God. What does the fact of prayer suggest about the nature and character of God? In a subsequent chapter, I address this question by probing prayer texts for underlying characterizations of God. Here, however, I want to turn the question around and ask it from a different perspective, that of the Hebrew Bible. What is it in the nature and character of God that both

1. F. Heiler, *Prayer: A Study in the History and Psychology of Religion* (Oxford: Oxford Univ. Press, 1932), 3.
2. Cf. Terrien, *Elusive Presence: Toward a New Biblical Theology* (New York: Harper and Row, 1978).

summons forth and enables the response of prayer? Such a question is all-encompassing, and any attempt to answer it completely will inevitably fall short of the mark. Here I wish only to call attention to certain fundamental Hebraic assumptions that one may consider entirely obvious, but are nonetheless centrally important. I restrict my comments to the idea of God's *relatedness,* first to humanity, and second to the world.

At the outset I acknowledge my debt in following this line of thought to the work of T. Fretheim in *The Suffering of God.*[3] The qualities that are evident in divine suffering, especially those associated with God's intimate relationship with the world, are understandably not different from those that make God receptive to prayer. In his pursuit of this subject Fretheim has therefore traversed some of the same ground, often with considerable attention to detail, that I will cover here. Although I proceed with the benefit of his analysis, I have not reproduced the supporting data for his conclusions. For the various twists and turns that some of these issues take one may consult his discussion for further clarification. For my purposes I wish to follow in his tracks for a bit, if only in a rather general way, departing where appropriate to follow the paths particularly pertinent to the subject of prayer.

GOD'S RELATEDNESS TO HUMANITY

I begin with the reminder that when the Hebrew Bible speaks of God, it almost always resorts to the language of metaphor.[4] By comparing God to other objects, both personal and nonpersonal, the Hebrew Bible assists the reader in constructing a portrait of God. The majority of these metaphors are drawn from the human sphere, thus anchoring the image of God in human experience. Hence God is described as possessing both human form (e.g., face, nose, hands, legs) and human emotions (e.g., love and hate, joy and anger). The texts witnessing to these characteristics are so pervasive throughout the Hebrew Bible that examples need not be cited here.

Most important for the discussion at hand are metaphors that suggest both the form and means of human communication and response. God is described as having a mouth, therefore speaking;

---

3. T. Fretheim, *The Suffering of God: An Old Testament Perspective* (OBT; Philadelphia: Fortress, 1984). For the discussion that follows see esp. chaps. 1–3.
4. Cf. Fretheim, *Suffering of God,* 5.

ears, therefore hearing; eyes, therefore seeing. The following texts, for example, are from the Psalms, Israel's official prayer literature.

> Incline your ear to me, rescue me speedily. . . .
> But you heard my supplications
>   when I cried out to you for help. (Ps 31:2, 22, NRSV)

> To you, O LORD, I call;
>   my rock, do not refuse to hear me,
>   for if you are silent to me,
> I shall be like those who go down to the Pit. (Ps 28:1, NRSV)

> The eyes of the LORD are on the righteous,
>   and his ears are open to their cry. (Ps 34:15, NRSV)

> The mighty one, God the LORD,
>   speaks and summons the earth. . . .
> Our God comes and does not keep silence. (Ps 50:1, 3, NRSV)

Such metaphors promote the understanding of divine-human relatedness. It is significant that they also function as foundational arguments in the effort to describe who this God is in contrast to other gods, and why communication to and from this deity promises more than can be had in the religions of Israel's neighbors. When temptations arise to stray toward other gods, the reminder of their basic inability to communicate is meant to discourage the Israelite from turning to them.

One may consider, for example, the polemics against idolatry in Isaiah (40:18-20; 41:7; 44:9-20; 45:20; 46:5-7). To those in Babylonian exile who, in their despair and disillusionment, shop for alternatives to fidelity to God, Isaiah poses the question, "To whom will you liken God or what likeness will you compare with God?" (40:18; cf. v. 25; 46:5). The idol? How silly, the prophet charges. Consider how such gods are *made* (cf. Isa 44:13-18). These deaf, dumb, and blind gods, cut down and carved out and hammered into shape, "can do no good" (Isa 44:10, NRSV). A block of wood is a poor substitute for a living God. "If one cries out to it, it does not answer or save anyone from trouble" (Isa 46:7; cf. 44:10, NRSV).

Such is the fundamental conviction that calls forth fidelity to the LORD alone. In times of distress when devotees of other gods mock such loyalty, the worshiping community is encouraged to reaffirm the real difference between the LORD and all other contenders for the position:

Why should the nations say,
  "Where is their God?"
Our God is in the heavens;
  he does whatever he pleases.
Their idols are silver and gold,
  the work of human hands.
They have mouths, but do not speak;
  eyes, but do not see.
They have ears, but do not hear;
  noses, but do not smell.
They have hands, but do not feel;
  feet, but do not walk;
  they make no sound in their throats.
Those who make them are like them;
  so are all who trust in them. (Ps 115:2-8, NRSV)

These are some of the more important metaphors appropriated in the Hebrew Bible to describe God. But what does this language mean when it describes God as having ears and eyes and a mouth? The question is multifaceted, and justifiably brings into focus a whole range of issues and problems relating to the function of metaphoric language in general.

Fretheim has pursued several of the key questions.[5] Especially helpful is his counsel that when one analyzes the "God-talk" of the Hebrew Bible it is important to distinguish between two types of images: (1) images of God that are "unfailingly non-contingent"; that is, "God will be this kind of God wherever God is being God"; and (2) images that "move around with people and their stories, and are affected by them" (e.g., the wrath of God; p. 31).

Applying this counsel to the subject of prayer, I will try to show that these anthropomorphic metaphors portray God as consistently personal and related to humanity and the world—wherever God is being God, God is expected to be this way. This relatedness has elements of contingency, occasions when for reasons specified (e.g., sin) and sometimes unspecified, communication to and from God is in question. In such times, however, prayer is seldom silenced. Rather, it often increases in intensity, especially in times of crisis, a testimony to the unfailing conviction that God will ultimately hear. But before investigating these maters I must first clarify a pre-

---

5. Ibid., 7–12. Note esp. the discussion of the relative value of metaphors, and the "varying degrees of correspondence" between the two terms of a metaphor, from those with "low" revelatory capacity to those with higher, more "controlling" capacities.

liminary question concerning what Fretheim calls "the relationship between metaphor and essential definition."

Following Fretheim, I begin by reflecting on the relationship between metaphor and reality or literality (pp. 7-8). It is obvious that metaphors are not to be taken in a literal sense. There are clear continuities between the two terms of a metaphor, some particular thought or understanding that the comparison is intended to illumine. There are also some discontinuities, points at which the comparison breaks down. If one does not recognize these discontinuities, the metaphor may distort rather than illumine. Hence one must be careful to avoid the trap of thinking that God literally possesses human attributes and the limitations inherent in them. Yet one must also be careful not to set metaphor over against literality as if they had no connection, as if metaphor were only decorative or illustrative speech, perhaps something to be appreciated as literary art but not to be taken seriously. A particular literalness is intended, particular information is conveyed, that is true and real. For example, the metaphors concerning idolatry convey information that is authentic and worthy of trust: God does see and hear and communicate. In this sense, one can describe metaphors as "reality depicting."[6]

I may sharpen this point with reference to the subject of prayer in the following way. The reality behind anthropomorphic metaphors for God is that the divine-human relationship functions as a "relationship of reciprocity."[7] More specifically, in prayer this reciprocity is especially manifest in the form of dialogue between God and humanity. God speaks and acts and listens. People speak and act and listen in response. Such interchanges, Greenberg observes,

> reveal God as sentient, willing, purposeful—as having the attributes of a person; to express communication with such a being, biblical man employs the language of interhuman intercourse, since that is the only

6. Ibid., 7. On "reality depiction" as a function of metaphorical religious language, see J. M. Soskice, *Metaphor and Religious Language* (Oxford: Clarendon, 1985), 97–117.

7. A. Heschel, *The Prophets* (2 vols.; New York: Harper and Row, 1962), 2.9. I am indebted to Fretheim's discussion for calling this phrase and concept to my attention. For his use of the expression see *Suffering of God*, 35–44. A similar emphasis informs H. G. Reventlow's discussion of prayer, though he makes the point in a much different way. Note especially his description of much of Western theology as heavily influenced by an Aristotelian metaphysic that runs contrary to the biblical perspective of a personal God with whom humanity may have direct and meaningful communication (*Gebet im Alten Testament* [Stuttgart: Kohlhammer, 1986], 9–80).

model available for interpersonal communication. Receiving God's address, man is "you" to God's "I"; addressing God, man is "I" to God's "you."[8]

Prayer in this sense necessarily involves the mutual participation of both divine and human partners in the task of communication. If one or the other fails to participate, if there is an "I" but no "you," then dialogue becomes monologue (or reflection, meditation, soliloquy), and the result for both parties is something less than could have been. Impediments may certainly hinder or halt the communication, even when it is desired. From God's perspective, human disobedience may jeopardize the dialogue (e.g., Isa 1:15; Jer 7:16; 11:11, 14; 14:11-12; Ezek 8:18; Mic 3:4). The wicked who masquerade as God's partners, who have God "near in their mouths yet far from their hearts" (Jer 12:2, NRSV), will not be privy either to God's presence or to God's hearing. From the human perspective, confession may remove sin as a barrier to communication with God (e.g., see the counsel of Job's friends, who follow the traditional understanding: 8:5-6; 22:27; 33:26). Even so, unknown or unaccepted blockage may remain, severely straining divine-human reciprocity (routinely in lament situations). On these occasions prayer may appear ineffective (e.g., Lam 3:8; Ps 22:2), perhaps even dangerous (e.g., Eccl 5:2). Yet even in these situations an underlying trust in God's ultimate receptivity to the human plight sustains the efforts of stubborn pray-ers (e.g., Job, Jeremiah, the suppliant of Psalm 88).

To summarize briefly, in this intersection between divine initiative and human response, relationship takes on concrete form. Such relationship achieves its clearest form in prayer. Indeed, in this respect prayer may serve as a microcosm of one of the Hebrew Bible's most important theological claims: the relatedness of God and humanity.

GOD'S RELATEDNESS TO THE WORLD

God's relatedness to humanity is itself part of a larger, and logically prior, fundamental Hebraic assumption, namely, God's relatedness to the world. Fretheim calls attention to two basic perspectives on God's relationship with the world, both of which have

---

8. M. Greenberg, *Biblical Prose Prayer As a Window to the Popular Religion of Ancient Israel* (Berkeley, Los Angeles, London: Univ. of California Press, 1983), 20.

significant repercussions for understanding the possibilities of prayer (pp. 34–44).

First, in terms of "spatial realities," the Hebrew Bible testifies broadly to a bipartite structure within the created order. This structure is clearly conceptualized, for example, in Ps 115:16: "The heavens are the LORD's heavens, but the earth he has given to human beings" (p. 37, NRSV). These two spatial areas, heaven and earth, prescribe the domains for God and humanity respectively. Yet for relationship to occur, for meaningful and substantive communication to take place, some interchange between these areas must be possible. Although God resides in the heavens and from this lofty abode looks down or hears or speaks, one ought not overstate the separateness of God's place from humanity's place. The Hebrew Bible does not equate separateness either with inaccessibility or with "unaffectability" (p. 39). Here Fretheim makes the point specifically with reference to prayer: "The prayers of the people are heard in heaven (cf. 1 Kings 8) . . . God is affected in many ways by what happens on earth (ibid.).

A second perspective concerns God's relationship to time. Within the created order God relates to the temporal sequences—past, present, future—of the world (pp. 39–44). Fretheim examines a number of texts that address this issue from a variety of angles. Most important for my focus are texts that relate to divine wrath and the planning and execution of divine judgment (e.g., God's "planning" for judgment, Jer 18:11; cf. 26:3; 49:20, 30; 50:45; Mic 2:3; 4:12; the time of God's anger, Pss 103:9; 30:5; Isa 54:7-8) (pp. 40–42). His point is that such references make sense only when understood temporally, that is, one can speak of God's *planning* divine judgment in response to a time of provocation, a time of *execution* of the judgment, and a time of *reversal* or *withdrawal* of the judgment (p. 42). Although it is not his primary concern, Fretheim does specifically call attention to the importance of the temporal delay between the planning of divine judgment and its subsequent execution.

During this delay one encounters instances of what Fretheim calls "divine consultation," where the human response to God's announced or planned intentions is not only entertained but allowed to have influence (pp. 49–53). "The interaction between God and people will determine whether the plan is put into effect" (p. 41). As illustration he cites texts that speak of God's interaction with prophetic leaders (e.g., Gen 18:7-22; Exod 32:7-14; Num 14:11-20). In these specific texts and in others that I will subsequently consider, what Fretheim terms "consultation" one may take as prime examples of prayer, specifically prayers for justice. As Staudt has noticed, such prayers are positioned within narrative contexts precisely in the temporal hiatus between the announcement of divine intentions and their subsequent fulfillment. In the overall narrative development they suggest that the fulfillment of God's word is "significantly conditioned by the people to whom and for whom that word was spoken."[9]

Both these issues—God's relationship to space and to time—bring into focus a third perspective that is especially relevant for the present discussion: God's power.[10] If God is reachable, and if having reached God through the normal channels of divine-human communication one can say that God is affected or moved by what is heard, then it is crucial that one have reason to believe that God has the power to respond to that which has transpired in the world.

In this respect the question put to Sarah and Abraham in Gen 18:14 becomes paradigmatic for all who would engage God in prayer: "Is anything too wonderful for the Lord?"[11] How this question is answered determines the kind of response one will make to God. On the one hand, if the assumption, however clearly or vaguely articulated, is yes, some things are impossible, too hard, even for God, then one is constrained to acknowledge that in this world some things are simply static, sometimes perhaps hopeless, and impervious to divine alteration. If the question is answered yes, then the relationship to God and world is reduced to an affirmation of what is. To the extent that it remains a living practice, prayer becomes a means by which people accommodate themselves to the unchanging and unchangeable powers that control their lives.

On the other hand, if basic assumptions about God's power in relationship to the world and humanity permit and encourage a negative response to this question, then the expectations differ radically. If nothing is impossible for God, then God has power to effect change, to create possibilities where the world suggests only impossibilities. In the case of Sarah and Abraham, God can provide a child against seemingly insurmountable physical odds. If God possesses and makes available such power, then the divine-human

---

9. E. Staudt, "Prayer and the People in the Deuteronomist" (Ph.D. diss., Vanderbilt University, 1980), 338.

10. Cf. Fretheim's discussion of "presence and power" (*Suffering of God,* 60–78).

11. Cf. W. Brueggemann, "'Impossibility' and Epistemology in the Faith Tradition of Abraham and Sarah (Gen. 18:1-15)" *ZAW* 94 (1982): 615–34.

relationship is significantly altered, and requests, petitions, and expectations directed to God take on new urgency and new hope. The acknowledgment of divine power positions humanity, rather uncomfortably at times, at the point of a double-edged sword. God has power to give or to take, to do good or harm, or—to use the language so frequently attested in the Hebrew Bible—to bless or to curse. From humanity's standpoint it is crucial *how* divine power will be manifest, more specifically, how to predict its various displays and to live accordingly, or how to *effect* its display, perhaps even alter its display when one perceives it to be working contrary to assumed standards of justice and fairplay. Here also perceptions about God's relationship to the world are crucial.

Once again I follow a suggestion from Fretheim. He notes quite rightly that one can immediately eliminate two possible understandings of the God-world relationship as far as the Hebrew Bible is concerned (p. 34). First, Israel never accepts the claims of pantheism. God is not identified with the world, nor is everything in the world so endowed with divinity that God and world are ultimately collapsed into one another. From Israel's perspective God is creator of the world and exercises authority over all creation as sovereign Lord. Hence God does not equal the world or the truth claims of the world. God's truth and the world's conception of truth are not necessarily the same.

Second, Israel also rejects the claims of dualism. Although separate, God and world are not independent of one another. The world is dependent on God for both its origin and its sustenance. Further, God and world are not in opposition to one another. God judges the created world as "very good." The world is "not anti-God either in principle or actuality, however much evil may be said to have permeated its life" (p. 34). Hence God is not aloof from the world or disinterested in its truth claims.

If Israel rejects both these viewpoints, the question becomes where between these two extreme perspectives does Israel's understanding of the God-world relationship lie? I follow Fretheim's suggestion a step further before branching off to focus the issue specifically on the subject of prayer.

Fretheim proposes two models in answer to this question (pp. 34–44). On the one hand, one may understand the God-world relationship in terms of a monarchical analogy. That is, one may view the relationship along the lines of king-subject. Such an understanding emphasizes the discontinuity between God and people. God is sovereign, free, and in control. The people are, correspondingly, the ruled over, the submissive, the controlled. On the other hand, one may point to a covenantal model of relationship, which represents a decidedly different perspective.[12] The emphasis here is on continuity rather than discontinuity, interrelatedness rather than separateness, intimacy with God rather than distance, enmity, or any other form of disinterest. Although Fretheim is most concerned to develop the latter model as the major perspective within which one can understand the issue of God's suffering, both models describe accurately the perspectives shaping certain major channels of divine-human communication in the Hebrew Bible.

A monarchical mode of divine-human relationship is clearly implicit, for example, in the Priestly imagery of temple worship. M. Haran has noted that the one epithet reserved exclusively for the priests is "servants of the LORD" *(mĕšārĕtê Yhwh)*.[13] Hence they are described as "standing before the LORD to serve" [*šrt*] (e.g., Deut 10:8; 17:12; 18:5, 7) or "drawing near to the LORD to serve" [*šrt*] (e.g., Ezek 40:46; 43:19; 44:15; cf. 44:16).[14] In all these cases one may understand the use of *šrt,* "to serve," as more than merely conventional language. In Haran's view it represents the "actual expression of the priest's functional idiosyncrasy."[15] In essence, priesthood is "the most exalted and fullest manifestation of divine service in ancient Israel."[16] Under the leadership of these "servants" of God, worship in the temple takes on characteristics directly analogous to the concept of serving human rulers. Worshipers are to prostrate themselves before God, bowing their heads, stretching out their hands and feet in bodily gestures of humility. Moreover, they are to offer tribute to God, especially in the form of sacrifice and offering, just as one would do before a human ruler to whom one has recognized obligations.[17]

12. Fretheim's preferred term for this model is "organismic." But the assymetry in "monarchical" and "organismic" is bothersome. The Hebrew Bible clearly presents the view that God is king and Israel is subject; hence the "monarchical" model is certainly rooted in a Hebraic way of viewing things. The word "organismic," however, is modern and seems to be not so well rooted in biblical thinking. I believe the reciprocity, mutuality, and intimacy of which Fretheim speaks is better represented by the word "covenantal." For the importance of prayer in the maintenance of covenant partnership with God, see my discussion on pp. 261–63.

13. M. Haran, "Priesthood, Temple, Divine Service: Some Observations on Institutions and Practice of Worship," *HAR* 7 (1983): 122.

14. Ibid.

15. Ibid., 122–23.

16. Ibid., 122.

17. On this point compare the observations of M. Greenberg ("On the Refinement of the Conception of Prayer in Hebrew Scripture," *Association for Jewish Studies* 1

One must take care not to overextend the monarchical analogy. For example, Israel's obligations to God in worship clearly have a different quality than the enforced obedience that often characterizes the obligation between king and subject. Israel's obligation is the response of loyal obedience to a God who has delivered them not only from Egypt but from oppressive situations wherever they arise. Such experiences become signs of God's "unending love" *(ḥesed)*. This perception of *who* God is and *what* God has done and *why* God has acted in such a way lends to Israel's worship the quality of "returned love."[18]

Even so, one may speculate whether the monarchical aspects of temple worship might have resulted in or secured a certain degree of submissiveness from the worshiper, perhaps even a certain measure of control over the worshiper. For example, in a service of worship where the distribution of power between God and people is so clearly unequal, and where the ceremonial regulations are so carefully stipulated and controlled, is it reasonable to expect that the worshiper would or could ever challenge or confront the God on the throne? In this respect the role of prayer within the temple is open to question.

Further pause is occasioned by the recognition that the extensive Priestly legislation concerning the practice of worship includes no requirement to pray, nor is there conclusive evidence that priests themselves ever engaged in or promoted the practice of prayer. There are no general instructions concerning how one should pray, when one should pray, where one should pray, or even if one should pray.[19] Indeed, if Haran is correct, prayer is "a gesture of secondary order" in the temple, a substitute for sacrifice reserved for the poor who could not afford the required burnt, peace, or grain offerings.[20] In such cases the poor would have access to formulaic prayers like those in the Psalter whose conventional language rather carefully

---

[1976]: 64–74) and those of Haran ("Priesthood," 131–34). Greenberg also understands prayer to be a part of the service *('ăbōdāh)* rendered in the house of God. Haran argues, however, that even though prayer may have occurred, it was in no way obligatory as were other forms of service such as sacrifice and prostration. On the importance of this issue for the present discussion, see pp. 273–75.

18. Cf. Greenberg, "Refinement," 68.

19. Cf. Haran, "Priesthood," 129–31. The case here for the lack of prayer in the Priestly tradition is stated rather strongly. Haran acknowledges, however (p. 131 n. 16), that liturgies accompanying the bringing of the firstfruits (Deut 26:1-10), the tithe of the third year (Deut 26:13-15), and the Day of Atonement (Leviticus 16–21) constitute "exceptions" in the Priestly legislation.

20. Ibid., 129.

prescribes the proper response before the throne of God. On balance, however, Haran suggests a very restricted role for prayer in temple worship:

> In the biblical period itself, that is, at its pre-exilic stage, prayer belonged to the periphery of cult and was not a part of cultic activity. Its place was outside the priestly circle, which held sole responsibility for all cultic matters within the temple precincts.[21]

Yet another consideration in this regard is the physical structure of the temple itself. Its tripartite division into porch *('ûlām)*, nave *(hêkāl)*, and inner sanctuary *(dĕbîr)* clearly functions to restrict immediacy to the most sacred symbols of God's presence to all but a select few (cf. 1 Kgs 6:1-22; 2 Chr 3:1-17). One may observe here a further manifestation of the monarchical perspective of the service of God—the architecture of controlled access to the divine, reinforcing the distance, the discontinuity, between holy God and unholy people.

By contrast, the covenantal model promotes a different level of divine-human interchange. Central to the model is the perception that God is integrally related to the world; God is accessible, personal, and powerful within the world's time and space. Before such a God the requirements of distance and caution give way to perceptions of connectedness, mutuality, equality, even intimacy. Such are the impulses leading to prayer, a form of interaction with the deity that requires no priestly supervision, no holy place, no special time. It is indeed a channel of communication open to all members of society, regardless of social status or official position, at any time.

This open and intimate accessibility to God has at least two important consequences. First, given the restrictions inherent in temple worship and the corresponding lack of obligatory prayer

---

21. Ibid., 131. In this judgment Haran concurs with the opinion of Y. Kaufmann, who portrays the priestly service in the temple as "soundless worship":

> In the cultic ceremony of the priestly code, all functions of the priest are carried out in silence without the accompaniment of any utterance, song, or recitation . . . there also is no room for prayer. Not only does the priest not offer supplication but neither does he offer a prayer of thanksgiving during the holy service . . . Words spoken by the priest are never part of the cultic act and always are uttered outside the sanctuary.

(Y. Kaufmann, *Toldot ha-Emmunah ha-Yisraelit* [Tel Aviv: Dvir, 1927], 2.476–77. The translation quoted here is from S. Talmon, "The Emergence of Institutionalized Prayer in Israel in the Light of the Qumran Literature," *Qumran,* ed. M. Delcor [Paris: Duculot, 1978], 268).

within its ritual requirements, one can imagine that the ordinary person could have perceived a seemingly unbridgeable distance between everyday concerns and the need for divine attention. Prayer serves as an important means of narrowing this distance between holy God and unholy people—in Greenberg's view, ensuring "the permanent link of the commoner to the transcendent realm."[22]

In a second area a covenantal relationship between God and world, especially as manifest in open and unrestricted human discourse with God, lends itself to notions of egalitarianism. On the one hand, it fosters the idea that humans can address God familiarly, apparently with no concerns, no emotions, considered off-limits or inappropriate. One clear evidence pointing in this direction to which I have previously alluded is the frequency with which narrative prayers begin with the casual introduction "and X said [*'āmar*] to God." On the other hand, as Greenberg has suggested, prayer may also have promoted certain egalitarian tendencies within Israelite social structures.[23] To grant the commoner an avenue of access to God roughly equivalent in intimacy to that of the priests is to blur the class distinctions between the official and the unofficial, the titled and the untitled.

In Greenberg's opinion the practical effect of this egalitarianism could have had immediate and perhaps potentially far-ranging consequences. In the first instance the effect would have been "to apply to the commoner a standard of conduct proper in the first instance to priests only," essentially promoting the biblical ideal of the covenanted people as a "kingdom of priests, a holy nation" (Exod 19:6).[24] Such egalitarian notions, Greenberg suggests, may well have prepared the way for the subsequent democratization of worship in the institution of the synagogue, where lay persons and the life of prayer are elevated to new levels of importance.[25]

Following the suggestions of Haran and Greenberg, I venture a step further to reflect on how differing perspectives on the God-world relationship may have influenced the institutionalization of prayer. I have noted that the monarchical emphasis on discontinuity finds particular representation in temple worship, where

22. Greenberg, *Prose Prayer,* 52.
23. Ibid., 52–53.
24. Ibid., 52.
25. Ibid., 53.

priests exercise the controlling influence. Here it is ritual that provides the primary avenue to God, particularly the ritual of sacrifice, which must be offered in its various forms on set occasions, always at a holy place, and according to carefully prescribed instructions. Although prayer would surely not have been wholly lacking in the people's worship, it seems to have been predominantly offered in conjunction with and in support of the primary tribute of sacrifice (e.g., Isa 1:13-14). As Haran has suggested, such prayer does not involve explicit obligation and so appears to have been of secondary importance. Subsequently, Greenberg suggests, with the emergence of the synagogue, prayer attains a more prominent place within formal worship.

I need not enter the debate concerning the historical origins of the synagogue, whether it is to be traced to the Babylonian exile or, as is more widely believed, only much later to the Persian period or after. Nevertheless, one can speak in general terms of a transition in the orientation of Israel's worship from sacrifice to prayer. With this transition the institutional role of prayer also begins to shift. Just when this transition begins and when it may have achieved its most complete form is open to question. S. Talmon has proposed that if one understands by "institutionalized prayer" the "establishment of a definite order of prescribed prayers in fixed formulations which are to be uttered according to a detailed time-schedule," then it is not until one comes to the Qumran literature that prayer finally attains such prominence.[26] Even so, with Greenberg, Talmon recognizes in the emergence of the synagogue the beginnings of a decisive effort to cope with historical circumstances, especially the destruction of the temple, that lead to the cessation of sacrifice as the primary approach to God. In this connection few would dispute Haran's generalization that, in contrast to the temple, the synagogue represents "mainly a gathering place for praying."[27]

At the risk of unfairly simplifying a host of complex issues, one might propose that temple worship and synagogue worship represent two of the more important historical manifestations of the changing perceptions concerning God's relatedness to the world. To highlight the principal metaphors that serve to articulate these perceptions, particularly as they bear on the practice of prayer within institutional settings, the following points of comparison are useful.

26. Talmon, "Emergence," 273ff. The quotation is from p. 267.
27. Haran, "Priesthood," 127.

Temple	*Synagogue*
1. Monarchical mode of of relating to God	1. Covenantal mode of of relating to God
2. Sacrifice as *the* principal avenue of communication	2. Prayer as *a* principal means of communication
3. Controlling metaphors: distance, discontinuity, control	3. Controlling metaphors: immediacy, continuity, mutuality

To summarize, I have attempted to show that the Hebrew Bible mainly uses metaphoric language to portray the God to whom prayer is offered. These metaphors are essentially anthropomorphic in character, drawn primarily from the human sphere of experience, and as such reinforce the ideal of a relationship of reciprocity between God and humanity. Although such metaphors cannot be taken literally, they do function to portray an essential reality about God. God does see and hear and speak. Communication to and from this God is possible; indeed, such communication is both summoned forth and enabled by this God who, in contrast to other deities, invites and responds to the mutual interchange of divine-human dialogue.

Further, the God to whom one directs prayer is related to the world in which humanity must live out its experiences. In Hebraic understanding God is neither totally identified with the world and its truth claims (pantheism) nor totally divorced from the world (dualism). Rather, with a number of analogies such as those labeled monarchical and covenantal, the Hebrew Bible affirms that God is both powerful to effect change in the world and accessible within the world to personal appeal. On occasion such divine power holds sovereign sway over those who would approach the throne, creating distance, requiring submission and obedience. On other occasions such power is brokered through mutual participation of the divine and the human, creating accessibility to the throne unrestricted by distance, control, or protocol. Although the institutional settings within which one communicates with God change in response to historical and other factors, a fundamental perception about God's relatedness remains anchored in Hebraic consciousness. "In the beginning God," sovereign and personal, powerful yet open to rigorous discourse with humanity; and from the beginning this God is both the source and the sustenance of prayer.

CHAPTER 4

Prayer
and the Depiction
of Character

As discourse between people and God, prayer plays an important role in portraying both human and divine character. What people say to God—their petitions and their praise, their desires and the life situations that bring them into articulation—reveal motives, attitudes, and morality. Likewise, the ascriptions addressed to God in prayer (e.g., "loving," "just," "merciful," "sovereign") reveal assumptions about divine character and divine receptiveness to human concerns, assumptions that a narrative situation may confirm, modify, or refute by supplying or withholding a divine response. It is part of the art of Hebrew narrative that such recorded dialogues enable the reader to witness the two-way traffic between heaven and earth and thus enter into the process of understanding the character of the parties involved.

Literary studies, especially those by R. Alter, A. Berlin, and M. Sternberg, have stressed that the rhetorical art of characterization in Hebrew narrative necessarily summons the reader to a "process of discovery."[1] No single narrative situation provides the full portrait of a character. In one scene the reader draws certain inferences and impressions from a character's actions that may be confirmed or challenged by information from another situation. The impression produced on one's first encounter with a character in biblical drama is seldom the same as that which remains after one's last encounter.[2] For a rounded or full portrait one must work through the complete

1. R. Alter, *The Art of Biblical Narrative* (New York: Basic Books, 1981); A. Berlin, *Poetics and Interpretation of Biblical Narrative* (Sheffield: Almond, 1983); M. Sternberg, *The Poetics of Biblical Narrative: Ideological Literature and the Drama of Reading* (Bloomington: Indiana Univ. Press, 1985). The expression "process of discovery" is from Sternberg, *Poetics,* 323.

2. Sternberg, *Poetics,* 326.

set of narrative depictions to move from what Sternberg has called "truth to whole truth."[3]

Biblical prayer is but one of the means afforded in Hebrew narrative for building character portraits. By itself a person's prayer can reveal only part of his or her character. One must weigh information gained from this source against additional information coded in other rhetorical techniques that may be at work shaping a character's presentation elsewhere.[4] Yet prayer is an important resource that scholars have unfortunately not addressed adequately in their descriptions of the art of characterization.

Alter provides some help in addressing this matter in his discussion of the primacy of dialogue over narration in Hebrew discourse. In his view biblical writers "are often less concerned with actions in themselves than with how [an] individual character responds to actions or produces them; direct speech is made the chief instrument for revealing the varied and at times nuanced relations of the personages to the actions in which they are implicated."[5] Stylistically such an interest is manifest in the preference for "narration-through-dialogue," where the standard practice of biblical narrative is to limit scenes to two characters at a time.[6] Through the verbal interchange of these two characters one can discern what is significant about each for a particular situation.

My intention in this and the next chapter is to follow Alter's suggestion concerning direct speech as a means of depicting character. Especially in two-sided dialogues, which provide the contribution of both human and divine participants, direct speech may indeed reveal important character traits of the parties involved. But one should make similar probes into one-sided dialogues, which

3. Ibid., 230–63.

4. In describing and illustrating some of these techniques, Alter *(Art of Biblical Narrative,* 116–17) has suggested that one think of them in terms of an ascending scale relative to their capacities for explicitness and certainty. At the lower end of the scale are depictions of characters by means of their appearance or action. Physical descriptions or reports of a person's acts or conduct provide the most implicit and the least certain portrayals, leaving the reader to infer how such information contributes to the intelligibility of the character. At the top of the scale a reliable and omniscient narrator sometimes provides an account of what characters feel, intend, desire. In between these two poles of the spectrum, one encounters direct speech, either by the characters themselves or by others about them. In this middle category one is able to move from inference to weighing the claims between speech and action, yet without the security of certainty that narratorial supplement can offer.

5. Alter, *Art of Biblical Narrative,* 66.

6. Ibid., 72.

assume God's participation in the exchange, even though it is word-less. In such cases the narrative's report of subsequent divine action may provide God's involvement in the interchange.[7]

In this chapter I focus primarily on the depiction of human rather than divine character. I look at a number of texts where a person's prayer may serve to emphasize certain admirable qualities of faith and practice (e.g., Solomon's wisdom; Hezekiah's piety) or to con-firm one's particular status as a divine representative (e.g., the pro-phets as pray-ers; Elijah as a "man of God"). With such texts I contrast a second set in which the content of one's prayers may function to parody the faithful (e.g., Jacob) or to hold up the pray-er for rebuke, hence a sort of negative paradigm (e.g., Jonah). Finally, I suggest that prayer's ability to characterize and depict essential qualities is not limited to persons only. At least in one notable case—the prayer of Solomon in 1 Kings 8—the act of prayer may serve to emphasize not so much the character of the pray-er as that of the institution in which it has its setting. Thus Solomon's prayer builds the image of the temple as a house of prayer.

PRAYER AS A MEANS OF CONFIRMING STATUS

The general understanding of the prophet as especially skilled in the practice of prayer is frequently registered in Hebrew Bible stud-ies. To cite one opinion, A. Johnson has argued in two influential publications that with respect to cultic duties, prophet and priest are distinguished by their different responsibilities.[8] While the priest exercises sole prerogative in matters relating to sacrifice, the prophet functions as a specialist in prayer. The prophets' unique privilege in this regard is the dividend of their peculiar access to the name of God. Johnson argues that it is the prophet, not the priest, who is able "to call upon the name of *[qārā' běšēm]* the LORD," thus interceding with God on the people's behalf in times of national or personal distress.[9]

---

7. Ibid., 84ff. As an example of "one-sided dialogue," Alter points to Hannah's prayer for a son in 1 Sam 1:11. No divine response is provided Hannah, yet by the narrative's end the reader is provided confirmation of the success of her efforts: "Elkanah knew Hannah his wife, *and the* LORD *remembered her.* In due time Hannah conceived and bore a son" (vv. 19–20, NRSV).

8. A. Johnson, *The Cultic Prophet in Ancient Israel* (2d ed.; Cardiff: Univ. of Wales, 1962), 58–60; idem, *The Cultic Prophet and Israel's Psalmody* (Cardiff: Univ. of Wales, 1979), 3, 68, et passim.

9. On the weakness of this theory as it has come to be applied to the prophets in general, see S. Balentine, "The Prophet as Intercessor: A Reassessment," *JBL* 103 (1984): 161–73.

With respect specifically to the issue of intercession, the Hebrew vocabulary carrying this theme (e.g., *pālal, pāga', dāraš, qārā' běšēm, 'āmad lipnê Yhwh*) suggests that Moses, Samuel, and Jeremiah are three intercessors par excellence in the Hebrew Bible. Thus when God tells Jeremiah, "Though Moses and Samuel stood before me, yet my heart would not turn toward this people" (Jer 15:1, NRSV), the reader has sufficient information accumulated already from previous encounters with these persons to know that it is especially their abilities as pray-ers that brings them together in this particular comparison. Jeremiah's intercessory efforts are frequently attested (e.g., Jer 7:16; 11:14; 14:11; 37:3; 42:4; cf. vv. 2, 20). These, along with his particularly poignant confessions, are instrumental in shaping the portrait of Jeremiah as a pray-er.[10] Further, Moses is specifically described as interceding with the LORD on two occasions (Num 21:7; Deut 9:20). In several other cases intercession is rather clearly implied, even though the technical vocabulary that usually introduces it is lacking (e.g., Exod 32:11-14, 31-34; Num 14:13-19). Similarly, three passages specifically describe Samuel as praying to the LORD on behalf of others (1 Sam 7:5; 12:18-19, 23). As the account in 1 Samuel 12 makes clear, Samuel's direct link to God is a key factor in confirming his status as worthy of respect, even awe, on a level equal to that of none other than God (cf. v. 18, NRSV: "and all the people greatly feared the LORD *and* Samuel").

The case here is made only in general terms. For particular persons like Moses, Samuel, and Jeremiah the text sufficiently describes their practice of prayer so that the reader has adequate information to fill in the gap when the simple allusion to "standing before the LORD" is the only reference to their common function. To make the point in more specific terms I consider in greater detail the role of prayer in the case of Elijah.

THE EXAMPLE OF ELIJAH

Elijah's capacity as a pray-er looms especially important in two incidents. Elijah's prayer for the son of the widow from Zarephath (1 Kgs 17:17-24) stands as a self-contained narrative, and is usually reckoned, along with other similar anecdotal stories about his private life (e.g., 17:2-7, 14-16; 19:4-8; 2 Kgs 1:9-16), to be part of the popular hagiography that accrued to the Elijah traditions.[11] This

---

10. Cf. S. Balentine, "Jeremiah, Prophet of Prayer," *RevExp* 78 (1981): 331–44. For further discussion of these texts, see chap. 7.
11. See, e.g., G. Fohrer, *Elia* (Zurich: Zwingli Verlag, 1957), 44–45, 52–53. For a summary of the critical discussion of the Elijah narratives, see J. Gray, *I and II Kings* (OTL; 2d ed.; Philadelphia: Westminster, 1970), 371–77.

historical evaluation notwithstanding, these verses function within their present narrative context to draw attention to the special powers of this divine representative and thus to prepare the way for understanding his performance in subsequent episodes of the story. The backdrop for this particular scene is provided by Elijah's announcement to Ahab of an imminent famine in the land (17:1). The narrative will return to this theme in chapter 18, where Elijah demonstrates dramatically that his God, and his God alone, has the power to break the drought. Sandwiched between this announcement of doom and its ultimate resolution, the scene in 17:17-24 cuts away momentarily from the larger episode to provide important confirmation of Elijah's unique link to God.

The immediate issue is the serious illness of the widow's son, an illness that has left him seemingly lifeless. The woman reasons that her previous encounter with this prophet (cf. vv. 8-16) has brought her into such close contact with the presence of a holy God that some hidden sin on her part has been uncovered for which her son is now being punished. Thus her opening address to Elijah:

> What have I to do with you, man of God *['îš hā'ĕlōhîm]* that you have come to me to call attention to my sin and to cause the death *[lĕhāmît]* of my son? (v. 18)

To this question and implicit accusation Elijah makes no substantive response, except to ask that the child be handed over to him; then he retreats with the child to the upper chamber of his quarters.

The following scene takes place in private, away from the mother's view, but not from the reader's, who is allowed to eavesdrop on a private moment of interchange between God and Elijah:

> And he called to the LORD *[wayyiqrā' 'el Yhwh]* and said, "O LORD my God, have you brought evil *[hărē'ôtā]* even upon the widow with whom I am dwelling to cause the death *[lĕhāmît]* of her son?" (v. 20)

Although the widow seems to have drawn the immediate conclusion that her son's condition is the result of some unwitting sin on her part, Elijah apparently does not share this assumption, or if he does he will not let it go unchallenged. Can it be that the LORD has brought "evil" in order "to cause death?" Elijah has no answer for the woman's charge—only questions for God.[12]

---

12. The prefacing of Elijah's question with the interrogative *ha*, which is used primarily with questions where one is uncertain of the answer, contributes to the suggestion that Elijah is in real doubt concerning God's intentions. Cf. GKC, par. 150d.

What follows next is Elijah's symbolic action of stretching himself upon the child three times, in a manner reminiscent of contactual magic known in Mesopotamia and Canaan. This act is accompanied by a second address to God, this time in the form of petition:

> And he called to the Lord *[wayyiqrā' 'el Yhwh]* and said, "O Lord my God, let the breath *[nepeš]* of this child be restored within him." (v. 21)

Without interruption, the divine response comes immediately, granting Elijah's request in exactly the terms it was presented: the breath of the child is restored and he revives (v. 22).

The final scene shifts back to the mother, who has waited silently and anxiously throughout Elijah's absence. Now Elijah brings the boy back down to his mother and presents him to her with words for her ears that no doubt the message conveyed by her eyes did not need: "See, your son is alive" (v. 23, NRSV).

The final words belong to the mother, providing not only an appropriate closure for this episode but, more importantly, also the key to its primary purpose within the Elijah narratives:

> Now I know that you are a man of God *['îš 'ĕlōhîm]*, and the word of the Lord in your mouth is truth. (v. 24, NRSV).

This response completes the widow's transition from challenging Elijah's status to confirming it. From her initial question "What have I to do with you, *man of God?*" to her final affirmation *"Now* I know that you are a *man of God,"* both she and the reader have come to recognize Elijah's special link to God. For her the confession can only have come in response to the miraculous healing of her son. But for the reader who has listened in on the private moment of Elijah's tête-à-tête with God, the miracle of healing is but the outcome of an important previous activity. This "man of God" is a pray-er. Therein lies the secret to his great power.

This scene from near the beginning of the Elijah narratives provides the first description of Elijah as "man of God." The same description is made at only one other juncture in the present narrative sequence, 2 Kgs 1:9-16, an episode placed, rather appropriately, just at the end of Elijah's public ministry. What the woman has confessed in a private encounter the messengers of Ahaziah are made to learn in a much more public engagement with the prophet. Sent from Ahaziah to inquire (*drš*; cf. vv. 2, 3, 6, 16 [twice]) of Baalzebub, these messengers learn in a fateful way, on three separate occasions, that to inquire of any god other than the Lord, by means of anyone other than this designated "man of God" (the phrase repeats five times in vv. 9-13), is to play with fire (indeed, quite literally). Thus both the narrative's introduction to Elijah and its closing presentation make Elijah's role as "man of God" a primary defining epithet. In both cases the prophet's ability "to call on the name of God," to "inquire" of God, serves to supplement the portraiture and give substance to its primary focus.

In these opening and concluding presentations of Elijah, the narrative perception of his special status has moved from a private acknowledgment to public witness. The climactic moment in this progression occurs in Elijah's contest with the prophets of Baal on Mt. Carmel. Here too the prophet and his activities are portrayed in close association with the practice of prayer.

My immediate focus is on the prayer of Elijah recorded in 1 Kgs 18:36-37, which is set within the context of verses 17-40, the dramatic encounter with the prophets of Baal. The relation of these verses to the rest of chapter 18, and of the whole to chapter 19, is much debated.[13] Even so, the literary unity of verses 17-40 is evident, and apart from some indications of editorial reworking in verses 36-37 (about which I shall comment), I need not enter into the debate about the text's compositional and redactional history.

As a literary unit the episode on Mt. Carmel poses a two-pronged test. At one level what is clearly to be established is the question of which deity has legitimate claim to the title "God." Thus as Elijah sets the ground rules for the contest with the Baal prophets, he lays down the criterion for determining the winner: "you call on the name of your god *[qĕrā'tem bĕšēm 'ĕlōhêkem]* and I will call on the name of the Lord *['eqrā' bĕšēm Yhwh];* the god who answers by fire is indeed God" (v. 24; cf. v. 21, NRSV). At a second level the contest is to determine who has legitimate claim to the title "prophet," the 450 prophets of Baal *[nĕbî'ê habba'al],* or Elijah, the lone aspirant to the title "prophet of the Lord" *[nābî' laYhwh,* v. 22). At this level the contest is designed primarily to determine who is effective in the art of summoning the deity. Both groups are to engage in "calling on the name" of their god (vv. 24-25, 26; cf. vv. 27-28). The winner, that is, the true prophet, will be the one(s) whose pleas are answered (v. 24). The judges in the contest will be the people, more specifically "all the people" as the narrative repeatedly states, thus stressing the public arena for the confrontation (cf. vv. 20, 24, 30, 39).

13. For the relevant literature on this question, see n. 11.

Presented with the decision to make, this audience remains silent (v. 21), agreeing only to the rules of the contest (v. 24). They will not speak again until they are persuaded to voice their judgment (v. 39). The Baal prophets are the first to take up the challenge. They prepare the bull for the fiery response from Baal that they are meant to induce, and they proceed to call on the name of their god for the desired results (v. 26). But as the text makes comically clear, try as they will from morning to noon, neither their physical stamina nor their symbolic blood-letting is able to secure a response. At both the beginning and the end of their efforts the outcome is the same: "there was no voice and there was no one answering" (vv. 26, 29). As the narrative states in a final reference to their failure, no one was any longer paying attention (v. 29).

Elijah, who apart from one mocking intrusion (v. 27) has been content to observe this ordeal silently from the sidelines, now summons the people to draw near to witness his own efforts to secure the victory. His preparation is twofold. First he prepares the altar and the trench around it, the bull that is to be laid upon the altar, and the water that is to be poured over and around the whole. As intriguing as these details are, it is what follows in the second half of his preparation that provides the primary focus of my present concern. Here the text permits yet another glimpse of Elijah at prayer.

> And Elijah the prophet drew near and said, "O LORD, God of Abraham, Isaac, and Israel, today let it be known that you are God *['attāh 'Ĕlōhîm]* in Israel *and that I am your servant,* and that I have done all these things according to your word. Answer me O LORD, answer me, so that this people will know that you, LORD, are God *['attāh Yhwh* and that you have turned their hearts back." (vv. 36-37).

In form and content Elijah's prayer anticipates victory in the contest at hand on both the levels suggested previously. At the first level, the opening invocation calling upon the "LORD, God of Abraham, Isaac, and Israel," sets forth clearly the assertion that this Yahweh God will have the only legitimate claim to the title "God." The prayer returns to this emphasis twice more, making explicit the linkage that the test is designed to solidify: let it be known that "you are God." This emphasis is signaled yet again, this time by way of the people's public affirmation as they respond to the success of Elijah's prayer with words that mirror Elijah's own plea: "And all the people . . . said 'The LORD is God. The LORD is God'" (v. 39: *Yhwh hû' hā'ĕlōhîm Yhwh hû' hā'ĕlōhîm).*

Most commentators recognize that Elijah's prayer and indeed the larger context of the contest on Carmel serve the interest of a polemical attack against worship of any god save the Lord. This polemic is surely a primary focus in the narrative. Less often noted, however, is that just as the Lord's status is vindicated, so also is Elijah's. In this respect I call attention to Elijah's petition that the people may learn that the Lord is God in Israel *"and that I am your servant."* This emphasis appears only in verse 36; it is not repeated in the people's affirmation recorded in verse 39. For this and other reasons that R. Smend, for example, has cited, one can argue that verse 36 is more explicit in its language than verse 37 and thus appears to be a secondary addition.[14] Even so, one may suggest that the editing of Elijah's prayer has functioned to call attention to an important if secondary aspect of what is being decided at Carmel. Not only is the Lord confirmed but also Elijah "the prophet," the "servant," especially with reference to his peculiar ability to "call upon the name" of God.

One should not press the point too far. Yet, given the cumulative evidence throughout the Elijah narratives of this prophet's special gifts as a pray-er, the view may be justified that prayer is one of the defining traits of this important figure in Israelite tradition. Taken as a whole, the Elijah narratives trace both the private and public recognition of the Lord's sole claim to divinity *and* of Elijah's special links to this God through the practice of prayer.

The Example of Solomon

One of the key traits that the biblical narratives attribute to Solomon is wisdom. The foundation for this ascription comes in 1 Kgs 3:4-15, a key text located strategically within the present sequencing of the narratives at the beginning of Solomon's reign. In this regard the epithet "wisdom" serves as a "proleptic portrait"[15] of the king that receives exposition and context from the narrative accounts of Solomon's various displays of wisdom in the scenes that follow in chapters 4–11. For my present purposes it is significant that this first characterization comes about as the product of a divine-human interchange that has the look of prayer.

---

14. R. Smend, "Das Wort Jahwes an Elia. Erwägungen zur Komposition von 1 Reg. XVII–XIX," VTSup 25 (1975): 526–27. Smend notes further, for example, that the address in v. 36 is "Yahweh, God of Abraham, Isaac, and Israel" whereas in v. 37 it is only "Yahweh."

15. Sternberg, *Poetics,* 338.

I have carefully phrased this last sentence. Solomon's address to God in verses 6-9 has the *look* of prayer. Yet two features of this particular narrative scene caution against too close an identification: (1) God, not Solomon, initiates the exchange here, thus distinguishing it from most other prayer texts, where the human partner makes the initial approach; and (2) one can describe the form of the narrative as a "report of a dream epiphany."[16] Such forms occur frequently in the Pentateuch, typically consisting of a report that the deity has appeared *(rā'āh, nipal)* to someone, following which a message is delivered or a dialogue with the recipient of the vision is begun. These formal features are enough for some to decide against seeing this text as a prayer in the same sense as those which have been discussed thus far.[17] Indeed, one should not overlook these differences.

Yet several commentators have noted that Solomon's address to God has the "generic element" of a prayer of petition, and I am inclined to follow this interpretation here.[18] This address is a good illustration of the biblical preference for direct discourse. On some occasions, as Alter has noted, this preference is so pronounced that even thought may be rendered as actual speech.[19] One is invited here, as in the interchanges previously examined, to probe for clues to characterizations that speech may reveal.[20]

The context for Solomon's address to God is a dream encounter at Gibeon. He has come to this ancient Levitical city to sacrifice at the great high place, because, as the preceding verses make clear, at this time "no house had yet been built for the name of the LORD" (1 Kgs 3:2). Subsequently, when Solomon awakes from this dream, he

---

16. Cf. B.O. Long, *1 Kings: with an Introduction to Historical Literature* (FOTL; Grand Rapids: Eerdmans, 1984), 65–66.

17. See, e.g., A. Wendel (*Das freie Laiengebet im vorexilischen Israel* [Leipzig: Eduard Pfeiffer, 1931], 9), who labels this as *aussergebetliche.*

18. Cf. Long, *1 Kings,* 65–66. J. Corvin ("Stylistic and Functional Study," [Ph.D. diss., Emory University, 1972], 159–62) lists this as a "conversational prayer" (cf. 123, a "dream prayer"). As examples of other conversational prayers employing a vision, he cites Gen 20:3ff. and Gen 15:1ff. M. Greenberg (*Biblical Prose Prayer as a Window to the Popular Religion of Ancient Israel* [Berkeley: Univ. of California Press, 1983], 59) lists 1 Kgs 3:6-9 among his "ad hoc" prayers, but he does not comment on it.

19. Alter, *Art of Biblical Narrative,* 67.

20. Alter cites as an example 2 Sam 2:1, where David's inquiry of God by consulting an oracle is reported as dialogue, even though the common means of such a consultation—drawing lots, divining through the Urim and Thummim— were not primarily verbal (*Art of Biblical Narrative,* 69).

will journey to Jerusalem to offer sacrifices there (v. 15). At this point the change in venue signals not only the transfer of worship from Gibeon to Jerusalem but also a change in Solomon. He receives the dream as one who "loved the LORD" and followed in the footsteps of his father David (v. 3). He emerges from the dream as one unparalleled in the gifts of wisdom, thus specially equipped to fulfill the responsibilities of kingship in Jerusalem. As the narrative strives to make clear, this special divine endowment comes about precisely because of what Solomon "asks" God, or more specifically, does not ask, in the dream dialogue reported here.

God initiates the dialogue with an invitation to petition: "Ask *[šĕ'al]* what I should give you" (v. 5). Solomon's response is recorded in verses 6-9. The petition proper, however, does not come until verse 9. It is artfully delayed until an introductory statement can set the proper context for its hearing. Solomon begins by focusing on the relationship between the LORD and his father David. David is described as God's "servant" *('abdĕkā)* who walked *before* God *(lĕpānêkā)* in fidelity *(be'ĕmet),* in righteousness *(ûbiṣdāqāh),* and with an uprightness of heart *(ûbĕyišrat lēbāb).* His reward for such loyalty was God's unending love *(ḥesed gādôl),* extended toward him *('āśîtā)* and kept for him *(tišmor lô)* at every juncture along the way. This covenant fidelity, both David's and the LORD's, has resulted in the promise of a son to carry on this relationship and to preserve its integrity according to these same terms. It is this son, designated by God to sit on the father's throne, who now addresses God boldly with petition.

The transition from Solomon's statement about God's past fidelity to the petition for the continuation of this fidelity in the present is signaled by the formulaic "and now" (v. 7).[21] Solomon had previously addressed God simply as "you" (v. 6: *'attāh).* Now he strengthens the invocation with ascriptions that serve to make explicit the kindred relationship between God and David and God

---

21. Long (*1 Kings,* 255) identifies this as a "transition formula" regularly occurring in "stylized petitions" between an opening statement of transgression against God or of God's past faithfulness and the petition prayer. Corvin ("Stylistic and Functional Study," 206–11) cites this as a recurring stylistic feature in "formal prayers"; M. Weinfeld (*Deuteronomy and the Deuteronomic School* [Oxford: Clarendon, 1972], 175–76) describes it as a recurring rhetorical device in deuteronomic orations; cf. E. Staudt, "Prayer and the People in the Deuteronomist" (Ph.D. diss., Vanderbilt University, 1980), e.g., 216. See further H. A. Brongers, "Bemerkungen zum Gebrauch des adverbialen *wĕ'attāh* im Alten Testament," *VT* 15 (1965): 289–99.

and himself: "And now O LORD, my God, you, you have made your servant king *[wĕ'attāh Yhwh 'ĕlōhāy 'attāh himlaktā 'et 'abdĕkā]* in place of David my father." Although he is David's son and God's designated appointee as king, Solomon nevertheless describes himself as small *(qāṭōn)* and as lacking the knowledge *(lō' 'ēda')* to fulfill the responsibilities that accrue to his position. This introduction, carefully setting forth both Solomon's claim to and need of divine assistance, leads finally to his specific petition. In his words, he is God's servant *('abdĕkā)* just as David was, set in the midst of God's people *('ammĕkā)* just as David was. The immediate need is for God to maintain fidelity to this servant and to equip him for the leadership of a people who are too many in number for such a one to lead if left to his own resources (cf. v. 8).

The petition in verse 9 brings all these concerns into sharper focus. Solomon begins by once again identifying himself as God's servant *('abdĕkā)*. He concludes by alluding once more to this "great people" *('ammĕkā hakkābēd)* that he is now called on to govern. God had asked "What shall I give to you" *[māh 'etten lāk]*? Solomon's request is now framed so that what he asks is integrally related to his position as a servant before God's people.

> Give *[nātatā]* to your servant an understanding mind *[lēb sōmēa']* to govern your people, to discern *[lĕhābîn]* between good and evil. For who is able to govern this your great people?

The petition itself is central to the meaning and function of Solomon's prayer. Before considering its substance, however, note the divine response that follows in verses 10-14. The narrator states that what Solomon asked was "good in the eyes of God." God confirms this external evaluation in a divine speech that repeatedly defines goodness in terms of the substance of Solomon's "asking" *(šā'al)*. Because of what he *did not* ask for *(lō' šā'altā;* note the phrase repeats 4 times)—long life, riches, the life of his enemies—and because of what he *did* ask for *(šā'altā* [twice]), God will grant both stated and omitted requests. God will give Solomon a heart of wisdom and understanding unequalled by any who came before him or who will come after him, *and* God will give him riches, honor, and long life. All this, provided that Solomon will practice the piety and faithfulness of the inheritance to which he has laid claim in his prayer; that is, that he take care to keep the statutes and commandments "just as David your father did" (v. 14).

I suggest that Solomon's prayer for wisdom constitutes the pri-

mary focus in this text.[22] Solomon's prayer at Gibeon affords the
reader an important opportunity for reassessing the king's character
at a point in the narrative where it has most been called into doubt.
After the preceding account of Solomon's solidification of the kingship (1 Kgs 2:12-46), with its candid reports of Solomon's involve-
ments in the murders of Adonijah, Joab, and Shimei, and his ban-
ishment of Abiathar the priest, the general portraiture of the king is
hardly inspiring.

Beginning with 1 Kgs 3:16, the narrative proceeds to describe a
more desirable figure: administering judgments wisely, implement-
ing judicious and effective administrative policies, supervising the
construction of first the temple, then his own palace. A very
changed character indeed occupies center stage in these subsequent
scenes. Were it not for the insider's view into the experience at
Gibeon that the narrator has given, one would have difficulty in
understanding how the two parts of the narrative are connected.

Having witnessed Solomon at prayer, however, one is now afforded the opportunity of a more positive appraisal. Solomon the
pray-er is pleasing to God not because of what he requests but
precisely because of what he does not request. As a true servant he is
desirous not of personal gain but of the gift of discernment, that he
may properly fulfill his God-appointed responsibilities. He is the
model king and, I may add, the model pray-er.[23] Those who would
follow his lead, provided they do not lose sight of the important
proviso stipulated in 3:14 (as Solomon subsequently did), may anticipate that God will guide their paths in the way of wisdom and
understanding.

---

22. At issue here is the assessment of the influence on this text of certain
extrabiblical parallels. S. Herrmann has argued on the basis of comparison with
Egyptian royal texts *(Königsnovelle)* that the primary emphasis in 1 Kings 3 is
Solomon's revelatory preparation for the building of a new sanctuary ("Die
Königsnovelle in Ägypten und Israel," *Wissenschaftliche Zeitschrift der Karl Marx
Universität Leipzig* 3 [1953–54]: 51–62). Weinfeld has cited additional parallels in
a number of Mesopotamian texts *(Deuteronomic School,* 247–50). In an argument
I find persuasive, however, Weinfeld concludes that neither Egyptian nor
Mesopotamian texts provide actual parallels to 1 Kings 3. In his view, what we
have here is only the framework of a common pattern. This pattern is utilized in 1
Kings 3, he contends, merely as a vehicle for conveying Solomon's special divine
endowment with wisdom (ibid., 253–54).

23. Cf. T. Veijola ("Das Klagegebet in Literatur und Leben der Exilsgeneration:
Am Beispiel einiger Prosatexte," VTSup 36 [1985], 289) who has argued that the
portrait of the praying king (e.g., David, Solomon, Hezekiah) originates in
Deuteronomistic piety against the backdrop of the practice of lament in exile.

THE EXAMPLE OF HEZEKIAH

Like Solomon, Hezekiah is presented as an exemplary king: "He did what was right in the sight of the LORD just as his ancestor David had done" (2 Kgs 18:3, NRSV). He too is accorded praise of the highest order: "there was no one like him among all the kings of Judah after him, or among those who were before him" (v. 5, NRSV). Unlike the narrative presentation of Solomon, however, where the timely insertion of prayer in effect rescues a positive character assessment from a portraiture that begins to take shape along very different lines, Hezekiah's character strengths are stated clearly upon his first introduction in the narrative (cf. vv. 1-8, NRSV). With this introduction the narrative proceeds to focus on two particular incidents during Hezekiah's reign when circumstances presented a serious challenge to his fidelity to God. The king reacts to both situations with prayer, thus affording the reader an opportunity not to reassess his piety, as in the case of Solomon, but to reaffirm it. One of these incidents, the Assyrians' siege of Jerusalem in 701 B.C.E., provides the occasion for Hezekiah's prayer recorded in 2 Kgs 19:15-19. Although this prayer does provide a glimpse into the king's faithfulness and piety, its rhetorical structure serves to emphasize God's character rather than Hezekiah's. For this reason I reserve it for discussion in the next chapter. Here I focus on the prayer recorded in 2 Kgs 20:2-3 (= Isa 38:2-3), set on the occasion of Hezekiah's "sickness unto death."

The episode is placed immediately after the account of the miraculous deliverance of Jerusalem from the siege of Sennacherib in 701 B.C.E. (2 Kgs 18:17—19:37). On that occasion Hezekiah had exhibited the effectiveness of prayer by calling on God to save the city (cf. 19:9). Through the prophet Isaiah the LORD had responded by announcing that Hezekiah's prayer had been heard and his request would be granted (cf. 19:20-34). When on the heels of this prayer the narrative reports the miraculous slaying of 185,000 Assyrians by the angel of the LORD (19:35), one is prepared to understand this slaughter as the response to Hezekiah's prayer, thus a confirmation of his status as one whose fidelity to God secured the victory for him and his people.

No sooner is this neat connection made between Hezekiah's piety and his success than the narrative turns to report a subsequent episode that seems to call it into question: "In those days Hezekiah became sick unto death" (20:1: *ḥālāh ḥizqîyyāhû lāmût).* No explanation is offered. The accompanying oracle from Isaiah registering God's assessment that Hezekiah is not to recover does little to soften the jarring impact of this report of the imminent death of so faithful a servant. Although the text provides few details, the instruction to Hezekiah to "set his house in order" suggests that the death is unexpected.[24] This instruction further contributes to the impression that God's intentions here do not square with public expectation. Are not righteousness and fidelity to be rewarded with long life and prosperity?

Hezekiah's response is to pray. He turns his face to the wall, a posture indicating the privacy of the address to follow, perhaps also symbolic of his turning away from the world to place his trust in God alone.[25] No one is to hear this prayer save God (and now the reader). The prayer itself is introduced with the phrase "and he prayed to the LORD" *(wayyitpallēl 'el Yhwh),* language commonly used to mark formal prayers and, quite often, prayers that employ typical Deuteronomistic concerns.[26] The content of Hezekiah's prayer, like that of Solomon's in 1 Kings 3, identifies it closely with concerns of the Deuteronomistic tradition.

The prayer is notable as much for what it does not articulate as for what it does. Hezekiah does not petition for healing, neither does he confess sin or plead for forgiveness. Rather he petitions God not to forget his faithfulness:

> Please, O LORD, remember now how I have walked
> before you in fidelity *[be'ĕmet]*
> and with a whole heart *[ûblēbāb šālēm]*
> and the good *[haṭṭôb]* that
> I have done in your eyes.

With the mention of but these three qualities—fidelity, a perfect or wholly committed heart, and good deeds—Hezekiah falls silent, his words now replaced with "great weeping" *(běkî gādôl).* Hezekiah's

---

24. Cf. Gray, *I and II Kings,* 697. The parallel version of this account in Isaiah attributes a thanksgiving psalm to Hezekiah (38:9-20) that makes this point more explicitly by its reference in v. 10 to the "noontide of my days," lit. "half of my days." The psalm goes on to supply a reason for Hezekiah's illness (v. 17), thus neutralizing the incongruity of divine action that is apparent in the Kings account.

25. Gray, *I and II Kings,* 697.

26. Corvin, "Stylistic and Functional Study," 32–34. For further discussion see E. A. Speiser, "The Stem *PLL* in Hebrew," *JBL* 82 (1963): 301–6; D. R. Ap-Thomas, "Notes on Some Terms Relating to Prayer," *VT* 6 (1956): 230–31; H. P. Stähli, *"pll,"* *THAT* 1.427–32; P. A. H. de Boer, *De Voorbede in Het Oude Testament* (*OTS* 3; Leiden: Brill, 1943), 120–36; Balentine, "Prophet as Intercessor," 162–73; J. F. A. Sawyer, "Types of Prayer in the Old Testament: Some Semantic Observations on Hitpallel, Hithannen, etc.," *Semitics* 7 (1980): 131–34.

recommendation of himself in these terms serves to link him (with typical Deuteronomistic language) to David (cf. 1 Kgs 3:6; 9:4; 14:8; 15:3) and to the dynastic promises that God had made to him.[27]

God's response to Hezekiah (vv. 4-6) is framed rhetorically to emphasize that precisely the king's linkage to the royal standard of conduct exemplified in David now justifies and secures God's positive intervention. Isaiah is instructed to return to Hezekiah, identified as the "prince of my people" (NRSV), with words from "the LORD, God of your father David." This God, experienced precisely in these special historical commitments, will act now "for my own sake and for the sake of my servant David" (v. 6). What Hezekiah did not request is precisely what God will provide: healing (v. 5) and an extension of his life by fifteen years (v. 6). A third provision is added to these two: the deliverance of the king and the city from the Assyrians (v. 6).[28]

Hezekiah's prayer functions on several levels to contribute significantly to the narratives within which it is set.[29] I suggest that one

27. Weinfeld, *Deuteronomic School,* 334–35. See further Staudt, "Prayer and the People," 311–12.

28. There is some chronological distortion here, for the deliverance that Hezekiah is promised appears in fact to have already occurred (cf. 2 Kgs 19:35-36). I am grateful to my colleague Keat Wiles for this observation and for calling to my attention B. Halpern's suggestion that behind the Deuteronomistic historian's portrait of Hezekiah stands a source written in Hezekiah's (or Manasseh's) court ("Sacred History and Ideology: Chronicles' Thematic Structure—Indications of an Earlier Source," *The Creation of Sacred Literature,* ed. R. E. Friedman [Berkeley: Univ. of California Press, 1981], 35–54). Such a source might understandably emphasize Hezekiah's piety as a causative factor in the resolution of the Assyrian crisis, even at the expense of chronological precision. Halpern has pursued further the idea of the Deuteronomistic historian's methodology in *The First Historians: The Hebrew Bible and History* (San Francisco: Harper and Row, 1988); see esp. 207–35.

29. For example, at one level it draws attention to the role of the prophet as a divine messenger and as a worker of signs and wonders (cf. vv. 7-11) in the interest of confirming divine oracles. This is at work in the Hezekiah traditions located in 2 Kings, but it is even more to the fore in the inclusion of these traditions in the Isaiah materials (cf. Isaiah 36–38; see, e.g., R. E. Clements, *Isaiah 1–39* [New Century Bible Commentary; Grand Rapids: Eerdmans, 1980], 289). On another level the prolongation of Hezekiah's life serves to provide an important alteration in the course of historical events as depicted in Kings. During these additional years one is encouraged to understand that (1) the Babylonians rather than the Assyrians become God's agents of doom (cf. 2 Kgs 20:16-19); and (2) Manasseh, age twelve at the time of his accession to the throne according to 2 Kgs 21:1, is born, thus securing that there would be no premature break in the Davidic dynasty or in God's covenant promises upon which it was founded. In this regard, Staudt has suggested that Hezekiah's petition secures a "schedule change" in the course of the fulfillment of the divine plan for Judah ("Prayer and the People," 318).

important function is to provide a portraiture of the king himself. Hezekiah is the epitome of the faithful devotee of God. His success in matters of both national (cf. 2 Kgs 19:15-19) and personal crisis is the mark of his piety and devotion.[30] To allow the reader to see this connection more clearly, the narrator does not restrict the report simply to the record of Hezekiah's activities. Rather, the reader is permitted to listen in on private moments of prayer designed by their careful rhetoric to illustrate the selflessness of one who places himself completely and securely at God's disposal. His is the ideal posture before God, the paradigm of the effective pray-er.

PRAYER AS A MEANS OF CARICATURE

THE EXAMPLE OF JACOB

Just as prayer may serve to confirm one's status, it may also function subtly to caricature or parody. One of the clearest examples of this function occurs in Jacob's prayer in Gen 32:9-12 (MT vv. 10-13). As part of the larger narrative concerning his preparation to meet Esau, Jacob's prayer represents but one of several attempts to control his own destiny through a shrewd combination of cunning and piety. In this regard the prayer contributes to the general narrative portraiture of *yāʿaqōb*, "Jacob," the "supplanter," the "grasper," the "exploiter" (Gen 25:22-23; cf. 27:36).

The larger narrative complex in Gen 27:41—33:17 provides the backdrop for Jacob's prayer.[31] The pertinent episodes in the developing drama may be summarized as follows: (1) Jacob flees to Haran to escape the wrath of Esau, whom he has cheated out of Isaac's blessing (27:41-45). (2) While in Haran with Laban (chaps. 29-31), Jacob takes Leah and Rachel as wives, and in the bargain cleverly tricks Laban out of his flocks (cf. 30:37-43). Just as his favored status with Laban begins to expire, he is instructed by God to return home to Canaan, a journey he is to undertake with the

---

30. Cf. Clements, *Isaiah 1-39,* 289.

31. The general consensus is that this section of the text, including Jacob's prayer in 32:9-12, derives from J, or perhaps JE. See, e.g., O. Eissfeldt, *The Old Testament: An Introduction* (New York: Harper and Row, 1965), 199; E. A. Speiser, *Genesis* (AB; Garden City, N.Y.: Doubleday, 1964), 255; G. von Rad, *Genesis* (OTL; rev. ed.; Philadelphia: Westminster, 1972), 316–19; M. Noth, *A History of Pentateuchal Traditions* (Englewood Cliffs, N.J.: Prentice-Hall, 1972); C. Westermann, *Genesis 12-36* (Minneapolis: Augsburg, 1985), 504; H. Gunkel, *Genesis* (3d ed.; Göttingen: Vandenhoeck und Ruprecht, 1964), 355–65; G. Coats, *Genesis; with and Introduction to Narrative Literature* (FOTL; Grand Rapids: Eerdmans, 1983), 224–28.

promise of divine presence to accompany him (31:3). (3) Jacob's preparations to meet Esau (chap. 32) involve a series of activities: sending messengers ahead with gifts (32:3-5); dividing his camp into two companies (32:7-8), each one bearing gifts (32:13-21); prayer (32:9-12); and last, a preparation not of his own making, his encounter with the mysterious assailant at the Jabbok River (32:22-32). (4) The final scene is the long-anticipated encounter with Esau (chap. 33).

My particular focus is on the acts of preparation described in Genesis 32. Combining pragmatism and piety, Jacob initiates a series of maneuvers in the hopes of securing control over his situation. First he instructs messengers to go before him to tell Esau of the numerous possessions he has acquired in Haran. Such a report he hopes might secure Esau's favorable disposition *(ḥēn)* toward him (vv. 3-5). The messengers return with a report of their own, however, which in its ambiguity leaves the success of their mission much in question: "he [Esau] is coming to meet you, *and four hundred men are with him"* (v. 6, NRSV). Does Esau seek reunion or retaliation? The report is unclear. Yet Jacob assumes the worst and is "greatly afraid." What follows are a series of acts, linked syntactically with *waw* consecutives, that show his preparations for all eventualities: "And Jacob was afraid . . . and he divided the people with him . . . and he said, 'If Esau comes to the one company and destroys it, then the company that is left may yet escape,' and Jacob said, 'God of my father Abraham. . . .'" (vv. 7-8).

With these last words Jacob turns to address God. Yet his approach to God—"and Jacob said *[wayyō'mer]"*—is hardly distinguishable in its beginning from the preceding interhuman conversations that have thus far occupied his attention. At one point he speaks *(lē'mōr)* to his messengers, instructing them to speak *(tō'měrûn)* to Esau the words Jacob has spoken *('āmar)* to them (v. 5). These messengers then return speaking *(lē'mōr)* their report (v. 6), to which Jacob responds by dividing his company and articulating *(wayyō'mer)* his rationale (v. 9). Following these several interchanges Jacob then turns, in the usual way of human conversation, to speak to God.

Corvin has suggested that the *'āmar* terminology is typical of conversational prayers, in which the pray-er's informality signals a high degree of intimacy in the divine-human relationship.[32] In most

---

32. Corvin, "Stylistic and Functional Study," 31, 159. In Gen 32:9-12 Corvin finds a "formal prayer," even though he observes it "lacks the normal characteristics of formal prayers" (261).

instances such an approach reinforces a positive assessment of the pray-er. In Jacob's case, however, I am inclined to see the approach differently. His converation with God is but one of several in which he engages, each one designed to implement different aspects of his planning. If one looks beyond the prayer, one finds an additional signal pointing toward this understanding. Upon the conclusion of his address to God, Jacob returns almost immediately to his previous conversation partners with no apparent shift in his basic orientation to the crisis (cf. 32:13-21).

The prayer itself is shaped as a petition consisting of four primary parts: address to God (v. 9), statement of humility (v. 10), petition (v. 11a), motivation for divine response (vv. 11b–12)[33]. As Greenberg has observed, the words that give content to this form constitute a "model of rhetoric" designed adroitly to persuade God that Jacob's interests and God's coincide.[34] Several elements of Jacob's prayer support this evaluation.

Although Jacob's invocation is introduced as only a familiar conversation, it is in fact marked off from preceding interchanges. Here he addresses God. But his invocation of God is also carefully formulated. On the one hand he addresses the God of the great patriarchal figures, "God of my father Abraham and God of my father Isaac" (NRSV), joining this identification of God with the special name "LORD" (YHWH).[35] In this way he positions himself in the succession of his forebears, as preserver of their faith and so as worthy recipient of the same divine care and attention to which they had been privileged. On the other hand these opening words, which in themselves need not imply anything other than the basis of Jacob's relationship to God, are immediately supplemented with language that seeks to define this relationship in ways particularly advantageous for Jacob. The God Jacob addresses is identified as the one who has made certain specific promises to him, promises that Jacob now recalls by quoting God's words to God:

> O LORD who said to me, "Return to your country and to your kindred, and I will do you good." (v. 9, NRSV)

The stress is clearly on Jacob's return to Canaan. For obvious

---

33. H. G. Reventlow *(Gebet im Alten Testament* [Stuttgart: Kohlhammer, 1986], 97–98) finds the *Urform* (original form) of prayer in Genesis 32 in vv. 10a, 12. In this form its basic component parts—address to God, petition for deliverance, portrayal of need—reflect the three most important elements of lament.

34. Greenberg, *Prose Prayer,* 14.

35. Reventlow *(Gebet,* 97) sees "LORD" as a secondary addition.

reasons Jacob does not allude to the real reason he finds himself just now outside the land of promise and in such dire straits (i.e., his cheating of Esau). His more immediate concern is how to secure safe passage back across the border. Toward this end Jacob reminds God of an earlier commitment. Jacob's view is that God has promised to "do good" *('êṭîbāh)* by him. Rhetorically this emphasis shapes the whole of Jacob's prayer so as to present it as his primary concern.[36] In verse 9 and again at the conclusion of the prayer in verse 12 in a still stronger formulation ("you, you said *['atta 'āmartā]*, 'I will surely do you good'" *[hêṭēb 'êṭîb]*, Jacob presses God to keep faith with divine commitments. But Jacob's version of this commitment does not square exactly with God's.

The promise to which Jacob refers appears first in the Jacob narratives at Gen 28:15 (cf. v. 20) and again at 31:3.[37] Both texts are set within the context of Jacob's journey back to Canaan, the first occurring during his dream at Bethel, the second just as he is preparing to depart from Laban's household. In both cases God's commitment is expressed principally in terms of the promise of divine presence. Hence God promises "I am/will be with you" *('ānōkî 'immāk/'ehyeh 'immāk).* In Jacob's quotation of this promise, however, he has altered the substance of God's commitment. It is not "return to your country and to your kindred *and I will be with you,"* but "return . . . *and I will do you good."* The promise of presence in general terms has been recalled in more specific terms. In a real sense Jacob desires more than just God's presence on the journey, more than what he has already been promised. He desires a divine presence concretely manifested in terms of goodness.

Jacob's tampering with the divine promise is in keeping with the general lines of his character displayed thus far in the narrative. He is consistently portrayed as one who schemes and manipulates people and events for personal gain. From his emergence out of the womb, *ya'ăqōb,* "the supplanter," is pictured as grasping, exploiting, insisting. In the words of Brueggemann, "his life is trouble not only for himself but for those around him."[38] He negotiates with Esau for the birthright (Gen 25:29-34); he tricks Isaac out of the blessing, again at the expense of Esau (27:18-29), who is prompted thereby to observe: "Is he not rightly named Jacob *[ya'ăqōb],* for he

36. Cf. W. Brueggemann, *Genesis* (Interpretation; Atlanta: John Knox, 1982), 265.
37. Cf. C. Westermann, *The Promises to the Fathers: Studies on the Patriarchal Narratives* (Philadelphia: Fortress, 1980), 140–43.
38. Brueggemann, *Genesis,* 214.

has tricked me *[ya'ǎqĕbēnî]* these two times" (v. 36); he cleverly cheats Laban out of his own flocks (30:37-43). The character Jacob displays in his address to God reinforces this larger picture. Whereas previous episodes pit Jacob's wiles against human antagonists, here Jacob attempts to manipulate God. With carefully chosen words Jacob seeks to maneuver God to agree with his own version of the situation. God has ordered him to return *(šub)*; this is a divine mission, not just a shady brother's return to the scene of a former crime. God has promised to do him good, not just to accompany him on the journey.

As the prayer unfolds, the picture of Jacob is not changed, only supplemented. Verse 10 presents a statement feigning self-deprecation,[39] yet here too Jacob only flirts with the truth. He describes himself as one who is small *(qāṭōntî)*, a servant of God *('abdekā)*, yet undeserving of God's steadfast love and faithfulness. To secure this emphasis he credits God for the fact that he had previously crossed the Jordan with no more than his staff, and now he has become two companies. But, the mention of two companies *(lišnê maḥǎnôt)* recalls an earlier incident in Jacob's preparations to meet Esau. Verse 7 has already stated that Jacob has become two companies *(lišnê maḥǎnôt)* because he himself has divided his people and his possessions (acquired at Laban's expense) as part of his plan to obtain Esau's favor. Thus Jacob camouflages his own scheming as evidence of God's blessing.

The petition in verse 11 is for deliverance. In keeping with the character of similar petitions in lament psalms, Jacob addresses God in imperatival tones: "Deliver me now, I pray *[haṣṣîlēnî nā']*, from the hand of my brother Esau." After the manner of the "traditional prayer,"[40] this petition is followed by a *kî* ("for, because") clause that expresses the motivation for divine intervention. Jacob's motivations are not in the least disguised. He is afraid of Esau

---

39. Greenberg, *Prose Prayer,* 10.

40. The term is from A. Aejmelaeus, whose form-critical investigation suggests that the traditionally recurring features of individual complaint psalms are the imperative petition, address to Yahweh, and motivation clause introduced by *kî.* This form is found primarily in the Psalms; it is not frequent in prose prayers. She finds one example in Gen 32:12, which she understands to be an important link between "profane petitions" and psalm petitions. In her judgment the presence of such a form in Genesis 32 means that the cultic form of petition grew out of a living practice, not vice versa (*The Traditional Prayer in the Psalms* [BZAW 167; Berlin: de Gruyter, 1986], 89–91). On the connections between profane petitions and petitions to God, see further E. Gerstenberger, *Der bittende Mensch* (Neukirchen: Neukirchener Verlag, 1980), 18–20, 127; Greenberg, *Prose Prayer,* 19–37.

(kî yārē' 'ānōkî), afraid that his coming will result in the slaying of the whole company. The same motivation previously led Jacob to prepare for the meeting with Esau by dividing his people and his possessions into two camps (v. 7). His rationale is that in this way perhaps he can protect at least half of his possessions. Thus Jacob's fear prompts him to act on two fronts. First, he relies on his own wits to devise a plan that will work against Esau. But in case this plan should fail—and he is still afraid, despite the plan as already conceived—it is prudent that he should turn secondly to God. Perhaps God will succeed where he may not.

As noted previously, the conclusion of Jacob's prayer in verse 12 is stylistically linked to its beginning in verse 9. The repetition of the verbal phrase "do you good," here strengthened to "surely do you good," once again signals Jacob's intent to hold God to his own skewed version of the promise. The latter half of Jacob's version—"and make your descendants as the sand of the sea"—corresponds more closely to the promise of increase found elsewhere in the narrative (e.g., 28:3, 14).[41] Even so, with Jacob's distortion of the promise as preface, the substance of the whole is colored in a self-serving way to motivate God toward fulfillment of a particular perception of the divine commitment.

The conclusion of Jacob's prayer receives no verbal response from God. Indeed, as verses 13-21 suggest, Jacob immediately resumes his own strategizing for the imminent encounter with Esau. He takes from what is "in his hand," that is, from his own resources, and prepares a gift for his brother. The gift is stipulated as "droves" or "moving herds" of livestock *('ēder)*, which he hands over to his servants. They are to pass on before him, drove by drove, with appropriate spacing in between them, as a parade of presents designed by their cumulative impression to win Esau's favor. Jacob is to remain behind, safely positioned to observe the outcome of it all without exposing himself to any risks. Little in this account suggests that Jacob's prayer has produced any change in his basic orientation to life. Both before and after his prayer he assumes the posture of one who is in control of his own destiny, commanding those under his authority (cf. vv. 5, 18-19) to implement his directives. As a whole verses 3-21 present a sequence of activities that describe Jacob's movements from planning to praying, and back to planning again. It is the picture of one who intends to leave nothing to chance, or perhaps, nothing to God!

---

41. Cf. Westermann, *Promises to the Fathers,* 149–55.

By the end of verse 21 Jacob's preparations are concluded. The whole of his activities has been carried out within a temporal framework that has alerted the reader that Esau is coming to meet him with four hundred men (v. 6). Yet just when one expects the narrative to bring Esau onto the scene, his arrival is delayed until 33:1. This delay allows for the reporting of one further episode, which serves ironically as Jacob's final preparation for the long-awaited encounter.

The text reporting Jacob's wrestling with the stranger at Jabbok (32:22-32) is one of the most extensively interpreted accounts in the patriarchal materials. It lends itself to a wide range of hermeneutical possibilities that I cannot begin to address here. But I shall try to discern its connection to the larger narrative, and particularly to Jacob's prayer.

The narrative itself suggests a chronological connection with the preceding events. The encounter takes place on "the same night" (v. 22: *ballayĕlāh hahû'),* that is, on the same night as he divided his company into droves (cf. v. 13), and presumably on the same day that he had prayed. When the wrestling match ends, the narrative reports that the sun was rising (v. 31; cf. v. 24); with no further temporal allusions, it goes on to report that Jacob lifted his eyes and "behold, Esau was coming" (33:1). Thus this dramatic episode is positioned as part of Jacob's eleventh-hour preparation.

During this nighttime interlude Jacob is left alone (v. 24). But he is not alone. Immediately a "man" *('îš)* is with him, locked with him in a wrestler's embrace. The identity of this assailant is kept intentionally unclear, yet several clues lead the reader to connect the assailant with God (cf. vv. 28, 30). This linkage invites the reader to understand Jacob wrestling, attempting to overpower, the deity whom he has just addressed in prayer. In the one encounter he has tried to manipulate God with words, in the other he tries to muscle God with brute strength. His struggle to obtain the blessing, by whatever means available to him, recalls his earlier quests with both Isaac (cf. 27:5-29) and God. Isaac had been duped, but God is an opponent of a different caliber. While God made no verbal response to Jacob's earlier petition, here the deity responds with unexpected force.

Surprisingly Jacob is not overcome. He wrestles through the night to a draw. But neither does he conquer, as he usually did in his previous encounters. For the first time Jacob does not control the situation. He does receive the blessing, but at significant cost. As F. Buechner has aptly put it, he is both blessed and broken by this "magnificent defeat at the hands of God."[42] That his brokenness applies to more than just the limp in his gait (cf. v. 25) is signaled by the change of name reported in verse 28. Jacob "the supplanter" comes away from this encounter as Israel, "the one with whom God has striven." The new name is meant to embody a new character, a change from one who seeks to control to one who is controlled.

In the present narrative the change manifests itself almost immediately. When at last Jacob lifts his eyes, he sees before him Esau and his men (33:1), and again he is thrust back into the reality of the crisis toward which all his preparation has been directed. His initial response seems at first unaltered from his original plans. He divides the children between Leah and Rachel, thus recalling his intentions to divide his people into two companies (33:1-2; cf. 32:7). Upon closer inspection, however, it becomes clear that this time his plan develops differently. Jacob's previous strategy had been to have his companies go on *before him,* winning Esau's favor with their presentation of gifts, and if not, providing a protective buffer for Jacob, who would remain behind. Now the plan suddenly takes on a new twist. Jacob goes *before them* (33:3), placing himself in the position of greatest vulnerability.

The narrative continues in chapter 33 to describe the reconciliation between Jacob and Esau. But this positive resolution has been anticipated by the sequence of episodes that have preceded. Jacob "the supplanter," the "exploiter," has now been sufficiently prepared, not by his own efforts, not even by his prayer, but by an unexpected assault on both his cunning and his piety.[43]

THE EXAMPLE OF JONAH

The characterization of "Jonah the son of Amittai" (Jonah 1:1) is achieved through a presentation of the paradoxical relationship between his pious affirmations and his conduct. He pronounces himself a "Hebrew" who fears "the LORD, the God of heaven, who

42. F. Buechner, *The Magnificent Defeat* (San Francisco: Harper and Row, 1966), 10–18.

43. As a caveat, I note that the combination of wit, cunning, and piety need not be portrayed only as a negative character trait. A classic example occurs in the prayer of Abraham's servant recorded in Gen 24:12-14, 26-27. In this instance both the servant's good sense and his piety are instrumental in securing the success of his mission to locate a wife for Isaac. By narrative's end not only the servant and Laban but also the reader are persuaded that God has been at work controlling the destinies of all the principal characters. For discussion of this account from a literary perspective, see Sternberg, *Poetics,* 131–52; note esp. his comments on the rhetoric of persuasiveness, 141–43, 148–52.

made the sea and the dry land" (1:9, NRSV), yet he flees to the sea to escape the commands of this God. He asks to be thrown into the sea (1:12) and then expresses thankfulness for being delivered from it (2:2-9; MT vv. 3-10). He proclaims a divine word of warning to the sinful Ninevites (3:4), then becomes angry when they heed the warning and confess their sins (4:1).

Nowhere is this discrepancy between word and act more clear than in his prayers, two of which this brief book records. Structurally these prayers are strategically positioned to show Jonah's response to two key episodes in the story. The first (2:2-9) provides his reaction to his deliverance from the sea, the second (4:2-3) his response to the sparing of the Ninevites. Both prayers posture a level of piety that, like Jacob's, is not exactly what it seems.

Before turning to these two specific texts, I note by way of introduction that prayer also serves as a literary leitmotif in characterizing the sailors and the Ninevites in chapters 1 and 3 respectively. Both groups "call out" in prayer (*qārā':* 1:14; 3:8). Both are described as "crying out" in their respective distresses (with *zā'aq:* 1:5; 3:8) with the identical hope "that we do not perish" *(wĕlō' nō'bēd:* 1:6; 3:9).[44] Both portray a common willingness to submit to the will of God and thus secure life in the face of death. In this way both groups serve as a foil to the reluctant and rebellious Jonah.

This contrast is particularly clear in the scene described in 1:4-16, which depicts Jonah as unresponsive and lethargic in the presence of impending calamity. While the sailors in their fear before the great storm at sea are praying to their gods, Jonah lies in a deep sleep within the bowels of the ship and has to be awakened by the captain. His posture strikes the captain as incredible: "What do you mean, you sleeper? Get up, call to your god *[qĕrā' 'el 'ĕlōhêkā]!* Perhaps the god will spare a thought for us so that we do not perish" (1:6). Awakened, Jonah remains silent and passive as the sailors in their frenzy cast lots to determine the source of their crisis. When Jonah at last speaks, his words mouth a confession of faith that his actions do little to confirm. He is a Hebrew, and he "fears" the LORD "who made the sea" (1:9), but to this God he makes no response, and the sea rages on. It is finally the sailors who discern the need to address the LORD, and it is ultimately their prayer for life before this God that stills the storm (cf. 1:4). In the end it is they who "fear" the LORD and their sacrifices and vows that seal their commitment

---

44. Cf. J. Magonet, *Form and Meaning: Studies in Literary Techniques in the Book of Jonah* (2d ed.; Sheffield: Almond, 1983), 20, 26.

(1:16). Throughout this episode the pagan mariners are described as the models of piety, whereas Jonah, the Hebrew, is presented as the model pagan.[45] Jonah too will ultimately offer vows and sacrifices to this God (cf. 2:9), thus finally approaching the level of piety exhibited by the sailors. But, as we shall see, even then his sense of commitment does not represent a comparable submission to the will of God.

The prayer recorded in 2:2-9 is commonly regarded as a secondary insertion, and for this reason is usually excerpted from the narrative and interpreted as an isolated unit.[46] Yet I am persuaded that efforts to defend the prayer's "suitability for the story as a whole" have merit.[47] Even if one grants that the prayer derives from

---

45. Cf. D. F. Payne ("Jonah from the Perspective of its Audience," *JSOT* 13 [1979]: 8–9), who suggests that perhaps it is not piety but only superstition that prompts the sailors' prayer. Do they indeed submit themselves to Israel's God, or are they simply exercising every means available, religious or practical, to save themselves from the storm? In any case, Payne also understands their behavior to serve as a foil to Jonah's.

46. H. W. Wolff conveniently summarizes the principal reasons under three headings: (1) The situation of the psalm does not fit the context, e.g., the psalm is more appropriate for the temple than the belly of a fish (cf. vv. 4b, 7b [MT vv. 5b, 8b]). (2) The language of the psalm is different than that of the narrative. Although the two prose prayers in the narrative (1:14; 4:2-3) are true lament prayers and share a common style and rhetoric with the larger narrative, the prayer of chap. 2 is in poetry and its language portrays Jonah's need in words quite different from 1:4—2:1. (3) The characterization of Jonah in the psalm is at odds with that which is presented elsewhere in the narrative. Can these pious words of thanksgiving belong to the stubborn and rebellious Jonah of chaps. 1 and 4? (H. W. Wolff, *Obadiah and Jonah* [Minneapolis: Augsburg, 1986], 128–31). With reference to the issue of characterization, Schmidt (*"De Deo": Studien zur Literarkritik und Theologie des Buches Jona, des Gesprächs zwischen Abraham und Jahwe in Gen. 18, 22ff. und von Hi. 1* [BZAW 143; Berlin: de Gruyter, 1976]) has argued that 2:2-10 comes from the final stages of the book's redaction. The original source (1:2; 3:3-10; 4:1, 5a, 6-11) shows no interest in Jonah's personality or character and instead focuses exclusively on God's universal mercy (cf. pp. 18–47). A second (1:1, 3-16; 2:1, 11) and third level of redaction (4:2-4) contribute the additional themes of divine power (cf. pp. 49, 66, 83) and the interrelationship between divine power with divine mercy (cf. pp. 119–20) respectively. Not until the final stage of redaction was the psalm in 2:2-10 inserted, and only then is the emphasis turned from God to Jonah. At this final stage Schmidt contends that the redactional emphasis corresponds with a common tendency (also displayed in Job 1 and Genesis 18) to transform stories whose original focus was on God's activities into stories focusing on human response.

47. See, e.g., O. Kaiser, "Wirklichkeit, Möglichkeit und Vorurteil: Ein Betrag zum Verständnis des Buches Jona," *EvT* 33 (1973): 91–103; G. H. Cohn, *Das Buch Jonah im Lichte der biblischen Erzählkunst* (Assen: Van Gorcum, 1969), 93–94; G. M. Landes, "The Kerygma of the Book of Jonah," *Int* 21 (1967): 3–31, from whom the phrase "suitability for the story as a whole" is quoted; Magonet, *Form and Meaning*, 39–54; J. S. Ackerman, "Satire and Symbolism in the Song of Jonah," *Traditions in Transformation: Turning Points in Biblical Faith*, ed. B.

a different author, and this is subject to challenge,[48] nevertheless the present arrangement of the book constrains one to search for its relation and contribution to the narrative in which it is set. J. Magonet has argued persuasively that the characterization of Jonah provided here is not contradictory to the traits he displays elsewhere in the narrative. Rather, one may see in this pious expression of thanksgiving the same paradoxical relationship between Jonah's words and his actions that the narrative as a whole is intent to portray.[49]

I begin by observing that the prayer occurs at a strategic place within the narrative's development. In response to God's first call to "arise and go to Nineveh," Jonah had arisen to flee *(wayyāqom . . . librōah)* to the sea (1:3). To God's second call, formulated with the identical command, Jonah responds by arising and going to Nineveh (3:3: *wayyāqom . . . wayyēlek)* as instructed. How is one to explain this transition from flight to obedience? It is Jonah's time in the belly of the fish, the interval of three days and nights, that provides the opportunity for reflection on this question.[50] The only clue to what transpires during this interval is Jonah's prayer.

At one level the form of the prayer itself bears witness to a transition in Jonah's circumstances. Structured as a typical thanksgiving psalm, the prayer traces Jonah's deliverance from a situation of distress and his resultant gratitude to God. The movement in such psalms is always from personal need to divine deliverance: "I called . . . the LORD answered me" (v. 2); "I went down . . . you brought me up" (v. 6); "my life was ebbing away . . . my prayer came to you" (v. 7); or, as framed in the opening and closing words of the prayer in Hebrew, *"I called . . . to the LORD"* (vv. 2, 9). This movement of a person to God, or better, of God's movement to the person, provides the motivation for thanksgiving. In Jonah's case, this movement is signaled by his intent to offer thanksgiving *(tôdāh),* sacrifice *('ezbĕhāh),* and the completion of his vows *(nādartî;* v. 9). By prayer's end Jonah seems to have come to the same level of commitment and piety as the sailors (cf. 1:16). Thus disgorged back on dry land he should be more receptive to the divine commission.

Halpern and J. Levenson (Winona Lake, Ind.: Eisenbrauns, 1981), 213–46.

48. Cf. Magonet (*Form and Meaning,* 39–54), who argues on both stylistical and thematic grounds that the psalm was composed by the author of the book and included by the author at this particular juncture in the narrative.

49. Ibid., 52–53.

50. Cf. A. Lacoque and P. Lacoque, *The Jonah Complex* (Atlanta: John Knox, 1981), 52.

As Magonet has observed, however, the rhetoric of this prayer suggests that Jonah's transformation is more complicated, his intentions more ambiguous, than might first appear.[51] For example, he offers no hint of repentance for fleeing from God. His prayer acknowledges no culpability for his present distress. He is not overcome by the waters of the sea because he has fled from God, but because *"you* cast me into the deep, into the heart of the seas" (v. 3, NRSV). Nor does the text mention the mission to Nineveh or his intent now to complete this mission. Rather his final oath suggests that he is intent on heading for Jerusalem to offer sacrifices and vows in the temple toward which he has looked so longingly (cf. vv. 4, 7) throughout his prayer. Magonet sees here a "retreat into piety" that may be reckoned as yet another attempt to flee from God: "when flight from God did not work, there is always flight to God, or to that convenient God who makes no demands beyond those the worshipper can comfortably offer."[52]

One may even note a hint of self-centeredness in Jonah's approach to God at several places. His opening words are nearly identical to the call of Ps 120:1, which in Hebrew is arranged as follows: "Unto the LORD in my distress I called, and the LORD answered me."[53] In Jonah's prayer, however, the word order is altered, the position of the pray-er replacing the position of the LORD in the syntactical sequence: *"I* called from my distress unto the *LORD,* and the LORD answered me." Jonah continues in the same vein a few verses later: "then *I, I* said, *'I* am driven from your presence, how can *I* look again toward your holy temple?'" (v. 4).[54] Structurally these opening verses constitute one of two prayers within this psalm. Following this first prayer in which Jonah's emphatic "I" has so prominent a position, there is no mention of divine intervention. Instead, the text proceeds to describe Jonah's continuing descent into the depths of the sea (v. 6). Only when he has reached this lowest level, far beyond the level of his initial address to God, does God intervene to raise Jonah to safety (v. 6).[55]

---

51. Magonet, *Form and Meaning,* 52–53.

52. Ibid., 179.

53. On this and other examples of inner-biblical comparisons throughout Jonah's prayer, see J. M. Sasson, *Jonah* (AB: Garden City, N.Y.: Doubleday, 1990), 164, 168–201.

54. Magonet, *Form and Meaning,* 46–47.

55. Ibid., 41–42. Sasson (*Jonah,* 182–83) sees in the two contrasting verbs *yārad,* "descend," and *he'ĕlāh,* "lift up," the "psychological center of the psalm." See further J. T. Walsh ("Jonah 2, 3-10: A Rhetorical Critical Study," *Biblica* 63 [1982]: 226–27), who sees in this rhetoric an emphasis on Jonah's "sinking," an emphasis that reflects his sense of separation from God. From Jonah's perspective

With his deliverance Jonah resumes his prayer, but now the construction of his sentences changes. He speaks of himself in the third rather than the first person—"when it ebbed away from me, my life"—and then not as most translations have it, "I remembered the LORD," but instead "the LORD, I remembered" (v. 7). It is interesting to consider Magonet's interpretation of these switches from first to third person. He suggests that they are representative of Jonah's slow realization that his own self-centeredness cannot lay claim to God's beneficence. With this lesson in hand Jonah then comes as a transformed "I" to offer the voice of thanksgiving and gratitude, and to proclaim the appropriate confession, "Deliverance belongs to the LORD" (v. 9). Magonet suggests, "for all his selfishness and absurdity even Jonah . . . is capable of crying to God and of a limited degree of change in response to God's command and teaching."[56]

Still, I must come back to an earlier observation. Throughout his prayer Jonah has offered no hint that he is prepared at last to take up the mission to Nineveh. If one interprets the prayer as a self-contained text, as is commonly done, one has the impression that the crisis has passed, the transformation has been completed, and the appropriate response of gratitude has been offered. From this perspective one could understand that Jonah would consider the experience closed. But the narrative context that frames the prayer permits a different view. "Then Jonah prayed to the LORD his God from the belly of the fish" (2:1, NRSV). And the LORD's response? "The Lord spoke to the fish and it *vomited* out Jonah upon the dry land" (2:10).[57] One is hard-pressed to find here much confirmation for Jonah the pray-er. One suspects that God does not yet consider this messenger to have attained the level of commitment that his piety pretends. As the narrative in chapter 3 draws attention back to original concerns (i.e., the mission to Nineveh), the reader is given yet another view of the incongruities between Jonah's words and his actions. Again Jonah will pray, and once again the divine response will have the final claim on one's understanding of his words.

Jonah's second prayer is recorded in 4:2-3. Like his first address

---

the psalm bespeaks the "tragedy of abandonment" that, given his preoccupation with self, he interprets as "unwarranted moral separation."

56. Magonet, *Form and Meaning,* 53.

57. Sasson notes that of the Hebrew verbs available to the poet to convey ejection (e.g. *hôṣî', pālaṭ),* the choice of the "loathsome" verb *qî',* "vomit, regurgitate," serves to add yet one more indignity to Jonah's already pitiful situation (*Jonah,* 220).

to God, this prayer also follows a key episode in the drama and thus provides commentary on Jonah's reaction to it. Chapter 3 has reported that at long last Jonah has taken up the call to go to Nineveh. To his words warning that the city is soon to be overthrown, the people respond immediately by believing in God and proclaiming a fast (3:5). The king joins in this response, replacing his royal robe with the mourner's sackcloth, abandoning the royal throne to sit among the ashes of the penitent (3:6). By decree he extends the fast to "human beings and animals," summoning all to pray to God *(yiqrě'û 'el 'ělōhîm)* and to turn from their evil and violence (3:8). The king voices the hope that underlies the actions of all: "Who knows, God may yet repent and turn from fierce anger, so that we do not perish" (3:9). Their prayer, like that of the sailors in chapter 1 (cf. 1:14), is effective. When God sees how they turn from their evil ways, God responds by repenting and turning from the anger that threatens to destroy them (3:10). By the end of chapter 3 the mission to Nineveh is complete, and its intent has been accomplished in God's eyes. All that remains now is Jonah's response.

Jonah's response to these developments contrasts directly to God's. Although God is pleased with the response of the Ninevites and has turned away from anger, Jonah is angry and exceedingly displeased (4:1). In his anger he prays, and once again his rhetoric suggests a measure of self-concern that betrays his true feelings:

> O LORD, is this not what *I* said when *I* was still in *my* country? Therefore *I* fled hastily to Tarshish because *I* knew that you are a gracious God, merciful, slow to anger, and abounding in steadfast love, and repenting of evil. Now LORD, take *my* life from *me*, for *my* death is better than *my* life. (4:2-3)

H. W. Wolff has noted that Jonah's words here betray the same self-concern that has characterized his speech throughout the book. Although he begins his address on the same submissive note as the sailors *('ānnāh Yhwh;* cf. 1:14) and continues with a traditional declaration affirming God's great mercy and love,[58] he pushes his own concerns in direct opposition to this merciful God. Five times in verse 2, and four times in verse 3, his preoccupation with self

---

58. On Jonah's use and adaptation of this formula, esp. as it relates to the reference in Joel 2:13, see M. Fishbane, *Biblical Interpretation in Ancient Israel* (Oxford: Clarendon, 1985), 345–47; T. B. Dozeman, "Inner-Biblical Interpretation of Yahweh's Gracious and Compassionate Character," *JBL* 108 (1989): 207–23. For an assessment of how this issue contributes to the universalistic message of the book, see J. Day, "Problems in the Book of Jonah," *OTS* 26 (1990): 44–47.

motivates his prayer.[59] "Is this not what *I* said when *I* was still in *my* country? . . . because *I* knew. . . . Take *my* life . . . for *my* death is better than *my* life."[60] The issue as framed here is no longer the Ninevites' evil but "this great evil" (4:1) that has resulted in their forgiveness. God's "fierce anger" has clearly now been assuaged, but Jonah's anger, which becomes apparent in the aftermath of God's display of mercy, burns unabated.

Only with Jonah's prayer is one permitted at last to understand clearly the reasons for his fleeing from God. He has resisted not because he feared that the message he was ordered to deliver would be hostilely received or denied, but because he knew that it would be effective—that should the Ninevites repent, they would certainly secure God's forgiveness. Jonah knows this, for God is "gracious and merciful," just as he knows that God is maker of the sea, but here as before he resists this God and places himself in opposition to God's will. To forgive the sinful Ninevites would be a travesty of justice, from Jonah's perspective. For him it would be better to die than to be party to such an event.

Yet this prayer is designed to emphasize not so much Jonah's perception of God but God's perception of Jonah and those like him who would disguise ruthlessness as piety. "Is it right for you to be angry?" (NRSV).[61] The question from God in response to Jonah's prayer is repeated (4:4, 9), and by means of this question the entire episode is drawn to a pointed close. To the first question Jonah remains silent, seething in his anger under the shade of a self-made booth outside the city. God proceeds to supply an additional means of shade to "save" Jonah from "his evil" (4:6). But again God's intentions and Jonah's understanding of them are far apart. Jonah's anger is momentarily replaced by "great joy" (4:6). Yet his joy is in his comfort rather than in appreciation for the witness to God's mercy that the shade provides. As soon as such comfort is removed, Jonah's joy vanishes, and in its place returns the anger that chooses

---

59. H. W. Wolff, *Studien zum Jonabuch* (Neukirchen: Neukirchener Verlag, 1965), 118; cf. Magonet, *Form and Meaning,* 97; Sasson, *Jonah,* 278.

60. Hebrew literature attests relatively few instances of the striking request of God to shorten life. Sasson discusses the texts and their relevance for Jonah (*Jonah,* 283–86).

61. On this question see S. H. Blank, "'Dost Thou Do Well To Be Angry?' A Study in Self Pity," *HUCA* 26 (1965): 29–41. Blank interprets the question as a device for setting up against Jonah's self-pity "the high tragedy of God's own hurt" (41). What is portrayed here is God's internal conflict between justice and commitment.

death over life. Again God puts the question, "Is it right for you to be angry?" (NRSV). Jonah's response, his final words in the book, is dominated as before with his affirmation of anger and his preference for death (4:9). The final words of the book belong not to Jonah but to God, however, and they shape the divine perspective in terms of mercy rather than anger, life rather than death:

> And I, should I not pity *['āḥûs]* Nineveh the great city in which there are more than a hundred and twenty thousand persons who do not know their right hand from their left, and also many animals? (4:11)

This final question rounds off the Jonah story. No further words come from Jonah; thus one is left to wonder if he ever brought himself into alignment with the divine perspective.[62] The witness of the book thus far does not encourage a positive evaluation. To his first prayer God responds by ordering the fish to vomit him onto the land. To his second prayer God responds with a rebuke and a challenge. In his activities Jonah has acted in ways that pretend piety but disclose rebellion. He becomes in this way a negative paradigm for all would-be pray-ers. In contrast to the sailors and the Ninevites, he is portrayed on the one hand as unresponsive to God's will and on the other as promoting self-concerns rather than divine concerns.

If one compares Jonah to other Hebrew models of prayer, he fares little better. His preference for death over life recalls a similar despair of Elijah, whose prayers are in large part responsible for his reputation as a great "man of God." Yet the irony is that whereas Elijah's wish to die (cf. 1 Kgs 19:10) comes after his apparent failure as a prophet, Jonah's is the response to a dramatic success.[63] Further, Jonah's mission to a sinful city threatened with destruction has close parallels with Abraham's concern over the fate of Sodom and Gomorrah (Gen 18:22-23), a text on which I will subsequently focus in some detail. But here too the comparison serves ironically to caricature Jonah rather than to confirm him. Abraham argues for the sparing of the sinful city, even if it requires a new understanding of what it means for God to be truly righteous. By contrast, Jonah, when faced with the message to the sinful Ninevites, sees the issue quite differently. Jonah urges justice, even if it means suspending divine mercy, in accordance with a prepackaged piety that resists

---

62. Sasson notes that postbiblical midrash speculates that Jonah did finally come to respond positively to God's question (*Jonah*, 320).
63. Cf. Magonet, *Form and Meaning*, 102.

any divine restructuring.[64] In these ways Jonah's prayers place him in the camp of Jacob, in opposition to God and feigning piety when obedience is required. In Jacob's case only a physical contest of strength leaves him finally submissive, broken, and ready for blessing. In Jonah's case the final verdict is suspended, leaving the reader to ponder the issues and judge the final response.

THE TEMPLE AS A HOUSE OF PRAYER

The argument in the preceding sections has been that prayer often functions within a narrative context as a literary vehicle for characterizing individuals. Elijah is a "man of God" because he can work miracles. But the narrative invites one to understand his wondrous powers in relation to his ability to pray. Solomon is a wise king, Hezekiah, a genuinely faithful one, because at special moments of encounter with God they do not pray for themselves but rather submit themselves unreservedly to God's will. By contrast, characters like Jacob and Jonah are not submissive. In their efforts to pass off cunning and self-interest as acceptable forms of piety, their prayers serve as negative examples of true devotion. In each of these examples a person's speech acts as a mirror reflecting inner thoughts and intentions.

In this final section I present the argument in a slightly different way. Here I suggest that prayer may serve as a defining characteristic of a place rather than a person. The evidence in support of this view comes from one of the longest recorded prayers in the Hebrew Bible, Solomon's dedicatory prayer for the temple in 1 Kgs 8:22-53. Although one hears the prayer as the words of Solomon, the prayer does not focus primarily on Solomon himself. "What is most unusual about Solomon's prayer," observes G. Savran, "is that it is not a petitionary response to a problem, an expression of thanksgiving, or praise for some moment of deliverance. It is, rather, a prayer

---

64. Cf. ibid., 110. On the important issue of Jonah's view of God's justice, see T. Fretheim, "Jonah and Theodicy," *ZAW* 90 (1978): 227–37. From another perspective J. Miles ("Laughing at the Bible: Jonah as Parody," *JQR* 65 [1974–75]: 168–81) suggests that the substance of Jonah's objection in chap. 4 is that "God is so intransigently godlike." In this connection Miles compares Jonah's prayer to that of Sholom Aleichem's Tevye: "Oh thou Father of the Universe, our dear God in Heaven. We have lived through a Kishinev and a Constitution, through pogroms and disasters of every kind. I am only surprised, if you will forgive me for saying this, that you haven't changed by a hair. May the Evil Eye spare you" (178).

about prayer."[65] To rephrase this point more in keeping with my emphasis here: it is a prayer about the temple as the preeminent *place* of prayer.

Although I focus specifically on verses 22-53, I begin by noting the larger context of 1 Kings 8 in which these verses are set. Upon the completion of the temple, Solomon assembles the people in Jerusalem for the formal ceremony of dedication. The ark is brought into the temple and set in its place in the inner sanctuary. Sacrifices are offered, and the glory of the LORD fills the house (vv. 1-11). Following these opening ceremonies, Solomon addresses the congregation with four distinguishable speeches. The first address (vv. 12-13) is cast as poetry, unlike the rest of the chapter, and most have regarded it for this and other reasons to be the oldest material in 1 Kings 8.[66] In this regard the stress placed on the temple as a dwelling place for God is particularly interesting. The building in which Solomon stands is described first as a "royal house" *(bêt zĕbul),* then as "a place for your dwelling." It is precisely this image of the temple as a place of residence for God that stands at odds with the remainder of Solomon's address.

The second and fourth addresses (vv. 14-21, 54-61) are introduced as words of blessing and as such provide a rhetorical frame for the series of petitions that constitute the core of Solomon's third address. In verses 14-21 Solomon praises God for the fulfillment of the covenant promises given to David (cf. 2 Sam 7:8-16), particularly as they have been realized in Solomon's completion of the temple, here specifically described as the "house for the name of the LORD" (v. 20; cf. vv. 17-19). In the concluding blessing Solomon stresses God's faithfulness to the promises given through Moses, particularly the promise of "rest" (v. 56: *mĕnûḥāh).* Both blessings are constructed with Deuteronomistic language and reflect the ideological concerns of the exilic period.[67] These concerns are par-

65. G. Savran, "1 and 2 Kings," *The Literary Guide to the Bible,* ed. R. Alter and F. Kermode (Cambridge: Belknap, 1987), 157.

66. LXX has a fuller version of the address and adds that these words are taken from "the Book of the Song" (LXX 8:53). This addition suggests that what is found here is an excerpt from another source, a source usually recognized to be earlier than the immediate context.

67. See J. Levenson, "From Temple to Synagogue: 1 Kings 8," *Traditions in Transformation: Turning Points in Biblical Faith,* ed. B. Halpern and J. Levenson (Winona Lake, Ind.: Eisenbrauns, 1981), 143–66. Following F. M. Cross *(Canaanite Myth and Hebrew Epic* [Cambridge: Harvard Univ. Press, 1973], 278–85), Levenson sees 1 Kgs 8:15-21 as belonging to the first, or preexilic, edition of Dtr (the Deuteronomist). With respect to the blessing in 1 Kgs 8:54-61 Levenson is of

ticularly clear in the repeated stress on the temple not as a place for God's dwelling but as a place for the "name" of God. Such an emphasis, as G. von Rad and others have noted, marks a change in the theological conception of the sanctuary.[68] In contrast to the Priestly emphasis on Zion and the ark as symbolically embodying the divine presence, the Deuteronomists press the view that only God's *name* is placed on the temple. With the destruction of the temple in 586 B.C.E., this advocation of a "Name theology," as von Rad calls it, serves as one means of securing access to God even when the temple itself can no longer function as the place of worship.

Solomon's third address (vv. 22-53) brings the issues just noted into still clearer focus with a series of petitions. As the rhetoric of the speech makes clear, the primary concern is that God "in heaven" (vv. 30, 32, 34, 36, 39, 43, 45, 49) will hear the prayers and supplications (vv. 28-29, 30, 33, 35, 38, 42, 44-45, 47-48, 49, 52) of Solomon (vv. 28, 30) and of all God's people (vv. 30, 38; cf. v. 41) whenever they are offered "toward this house/place" that bears the divine name (vv. 29-31, 33, 35, 38, 42, 44, 48). The overwhelming preoccupation with the temple as a place of prayer is signaled in Solomon's opening petitions. First articulated in verse 25 and repeated in verse 26 is Solomon's petition to God, in keeping with the themes sounded in his opening invocation (vv. 23-24), to keep faith with the promises to David and thus to secure the dynasty in the succession of his sons, provided they continue to walk in the ways of God. As Solomon's elaboration of this petition in verses 28-30 makes plain, however, his primary intent here is not simply to secure his place in the Davidic dynasty. The focus in these verses shifts away from David, indeed away from Solomon himself, to petition God to be ever responsive to the temple as the conduit through which the prayers of the needy are channeled heavenward. As verbal confirmation of this emphasis three primary groups of words are repeated throughout these verses: (1) prayer (*tĕpillāh:* v. 28 [3 times], v. 29 [twice], v. 30), supplication *(tĕhinnāh:* vv. 28, 30), cry *(rinnāh:* v. 28); (2) hear (*šāma':* vv. 28, 29, 30 [3 times]); and (3) "this house/place" (*bêt:* v. 29; *māqôm:* v. 29 [twice], v. 30

---

the opinion that it is "a collection of Deuteronomic cliches" (163) which probably derives from a second, exilic, edition of Dtr (Dtr. 2).

68. G. von Rad, *Studies in Deuteronomy* (SBT 1/9; London: SCM, 1953), 37–44. See further Weinfeld, *Deuteronomic School,* 190–209, and the glossary of deuteronomic phraseology for "Centralization of Worship—the Chosen Place and the 'Name' Theology," 324–26.

[twice]). These themes—prayer, hearing, house/place—are framed and focused by Solomon's opening and closing words that God "turn" (v. 28) and "forgive" (v. 30).

This last word—"forgive"—provides a rhetorical bridge to the remainder of Solomon's third address. In verses 31-53 Solomon specifies seven occasions when prayer is to be offered in or toward the temple. In all but two of these occasions (vv. 41-43, 44-45) the petition that God "hear" and "forgive" remains consistent. It is frequently argued that both these exceptions, along with the occasion described in verses 46-53, represent a later supplement to verses 31ff.[69] Here one need not be overly distracted by such issues; whatever their redactional history, verses 31-53 may be taken as a rhetorical unity. In support of this view A. Gamper has argued for their internal integrity on the basis of a common structural pattern.[70] He finds the framing piece in the inclusio marked in verse 31 and again in verse 46 by the verb *ḥāṭā'*, "to sin": "If someone *sins* against a neighbor . . . if they *sin* against you." Within this framework the substance of the whole is carried by the sevenfold repetition of the phrase "you, you hear" (*'attāh tišma':* vv. 32, 34, 36, 39, 43; *šāma'tā:* vv. 45, 49) and a like number of references to the temple (vv. 31, 33, 35, 38, 42, 44, 48). With this structure, the primary emphasis throughout these verses is constant: when one sins, the temple provides a means of addressing God and securing a hearing.

In keeping with Gamper's observations I illustrate the rhetorical structure of these verses by presenting their central concerns as follows:

(1)   If someone sins against a neighbor and is made to take an oath and comes and swears before your altar *in this house, then you, you hear in heaven* and act. (vv. 31-32)

(2)   When your people Israel are defeated before an enemy because they have sinned against you, and they return to you and confess your name and pray and make supplication to you *in this house, then you, you hear in heaven* and forgive. (vv. 33-34)

---

69. So, e.g., vv. 41-43 may be taken as an expansion of v. 40; vv. 44-45 refer to a situation previously addressed in vv. 33-34; and vv. 46-53 allude to prayer during a time of captivity and to a hope for restoration that appears to derive from the late exilic or postexilic period. For a summary of the various positions taken on these verses, see Levenson, "From Temple to Synagogue," 152–53; Reventlow, *Gebet*, 270–71.

70. A. Gamper, "Die heilsgeschichtliche Bedeutung des Solomonischen Tempelweihgebets," *ZKT* 85 (1963): 56.

(3)   When heaven is shut up and there is not rain because they have sinned against you, and they pray *toward this place* and confess your name and turn back from their sin because you afflicted them,[71] *then you, you hear in heaven* and forgive. (vv. 35-36)

(4)   If there is famine in the land, or if there is plague, or blight, or mildew, or locusts, or caterpillar; or if their enemy besiege them in any of their cities; whatever plague or illness there is, every prayer, every supplication made by any person, by all your people Israel . . . *then hear you, you in heaven the place of your dwelling* and forgive. (vv. 37-40)

(5)   Also if a foreigner who is not of your people Israel . . . comes and prays *toward this house, then you, you hear in heaven the place of your dwelling* and act. (vv. 41-43)

(6)   When your people go out to war against their enemy . . . and they pray to the LORD toward the direction of the city that you have chosen and *toward the house that I have built for your name, then you will hear in heaven* their prayer and their supplication and do them justice. (vv. 44-45)

(7)   When they sin against you . . . and return to you with all their heart and all their soul . . . and they pray to you in the direction of the land you gave to their ancestors, the city that you have chosen and *the house that I built for your name, then hear in heaven* the place of your dwelling their prayer and their supplication and do them justice. Forgive your people. (vv. 46-53)

As the rhetoric of his petitions makes clear, Solomon's primary concern is that God will hear "in heaven" the prayers and supplications directed toward the temple. In famine and pestilence, personal illness and corporate defeat, even captivity (cf. v. 46) in the ravages of war, all people, including foreigners attracted to faith in Israel's God, are to pray toward the temple, and God in heaven is petitioned to hear and forgive and restore. Two issues emerge as fundamentally important in this emphasis.

First, as already mentioned, verses 12-13 are probably the oldest part of 1 Kings 8. These verses reflect an old temple theology that stresses the physical manifestation of God in an earthly residence. It is precisely this emphasis, however, that Solomon's third address calls in question. Throughout his speech every reference to *měqôm šibtěkā,* "place of your dwelling," is accompanied by the term *haššāmayim,* "the heavens" (vv. 30, 39, 43, 49),[72] thus articulating the view that no physical structure can contain the God of heaven and earth (cf. v. 23). The same emphasis emerges from the repeated

71. Reading *te'annēm* with LXX.
72. Cf. S. B. Wheeler, "Prayer and Temple in the Dedication Speech of Solomon, I Kings 8:14-61" (Ph.D. diss., Columbia University, 1977).

reference to the house "built for my name" (vv. 44, 48; cf. the additional references in Solomon's second address: vv. 17-20). Indeed, this push for a different view has been anticipated in Solomon's rhetorical question in verse 27: "But will God indeed dwell on the earth? Even heaven and the highest heaven cannot contain you, much less this house that I have built." Such an emphasis is clearly in line with exilic concerns and is one of the key clues for tying this prayer, like the addresses in verses 14-21 and verses 54-61, to the Deuteronomistic redactors.[73] This emphasis recalls here the similar polemic in Third Isaiah:

> Thus says the LORD: "Heaven is my throne and the earth is my footstool; what is the house that you would build for me, and what is my resting place?" (Isa 66:1, NRSV)

I can agree with Westermann's evaluation that "these words from the Deuteronomic account of the prayer at the consecration of the temple may come from about the same time as Isa 66:1f."[74]

Second, not only does Solomon's prayer promote a different view of the temple as merely the earthly conduit for God's presence on earth, but it also suggests a different perception of the primary function of the temple. In contrast to the view that the temple is the center for sacrifice, here it is described as the center for prayer. What Solomon offers before the altar of the LORD (v. 22: *mizēbaḥ*), the heart of the sacrificial area, is "prayer and supplication" (v. 54).[75] Not once in all his address does he mention sacrifice. Instead the repeated petition is that the "prayers and supplications" of

---

73. See, e.g., Staudt, "Prayer and the People," 222–57; Weinfeld, *Deuteronomic School,* 35–37 (note esp. the listing of Deuteronomic phraseology in 1 Kings 8, p. 36); Levenson, "From Temple to Synagogue," 154–63; Reventlow, *Gebet,* 269.

74. C. Westermann, *Isaiah 40–66* (OTL; Philadelphia: Westminster, 1969), 413. Cf. Levenson ("From Temple to Synagogue," 159), who makes the same point.

75. In the parallel account of the prayer in 2 Chronicles 6, Solomon is positioned not at the altar *(mizbēaḥ)* but rather "in the midst of the court" (6:13: *ha'ăzārāh*). M. Throntveit (*When Kings Speak: Royal Speech and Royal Prayer in Chronicles,* Society of Biblical Literature Dissertation Serires [Atlanta: Scholars Press, 1987], 58–61) does not comment on the above alteration in the Chronicles account. He does observe, however, that 1 Kgs 8:50-53 has been virtually eliminated in the Chronicles version and has been replaced by material from Ps 132:8-10, 1 (2 Chr 6:41-42). Following H. G. M. Williamson (*Israel in the Book of Chronicles* [Cambridge: Cambridge Univ. Press, 1977], 64–66), he suggests the purpose of such a change was to focus attention on David—his faithfulness to the ark, his receipt of the promise of an external dynasty, and the fulfillment of these promises in the building of the temple—and not simply on Solomon. In this way the prayer in Chronicles functions as a "timeless paradigm" applicable to any period in history and not simply that of Solomon. Whenever prayers are offered at or toward this temple the people can be assured of God's continual hearing.

God's people be heard (vv. 28-30, 33, 35, 38, 42, 44-45, 47-48, 49, 52). Although the larger context of 1 Kings 8 clearly affirms sacrifice in the temple (cf. vv. 5, 62–64), Solomon's address puts the emphasis elsewhere.

This emphasis on prayer in the temple is particularly striking, as I noted in chapter 3. In Haran's view, "in the biblical period itself, that is, at its pre-exilic stage, prayer belonged to the periphery of cult and was not part of cultic activity. Its place was outside the priestly circle, which held sole responsibility for all cultic matters within the temple precincts."[76] According to Priestly legislation, what is mandatory in the temple is sacrifice; prayer itself is considered "a gesture of secondary importance."[77] But prayer as represented and promoted by Solomon is clearly much more than a secondary gesture. It is the principal act that binds God and humanity together.

Since it stands in such contrast to a dominant view of the temple's primary function, Solomon's emphasis on prayer suggests concerns originating, as Haran observes, "outside the priestly circle." Where then may one look to find the source of this idea? Again the best evidence points to the exilic period, for here also this reinterpretation of the temple emerges. Nowhere is this more clearly stated than in Third Isaiah:[78]

> And the foreigners who join themselves to the LORD, to minister to the LORD, to love the name of the LORD, and to be the LORD's servants, everyone who keeps the Sabbath and does not profane it and holds fast my covenant: these I will bring to my holy mountain and make them joyful in my *house of prayer;* their burnt offerings and their sacrifices will be accepted on my altar; for my house will be called *a house of prayer* for all peoples. (Isa 56:6-7)

Again the prophet does not deny the role of sacrifice in the temple, yet the idea of the temple as a house of prayer clearly fixes the prophet's attention.

Can one be more specific in locating the locus of this concern? Critical opinion favors the attribution of Solomon's prayer to the Deuteronomistic redactors.[79] Years ago M. Noth observed that one

---

76. M. Haran, "Priesthood, Temple, Divine Service: Some Observations on Institutions and Practice of Worship," *HAR* 7 (1983): 131.

77. Ibid., 129.

78. Cf. Levenson, "From Temple to Synagogue," 159.

79. Levenson assigns this to "Dtr 2," i.e., to the second, or exilic, edition of Deuteronomistic redaction ("From Temple to Synagogue," 160–63).

of the telling characteristics of Deuteronomistic redaction was the tendency to use prayer as a literary vehicle for conveying theological and ideological perspectives.[80] He noted particularly speeches attributed to major characters that served to provide historical retrospect and interpretation at crucial junctures within Israel's history. He pointed in this regard to the speeches of Joshua (Joshua 23), Samuel (1 Samuel 12), and, significantly, to the address of Solomon in 1 Kings 8. Others have advanced his argument in ways both general and specific, providing along the way a reservoir of data suggesting that in both its language and its theology Solomon's prayer can be clearly connected with the Deuteronomists.[81]

Staudt has suggested that 1 Kings 8 is "the key that will completely unlock Deuteronomistic prayer."[82] The emphasis on the temple as a place of prayer is in keeping with the Deuteronomists' concern to establish a place and a role for the people in participating with and influencing God in the fulfillment of the divine plan for history. Prayer at the temple affords the people just this opportunity. Whatever the crises that threaten their stability, and whatever the rupture in the relationship with God that they might precipitate, all people may come to the temple to pray. If people seek forgiveness and commit themselves to walk in God's ways, they can expect that God in heaven will hear their prayers, forgive them, and act on their behalf. Such activity is to take place preeminently at the temple. In this sense the temple as a house of prayer becomes the focal point in the relationship with God.[83]

In view of the claim that Solomon's prayer in 1 Kings 8 represents Deuteronomistic interests, I return to the similar suggestions made at various points in the preceding discussion of prayers in this chapter. In presenting the prayers of Elijah the "man of God," and Solomon and Hezekiah the faithful kings, I mentioned the suggestion that the portrait of each has also received some editorial shaping at the hands of the Deuteronomists. One could challenge the suggestions of editorial influence, by the Deuteronomists or by any other source, at a number of points and for a variety of reasons.

---

80. M. Noth, *Überlieferungsgeschichtliche Studien* (1943; Tübingen: Max Niemeyer, 1957), 5–6.

81. E.g. Weinfeld, *Deuteronomic School,* 32–58; Staudt, "Prayer and the People," 209–54; O. Plöger, "Reden und Gebete im deuteronimistischen und chronistischen Geschichtswerk," *Festschrift für Gunther Dehn,* ed. W. Schneemelcher (Neukirchen: Kreis Moers, 1957), 35–49.

82. Staudt, "Prayer and the People," 337.

83. Ibid., 336.

For this reason I have intentionally sought not to let such claims or suggestions be the controlling influence in the discussion of how these prayers function in their respective literary contexts. Yet one should not overlook the frequency with which such critical claims are made for these texts. Can one talk with reasonable certainty, as Staudt proposes, of "Deuteronomistic prayer"? Is it possible that prayer surfaces as a particular narrative medium in one tradition more than another, and with recognizable characteristics that emerge out of particular historical situations? I need not attempt to decide the question here. If, however, Noth and others who have followed his lead have stated the matter correctly, then one might conclude that the literary art of these prayers, to which scholars have begun to sensitize themselves, is congruous with the intentional designs at work in their redactional history.

CHAPTER 5

Prayer
and the Characterization
of God

In the preceding chapter I suggested that prayer functions in
Hebrew narrative as one of the literary means for portraying character. Thus I sought to demonstrate that what one says to God (or,
as in the case of Solomon and Hezekiah, what one does not say)
reveals inner desires, intentions, motives. Such direct speech, as
Alter observes, is one of the principal narrative techniques that
assist the reader in evaluating the relationship between what characters say and what they do.[1] On the one hand the prayers of Elijah
reflect a correspondence between speech and action that is quite
close. Hence one can accept unreservedly the characterization of
this prophet as a true "man of God." On the other hand the prayers
of Jacob and Jonah articulate a level of piety that contrasts with
their behavior. Only by recognizing this contradiction between
speech and action can one assess their true character.

In this chapter I extend this observation by suggesting that prayer
may serve also as a means of delineating divine character. Not only
what one says *to* God but also what one says *about* God provides
insight into God's identity. This is particularly true in a number of
late narrative prayers that M. Weinfeld has described as "liturgical
orations."[2] Such prayers appear in the text not as the words of an
individual delivered in some concrete circumstance, but as "literary
programmatic creations" put into the mouths of certain pray-ers for
the purpose of conveying the ideological and theological concerns
of the editors.[3] Corvin has similarly noted such prayers, describing

1. Alter, *Art of Biblical Narrative*, 66.
2. M. Weinfeld, *Deuteronomy and the Deuteronomic School* (Oxford: Clarendon,
1972), 32–45.
3. Ibid., 51–52.

them as "formal" rather than "contextual."[4] That is, they exhibit a loose connection with the narrative framework into which they are inserted, thus giving the impression that they were consciously composed as independent literary creations. Whereas Corvin locates such formal prayers generally in the monarchical and post-monarchical period, Weinfeld explicitly relates them to Deuteronomy and to the specific redactional interests of the Deuteronomistic editors.[5]

The most distinctive stylistic feature of these prayers is their rhetorical preoccupation with God. In this regard both Weinfeld and more recently M. Throntveit have contributed important observations. In describing the oratorical style of the Deuteronomic school, Weinfeld has identified a number of prayers in the Deuteronomic historiography (2 Sam 7:22-24; 1 Kgs 8:23; 2 Kgs 19:15-19) and in the Deuteronomic stratum in Jeremiah (32:17-23) that serve in effect as liturgical proclamations of the uniqueness of God. Weinfeld contends that the same theme is present in the later prayers of Nehemiah, Daniel, and Chronicles (e.g., Neh 1:5; 9:6, 32; Dan 9:4; 1 Chr 29:11; 2 Chr 2:11; 20:6), where it is buttressed by an emphasis on God's creation of the world.[6] Throntveit's analysis of royal prayer in Chronicles leads him to a similar conclusion. He argues that in prayers unique to Chronicles (i.e., they have no parallel in Samuel–Kings; e.g., 1 Chr 29:10-19; 2 Chr 14:10; 20:6-12), the particular theological *Tendenz* is to stress the omnipotence of God over against the dependence of humanity.[7]

In this chapter I build upon the suggestions of Weinfeld and Throntveit by analyzing a selection of prayers that seem rather clearly crafted to proclaim God's sovereignty. Such an emphasis shapes prayers that present two kinds of petitions. First are petitions for divine intervention, particularly in contexts reporting military crises. A prime example of such a prayer occurs in 2 Kgs 19:15-19. A second type of petition is for divine forgiveness. The prayers of penitence recorded in Ezra 9, Nehemiah 9, and Daniel 9 particularly model this concern. In both these groups of prayer the rhetorical focus on God is so pronounced that the pray-ers them-

---

4. J. Corvin, "Stylistic and Functional Study of the Prose Prayers in the Historical Narratives of the Old Testament" (Ph.D. diss., Emory University, 1972), 203–11.

5. Ibid., 204; Weinfeld, *Deuteronomic School,* 43.

6. Weinfeld, *Deuteronomic School,* 39–43.

7. M. Throntveit, *When Kings Speak: Royal Speech and Royal Prayer in Chronicles* (Atlanta: Scholars Press, 1987), 62–75, 88, 93–96.

selves recede into the background. Their petitions therefore reflect not so much their own inner character as that of the God to whom they are addressed.

PRAYERS FOR DIVINE INTERVENTION

HEZEKIAH'S PRAYER (2 KGS 19:15-19)

The general context of Hezekiah's prayer is the Assyrian siege of Jerusalem in 701 B.C.E. It has long been recognized that the events described here are presented in three accounts, usually identified as the A account (2 Kgs 18:13-16) and the B accounts: B¹ (2 Kgs 18:17—19:9a and 19:36-37) and B² (2 Kgs 19:9b-35). The reasons for these divisions have been discussed at length by a host of commentators and need not be repeated here.[8]

For my purposes two points are particularly important: (1) Hezekiah's prayer in 2 Kgs 19:15-19 occurs within the B² account, which describes the defeat of the Assyrians at the hands of the angel of the LORD, who slew 185,000 in a miraculous nocturnal assault. (2) Of the three accounts, only the B² account records the prayer of Hezekiah.[9] This account relates that upon receiving the letter of threats from Sennacherib, Hezekiah read it and went immediately to the house of God. There he spread it before the LORD and prayed a lengthy prayer, the substance of which is recorded in verses 15-19. This prayer gives a portrait of Hezekiah as a faithful and trusting servant, who at the first sign of crisis approaches God directly with the intent of securing positive and immediate response. As noted in preceding discussions, the report of his similar conduct in 2 Kgs 20:2-3 further strengthens this portrait of Hezekiah's piety.[10] (3) Finally, the general scholarly consensus assigns Hezekiah's prayer and the B² framework of which it is part to the Deuteronomists, or at least to Josianic redactors who share the concerns of the Deuter-

---

8. See, e.g., B. Childs, *Isaiah and the Assyrian Crisis* (SBT 2/3; London: SCM, 1967); R. Clements, *Isaiah and the Deliverance of Jerusalem* (Sheffield: JSOT Press, 1980).

9. In the A account, 2 Kgs 18:13-16, Sennacherib withdraws from Jerusalem after receiving tribute from Hezekiah, and the city is spared. The B¹ account, 2 Kgs 18:17—19:19a and 19:36–37, also concludes that Sennacherib spared Jerusalem, though the outcome is reported in somewhat different terms. Here we are informed that Hezekiah's response was to rend his garments, cover himself with sackcloth, and go into the house of God. From this position he summoned Isaiah to "lift up a prayer" of intercession (19:4: *nāśā'tā tĕpillāh)* on behalf of the people. This prayer, however, is not recorded.

10. See pp. 61–64.

onomic movement.[11] Thus Weinfeld lists it among his "liturgical orations" as a "religious declaration in the language of deuteronomic religio-national ideology."[12]

Verses 9-13 provide the immediate literary backdrop for the prayer. Messengers are sent from the Rabshakeh to Hezekiah with words designed to raise doubts and undermine trust in God's ability to deliver the Israelites from the impending Assyrian attack. Three clusters of words carry the major ideas: *bāṭaḥ*, "trust"; *'ĕlōhêkā* versus *'ĕlōhê haggôyim*, "your God" versus "the gods of the nations"; and *nāṣal*, "deliver." Around these key expressions the message to Hezekiah develops:

> Do not let your God *['ĕlōhêkā]* in whom you are trusting *[bōṭēaḥ]* deceive you. . . . You have heard what the kings of Assyria have done to all the lands . . . and you, will you be delivered *[wĕ'attāh tinnāṣēl]?* Have the gods of the nations delivered them *[hahiṣṣîlû 'ōtām 'ĕlōhê haggôyim]?*

Hezekiah's response is to pray:

> O LORD, God of Israel, enthroned on the cherubim, you are God, you alone of all kingdoms of the earth; you have made heaven and earth. Incline, LORD, your ear and hear; open, LORD, your eyes and see; and hear the words of Sennacherib that he has sent to mock the living God. Truly, LORD, the kings of Assyria have laid waste the nations and their lands, and have cast their gods into the fire, for they were not gods, but the work of human hands, wood and stone, and they destroyed them. But now, LORD our God, save us from his hand, and all the kingdoms of the earth will know that you, LORD, are God alone. (vv. 15-19)

In both its form and its rhetoric this prayer is carefully designed to affirm that the LORD, and the LORD alone, can be trusted to deliver the people. With respect to its form the prayer consists of five elements: (1) invocation (v. 15a); (2) declaration of the LORD's exclusive sovereignty (v. 15b); (3) petition (v. 16); (4) declaration of the nations' gods as "not gods" (vv. 17-18); and (5) petition (v. 19). Thus, following the opening invocation, the prayer moves back and forth between the two poles of declaration and petition, each petition prefaced with a declarative statement setting forth the basis upon which God should consider and respond to the request. Mov-

---

11. So Clements, *Isaiah and Deliverance,* 90–108.

12. Weinfeld, *Deuteronomic School,* 39, 52. See further E. Staudt, "Prayer and the People in the Deuteronomist" (Ph.D. diss., Vanderbilt University, 1980), 296–310.

ing beyond the prayer to the verses immediately following, one finds that God's positive response is delivered by Isaiah and is directed in three oracles to (1) the king of Assyria (vv. 21-34); (2) Hezekiah (vv. 29-31); and (3) the people (vv. 32-34). Verse 35 provides the final dramatic conclusion.

Within this formal structure the rhetorical emphasis of Hezekiah's prayer focuses decidedly on God. Coming on the heels of the invocation, the introduction to the prayer, and the opening descriptive statement of verse 14, the declaration of verse 15b provides a fourth successive reference to "the LORD" *(Yhwh),* the special god to whom Hezekiah appeals. Thus, "Hezekiah went up to the house of the LORD," and "he spread it [the message of Sennacherib] before the LORD," and he prayed "before the LORD," and "he said LORD, God of Israel. . . ." The declaration builds on this fourfold repetition of the name "LORD" to proclaim that the LORD and the LORD alone *(lĕbaddĕkā)* is God, God of all kingdoms of the earth *(lĕkōl mamlĕkôt hā'āreṣ).* This emphasis on the LORD's "unity and exclusive sovereignty" incorporates typical Deuteronomic language, here supplemented, as Weinfeld has observed, by a "cosmogonic element" that declares this sovereign God to be also maker of "heaven and earth."[13]

The petition in verse 16 appeals to this LORD, sovereign and powerful, to hear and respond to the challenges of Sennacherib. In keeping with the rhetorical emphasis established by preceding verses, the petition is laced with successive references to the name *Yhwh:* "Incline, LORD, your ear and hear; open, LORD, your eyes and see." The petition calls for response specifically to Sennacherib's words designed to mock *(ḥārāp, hiphil;* note the repetition of this word in vv. 4, 16, 22, 23), that is, to cast suspicion on and to denegrate the living God *('ĕlōhîm ḥāy).*

The latter phrase, *'ĕlōhîm ḥāy,* stands in immediate juxtaposition with the following words introducing verse 17, *'omnām Yhwh,* "Truly, LORD." At one level the two expressions serve rhetorically to draw attention to the concern underlying Hezekiah's prayer. Is the LORD truly a living God, sovereign and powerful as confessed by successive generations of the community of faith? Can the LORD be trusted? Or will the taunts of Sennacherib be substantiated?

On another level the words serve literarily to introduce the second statement of declaration in verses 17-18. This second declaration functions to remind the LORD of the status of the gods of the

---

13. Weinfeld, *Deuteronomic School,* 39.

nations—they are "not gods" (v. 18: *lō' 'ĕlōhîm),* the work of human hands *(ma'ăśēh yĕdê 'ādām)*—and at the same time to contrast their nothingness with the LORD. The contrast and the polemic implicit in it are carried rhetorically by the two phrases *'ĕlōhîm ḥāy,* "living God," and *lō' 'ĕlōhîm,* "not gods," and by the characteristics that accrue to each. Of the living God it is confessed and hoped that (1) it is the God of Israel; (2) *Yhwh* is maker *('āśāh)* of heaven and earth *(haššāmayim wĕ'et hā'āreṣ);* and (3) all kingdoms of the earth *(kōl mamlĕkôt hā'āreṣ)* fall under the LORD's dominion. Over against this confession are the observations that (1) the gods *('ĕlōhîm)* of the nations have been cast into the fire because they were "not gods" *(lō' 'ĕlōhîm);* (2) these gods are not the *makers* of heaven and earth; rather they are *made (ma'ăśēh)* by earthly hands; and (3) these constructed gods have no influence over the kingdoms of the earth; rather they fall under the dominion of the kings of Assyria *(malkê 'Aššûr).* By stating the contrast between God and the "not gods" so clearly, and from a variety of perspectives, Hezekiah's declaration effectively seeks to petition God to act now in a manner consistent with the divine character. In other words, the LORD's reputation as a living God is at stake.

The second and final petition occurs in verse 19. It is introduced by the words "but now" *(wĕ'attāh),* a rhetorical formula frequent in prayers indicating the important transition point from preliminary overtures to God to specific petitions.[14] The petition itself is just two words in Hebrew: *hôšî'ēnû nā',* "Save us, now." This petition for deliverance makes explicit the intervention implied by the petition in verse 16 that God "hear" and "see." In keeping with rhetorical emphases at work throughout the prayer, the petition is accompanied by key words and phrases that acclaim the LORD as sovereign God, God alone *('attāh Yhwh 'ĕlōhîm lĕbaddĕkā),* God over all the kingdoms of the earth *(kōl mamlĕkôt hā'āreṣ).*

Thus, through a structured prayer that moves between petition and supporting arguments, Hezekiah seeks to secure divine deliverance from the Assyrian crisis. As noted, the prayer represents a literary creation of the Deuteronomists, and as such it supplies a certain religious perspective from which one may interpret the historical account of the siege of Jerusalem in 701. On one level the prayer clearly functions within its larger literary context as the turning point in the resolution of the Assyrian threat. Thus the

14. See chap. 4 n. 21.

narrative develops broadly in the following way: (1) crisis (vv. 9-13); (2) prayer for deliverance (vv. 14-19); (3) resolution of crisis (vv. 20-35). From this perspective, the deliverance from the Assyrians is interpreted to be the direct result of Hezekiah's petition. At another level one may understand the rhetorical framework of this prayer to complement its contribution to the larger narrative. The chiastic arrangement of the introduction and the conclusion makes a major theological statement in support of the sovereignty of God.

Diagram 1

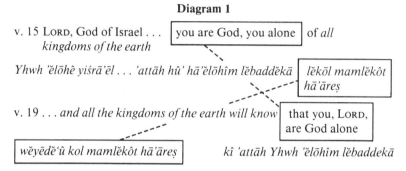

v. 15 LORD, God of Israel . . . | you are God, you alone | of *all kingdoms of the earth*

Yhwh 'ĕlōhê yiśrā'ēl . . . *'attāh hû' hā'ĕlōhîm lĕbaddĕkā* | *lĕkōl mamlĕkôt hā'āreṣ*

v. 19 . . . *and all the kingdoms of the earth will know* | that you, LORD, are God alone

wĕyēdĕ'û kol mamlĕkôt hā'āreṣ | *kî 'attāh Yhwh 'ĕlōhîm lĕbaddekā*

In between these two framing pieces, and in support of them, two supplementary clusters of words and phrases serve to develop the argument. One is the repetition of the word *Yhwh* throughout the prayer (seven times in all, missing only in v. 18). The other is the less frequent repetition of the word *'ĕlōhîm* (once in v. 16 and twice in v. 18), setting forth the contrast between the living God (*'ĕlōhîm ḥāy*) and their gods (*'ĕlōhêhem*), who are "not gods" (*lō' 'ĕlōhîm*) as evidenced by their being cast into the fire. Diagram 2 illustrates the structure.

To summarize, the position of this prayer within the larger narrative and the rhetoric that conveys its message work together to inform the reader that the LORD, sovereign God of all kingdoms of the earth, can and will deliver Israel from the Assyrian crisis. The narrative could have been structured without the prayer, moving directly from a description of the threat to its resolution. That Jerusalem was indeed finally spared in 701 B.C.E. all the traditions agree. Yet the inclusion of this fairly lengthy prayer affords the editors an opportunity to shape the readers' understanding of these events in particular ways. By attributing such a prayer to Hezekiah they not only promote prayer as the effective and paradigmatic response of a faithful servant; they also proclaim their theological

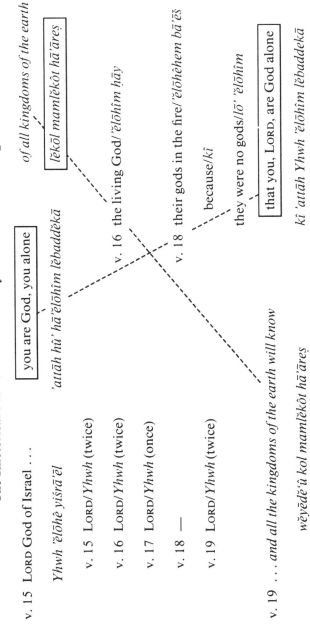

Diagram 2
The Rhetorical Framework of the Prayer of Hezekiah in 2 Kgs 19:15-19

v. 15 Lᴏʀᴅ God of Israel . . .

Yhwh ʾĕlōhê yiśrāʾēl

v. 15 Lᴏʀᴅ/Yhwh (twice)

v. 16 Lᴏʀᴅ/Yhwh (twice)

v. 17 Lᴏʀᴅ/Yhwh (once)

v. 18 —

v. 19 Lᴏʀᴅ/Yhwh (twice)

v. 19 . . . and all the kingdoms of the earth will know

wĕyēdĕʿû kol mamlĕkōt hāʾāreṣ

you are God, you alone

ʾattāh hûʾ hāʾĕlōhîm lĕbaddĕkā

of all kingdoms of the earth

lĕkōl mamlĕkōt hāʾāreṣ

v. 16 the living God/ʾĕlōhîm ḥāy

v. 18 their gods in the fire/ʾĕlōhêhem bāʾēš

because/kî

they were no gods/lōʾ ʾĕlōhîm

that you, Lᴏʀᴅ, are God alone

kî ʾattāh Yhwh ʾĕlōhîm lĕbaddĕkā

convictions concerning the LORD's unrivaled status among all gods and hostile nations.

THE PRAYERS OF ASA AND JEHOSHAPHAT (2 CHR 14:11; 20:5-12)

Both the rhetoric and the context of Hezekiah's prayer are closely paralleled in two other texts in Chronicles: the prayer of Asa in 2 Chr 14:11 (MT v. 10), and the prayer of Jehoshaphat in 2 Chr 20:5-12. Neither prayer occurs in Samuel–Kings, hence one may assume that both were composed by the Chronicler, who, like the Deuteronomistic redactors, frequently uses prayer as the preferred medium of discourse. With respect both to their literary form and to their content, these prayers illustrate the far-ranging influence of Deuteronomistic concerns on postexilic piety.[15]

Asa's prayer is set against the background of a confrontation with Zerah and the million-strong forces of the Ethiopian army (v. 9). With rapid strokes the successive stages in the drama are described: "And Zerah the Ethiopian came out against them . . . and Asa went out to meet him, and they drew up their line for battle" (vv. 9-10). But just before the moment of engagement the narrative slows its pace to provide an account of Asa's prayer for God's help (v. 11). Immediately following this brief interlude the narrative returns the focus to the crisis at hand, reporting that Asa's petition has been successful: "And the LORD defeated the Ethiopians" (v. 12).

This portrait of Asa at prayer serves to illustrate a degree of personal piety and commitment that the larger narrative context has already ascribed to the king. Verses 1-8 introduce Asa as one who did what was "good and right in the eyes of the LORD his God" (v. 2, NRSV). Such an evaluation is based not only on his support of religious reform but also on his advocacy of seeking the LORD (*drš*, vv. 4, 7; MT vv. 3, 6) so that Judah may have rest all around from its enemies.[16] With these recommendations Asa himself is portrayed as

---

15. Cf. M. Noth, *The Chronicler's History* (Sheffield: JSOT Press, 1987), 80–81; O. Plöger, "Reden und Gebete in deuteronomistischen und chronistischen Geschichtswerk," *Festschrift für Günther Dehn,* ed. W. Schneemelcher (Neukirchen: Kreis Moers, 1957), 35–49.

16. On the importance of *drš* in Chronicles, see G. E. Schaeffer, "The Significance of Seeking God in the Purpose of the Chronicler" (Th.D. diss., Southern Baptist Theological Seminary, 1972); S. Wagner, *"drš," TDOT* 3.300–305; G. Gerleman and E. Ruprecht, *"drš," THAT* 1.460–67. P. Welten has noted that in Chronicles "seeking God" is an important prerequisite for prosperity and success (*ṣlḥ; Geschichte und Geschichtsdarstellung in den Chronikbüchern* [Neukirchen-Vluyn: Neukirchen Verlag, 1973], 17–18, 50–51). Indeed, in Chronicles prosperity is

most clearly embodying exemplary piety as he calls out to the LORD in a particular moment of real crisis.

Yet here, as in Hezekiah's prayer, the rhetoric of Asa's plea serves to emphasize not so much his own qualities as his dependence on the LORD.[17] The prayer consists of an introduction followed by alternating declarations of faith and petitions:

Introduction:	And Asa called to *the LORD his God* and said
Declaration:	*LORD*, there is none like you to help, either the strong or the powerless.
Petition:	Help us, *O LORD our God*, for upon you we have relied and in your name we have come against this multitude.
Declaration:	*LORD, our God you are*,
Petition:	let no mortal prevent you.

The italicized phrases show that at every juncture the prayer is introduced by the invocation "LORD." The invocation grows rhetorically with the addition of elements that increase the weight of the address. Asa begins by calling on "the LORD *his God*," then petitions "the LORD *our God*," and concludes with the declaration that binds king and community in mutual confession, "LORD, *our God you are*."

A similar rhetorical emphasis is evident in Jehoshaphat's prayer, though it is achieved in a somewhat different manner. Again the context is military confrontation. Specifically, a coalition of enemy forces from Moab, Ammon, and Edom prepare to wage war against Jehoshaphat (2 Chr 20:1-2). The report that follows is framed by Jehoshaphat's fear (v. 3) and the ultimate dismissal of this fear by an oracle from Jahaziel the Levite announcing that "the battle is not yours but God's" (vv. 15-17, NRSV). The key to this promise of deliverance is Jehoshaphat's prayer in verses 5-12.

The form of Jehoshaphat's prayer is often compared with psalms of corporate lament (e.g., Psalms 44, 60, 74, 79, 83, 89).[18] Indeed, the typical features of lament are often identified in Jehoshaphat's prayer: verse 6a, address; verses 6-7, recitation of God's past acts;

---

granted only to those kings who, like Asa, have sought God: Solomon (2 Chr 7:11), Jehoshaphat (2 Chr 20:20), Uzziah (2 Chr 26:5), and Hezekiah (2 Chr 31:21).

17. Cf. J. Myers, *II Chronicles* (AB; Garden City, N.Y.: Doubleday, 1965), 85; Throntveit, *When Kings Speak*, 63.

18. Cf. O. Eissfeldt, *The Old Testament: An Introduction* (New York: Harper and Row, 1965), 112–13.

verses 8-9, protestation of innocence and statement of trust; verses 10-11, complaint; verse 12, petition.

This prayer is distinctive, however, in its repetition of the vocative "LORD"/"our God" at three junctures during the address (vv. 6, 7, 12). Further, each vocative is associated with the particle *hălō'*. It is common to translate each of these statements as questions.

O LORD, God of our ancestors are you not God in heaven *[hălō' 'attāh 'ĕlōhîm baššāmayim]?*
Are you not ruler of all the kingdoms of the nations *[wĕ'attāh môšēl bĕkōl mamlĕkôt haggôyim]?* (v. 6)
Are you not our God *[hălō' 'attāh 'ĕlōhênû]* who drove out the inhabitants of the land? (v. 7)
Our God, will you not execute judgment against them *['ĕlōhênû hălō' tišpot bām]?* (v. 12)

While vocatives are not uncommon in lament prayers, they typically introduce hard questions or urgent petitions that express the pray-er's awareness of separation from God.[19] In Jehoshaphat's prayer, however, the use of the particle *hălō'* sets these vocatives in a different light. *Hălō'* is normally used in sentences where one would expect an affirmative answer or a positive response. Indeed, often in Kings and Chronicles, *hălō'* functions not to introduce a question but to stress a positive assertion.[20] In such cases it is appropriately translated with interjections like "surely," "truly," "indeed," and so on. For example, the NJPS treats the verses in question as statements full of confidence, not despair.[21]

v. 6   LORD God of our fathers, *truly* You are the God in heaven and You rule over the kingdoms of the nations.

Similarly, verse 12, which is often taken as a plea for help, one can appropriately render as an unqualified affirmation of the help God will certainly provide: "O our God, *surely* You will punish them" (NJPS). Such language hardly resembles the imperative petitions

---

19. See, e.g., Ps 80:3: "O God, restore us" (cf. vv. 4, 7, 14, 19); Ps 6:1-2: "O LORD, do not rebuke me in your anger, be gracious to me, O LORD" (cf. v. 4); Ps 22:1: "Why, O LORD, do you stand far off?" (cf. Pss 74:1; 88:14).

20. Cf. GKC, par. 150e; H. A. Brongers, "Some Remarks on the Biblical Particle *hălō'*," *OTS* 21 (1981): 177–89; M. Held, "Rhetorical Questions in Ugaritic and Biblical Hebrew," *ErIsr* 9 (1969): 71–79; M. L. Brown, "'Is It Not?' or 'Indeed!': *HL* in Northwest Semitic," *Maarav* 4 (1987): 201–19; B. Waltke and M. O'Connor, *An Introduction to Biblical Hebrew Syntax* (Winona Lake, Ind.: Eisenbrauns, 1990), 684–85.

21. Throntveit, *When Kings Speak,* 70.

that usually dominate in prayers of lamentation. Indeed, for the Chronicler's Jehoshaphat, such language serves as a declaration of doxology, not complaint.[22] But will God respond? Will the God of heaven, ruler over all kingdoms, dispossessor of the foreign inhabitants of the land, render now a judgment in accordance with this acknowledged divine stature? Jehoshaphat's affirmation of divine fidelity adds to the incentive for God's intervention. To strengthen still further his prayer Jehoshaphat represents the people as quoting Solomon's prayer at the temple: "If evil comes upon us . . . we will stand before this house and before you . . . and cry to you in our affliction and you will hear and save" (v. 9). For all these reasons then—because of who God is and because of what God has promised—God should act. No other resource is available to Jehoshaphat and his people. "This great multitude" threatens their existence, and they know not what to do save fix their hopes on God (v. 12).

Jahaziel's responding oracle of salvation (vv. 15-17) provides the final context for evaluating the prayer and all its concerns. The promise of God's presence (v. 17) makes clear God's intentions. From opening address to final affirmation the focus of the prayer has remained on "the LORD our God" (vv. 6, 12). That which began as doxology is finally affirmed by divine promise. By narrative's end the crisis has passed and all is at rest (cf. v. 30). The hymnic thanksgiving that marks finally the victory celebration—"Give thanks to the LORD, for his steadfast love is everlasting" (v. 21, NRSV)—serves as the poetic affirmation of the prayer's ringing proclamation of God's sovereignty and fidelity.

THE PRAYER OF DAVID (1 CHR 29:10-19)

Cast as David's final words before passing the responsibilities of the kingdom to Solomon, this prayer is characterized as both a blessing (v. 10) and praise (v. 13). In this regard it differs from the prayers of Hezekiah, Asa, and Jehoshaphat. David's petition is not for deliverance from an impending military confrontation, but for God's continuing supervision of Solomon and his subjects (vv. 18-19). Nevertheless, the rhetorical emphasis on God's sovereignty that prefaces and sustains David's prayer is sufficiently similar to

---

22. On the affinity between *hălō'* and the hymn of praise, see A. Schoors, *I Am God Your Savior: A Form-Critical Study of the Main Genres in Is. XL–LV* (VTSup 24; Leiden: Brill, 1973), 255; C. Westermann, *Isaiah 40–66* (OTL; Philadelphia: Westminster, 1969), 55–56.

the prayers just discussed to justify its consideration here rather than in the following section, where penitence and forgiveness are the primary foci.

In its present form the prayer divides into three primary parts.[23] Following the introduction and opening address (v. 10a) these develop as follows: verses 10-12, hymn of praise; verses 13-17, reflection on the people's dependence on God's generosity; verses 18-19, petition. As in the prayers previously examined, the repeated invocation "LORD" is distinctive here. The rhetorical framework of the prayer serves both to introduce and to promote the major theme:

v. 10   Blessed are you O LORD, the God of our ancestor Israel
v. 18   O LORD, the God of Abraham, Isaac, and Israel, our ancestors

NRSV

Between these framing pieces each component of the prayer is introduced with some form of the vocative that sustains this primary focus on the LORD. Thus the hymn begins "To you LORD" (v. 11); the reflections of verses 13-17 begin "And now, our God"; and finally, the petition of verses 18-19 is introduced with "O LORD, God of Abraham." Further, throughout each of these divisions the invocation occurs no less than three times (v. 11b: "to you LORD the kingdom;" v. 16: "LORD, our God"; v. 17: "I know, my God"). The total of six references to "LORD" *(Yhwh)* and five to "God" *('ĕlōhîm)* combine to give the impression that hardly a word may be spoken without first pausing to acknowledge the true object of the prayer's focus.

Yet even these repetitions are not sufficient; they are further buttressed by a string of attributes that pile praise upon praise. This is especially evident in verse 11, which lists five different ascriptions: "To you LORD are the greatness and the power and the glory and the eminence and the majesty." Added to these in verse 12 is the acknowledgment "you are ruler over all," and in verse 17 "you are examiner of the heart." Indeed, in the whole prayer invocations of the name or ascriptions of grandeur and sovereignty are lacking only in verses 14-15 and 19, and even here the use of the second

23. Throntveit (*When Kings Speak,* 94) suggests that vv. 14b, 16-17, and 19 are secondary. The remaining verses, 10-14a, 15, and 18 he holds to be the original creation of the Chronicler. Cf. R. Moses (*Untersuchungen zur Theologie des chronistischen Geschichtswerkes* [Freiburg: Herder, 1972], 105–7), who takes the entire prayer to be secondary.

person pronoun with reference to God sounds the same dominating theme: verse 14, "for from you the whole and from *your* hand we give *to you*"; verse 15, "for we are sojourners *before you*"; verse 19, "Give to Solomon my son a single mind to keep *your* commandments, *your* testimonies, *your* statutes."

Against this repeated emphasis on God's sovereignty and power, David's reflections on his and his people's status (vv. 13-17) serve in effect as praise in counterpoint. "Who am I and who are my people? . . . We are sojourners before you . . . our days on earth like a shadow" (vv. 14-15). Depicted as powerless and transient, these folk are by necessity dependent entirely on this great God from whose hand comes all that is. This contrast between the power and might of God and the people's weakness and dependence recalls similar emphases in the prayers of Asa and Jehoshaphat (2 Chr 14:11; 20:6, 12; cf. 1 Chr. 17:16) and, as Throntveit has observed, constitutes a major theme in the Chronicler's prayers.[24]

To summarize, the addresses of Hezekiah, Asa, Jehosaphat, and David are examples of exilic and postexilic prayers that function to characterize God rather than the pray-ers themselves. By repeatedly stressing God's exclusive sovereignty (2 Kgs 19:15, 19), God's creation of heaven and earth (2 Kgs 19:15; cf. 1 Chr 29:11), and God's power (2 Chr 14:11; 20:6, 12), the rhetoric of these prayers serves as proclamation.

That the Deuteronomistic redactors and the Chronicler should prefer to make such proclamations through the literary means of prayer is perhaps not surprising. As O. Plöger notes, this preference for prayer as a form of discourse may be connected with the heightened importance of the practice of prayer in the post–586 B.C.E. community, where sacrifice is no longer possible.[25] On the one hand such prayers, placed into the mouths of leading personages, must have served the beleaguered community as a model of an effective means of coping with their crises. On the other hand it is not so much the speakers who claim the attention in these addresses as the Almighty God to whom they have access. One prays to this God of heaven and earth, ruler over all nations, final judge over all human excesses. It is this God that these prayers repeatedly proclaim with the invocation "LORD, you are our God."

---

24. Throntveit, *When Kings Speak,* 94–95.

25. Plöger, "Reden und Gebete im deuteronomistischen und chronistischen Geschichtswerk," *Festschrift für Günther Dehn,* ed. W. Schneemelcher (Neukirchen: Kreis Moers, 1957), 45.

PRAYERS OF PENITENCE

Within the prose prayers of the Hebrew Bible, Ezra 9:6-15, Neh 1:5-11, 9:6-37, and Dan 9:4-19 constitute a distinct genre of "prayers of penitence." Although they exhibit similarities with other types of prayer in the Hebrew Bible (e.g., the lament), and although they make frequent use of language found in older parts of Scripture (particularly in Deuteronomic texts), they stand apart from the rest with respect to both their form and content.[26] W. S. Towner has summarized their distinctiveness in three primary areas.[27] (1) Of all prose prayers these alone are identified by the *Stichwort* (key word) *lĕhitwaddeh,* "to make confession" (Ezra 10:1; Neh 1:6; 9:3; Dan 9:4, 20). This *hithpael* form of the verb *yādāh* occurs just ten times in the Hebrew Bible with the meaning "confess," and of these, six occur in association with these four particular prayers. (2) These prayers are considerably more elaborate than the usual prose prayer and are ecclectic in their language, borrowing from earlier types of prayer and combining the various elements into a general structure that moves from ascription to confession and finally to petition. (3) Each prayer is penitential in character, and in this respect can be linked to the penitential program advocated in Solomon's temple prayer (cf. 1 Kgs 8:46-47, 49). Thus in Dan 9:5 the confession "We have sinned and acted perversely and wickedly" is almost a verbatim recollection of 1 Kgs 8:47. Similar acknowledgments of sin occur repeatedly in the prayers in Ezra and Nehemiah. Although these four prayers occur in writings that differ in tone and theology, Towner concludes that they provide a common theoretical basis for penitence analogous to those described by the Deuteronomistic editors.[28] In this regard he agrees with Noth, Plöger, Weinfeld, Reventlow, and others who see

---

26. On the relation of these prayers to the lament genre, see esp. C. Westermann, "Struktur und Geschichte der Klage im Alten Testament," *ZAW* 66 (1954), 44–80 (= "The Structure and History of the Lament in the Old Testament," *Praise and Lament in the Psalms* [Atlanta: John Knox, 1981], 165–213). For their use of other Scripture, cf. Weinfeld, *Deuteronomic School,* 39–43, 331; Plöger, "Reden und Gebete," 39–44; H. G. Reventlow, *Gebet im Alten Testament* (Stuttgart: Kohlhammer, 1986), 277–84. For lists of numerous borrowings from Deuteronomistic texts in Daniel 9, Ezra 9, and Nehemiah 9, see L. Hartman and A. Di Lella, *The Book of Daniel* (AB; Garden City, N.Y.: Doubleday, 1978), 248; J. Myers, *Ezra-Nehemiah* (AB; Garden City, N.Y.: Doubleday, 1965), 78–79, 167–69.

27. W. S. Towner, "Retributional Theology in the Apocalyptic Setting," *USQR* 26 (1971): 210–11.

28. Ibid., 211.

in late narrative prayers the continuing influence of Deuteronomistic perspectives on prayer and piety.[29]
   I agree that the penitence motif constitutes a common link between these prayers. In this section of the discussion, however, I
suggest that the theme of penitence attains clarity by being contrasted to a governing emphasis on God's sovereignty, mercy, and
justice. The nucleus of this emphasis occurs in a repeating ascription that proclaims the LORD as "the great and awesome God who
keeps covenant and steadfast love to those who love you and keep
your commandments" (Dan 9:4; Neh 1:5; 9:32). This emphasis
receives elaboration throughout these prayers in lengthy recollec-
tions contrasting God's faithfulness with Israel's willful and repeated disobedience. Within this framework contrition emerges as
the only appropriate response, yet the prayers focus on the merciful
and forgiving God who invites and accepts such response.

A PRAYER OF DANIEL (DAN 9:4-19)

   It has long been recognized that this prayer relates rather uneasily
to the basic narrative stratum of chapter 9.[30] I do not dispute the
cogency of these arguments; nevertheless, I want to press for understanding the prayer in relation to the narrative in which it is set. For
whatever reasons, chapter 9 now includes this important text, and
the narrative sequence therefore requires that one read through it
rather than around it. I will subsequently seek to understand its
contribution to the whole, but first I focus attention on the prayer's
rhetorical structure and its internal dynamics. Towner has sug-

---

29. Noth, *Chronicler's History,* 80–81; Plöger, "Reden und Gebete," 39–44;
Weinfeld, *Deuteronomic School,* 42–43; Reventlow, *Gebet,* 277–84.

30. Four general observations are commonly used in support of the argument that
the prayer is a late insertion: (1) Verses 1-2 and 20-27 constitute a thematic unity
that focuses on the meaning of Jeremiah's prophecy of seventy years as the time
allotted by God for the desolation of Jerusalem (cf. Jer 25:11-12). The prayer of
Daniel does not address this theme and thus appears to interrupt the logical
narrative sequence. (2) The prayer reads smoothly as an independent unit, and
thus has the appearance of what Corvin describes as "formal prayer" ("Sylistic
and Functional Study," 206–12; Corvin, however, does not discuss Daniel 9).
Further, the prayer's emphasis on confession and repentance does not fit well with
the context of vv. 2-3 and vv. 21-27. Given Daniel's quest for enlightenment
concerning Jeremiah's prophecy, one might have expected instead a prayer for
illumination. (3) The narrative in its present form contains duplications in vv. 3,
4a and again in vv. 20, 21 that betray an editor's attempt to integrate the prayer
into the original account. (4) The prayer is written in good Hebrew and in contrast
to the rest of chap. 9, it shows no indication of having been translated from an
original Aramaic text. For a convenient summary of the general arguments, see
Hartman and Di Lella, *Daniel,* 244–45. For arguments in favor of the prayer's
authenticity, see O. Plöger, *Das Buch Daniel* (Gütersloh: Gerd Mohn, 1965), 135;
B. Jones, "The Prayer of Daniel 9," *VT* 18 (1968): 488–93.

gested that prose prayers of penitence share a similar structure: ascription, confession, petition.[31] In Daniel 9 these basic elements are represented in verse 4, verses 5-14, and verses 15-19 respectively. The internal rhetoric of the prayer, however, suggests a dynamic contrasting of God and Israel to which such a neat demarcation of formal elements does not do justice. I may illustrate this contrast by focusing on verses 4-14 as a rhetorical unit. Following the introduction describing Daniel's preparations for prayer (v. 3), this unit moves in three groups of verses (4-6, 7-8, 9-11) to contrast the virtues of God with the failures of Israel. Each set of contrasts begins with "(to you/to) Adonai," which then introduces God's virtues, followed by statements describing Israel's sins.[32]

> v. 4   *Adonai,* the great and awesome God, who keeps covenant and steadfast love . . .
>> v. 5   we have sinned and acted perversely, done evil and rebelled and turned aside from your commandments and your ordinances.
>> v. 6   And we have not listened to your servants the prophets. . . .
> v. 7a   *To you Adonai,* righteousness *[haṣṣĕdāqāh],*
>> v. 7b   but to us shame. . . .
>> v. 8   . . . to us shame . . . to our kings, our officials, and to our ancestors in that we have sinned against you.
> v. 9a   *To Adonai our God* compassion *[hārahămîm]* and forgiveness *[hassĕlihôt]*
>> v. 9b   but we have rebelled against you.
>> v. 10   And we have not listened to the voice of the LORD our God. . . .
>> v. 11   And all Israel has transgressed your law and turned aside without listening to your voice . . . for we have sinned against you.[33]

This structure breaks off after verse 11, with verses 12-14 describing the curse and oath (cf. v. 11b) that God has brought upon the people as judgment for their disobedience. Yet here too the contrast so prominent in the preceding verses is echoed, though its order is inverted to allow the final note to fall on Israel's sin:

---

31. Towner, "Retributional Theology," 210.

32. I had already discerned this basic structure when I discovered the similar argument in M. Gilbert's "La prière de Daniel, Dn 9, 4-19," *Revue théologique de Louvain* 3 (1972): 297–303. My presentation has been sharpened by Gilbert's analysis.

33. Reading with several mss *lāk* instead of MT's *lô.*

v. 13b   . . . we have not appeased the LORD our God by turning aside
from our iniquities.
v. 14   . . . but righteous *[ṣaddîq]* is the LORD our
God . . .
v. 14b   . . . and we have not listened to his voice.

The confession element in these verses is unmistakable. Verse 5
introduces this theme with five different words describing Israel's
condition: sin *(ḥṭ')*, perverseness *('wn)*, wickedness *(ršʻ)*, rebellion
(mrd), turning aside *(swr)*. These expressions then are summarized
by two general confessions that repeat throughout this unit: we have
sinned (*ḥāṭā'nû:* vv. 5, 8, 11); we have not listened (*lō' šāma'nû:* vv.
6, 10, 14). Israel's guilt is made all the more apparent by being
contrasted with God's great mercy and justice. The character of this
"great and awesome God" provides the true measure of Israel's
guilt. God is a "keeper of covenant and steadfast love," righteous
(just), compassionate, and forgiving. The prayer proclaims these
virtues and the petition that follows lays claim to them.[34]

Verses 15-19 form a second rhetorical unit that presents two
requests for divine intervention. Each is introduced by the formulaic expression *wěʻattāh*, "and now" (vv. 15, 17). The first petition (vv. 15-16) is that God turn away from the divine anger and
wrath now manifest toward Jerusalem. The plea is framed and
supported by a double reference to the same contrast between God's
character and the people's failure that has dominated the first part
of the prayer. God is affirmed as the one whose favor has been
demonstrated in the deliverance from Egypt (v. 15a) and whose
actions toward Israel, even in judgment, have always been characterized by righteousness (*ṣědāqāh,* v. 16a). The people, however,
have sinned against God (*ḥṭ'*, vv. 15, 16; *ršʻ*, v. 15; *'wn*, v. 16) and so
have become a reproach to all around them. The second petition
(vv. 17-19) is for God now to turn toward the people and respond
positively to their cry for help. The plea is carried rhetorically by the
triple imperative "hear" *(šěmaʻ)*, each request supplemented by
additional language that builds toward the climactic final petition
for forgiveness:

Hear, our God . . . and cause your face to shine upon your desolate
sanctuary. . . .
Incline your ear, my God, and *hear,* open your eyes and see our desolation. . . .
Adonai *hear,* Adonai forgive, Adonai be attentive and act.

34. For discussion of the prayer's emphasis on God's virtues, see further J.
Goldingay, *Daniel* (WBC; Dallas: Word, 1989), 241–44.

Within these two petitions the motivation for divine response recalls the virtues of God that have been confessed repeatedly throughout the prayer. Seven times in these four verses the name of God is invoked, the most dramatic repetition occurring in the climactic final petition, where each plea that God "hear" and "forgive" and "be attentive" is prefaced by the vocative "Adonai." As J. Montgomery has noted, the rhetorical effect is to elevate this verse as the Kyrie eleison of the Hebrew Bible.[35] The phrase "for your own sake" occurs twice (vv. 17, 19), the full meaning of which verse 18 makes explicit: "for not according to our righteousness are we presenting our supplication before you, but according to your great compassion." With this last expression of faith the prayer ends as it begins, praising God's virtues of compassion, love, righteousness, and, most importantly for this special occasion, God's forgiveness (cf. vv. 4, 7, 9).

Having completed this analysis of the prayer's rhetorical structure, I now return to the previous question concerning its function in chapter 9. What does a prayer of penitence, stressing the sovereignty, compassion, and justice of God, contribute to the narrative in which it is set? Among the reasons for regarding the prayer as secondary,[36] the argument that it addresses issues unrelated to the surrounding narrative is perhaps the most necessary to resolve if one is to find some sense in the present arrangement of the chapter.

Without the prayer chapter 9 focuses on Daniel's quest to understand Jeremiah's prophecy concerning the end of the desolation of Jerusalem. As preparation for receiving God's revelation on this matter Daniel turns to prayer and fasting. The original narrative presumably suggested that Daniel prayed but did not record the words of his prayer. Next in this sequence is Gabriel's revelation, which provides a reinterpretation of Jeremiah's prediction. The seventy years before the end of desolation are now presented as "seventy weeks of years" (v. 24), that is, 490 years. At no point does Gabriel's announcement acknowledge the prayer for forgiveness.

If this stratum of the narrative is dated between 167 and 164 B.C.E., that is, after the desecration of the temple by Antiochus Epiphanes (Dan 9:26; cf. 1 Macc 1:29-35; 2 Macc 5:22-26) but before the temple's reconsecration by Judas Maccabeus, then one may understand that the author is concerned about the question of when the persecutions and oppressions that have ravaged Jerusalem

35. J. Montgomery, *A Critical and Exegetical Commentary on the Book of Daniel* (ICC; Edinburgh: T. and T. Clark, 1927), 368.
36. See n. 30.

will end. The seventy years prophesied by Jeremiah had long since passed without the realization of relief he had predicted. The revelation of Gabriel clarifies this issue. The seventy years are to be understood as seventy weeks of years. The focus of this interpretation is on the last of these "weeks," that is, on the final seven years (vv. 26-27). These years correspond roughly with the years of Antiochus's persecution in 169–164 B.C.E., and so also with the probable date of the author of the text. In this sense the revelation confirms that the end of Jerusalem's suffering is near. Still, the allotted time must run its full course as determined by God.

If the prayer of verses 4-19 is inserted into this narrative, the major lines of thought are presented as follows: concern about the duration of Jerusalem's oppression, prayer for forgiveness focusing on God's virtues vis-à-vis Israel's sin, and finally a return to the focus on the end of Jerusalem's plight. I have previously noted that the prayer is not acknowledged in Gabriel's revelation. Indeed, before Daniel has completed his plea the divine revelation is already on its way; it does not come in response to anything Daniel said. The revelation of the time allotted for Jerusalem's desolation remains unchanged. Further, the prayer does not secure divine forgiveness; the text does not mention it. Yet the prayer does offer rhetorical persuasion for believing that it will be granted by the repeated confession of God as righteous, compassionate, and forgiving.

Further, the prayer also makes a particular contribution with respect to the question of Jerusalem's future. The LORD is the "great and awesome God who keeps covenant and steadfast love." This proclamation grounds not only the hope for forgiveness but also the promise of ultimate restoration. God is a "keeper of covenant." With Gabriel's announcement that the desolations must run their allotted time "until the decreed end" (v. 27), the full meaning of God's covenant fidelity is defined in terms of the present crisis. God *will* maintain the covenant, not because of Daniel's prayer of penitence but for God's own sake. By so functioning as a literary vehicle proclaiming God's self-vindication, the prayer is appropriately linked, as G. Bornkamm suggests, with the *Gattung* of doxology.[37] Towner affirms this point: the prayer is "first and foremost a proclamation of God's being and a celebration of his power."[38] Such a

37. G. Bornkamm, "Lobpreis, Bekenntnis und Opfer," *Apophoreta: Festschrift für Ernst Haenchen* (BZNW 30; Berlin: Töpelmann, 1964), 60–63.
38. Towner, "Retributional Theology," 213. For Towner this view supports his argument that in Daniel the eschaton is not regarded primarily as God's

proclamation is not out of place in Daniel 9. What better way to confirm that the promise of Jerusalem's restoration is in safe hands?

THE PRAYERS OF EZRA AND NEHEMIAH (EZRA 9:6-15; NEH 1:5-11; 9:6-37)
Like Daniel 9, these three prayers focus on the theme of penitence. Like Daniel's prayer, they articulate this theme by contrasting Israel's guilt with God's great faithfulness, mercy, and justice. For example, the prayer in Nehemiah 1 is introduced with the same ascription noted in Dan 9:4: "LORD God, God of the heavens, the great and awesome God who keeps covenant and steadfast love to those who love you and keep your commandments" (Neh 1:5). This doxology introduces Nehemiah's petition that God hear the prayer of this servant on behalf of the people (*těhî nā' 'ozněkā qaššebet,* vv. 6, 11), for they have sinned (*ht',* v. 6 [3 times]) and acted perversely (*hbl,* v. 7) and have not kept the commandments (v. 7). The same doxology repeats in Neh 9:32 just at the crucial transition (note the use of *wě'attāh,* "and now") between the preliminary recollection of God's mercy and Israel's sin (vv. 1-31) and the petition that God now respond with continuing mercy to their present plea for help.

Only in Ezra 9 is this particular ascription lacking. Nevertheless, the central thesis of the prayer remains the same. Ezra's address begins with the vocative "O my God" (v. 6) and closes with the confession "LORD, God of Israel, righteous *[saddîq]* are you" (v. 15). Between these framing pieces the rhetorical emphasis of the prayer is carried by the repeated contrast between LORD/God (7 times: vv. 6, 8, 9 [2 times], 10, 13, 15), who is gracious (*hnn,* v. 8), ever-loving (*hsd,* v. 9), and righteous (*sdq,* v. 15), and the disobedient Israelites, whose perversity is variously described (*bšt,* "shame," vv. 6, 7; *klm,* "humiliation," v. 6; *'wn,* "iniquity," vv. 6, 7, 13; *'šm,* "guilt," vv. 6, 7, 13, 15; *'sb,* "forsaking," v. 10; *r'h,* "evil," v. 13).

Given the similarities in these texts, I shall explore their significance for the present discussion by focusing on one particular example. The prayer in Nehemiah 9 is not only the most elaborate of the three, but its rhetorical structure also provides an excellent opportunity to witness prayer's function in the literary art of char-

---

retributive act against sinners, but as a means of God's "vindicating himself in the introduction of his new age". The prayer in 9:4-19, therefore, is seen not as a device for influencing God's will but as "an act of piety, a *miswah,* part of the process by which men prepare themselves to cope with difficulties which form part of their present empirical experience" (p. 212). For further discussion of his views on the prayer's theological function, see *Daniel* (Interpretation; Atlanta: John Knox, 1984), 130–40.

acterizing God. In the remainder of this chapter, then, I will focus on Neh 9:6-37.

The compositional history of Nehemiah 9 is a matter of considerable debate. Noth's views concerning the Chronicler's responsibility for this prayer[39] have come under strong attack, especially by H. G. M. Williamson. Indeed, S. Japhet and Williamson have mounted strong criticisms of Noth's entire hypothesis concerning the Chronicler's authorship of materials in Ezra-Nehemiah.[40] For my purposes here, however, it is not necessary to decide for or against the Chronicler's authorship of the prayer; I am primarily interested in the internal dynamics of the text and in its relationship to the larger narrative context in which it is now located.

The observation of Williamson and others that Nehemiah 8–10 follows in general the sequence of a typical covenant renewal ceremony (proclamation of law, confession, renewal of commitment) provides a clear theological framework for understanding these texts.[41] Within this framework the prayer in chapter 9 occupies a position of central importance. Not only does it signal the people's

39. Noth (*Chronicler's History*, 80, 105) suggests that the prayers in Ezra 9 and Nehemiah 9 reflect the Chronicler's preference for casting important speeches in the style of the "Levitical sermon" which was popular in his own day. (Here he follows G. von Rad; cf. "Die levitische Predigt in den Büchern der Chronik," *Festschrift Otto Procksch* [Leipzig, 1934], 113–24 [= "The Levitical Sermon in I and II Chronicles," *The Problem of the Hexateuch and Other Essays* (New York: McGraw-Hill, 1966), 267–80].) Noth contends that the Chronicler's use of such prayers is reminiscent of the Deuteronomist, who used prayer speeches to promote theological and ideological concerns.

40. See H. G. M. Williamson, *Israel in the Books of Chronicles* (Cambridge: Cambridge Univ. Press, 1977), 5–70; idem, *Ezra-Nehemiah* (WBC; Waco: Word, 1985), xxiii–xxxv. For a less detailed presentation of Williamson's views, see his *Ezra and Nehemiah* (Old Testament Guides; Sheffield: JSOT Press, 1987), 20–29, 37–47. See S. Japhet, "The Supposed Common Authorship of Chronicles and Ezra-Nehemiah Investigated Anew," *VT* 18 (1968): 330–71; idem, *The Ideology of the Book of Chronicles and its Place in Biblical Thought* (Beiträge zur Erforschung des Alten Testaments und des Antiken Judentums 9; Frankfurt: Peter Lang, 1989). J. Blenkinsopp (*Ezra-Nehemiah* [Philadelphia: Westminster, 1988], 47–54) has returned to a more traditional view.

41. In Williamson's view the present theological arrangement of Nehemiah 8–10 took place at a first stage of redaction, which he dates ca. 400 B.C.E., i.e., *before* the work of the Chronicler (see the sources listed in n. 40). For similar views concerning the theological structure of Nehemiah 8–10, see K. Baltzer, *The Covenant Formulary* (Oxford: Basil Blackwell, 1971), 43–47; W. Th. In der Smitten, *Esra: Quellen, Überlieferung und Geschichte* (Assen: Van Gorcum, 1973), 35–53; U. Kellermann, *Nehemia: Quellen, Überlieferung und Geschichte* (BZAW 102; Berlin: Töpelmann, 1967), 90–92; D. J. McCarthy, "Covenant and Law in Chronicles-Nehemiah," *CBQ* 44 (1982): 25–44.

contrition for past failures, a crucial confession in the step toward recommitment; but it also proclaims that the God whose righteousness requires such fidelity is gracious and merciful to bring it to fruition. Both sides of the nature of God—righteousness and grace—constitute key themes in this prayer. An examination of the prayer's rhetorical structure illustrates these themes.

As in Daniel 9, in this prayer the rhetoric serves to contrast God's virtues with Israel's failures. The essential contrast is suggested in the opening and closing words of the prayer: "You are the LORD, you alone" (v. 6, NRSV) "and we are in great distress" (v. 37). Between these primary foci—God's sovereignty and Israel's distress—the contrast is sustained and developed through six rhetorical units that recount with alternating descriptions the sovereignty and mercy of God vis-à-vis Israel's repeated disobedience. These units may be presented summarily as follows:

I (vv. 6-8): You are the LORD alone. You have made the heavens. . . . (v. 6)
You are the LORD, the God who chose Abram . . . *for you are righteous [saddîq].* (vv. 7-8)

II (vv. 9-15): You saw the affliction of our ancestors in Egypt, and you heard their cries. . . . (v. 9)

III (vv. 16-18): But they and our ancestors acted presumptuously and they stiffened their neck and they refused to listen to your commandments. . . . (vv. 16-17)

But you are a God *forgiving [sělîhôt], gracious [hannûn],* and *merciful [rahûm], patient ['erek 'appaîm],* and *abounding in steadfast love [rab wěhesed],* and you did not forsake them. (v. 17)

Even when they made for themselves a molten calf . . . and they committed great blasphemies. . . . (v. 18)

IV (vv. 19-31): *But you in your great mercies [běrahǎmêkā] did not forsake them.* . . . (v. 19)

But they were disobedient and rebelled against you. . . .
And you gave them into the hand of their enemies . . . and they cried out to you . . . and you heard from heaven and *according to your great mercies [kěrahǎmêkā hārabbîm]* you (vv. 26-30) gave them saviors. . . .
But when they were relieved they turned back to do evil in your sight.

> And you gave them into the hand of their enemies
> . . . and they cried out again to you and you heard
> and delivered them *according to your mercies
> [kĕraḥămêkā]*. . . .
> But they did not listen and you gave them into the
> hand of the peoples of the land.
>
> *But in accordance with your great mercies [ûbĕraḥămekā
> hārabbîm]* you did not make an end of them and you
> did not forsake them because a God of grace *[ḥannûn]*
> and mercy *[raḥûm]* you are. (v. 31)

V (v. 32):   And now *[wĕ'attāh]*, our God, the great God, the mighty
and the awesome one, who keeps covenant and *stead-
fast love [ḥesed]*, do not treat lightly all the hardship
that has fallen on us. . . .

VI (vv. 33-37):   You are righteous *[ṣaddîq]* concerning all that has come
upon us . . . (v. 33)
and we have done evil. . . . (v. 33b)
Behold, we are slaves. . . . (v. 36a)
Behold, we are slaves. . . . (v. 36b)
. . . and in great distress we are. (v. 37b)

This overview clarifies how the rhetorical emphasis on God controls and shapes the penitential elements in the prayer. Each of the
six sections, except III (vv. 16-18), is introduced by a statement
proclaiming God's greatness. The phrase that repeats in four instances begins with the second person pronoun *'attāh*, "you," followed by the invocation of the divine name or a phrase or a clause
further defining God's special virtues. In section I (vv. 6-8) this
occurs twice, the first (v. 6) acclaiming God's "unity and exclusive
sovereignty"[42] in terms of creation: "You are the LORD, you alone.
You have made the heavens" *('attāh hû' Yhwh lĕbaddekā 'attā 'āśîtā
'et haššāmayim);* the second (v. 7), God's special election of Abraham: "You are the LORD, the God who chose Abram" *('attāh hû'
Yhwh hā'ĕlōhîm 'ăšer bāḥartā bĕ'abrām).* Between these references
a similar ascription declares God's sustenance of the created world
(v. 6c: *wĕ'attāh mĕḥayyeh 'et kūllām).*
Section II (vv. 9-15) continues this opening recitation with a
lengthy description of God's providential care in leading the people
out of Egypt. This historical retrospect is introduced with a verbal
phrase, "You saw *[wattēre']* the affliction of our ancestors," which is

---

42. Cf. Weinfeld, *Deuteronomic School,* 39.

then developed by a series of additional verbs elaborating God's specific act of provision.

> you heard their cries *[šm']* (v. 9b)
> you performed *[ntn]* signs and wonders (v. 10)
> the sea you divided *[bq']* before them (v. 11a)
> their pursuers you hurled *[šlk]* into the depths (v. 11b)
> by a pillar of cloud you led them *[nhh]* by day (v. 12)
> upon the mountain of Sinai you descended *[yrd]* (v. 13a)
> and you gave *[ntn]* to them right ordinances (v. 13b)
> and your holy Sabbath you made known *[yd']* to them (v. 14a)
> and commandments and statutes you commanded *[ṣwh]* to them (v. 14b)
> and bread from heaven you gave *[ntn]* to them (v. 15a)
> and water from the rock you brought forth *[yṣ']* for them (v. 15b)
> and you said *['mr]* to them to go in to possess the land (v. 15c)

Section IV (vv. 19-31) begins and ends with an almost identical description of God's great compassion: verse 19, "you in your great mercies" *('attāh běraḥǎmêkā hārabbîm);* verse 31, "But in accordance with your great mercies" *(ûběraḥǎmêkā hārabbîm).* The same language repeats twice more in this section (vv. 27c, 28c), thus sustaining the principal contrast between God's benevolence and Israel's continual rebellion. Section V (v. 32) prefaces the petition with the doxological acclamation of God as "the great God, the mighty and the awesome one, who keeps covenant and steadfast love." Finally section VI (vv. 33-37) returns to the motif of divine righteousness sounded first at the conclusion of section I, "You are righteous" (v. 33, *'attāh ṣaddîq;* cf. v. 8, *kî ṣaddîq 'āttāh).*

Section III (vv. 16-18) is the one part of the prayer that begins differently. Here attention focuses first and last not on God but on Israel: verse 16, "But *they* and *our* ancestors acted presumptuously . . ."; verse 18, "Even when *they* made for *themselves* a molten calf." In this section the emphasis on Israel's disobedience serves as a rhetorical frame for verse 17, where once again the theme of God's grace and mercy that has governed preceding sections provides the focal point for evaluating Israel's behavior. Despite their stubbornness, God's dealings with them have affirmed the divine characteristics of forgiveness *(slḥ),* grace *(ḥnn),* mercy *(rḥm),* patience *('rk 'pym),* and unending love *(ḥsd).*

With this structure section III stands juxtaposed to section IV, displaying an inverted order of development. I have attempted to highlight this development in the outline by bracketing the framing motifs of each. Whereas verses 16-18 unfold along the lines of

Israel's sin—God's mercy—Israel's sin, verses 19-31 reverse this order: God's mercy—Israel's repeated rebellion (vv. 26-30)—God's mercy. Verse 17, which had previously interrupted the recitation of Israel's disobedience in order to declare that God had not forsaken the people in accordance with the divine qualities of grace and mercy, now provides the rhetorical frame of verses 19-31. It is this God, "great in mercy," that has never forsaken Israel; even in the face of their repeated apostasy, God has not yet made an end of them.

Taken together these first four sections (vv. 6-31) provide the introduction to and the grounding for the petition that occurs in verse 32. As in previous prayers that I have analyzed, the transition to petition is marked by *wĕ'aṭṭāh,* "and now." But here, before the petition proper is articulated, yet another declaration of God's greatness once again affirms the unparalleled status of the God before whom the people now submit themselves: "And now, our God, the great God, the mighty and the awesome one, who keeps covenant and steadfast love." With this preface the petition is couched indirectly, as if to suggest that given their miserable record of failures, the people hardly dare portray themselves as deserving God's favor. Thus they ask only that God not count their present hardship as too insignificant to merit attention.

Following this brief petition, the prayer returns immediately to emphasize God's virtues—"You are righteous concerning all that has come upon us" (v. 33)—and to stress that it is only their own failings that have resulted in their present misery. In this final section (vv. 33-37) the contrast between God's character and Israel's sin that has dominated throughout the prayer is rounded off by the fourfold repetition of the pronoun *'ănaḥnû,* "we," which presents a final acknowledgement of guilt and its consequences:

We have done evil (*'ănaḥnû hiršā'nû,* v. 33b)
Behold, we are slaves today (*'ănaḥnû 'ăbādîm,* v. 36a)
Behold, we are slaves (*'ănaḥnû 'ăbādîm,* v. 36b)
. . . and in great distress we are (*bĕṣārāh gĕdôlāh 'ănāḥnû,* v. 37b)

The final words of the prayer in Hebrew—"in great distress *[bĕṣārāh]* we are"—serve rhetorically to link the people's present subjugation by the Persians to the "distress" of their forebears (*ṣārêhem;* cf. vv. 27-31) during the days of the judges. In that time their ancestors had cried out to God for relief, and they had been delivered, only to return to their evil ways and hence to a repetition of the cycle of oppression, plea for mercy, deliverance. This final section is presented as yet another stage in the continuation of this historical cycle, for once again disobedience has resulted in oppression by a foreign power.

Yet in what one may consider a dramatic departure from the cycle of the preceding era, this present lament breaks off just after the description of suffering without repeating the expected cry for help.[43] "Behold, we are slaves today—and the land that you gave to our ancestors to eat its fruit and its goodness . . . its abundant produce goes to the kings whom you have set over us in our sin . . . and in great distress we are" (vv. 36-37). Their future plight is left open. Will God deliver as in days gone by? The final outcome is not articulated. Nonetheless, the whole prayer has so emphasized God's power and covenant fidelity that these final woeful words cannot help but convey the hope that God's great mercies will ultimately secure their restoration. This hope then manifests itself concretely in a pledge to renewed faithfulness, the substance of which becomes the primary focus of chapter 10.

In the second half of this chapter I have attempted to show that in the so-called prose prayers of penitence, confessions of guilt and petitions for forgiveness attain their rhetorical effect by being set in contrast to proclamations of God's sovereignty, mercy, and justice. In this respect they are comparable in their emphases to the prayers of Hezekiah, Asa, Jehoshaphat, and David that I examined in the first half of the chapter. Taken as a group these prayers are all exilic and postexilic in origin and as such attest the emphasis on proclaiming the nature and character of God that emerges in late narrative prayers.

Westermann suggests that such an emphasis reflects what may be described as a third stage in the development of prayer.[44] The earliest stage has short cries of prayer or calls to God that require no cultic framework. Such prayers (e.g., Exod 18:10; Judg 15:18) occur in the middle of a narrative and give the impression of having emerged naturally from the situation in which they are spoken. In

---

43. Cf. H. G. M. Williamson, "Post-Exilic Historiography," *The Future of Biblical Studies,* ed. R. E. Friedman and H. G. M. Williamson (Atlanta: Scholars Press, 1987), 200–20; idem, "Structure and Historiography in Nehemiah 9," *Proceedings of the Ninth World Congress of Jewish Studies,* ed. D. Assaf (Jerusalem: Magnes, 1988), 117–31.

44. C. Westermann, "Gebet im Alten Testament," *BHH* 1.519–22; idem, *Elements of Old Testament Theology* (Atlanta: John Knox, 1982), 154–56.

the second or middle stage of prayer's development these short calls come together in the form of liturgical psalms. The *Sitz im Leben* of these prayers is the worship service of the settled community, where the unity between the congregation coming together to worship and the civil community held together by state and monarchy buttresses a consciousness of common belonging to God that appears in the prayers of this period as self-evident. With the dissolution of the monarchy and the cessation of worship in the temple, this self-evident sense of belonging to the community of faith is lost. In the prayers that emerge from the third stage (e.g., the long prose prayers of 1 Kings 8, Ezra 9, Nehemiah 9), this historical situation is reflected in the replacement of "self-evident belonging" by a "conscious and reflected belonging."[45]

Westermann's suggestions are confirmed in the prayers examined here. In the prayers of Hezekiah, Asa, and Jehoshaphat the sovereignty and power of God are proclaimed as the basis for hope in God's deliverance during times of crisis. Given the need of the post–586 B.C.E. community to understand God's intentions toward them vis-à-vis their domination first by the Babylonians and then by the Persians, these prayers provide major declarations of trust in the unparalleled resources for these confrontations made available by the Almighty God.

In the prayers of Daniel, Ezra, and Nehemiah a similar historical backdrop provides the impetus for the acknowledgment of guilt and the petition for restoration through forgiveness. In these prayers a repeating doxology ascribing to God unrivaled status as "a great and awesome God" (Dan 9:4; Neh 1:5; 9:32) is elaborated especially with affirmations of God's righteousness (*ṣĕdāqāh*, e.g., three times in Daniel 9: vv. 7, 14, 16; cf. v. 18) and mercy (*raḥûm*, e.g., six times in Nehemiah 9: vv. 17, 19, 27, 28, 31 [twice]). Such emphases summon forth penitence, for as each of these prayers affirms in a variety of ways, Israel's fidelity has nowhere been equal to God's great compassion.

In both groups of prayers it is not the pray-ers themselves who are the fixed point of attention, but God. This focus on God's great virtues is clearly "conscious and reflected," as Westermann has noted. Hence I have taken these texts as prime illustrations of the way prayer may contribute to the art of divine characterization.

One final word is in order. In the prayers of penitence God's

---

45. Westermann, *Elements,* 156.

sovereignty and righteousness are affirmed without question. Indeed, the justice of God's actions is repeatedly stressed (e.g., Dan 9:7, 14; Ezra 9:15; Neh 9:8, 33), rendering any response other than contrition completely inappropriate. These prayers are reminiscent of the great tradition of lament as embodied, for example, in the Psalms. As Westermann has pointed out, however, they also represent a transformation of the lament. Unlike so many psalms of lament, these prayers of penitence contain no protestation of innocence, no questioning of God's intentions. In fact the element of lament recedes almost completely in these prayers, the emphasis falling instead on confession of sin.[46] From first to last these are prayers of trustful submission.

In the prayers analyzed in the next chapter, however, precisely this element of lament and protest emerges as all-important. In these prayers God's sovereignty and power, God's mercy and righteousness, are very much in question, at least from the pray-er's perspective. Here too petitions are raised for divine intervention in times of great distress, and as the context of each prayer makes clear, much is at stake in how God responds. If God fails to respond as petitioned, the consequences for the pray-er will be severe. Not only will the suppliant find no relief from the crisis that threatens, but more importantly trust in God's character will be seriously jeopardized. To these prayers for divine justice I now turn.

46. Westermann, *Praise and Lament,* 206.

CHAPTER 6

Prayers
for Divine Justice

While the prayers of penitence examined in the previous chapter promote contrition and submission as the only legitimate response to the unquestioned justice and mercy of God, a significant number of other prayers in the Hebrew Bible are characterized by their insistence on nearly the opposite attitude. These prayers articulate the perception that suffering is either undeserved or too excessive to be acceptable as divine punishment for sinfulness. Hence they hurl at God questions and petitions designed to secure suffering's removal or at least its modification. Such prayers are preeminently displayed in the poetry of the Hebrew Bible's lament traditions, especially in the confessions of Jeremiah, in Job, in Habbakuk, and in the Psalms. This lament tradition is the focus of the next chapter.

Before turning to these prayers, I shall in this chapter retain for a little longer the focus on prose prayers, for here also, embedded within Hebrew Bible narratives, one finds a vital witness to prayer as a principal means of securing divine justice. Indeed, the narrative context of these prayers affords the opportunity to understand how vigorous engagement with God at critical points can affect the outcome of particular experiences. To illustrate this point I have selected five texts that raise questions of divine justice within a context of prayer: Gen 18:22-33; Exod 32:7-14; Num 11:4-34; 14:11-23; and Josh 7:7-9.

At the outset one should note that in all likelihood these texts derive from disparate historical origins. At least one is inclined toward this conclusion based on the prevailing critical theories concerning their authorship and dating. Gen 18:22-33 is generally thought to have originated in the exilic or postexilic period and from this point to have been inserted back into the Abraham tradition as part of its *Nachgeschichte*.[1] A similar exilic setting is also commonly suggested for the prayers in Exod 32:7-14; Josh 7:7-9; and Num 14:11-25, all of which many assign to the Deuteronomistic editors.[2]

A majority of commentators assign Num 11:4-34 (and some argue also Num 14:11-25) to the J source.[3] If the traditional dating of this source to the tenth-ninth century B.C.E. can be retained (a matter of serious debate), then this text would represent an early witness to this type of prayer. One cannot rule out that prayer could have functioned in this regard at an early period in Israel's history, whatever the arguments against dating this prayer or the J tradition to the tenth-ninth century. As A. von Soden, H. H. Schmid, and others have recognized, the social, cultural, and historical situations that produced the need for questioning divine justice, which emerged so sharply for Israel during the days of exile, were already present in Mesopotamia to a quite similar extent at least as early as the second millennium.[4] One can with good reason suppose, therefore, that the tradition of raising hard questions about divine justice in prayers of the sort represented in these five prose texts had a long and varied history.

I am not, however, concerned here to press for locating these texts

1. See, e.g., C. Westermann, *Genesis 12–36* (Minneapolis: Augsburg, 1985), 292. See further J. Blenkinsopp, "Abraham and the Righteous of Sodom," *JSS* 33 (1982): 119–32; L. Schmidt, *"De Deo": Studien zur Literarkritik und Theologie des Buches Jona, des Gesprächs zwischen Abraham und Jahwe in Gen 18, 22ff. und von Hi 1* (BZAW 143; Berlin: de Gruyter, 1976), 119ff.

2. For a representative sampling of the standard views on the literary history of these texts, see, e.g., G. Coats, *Rebellion in the Wilderness: The Murmuring Motif in the Wilderness Traditions of the Old Testament* (Nashville: Abingdon, 1968); A. Tunyogi, *The Rebellions of Israel* (Richmond: John Knox, 1969); V. Fritz, *Israel in der Wüste: Traditionsgeschichtliche Untersuchung der Wüstenüberlieferung des Jahwisten* (Marburg: N. G. Elwert, 1970); M. Noth, *Exodus* (OTL; Philadelphia: Westminster, 1962); idem, *A History of Pentateuchal Traditions* (Englewood Cliffs, N.J.: Prentice-Hall, 1972); B. Childs, *The Book of Exodus* (OTL; Philadelphia: Westminster, 1974).

3. On Num 14:11-25 see, e.g., Coats, *Rebellion,* 138–39, and more recently in *Moses: Heroic Man, Man of God* (Sheffield: JSOT Press, 1988), 122–23. In the latter work Coats has focused specifically on the "heroic" character of Moses' role as intercessor, which he finds to be most clearly expressed in the J traditions recounting the period of wilderness wandering (109–24). On Num 11:4-34 see, e.g., Fritz, *Israel in der Wüste,* 16–17; Coats, *Rebellion,* 96–98; M. Noth, *Numbers* (OTL; Philadelphia: Westminster, 1968), 83; cf. H. Seebass, "Num. XI, XIII und die Hypothese des Jahwisten," *VT* 28 (1978): 214–23.

4. W. von Soden, "Das Fragen nach der Gerechtigkeit Gottes im Alten Orient," *MDOG* 96 (1965): 41–59; H. H. Schmid, *Wesen und Geschichte der Weisheit* (Berlin: A. Töpelmann, 1966).

at a particular point in the historical development of prayer. What suggests their linkage is not common authorship but a common rhetorical function. Despite some differences in the details of their presentation, each of these texts functions within a literary context that has three essential features: (1) some crisis in the relationship between pray-er and God; (2) a response to the crisis in the form of a prayer that raises questions about divine justice and divine intentions; and (3) some resolution or at least explanation of the crisis that, within the narrative context, is depicted as the result of the pray-er's engagement with God. Simply stated, these texts all revolve around the themes of crisis, prayer, and resolution of crisis. Together they represent a significant witness to a tradition of piety embracing prayer as an appropriate response for those who would stand in "loyal opposition"[5] to God and to God's ways of executing justice. In this respect I suggest that one of the principal functions of these prose prayers, and also of the lament prayers on which I focus in the next chapter, is to address, to clarify, and sometimes to resolve the various concerns relating to theodicy.

In this chapter I address these three themes first rather generally with the hope of providing some overview of their presence in the five texts as a whole. I then concentrate in more detail on three of the texts—Num 11:4-34; Num 14:11-25; and Exod 32:7-14—in order to focus the discussion more sharply. The final section of the chapter is devoted to some general observations concerning prayer's function as a vehicle of theodicy. To this last discussion I shall have to return in chapter 7 before finalizing my conclusions.

THREE BASIC FEATURES

CRISIS

The crises described in these texts are not identical in their details, but they are similar in their effects. They present situations in which some serious breach in the relationship with God has occurred or threatens to occur, a breach that, if not addressed, will have dire results: either divine judgment, which may mean the destruction of the people; or human doubt, suspicion, or misunderstanding about God's character and intentions, which may mean that the level of trust in the divine-human relationship is seriously impaired. In either case the problems are serious and the stakes are

---

5. I take the phrase from G. Coats, "The King's Loyal Opposition: Obedience and Authority in Exodus 32–34," *Canon and Authority,* ed. G. Coats and B. O. Long (Philadelphia: Fortress, 1977), 91–109.

high. Both the quality and the duration of the relationship with God hang in the balance.

In Exodus 32, Genesis 18, and Numbers 14, for example, the crisis involves God's announced intentions to judge and annihilate a whole people. In Exodus and Numbers the sin of the Israelites, first in substituting a golden calf for a holy God, and subsequently in despising God and God's provisions during the time of wilderness wandering, prompts God to announce that the people will be destroyed and a new beginning will be made from Moses' seed (Exod 32:10; Num 14:12). In Genesis 18 the sin of Sodom and Gomorrah initiates God's announced intentions to judge. This announcement in turn prompts Abraham to intervene.

In Josh 7:7-8 the crisis is born out of confusion concerning God's intentions. In the aftermath of the defeat at Ai, Joshua questions a divine wrath that threatens not only to deny Israel possession of the promised land but also to undermine confidence in the God who stands behind this promise.[6] Does God deliver only to destroy? Or, as Joshua puts it, "Why have you brought this people across the Jordan at all, to hand us over to the Amorites, so as to destroy us?" (Josh 7:7, NRSV).

In Numbers 11 the people's complaint about lack of meat and Moses' own perception of the inordinate burden of his responsibility for their welfare prompt his anger with God. Why should he, a faithful servant, be caught in the middle between such a rebellious rabble and such a demanding God? His address to God, "If you are going to treat me like this, then kill me I pray," raises an ominous threat for the Israelites. Should this request be granted, they would be left with no mediator between themselves and God.

THE RESPONSE OF PRAYER

The response to each of these crisis situations is a direct and intentional address to God that, in my judgment, can be legitimately understood as prayer. Although the content of each of the prayers differs, they share a number of similarities in form.

(1) They are explicitly directed to God. Four of the texts invoke God's name, either at the beginning of the address (e.g., Exod 32:11: "LORD"; Josh 7:7: "Adonai LORD"), or at some point in the body of the prayer (e.g., Num 14:14: "LORD" [twice]; Gen 18:27, 30, 31:

6. J. A. Soggin sees here two originally independent narratives—7:1, 5b-26, the Achan narrative, and 7:2-5a, the Ai narrative—now woven together, with the former providing interpretation of the latter (*Joshua* [OTL; Philadelphia: Westminster, 1972], 96–97).

"Adonai"). Only Num 11:4–34 lacks a clearly articulated invocation. In this instance the introductory statement "And Moses said to the LORD" marks the response as prayer, and a second person address follows: "Why have you done evil *[hărē'ōtā]* to your servant?" (v. 11).

(2) On the heels of the invocation/direct address, questions are put to God. In every case the questions take issue with some dimension of divinely initiated evil or divine injustice. For example, two of the texts explicitly describe God's action as "evil" (*r'h:* Exod 32:12 [twice], 14; Num 11:11, 15).[7] The issue of justice is implicit in Moses' concern that God's intent to "kill this people like one person" (Num 14:15) will reflect negatively on God's reputation among the nations. In Gen 18:22–33 Abraham's insistence that divine justice be worked out in the differentiation of the righteous from the wicked at Sodom attains a level of explicitness unparalleled in the Hebrew Bible. Nowhere is the concern stated more sharply than in Abraham's question of verse 25: "Shall not the Judge *[šōpēṭ]* of all the earth do justice *[mišpāṭ]?*"

(3) Finally, each of the prayers in context receives some response from God, provided either by means of a first person reply direct from God (e.g., Gen 18:26, 28, etc.; Num 11:16–20, 23; 14:20–25; Josh 7:10–15), or by a third person report supplied by the narrator (Exod 32:14). This feature places these prayers within the framework of divine-human dialogue, depicting two partners participating as near equals in the discussion and resolution of issues of mutual concern. This dialogic framework for prayer reflects, as I suggested in chapter 3, a fundamental Hebraic understanding about the degree of reciprocity between creator and creature. Such "conversational prayers," as Corvin labels them, both permit and require of the pray-er a high level of participation with God in the process of accomplishing the divine will. I shall argue that especially this characteristic of prayer recommends it as an important vehicle for addressing the concerns of the theodicy.

---

7. Note the *tiqqun* (scribal correction) in v. 15, which suggests an emendation away from the attribution of evil to God in this particular case. The present text reads: "If you will deal thus with me, then kill me at once I pray, if I find favor in your eyes, that I may not look on *my* evil *[běrā'ātî]."* The original text, however, reads: "that I may not look on *your* evil *[běrā'ātekā]."* The uncorrected version makes no attempt to disguise the problem as seen from Moses' perspective. If God is to act in such a manner, to bring evil on a faithful (and undeserving) servant, then Moses does not wish to live to witness it. For a similar description of God's conduct as "evil" in a prayer I have already examined, see 1 Kgs 17:20.

RESOLUTION OR EXPLANATION OF THE CRISIS

Each text presented here contains some resolution or explanation of the crisis or functions within the context of a larger narrative whose rhetorical structure serves this purpose. For example, two of Moses' prayers (Exodus 32, Numbers 14) specify the resolution in terms identical to the petition for divine intervention. In Exodus 32 Moses petitions God to "repent concerning the evil" (v. 12: *wĕhinnāḥēm 'al hārā'āh lĕ'ammekā*), and the response provided is "God repented of the evil" (v. 14: *wayyinnāḥem Yhwh 'al hārā'āh*). In Numbers 14 the plea is that God "pardon *[sĕlah]* the inquity of the people" (v. 19), and the response is "I have pardoned *[sālaḥtî]* according to your word" (v. 20). In Numbers 11 Moses' question "Where am I to get meat to give to all this people?" (v. 13, NRSV) receives the response "the LORD will give you meat" (v. 18, NRSV). Although this response does not address Moses' question about God's evil intents (cf. vv. 11-12), it does effectively neutralize the principal crisis as far as the complaining Israelites are concerned. Similarly, Joshua's prayer (Josh 7:7-9) questioning why God has given them over to defeat is set within a larger unit that introduces the crisis with the notice that the "anger of the LORD burned hot against Israel" (v. 1: *wayyiḥar 'ap Yhwh*) and concludes with the announcement that subsequent to Joshua's prayer the LORD turned away from this divine anger (v. 26: *wayyāšāb Yhwh mēḥărôn 'appô*).

The resolution of Abraham's concern over the impending judgment of Sodom is provided in a slightly different way. Abraham's conversation with God has been inserted into a larger narrative encompassing Genesis 18-19. Although by the end of this conversation Abraham's concern that God be attentive to the righteous in Sodom is eased, not until Gen 19:17-29 is the effectiveness of Abraham's prayer clear.

The pattern common to all these texts—crisis, prayer, resolution—may now be delineated by focusing on the details of its exposition in three specific texts: Num 11:4-34; 14:11-23; and Exod 32:7-14.

EXAMPLES OF PRAYERS FOR JUSTICE

MOSES' COMPLAINTS CONCERNING DIVINE INTENTIONS (NUM 11:4-34)

Source analyses of Num 11:4–34 show some variation, but the general consensus is that the bulk of the narrative (except 7-9, 14-

17, and 24b-30) belongs to J.[8] The basic lines of the J account then develop as follows:

> The people complain; God's anger is provoked
> (vv. 4-6, 10: *wayyiḥar 'ap Yhwh*)
>
> > Moses' dialogue with God
> > (1) vv. 11-13, 18-20
> > (2) vv. 21-24a
>
> The complaint is resolved with a miraculous provision of quail that at the same time is a manifestation of divine anger
> (vv. 31-34; cf. v. 33: *wĕ'ap Yhwh ḥārāh).*

This outline illustrates that the framework of the narrative hinges on the peoples' complaint that provokes God's anger. Between the first statement of divine wrath in verse 10 and the final manifestation of this wrath in verse 33, Moses engages God in two dialogues that raise questions concerning God's intentions, questions that provide interpretive guides for understanding the overall narrative. A closer inspection of the narrative can clarify the function of these divine-human dialogues.

The narrative moves between the three major themes: complaint, prayer, and resolution of complaint. The complaint, described in verses 4-6 and 10, provides an important and necessary preface to Moses' prayer. In specific terms, the complaint involves the people's lack of meat, a concern that is accompanied by weeping *(bkh)* and a strong craving *(hit'awwû ta'ăwāh).* Although not as explicit as the parallel account in Exodus 16,[9] this complaint is no less serious, for as verse 20 makes clear these "weepers" have rejected *(m's)* God.

Even though the text clearly describes the people's behavior as complaint, it leaves some question about whether the complaint is directed against Moses or against God. Verse 10 suggests that Moses heard the complaint and responded to it, but the text is curiously ambiguous just at this juncture:

> And Moses heard *[wayyišma']* the people weeping . . . and the anger of the LORD burned exceedingly *[wayyiḥar 'ap Yhwh],* and in the eyes of Moses it was evil *[ûbĕ'ênê mōšeh rā'].*

8. For the basic arguments supporting this ascription to J, see n. 3.

9. The P account in Exodus 16 uses the verbal expression "to murmur against" *(lwn + 'l),* which Coats suggests ought to be understood as "rebel against" in the sense of a hostile, face-to-face confrontation (*Rebellion,* 24). For additional comparisons between Numbers 11 and the other traditions represented in the wilderness wandering narratives, see S. E. Balentine, "Prayer in the Wilderness Traditions: In Pursuit of Divine Justice," *HAR* 9 (1985): 53–74.

With *waw* consecutives linking the verbs *šm'* and *ḥrh,* one might expect to read that Moses heard and Moses was angry and in Moses' eyes[10] it was evil. But rather abruptly the subject of the second verb changes to "the LORD." With this shift in the focus of the narrative the intent of the last phrase becomes uncertain. What is *rā',* "evil," in the eyes of Moses—the people's crying or God's anger? The dialogue that follows between Moses and God leaves little doubt that from Moses' perspective the only legitimate target of this complaint is God. It is God's reputation that is, or ought to be, at stake here, not Moses'. Thus Moses turns to God with an address designed not simply to direct the complaint in the proper direction but also to raise serious questions about divine intentions.

Moses' address to God in verses 11-15 is introduced simply with *wayyō'mer,* "and he said," the language Corvin designates as characteristic of "conversational prayers." Such prayers, he maintains, are typically dominated by "question-centered dialogue," often initiated by the human partner for the purpose of raising some issue of "a theologico-philosophical nature," such as innocent suffering or proof of God's presence.[11] These general observations hold true for Num 11:11-12. Moses' prayer is initiated with a bold question that immediately focuses on the issue of *rā',* "evil," which verse 10 has introduced:

> . . . and in the eyes of Moses it was evil *[ûbĕ'ênê mōšeh rā']* (v. 10)
> and Moses said: "Why have you done evil to your servant?" *[lāmāh ḥărē'* (v. 11)

Indeed, this lead question introduces a series of questions to God that substantiate the description of this engagement as truly "question-centered":

> Why *[lāmmāh]* have I not found favor in your eyes?
> Did I *[he'ānōkî],* I conceive all these people, or did I *['im 'ānōkî],* I birth them?
> Where *[mē'ayin]* will I get meat to give to all this people?

Both in the specificity of their language and in their general context, these questions serve individually and collectively to place before God a strong note of protest.

---

10. Perhaps this is the thinking behind the proposed emendation in *BHS* to *bĕ'ênāyw,* "in his eyes."

11. J. Corvin, "Stylistic and Functional Study of the Prose Prayers in the Historical Narratives of the Old Testament" (Ph.D. diss., Emory University, 1972), 166–68.

Twice Moses' questions are prefaced with the word *lām(m)āh,* "Why?" Of the stock of Hebrew interrogative words available, none features more prominently in questions directed from people to God than *lām(m)āh.*[12] This "Why?" question is especially frequent in, though not limited to, contexts of lament and complaint, where a suppliant raises hard questions about something in the relationship with God that seems very wrong.[13] Thus frequently in psalms of lament questions about God's hiddenness are framed with *lām(m)āh* (cf. Pss 10:1; 22:2; 44:24; etc.). In other cases the question may raise the issue of innocent suffering (cf. Jer 15:18; 20:18; Job 7:20) or the perversion of justice (cf. Hab 1:3, 13). Although the questions are certainly more frequent in psalms of lament and in lament contexts like those that characterize Job, Habakkuk, and Jeremiah, they are not lacking in the narrative literature, especially on the lips of Moses, who, more than any other major character, so interrogates God.[14] In Num 11:11 Moses questions God about divine conduct that must seem, at least to Moses, to be contrary to God's character. Why is there *rā',* "evil," to your servant *(lĕ'abdekā)* rather than favor *(ḥēn)?* Do not servants merit more than this? Is not *rā'* the punishment reserved for the one who refuses to serve? After all, the people, not Moses, have done the crying and the petitioning. Why is God's anger directed against Moses rather than them? The whole idea of God doing evil to one of God's own seems incongruous.

The note of protest carried in these two "Why?" questions is heightened by a third question that follows in verse 12, this one expressed with the form *ha . . . 'im:* "Did I *[he'ānōkî],* I conceive all this people, or did I *['im 'ānōkî],* I birth them, that you should say to me, 'Carry them in your bosom'?" The form of the question, used in wisdom circles for pedagogical purposes and by prophets as a rhetorical means of disputing commonly held assumptions,[15] is used

---

12. Cf. S. E. Balentine, *The Hidden God: The Hiding of the Face of God in the Old Testament* (Oxford: Oxford Univ. Press, 1983), 118–19.

13. Cf. J. Barr, "'Why?' In Biblical Hebrew," *JTS* 36 (1985): 8. See further A. von Jepsen, "Warum? Eine lexikalische und theologische Studie," *Das Ferne und Nahe Wort: Festschrift Leonhard Rost,* ed. F. Maass (BZAW 105; Berlin: Töpelmann, 1967), 106–13.

14. Balentine, *Hidden God,* 118–19; Barr, "Why?" 18.

15. On its use in wisdom circles, see H. W. Wolff, *Amos the Prophet: The Man and His Background* (Philadelphia: Fortress, 1973), 6, 16. For its use in the prophets, see W. Brueggemann, "Jeremiah's Use of Rhetorical Questions," *JBL* 92 (1973): 358–74. Cf. A. Van Selms, "Motivated Interrogative Sentences in Biblical Hebrew," *Semitics* 2 (1971–72): 143–49; M. Held, "Rhetorical Questions in

here with the expectation of a negative response. The accusation in Moses' question has a double edge. First, Moses charges that the responsibility for these people properly belongs to God; Moses did not birth them, God did. Secondly, to the extent that Moses does bear some responsibility as God's specially appointed liaison with the people, his abilities are limited. He is no match as one man for "all this people." The latter phrase repeats several times throughout the narrative as Moses presses his complaint that "I am not able, I alone, to carry all this people for they are too heavy for me" (v. 14; cf. vv. 11, 12, 13).

It is not just the form of these questions, however, that conveys the note of protest in Moses' prayer. The questions themselves strike at the very heart of common assumptions about God's character. Two key ideas combine in verses 10 and 11 to focus the major concerns: the burning anger of God *(ḥrh + 'p)* and God doing evil *(r'', hiphil)*. Both these ideas, divine anger and divinely initiated evil, occur most frequently in Deuteronomistic literature and in the judgment speeches of the prophets, especially in Jeremiah. In both settings God's behavior is typically described as a justified reaction to a sinful people.[16]

One may draw similar conclusions with respect to *r''* and the noun derivatives *ra'* and *rā'āh.* God is the subject of *rā'āh (hiphil)* twelve times, about half of which connect God's intention to do evil specifically with the evil designs of the people.[17] The nouns *r'* and *r'h* combine with a number of verbs, again primarily in Deuteronomistic and prophetic texts, to describe God's "bringing evil" *(bw', hiphil,* some 31 times; 17 times in Jeremiah); "planning evil" *(ḥsb,* 5 times; *zmm,* once), "pronouncing evil upon" *(dbr,* 13 times); "doing evil" *('śh,* 4 times), "repaying [returning] evil" *(šlm,* 3 times; *šwb, hiphil,* twice), and so on. Here too God's actions are most frequently

Ugaritic and Biblical Hebrew," *ErIsr* 9 (1969): 71–79.

16. C. Westermann has evaluated the prophets as "messengers of anger" *(Boten des Zorns),* concluding that in Jeremiah, for example, where 56 words for divine anger occur in some 30 places (none more frequently than *'ap,* with 24 occurrences), in all cases where the anger of God is directed against Israel it is the consequence of the guilt of Israel ("Boten des Zorns: Der Begriff des Zornes Gottes in der Prophetie," *Die Botschaft und der Boten, Festschrift für Hans Walter Wolff,* ed. J. Jeremias and L. Perlitt [Neukirchen: Neukirchener Verlag, 1981]: 151–54).

17. Exod 5:22; Num 11:11; Josh 24:20; 1 Kgs 17:20; Jer 25:6, 29; 31:28; Mic 4:6; Zeph 1:12; Zech 8:14; Ps 44:3; Ruth 1:21. See further H. J. Stoebe, *"r'," THAT* 2.794–803.

set in the context of just and expected punishment for evil behavior.[18]

With respect to these ideas something like a party-line view developed, at least as early as the Deuteronomistic editors, if not considerably before them. That is, the outbreaking of divine anger and divinely ordained evil is primarily retributive in nature, the just reaction of a just God to specific manifestations of human sinfulness. In the course of Israel's history various challenges to the party line would arise, various "rumblings" of discontent as Crenshaw has suggested,[19] designed to test theological maxims against the realities of life. These challenges have traditionally been understood to have emerged principally in the exilic era, when the demise of stabilizing institutions is thought to have encouraged rampant skepticism among the general populace.[20] The text of Num 11:4-34, if one can date it in the tenth-ninth century, may suggest an important supplement to these traditional views concerning the questioning of divine justice.[21]

Of the twelve cases where God is the subject of *r" (hiphil)*, three put the issue in question form, all in direct address to God that may

18. Cf. E. Noort, "JHWH und das Böse: Bemerkungen zu einer Verhältnisbestimmung," *OTS* 23 (1984): 120–36.

19. J. L. Crenshaw, "Popular Questioning of the Justice of God in Ancient Israel," *ZAW* 82 (1970): 380–95.

20. J. Pedersen, "Scepticisme israélite," *RHPR* 10 (1930): 317–70; R. H. Pfeiffer, "The Peculiar Skepticism of Ecclesiastes," *JBL* 53 (1954): 100–109; E. Bishop, "A Pessimist in Palestine," *PEQ* 100 (1968): 3–41; J. Priest, "Humanism, Skepticism, and Pessimism in Israel," *JAAR* 36 (1968): 311–26. Hard questions about divine justice are especially frequent in Deuteronomistic texts, but it is typical of their perspective that these texts also seek to provide answers that reaffirm traditional views. With respect to the issue under consideration here, divinely initiated evil, Jer 16:10-13. may be taken as one example of the typical Deuteronomistic perspective:

> Question: And when you tell these people all these words and they say to you "Why has the Lord pronounced all this great evil against us?"
> Answer: Then you shall say: "Because your ancestors have forsaken me . . . and you, you have done more evil than your ancestors."

On the use of this particular form of the question-answer schema, see B. O. Long, "Two Question and Answer Schemata in the Prophets," *JBL* 90 (1971): 134–35.

21. Cf. my criticism and critique of the traditional view in *Hidden God,* 169–76. See further J. L. Crenshaw's discussion of the issue in which he asserts that skepticism belongs to Israel's thought from early times ("The Birth of Skepticism in Ancient Israel," *The Divine Helmsman: Studies on God's Control of Human Events, Presented to Lou H. Silberman,* ed. J. L. Crenshaw and S. Sandmel [New York: KTAV, 1980], 5–7).

be understood as prayer (Exod 5:22; Num 11:11; 1 Kgs 17:20). Two of these are especially important for the present discussion.[22] Both Exod 5:22 and Num 11:11 consist of prayers placed on the lips of Moses; both are texts usually attributed to J. The former is set in the context of Moses' initial failure with Pharaoh after which he raises with God the double question, "Why *[lāmmāh]* have you done evil to this people *[hărē'ōtāh lā'ām hazzeh]?* Why *[lāmmāh]* did you send me?" The rhetoric of the address makes clear the nature of the complaint. Moses charges that the evil he perceives in God is no different from the evil that the people now experience at the hands of Pharaoh: "For since I came to Pharaoh to speak in your name he has done evil to this people *[hēra' lā'ām hazzeh]"* (v. 23). Although its historical setting is different, this challenge to God is fundamentally similar to Moses' protest in Numbers 11. Here, in another text usually assigned to J, is a line of questioning similar to that in Numbers 11. If one can retain the traditional dating of this source, then Exod 5:22 is an early questioning of the party-line view that not only anticipates the Deuteronomistic ruminations but is perhaps even paradigmatic for them.[23]

God responds to Moses' complaint in Num 11:18-20. Moses is instructed to inform the people of the requirement for consecration in preparation for receipt of the meat they had been craving. Their complaint will be resolved. Moses' question—"Where am I to get the meat?"—will be answered. Now they will eat, because God will provide. Indeed, they will eat not one day or five days or even twenty, but a whole month of days until their gift becomes a burden, a punishment rather than a blessing. God supplies the reasons for the judgment: (1) because they have rejected *(m's)* God; (2) they have wept *(bkh)* before God; and (3) they have complained, saying, "Why *[lāmmāh]* did we come out of Egypt?" This quotation of the Israelites' complaint shows a subtle shift in rhetoric that reveals, along with the other reasons already given, God's interpretation of the people's behavior. As reported in verses 4-6 and again in verse

---

22. On the third text, 1 Kgs 17:20, see pp. 51–53.

23. Others have seen in the wilderness narratives an early form of the quest for divine justice so prominent later in Deuteronomistic texts (e.g., R. P. Carroll, "Rebellion and Dissent in Ancient Israelite Society," *ZAW* 89 [1979]: 176–204; R. Adamiak, *Justice and History in the Old Testament: The Evolution of Divine Retribution in the Historiographies of the Wilderness Generation* [Cleveland: John T. Zubal, 1982], e.g., 84–89), but without recognizing the importance of prayer as a literary vehicle for introducing the concern.

18, the substance of their complaint revolves around dietary concerns (*bāśār,* "meat," vv. 4, 18). In God's review of the complaint, however, the people are quoted as questioning not only their diet but also their entire exodus deliverance.

Taken as a whole, God's response in verses 18-20 explains the divine reaction as a justified punishment for the Israelites' rejection of God's leadership and their doubt about God's ability to provide for them. The response does not address Moses' question about God's evil intents. Nevertheless, the questions have been raised and rather fully articulated. From a literary perspective they provide a distraction to the blazing anger of God introduced in verse 10, shifting the focus of the reader, if only temporarily, away from the divine concern for punishment to a very human concern for clarity and understanding.

The second dialogue between Moses and God (vv. 21-24) takes up where the first one leaves off, with Moses pressing for further clarification about his responsibility in providing the meat God has promised. One of Moses' concerns, repeated several times in his first discourse with God, has to do with his individual responsibility for "all this people" (*kol hā'ām hazzeh;* vv. 11, 12, 13, 14). In this second address Moses raises the same issue by contrasting in stark terms the impossible statistics involved in the fulfilling of God's promise. A rather literal translation can best illustrate the emphasis the Hebrew syntax gives to the numbers Moses faces: "Six hundred thousand on foot, the people, among whom I am in their midst" (v. 21). Here too Moses sounds a note of protest. Is Moses alone to provide for all the people? Is Moses "in their midst" now to replace the LORD "in their midst" (cf. v. 20), and so to fulfill as proxy a rejected God's promise of sustenance?

God's response (v. 23) is couched in terms almost identical to the language in Exod 6:1, which, as already noted, records a similar prayer of protest from Moses: "Is the hand of the LORD shortened . . .? Now you will see. . . ." Once again the divine response makes little attempt to address Moses' questions directly. Rather, God's rhetorical counter-question calls attention to divine power and, by so doing, prepares Moses for the final manifestation of this power in the miraculous provision of quail (vv. 31-34).

To summarize, in Numbers 11 Moses addresses God directly in two places with "conversational prayer." By means of these prayers Moses engages God in close discussion of issues relating to the overall context, issues that, from Moses' perspective at least, need clarification. Moses questions God, God responds, and the narrative moves on to its conclusion, which is presented as having emerged out of their joint deliberations. The text thus assigns to Moses the work of both intercessor and interrogator in prayer. Both these responsibilities demand of the pray-er a high level of participation with God in the accomplishment of the divine will.

Moses' Intervention on Behalf of the People (Num 14:11-25)

The literary context of Moses' prayer in Numbers 14 is complicated. Without discussing in detail specific verses or portions of verses, I simply note that the basic framework of the narrative describes the congregation's rebellion against Moses and Aaron and God (vv. 1-10) and the pronouncement and execution of divine judgment (vv. 26-38). This material is usually assigned to P. Although most understand the intervening verses (11-25) to be supplemental material, opinion is divided as to whether they should be assigned to the Deuteronomistic editors or to J.[24] For my purpose it is not necessary to decide the question of authorship. It is sufficient to note (1) that Moses' prayer appears to derive from a different hand than the surrounding framework, hence to serve as a supplementation that alters the final perspective of the whole; and (2) that this prayer is shaped rhetorically by the same motifs already noted, namely, God's complaint, prayer, divine response. In this respect the development within verses 11-25 is as follows:

vv. 11-12: God's complaint and statement of intent to punish
            vv. 13-19: Moses' intervention with prayer for
                        forgiveness *(slḥ)*
vv. 20-25: God forgives *(slḥ)* according to Moses' request *and* punishes

Following the discussion of the internal dynamics of the prayer as outlined, I will return to the question of its function within the larger narrative framework.

I begin by observing that in verses 11-25 the divine complaint and response are rhetorically linked by the accusation and punishment of all those who have not believed in "the signs that I did" (*hā'ōtôt 'ăšer 'āśîtî;* vv. 11, 22). Taken together, the complaint and response describe God's punishment as typically quid pro quo: a guilty people receive a just punishment. The structure of this part of the narrative, however, does not permit a direct linkage between complaint and response, for wedged between the two is a lengthy

24. See n. 3.

dialogue between Moses and God. Couched in the form of a prayer for forgiveness, this dialogue creates a literary break between the introduction and the conclusion and thus an interruption in the cause-consequence sequence. One is to understand the consequence as emerging out of and in response to the intervention of Moses. Simply put, Moses' prayer influences the outcome of the story. Moses' prayer is addressed directly to God and is introduced with conversational language *(wayy'ōmer)*. Moses seeks from God a reconsideration of the divine plan to punish. To support his petition Moses offers three arguments. Each of Moses' arguments fits well against the backdrop of exilic concerns, and hence may serve as support for the view that the Deuteronomistic editors are responsible for this material.

First, Moses argues that God's reputation as a powerful, delivering God is at stake. The Egyptians will hear of the punishment of this people and will draw the wrong conclusions. They will spread the rumor that this God, who formerly led the Israelites out of Egypt by divine power (v. 13) and who led them by pillar of cloud and fire through the Reed Sea (v. 14; cf. Exod 13:21), is *now unable* to bring the people into the land that God has sworn to them (v. 16). The status of God's reputation among the nations is a concern expressed frequently in Deuteronomic and Deuteronomistic texts (e.g., Deut 9:28; Exod 32:12; cf. Ezek 20:14). It was during the exilic era that God's reputation was most in question, at least from the perspective of those who had to endure the exile. Ruled over by Babylonian powers whose very presence cast a pall over God's ability to protect and defend God's own, and faced with a distant, silent, seemingly defeated God, an exilic audience would be eager to know if God could be persuaded to intervene to protect God's standing among the nations *and* among God's own.

Moses' second argument questions the justice of God's apparent intent to "kill this people like one person" (v. 15). The question echoes the concern for justice with respect to the individual that is addressed in other texts of the exilic period. It is the question of Abraham in Gen 18:22-33 as he presses God to discriminate between the righteous and the wicked in the judgment of Sodom. Abraham clearly states the issue: "Shall not the Judge *[šōpēt]* of all the earth do justice *[mišpāt]?*" (Gen 18:25). Ezekiel reports that the same concern is circulating among the exiles: "The fathers have eaten sour grapes, and the children's teeth are set on edge" (Ezek 18:2). Both Abraham and Ezekiel argue for a divine justice that distinguishes between the righteous and the wicked at every level, whether between individuals and communities or children and parents.[25] Reeling under the judgment of Babylonian oppression, an exilic audience would be relieved to hear that in the execution of divine judgment God is ever mindful to discriminate between the innocent and the guilty. As long as this is so, the hope for ultimate justice does not die, not even in exile.

Finally, Moses contends that God's own nature requires that God be guided as much by grace as by the need for justice. The text has Moses quoting God to God, reminding God of the promise to be "slow to anger, abounding in loyalty *[ḥesed]*,[26] and a forgiver of iniquity." This formula appears in various contexts throughout the Hebrew Bible and with different functions. It is not an idea that is restricted to the exilic period, but for an exilic audience the description of a God who is characterized by loyal love as well as just punishment would be particularly welcome.[27]

In the progression of Moses' prayer these three arguments provide the introduction to and support for the petition for forgiveness. The petition is carried by the verb *slḥ*, "forgive," which is used in two primary contexts in the Hebrew Bible, always with God as the stated or implied subject of the action. First, it is frequent in Priestly texts where the priest offers a sin offering that will atone *(kpr)* for sins and result in the forgiveness of the guilty (e.g., Lev 4:20, 26, 31, 35). Second, *slḥ* occurs with notable regularity as a petition for forgiveness in prayer in a wide assortment of texts and contexts: in poetry (e.g., Pss 25:11; 86:5; 103:3; 130:4) and in narrative, as here in Numbers 14; in conversational prayers (e.g., Exod 34:9; Num 14:19) and in formal prayers (e.g., 1 Kgs 8:30, 35, 36; Neh 9:17; Dan 9:19). In some instances the petition is specifically linked to further actions on God's part (e.g., Exod 34:9: "forgive our sin and take us for your inheritance"; 1 Kgs 8:34: "forgive . . . and bring them again to the land"). In other cases the petition for forgiveness stands alone, though further divine involvement is implied (e.g., Num 14:19: "forgive . . . [and do not punish]").

In some prayers forgiveness is requested on the strength of con-

25. Cf. Schmidt, *"De Deo,"* 131ff.; Blenkinsopp, "Abraham and the Righteous of Sodom," 122–23.
26. Cf. K. Sakenfeld, "The Problem of Divine Forgiveness in Numbers 14," *CBQ* 37 (1975): 323–28; idem, *Faithfulness in Action: Loyalty in Biblical Perspective* (OBT; Philadelphia: Fortress, 1985), 73–76.
27. For form-critical and tradition-historical analysis of the formula, see J. Scharbert, "Formgeschichte und Exegese von Ex 34, 6f und seiner Parallelism," *Biblica* 38 (1957): 130–50; R. C. Dentan, "The Literary Affinities of Exodus XXXIV 6f," *VT* 13 (1963): 34–51; Sakenfeld, *Faithfulness in Action,* 47–52.

fession of sin (e.g., 1 Kgs 8:50; Dan 9:19), while in other prayers the petition is supported in other ways. In Numbers 14 Moses' petition of God's forgiveness is not based on repentance but rather on the fact that God is a loving God who ought to forgive if God is to act in a way consistent with divine character. Thus Moses' petition states the matter clearly, gathering together in summary fashion the crux of his request: "Forgive . . . according to the greatness of your steadfast love, just as you have pardoned this people from Egypt even until now" (v. 19, NRSV). It is a prayer for undeserved, yet expected, forgiveness.

God's initial response is immediate, brief, and positive: "I have forgiven *[sālaḥtî]"* (v. 20). The accompanying expression, "just as you have asked" *(kidbārekā),* links the response directly to Moses' petition. It is not, however, a blanket forgiveness, as verses 20-23 go on to make clear. The pardon will involve judgment, albeit in a modified form. God's intention as expressed in verses 11-12 had been to disinherit this people as a whole and start all over with Moses. Now, in the aftermath of Moses' prayer, God relents. The judgment is restricted to those who had seen the miraculous acts of deliverance and sustenance in Egypt and in the wilderness and yet had not heeded them. God would not punish this people indiscriminately, "like one person." Moses' prayer would achieve its goal.

Thus within its immediate literary setting in verses 11-25, this account suggests a narrative that moves from an announcement of divine judgment to an execution of divine judgment, with a significant prayer for forgiveness sandwiched between them. It is primarily this prayer that informs the image of a God who not only tolerates but invites participation in the accomplishing of divine will. It is an optimistic image both of humanity's potential to influence divine intentions and of God's openness to dialogue, counsel, and persuasion. If in fact directed to an audience in exile, this image promotes prayer as a legitimate and effective response to the concerns that erupt in Babylon about the availability of divine forgiveness, the justice of divine judgments, and the reliability of divine character.

To complete the investigation I now return briefly to examine the contribution of this particular unit to the larger narrative in Numbers 14. The Priestly framework of the narrative provides the themes of sin and punishment. If the basic source analysis previously outlined is reliable, however, it is striking that this Priestly frame is interrupted precisely at the point where the glory of the

LORD appears at the tent of meeting (v. 11). The divine revelation that one expects to follow in this situation is delayed until verses 26–38. This literary delay allows for the unfolding of a rather lengthy address from Moses to God in which fundamental questions concerning God's intentions are raised and ultimately resolved with an assurance of divine forgiveness. When the narrative returns to report the expected word of judgment from God, the reader has been prepared to receive it as a judgment tempered with divine love and limited by divine commitment to justice and fair play. The literary sequencing of the events may be illustrated as follows.

vv. 1-10:   The congregation's rebellion against the leadership of Moses and Aaron. They move to stone them, . . . and the glory of the LORD appears at the tent of meeting.

vv. 11-25:   Moses' intervention with prayer for forgiveness *(slḥ)*. God forgives *(slḥ)* according to Moses' request, *and* punishes.

vv. 26-38:   "And the LORD said to Moses and Aaron. . . ." Divine judgment pronounced.

The composite narrative of Numbers 14 is in agreement that disloyal behavior in the wilderness period resulted in God's punishment. But in its final form this judgment is attributed to a God who both judges and forgives, a God who can be addressed and moved to show mercy to a guilty people. In its final form, the narrative assigns to Moses' prayer a position of major importance. Positioned between the announcement of punishment and the execution of the punishment, the prayer occurs precisely at the point of literary climax and from this point shapes the final outcome of the story.

MOSES' PETITIONS AND ISRAEL'S SIN (EXOD 32:7-14)

The prayer of Moses in Exodus 32 functions within a myriad of ever-expanding contexts. Despite the obvious literary non sequiturs, the account reflects a thematic unity revolving around Israel's sin in the making of the golden calf (Exod 32:1-6) and God's response (Exodus 34). Taken as a unit then, Exodus 32–34 begins with a notice of Israel's sin, which puts the divine-human covenant in jeopardy, and ends with the reissuing of the commandments and the renewal of the covenant relationship. How this transition from disobedience to renewal takes place is the focus of the intervening texts.

To be more specific, God's instructions in verses 7-10 provide the immediate context for Moses' prayer. These instructions are introduced with the divine imperative "Go down" *(lek rēd)*. Given the present shaping of the Exodus narrative, this command signals an abrupt ending to a lengthy divine address concerning the construction of the tabernacle that began with Exod 25:1 and has continued uninterrupted to this point. Now God orders Moses to return to the people below, whose behavior in fashioning an unholy golden calf has made instructions for a holy tabernacle both impossible and unnecessary.

Their disobedience is clear; so too is God's intent to punish: "Now leave me alone so that my anger may burn against them *[wĕyiḥar 'appî bāhem]* and I may consume them *[wa'ăkallēm]* (v. 10). The general sense of God's intention to punish is clear. The use of the particular phrase "let me alone" (lit. "give me rest"), however, provides an intriguing introduction. So far as I can determine, this is the only instance of its use with God as subject of the action.[28] Because of its limited use it is probably impossible to retrieve completely what is intended here; nevertheless, the implication is that God needs Moses' permission, at least his silent consent, to carry through with these divine plans to destroy. In this sense the phrase is similar to the negative command that often calls forth the very action that ostensibly it seeks to prohibit. That is, God demands to be left alone, and that prompts Moses to do exactly the opposite— *not* to leave God alone. It is a form of invitation by prohibition, and in this instance, given what follows in Moses' address to God in verses 11-14, it is perhaps legitimate to understand it as an invitation to prayer. Such at any rate is the view offered in the paraphrase of Targum Onkelos: "Refrain from thy prayer."[29]

From this perspective the narrative alerts the reader to the drama of the moment. If Moses heeds these instructions by leaving God alone or by refraining from prayer, divine destruction will presumably be executed without interruption. If Moses does not follow orders, but instead engages God by responding to these announced intentions, *perhaps* the crisis can be averted.

Verses 11-14 clearly imply that from Moses' perspective God's announced intentions are both incomprehensible and unaccept-

28. The only other instance where this exact form occurs is in Judg 16:26, where Samson instructs the lad who has led him into Dagon's temple to leave him alone so that he might feel the pillars of the house.
29. Quoted from Childs, *Exodus,* 556.

able, and Moses does not let them go unchallenged. Rather, using words freighted with both accusation and petition, Moses seeks to turn God away from these divine plans. Following an invocation, Moses introduces his complaint with a repetition of the question "Why?" *(lām(m)āh),* the same protest-laden interrogative already encountered in Moses' prayer at Num 11:11-12.

> Why does your wrath burn hot against your people? (Exod 32:11)
> Why should the Egyptians say, "With evil intent God led them out . . .
> to kill them . . . and to consume them?" (v. 12)

The implicit protest of Moses' questions is strengthened dramatically by the explicit, thrice-repeated description of God's intentions as "evil" *(r'h).* In the first instance Moses attributes the charge to the Egyptians: "Why should the Egyptians say, 'With evil intent *[běrā'āh]* God led them out . . . to kill them . . . and to consume them?'" (v. 12). But then Moses takes up the charge himself, for it is not only the foreigners who, witnessing this display of divine anger, will conclude that God is acting for evil rather than good. "Turn from your fierce anger," Moses petitions, "and repent concerning the evil toward your people" (v. 12: *wěhinnāḥēm 'al hārā'āh).* Finally, in response to Moses' petition, the narrative supplies a third person perception confirming the charges of both the Egyptians and Moses: "And the LORD repented of the evil *[wayyinnāḥem Yhwh 'al hārā'āh]* that the LORD thought to do to the people" (v. 14).

Given this perception of divinely initiated evil, Moses' questions function not only as statements of protest but also as arguments intended to persuade a God for whom evil is not or should not be characteristic to relent and to change. As the narrative itself introduces the prayer, its intended purpose is to "soften the face of the LORD" (v. 11: *wayěḥal mōšeh 'et pěnê Yhwh).*[30]

Moses' questions flow directly into petition. The petition consists of three appeals, each directed to God in the same imperatival tone that had characterized God's instructions to Moses (cf. v. 7). The one formerly commanded by God now responds with commands of his own that the Almighty (1) turn away from *(šwb)* the burning wrath (v. 12a); (2) repent *(hinnāḥēm),* that is, reverse the decision

---

30. Cf. J. Reindl (*Das Angesicht Gottes im Sprachgebrauch des Alten Testaments* [Leipzig: St. Benno, 1970], 175–85), who presents this as a typical Deuteronomistic phrase used in contexts where a set pattern is at work: (1) God's anger is kindled and punishment is threatened; (2) an intercessor "softens" God's face; and (3) punishment is withdrawn.

concerning the evil to be directed toward the people (v. 12b); and (3) remember *(zĕkōr)* Abraham and the patriarchal ancestors and the divine promise to give them and their children an inheritance in the land of Canaan (v. 13).

Together Moses' questions and petitions mount three reasons why God should reconsider the announced plan of judgment. First, Moses contends that despite their disobedience, these people are *God's* people whom God has brought out of Egypt (v. 11). Second, Moses argues that should God follow through with the announced plans for judgment, some, notably the Egyptians, will misinterpret divine punishment as a divine failure to complete the goal of the Exodus from Egypt (v. 12). Third, Moses appeals to God's own character by reminding God that God has already taken an oath (v. 13: *nišba'tā lāhem bāk,* "you have sworn to them by your own self"), the violation of which would jeopardize trust in the divine character.[31]

Finally, the success of Moses' prayer is indicated in several ways. First, within the self-contained narrative of verses 7-14, Moses' prayer has clearly secured its desired end. Simply put, Moses petitions God to repent of the evil *(hinnāḥēm 'al hārā'āh)* that was directed toward the people (v. 12), and according to the narrative's conclusion God does just that (v. 14: *wayyinnāḥem . . . 'al hārā'āh).* Within the larger context of Exodus 32–34 this divine repentance takes on additional meaning, especially in the light of the subsequent restoration of the covenant relationship in Exodus 34.[32]

We may note a more subtle indication of Moses' success. In God's initial address to Moses (vv. 7-10), the narrator has God refer repeatedly to the people with terms that shift responsibility to Moses. The instructions to Moses are "Go down, for *your* people *['ammĕkā]* whom *you* brought out *[he'ĕlêtā]* from the land of Egypt have corrupted themselves" (v. 7). Subsequently, God responds, "I

---

31. A number of Deuteronomistic or Deuteronomistically influenced texts share one or more of these arguments. The same reasons given by Moses in Exodus 32 are also cited in Deut 9:25-29, though in different order. Similar arguments concerning God's reputation among the nations are used in Josh 7:9 and, as already seen, in Num 14:13-19, the latter text offering additional arguments based on common notions about divine justice and divine character. One may detect here a stock of legitimate reasons that pray-ers could use to seek to persuade God to modify or depart from plans for divine judgment.

32. On the semantic range of repentance *(nḥm)* and its theological function as a "controlling metaphor" for understanding divine activity in the Hebrew Bible see T. Fretheim, "The Repentance of God: A Key to Evaluating Old Testament God-Talk," *HBT* 10 (1988): 47–70.

have seen *this people [hā'ām hazzeh]*, and behold, *it* is a stiff-necked people *[wĕhinnēh 'am qĕšēh 'ōrep hû']*" (v. 9). It is a speech rather cleverly crafted to allow God to disavow any ownership of "this people." Yet it is precisely at this point that Moses takes issue with God:

> Why does *your* anger *['appĕkā]* burn hot against *your* people *[bĕ'ammekā]* whom *you* brought out [hôṣē'ta] from the land of Egypt? (v. 11)
>
> . . . repent of the evil toward *your* people *[lĕ'ammekā]*. (v. 12)
>
> Remember Abraham, Isaac, and Israel *your* servants *['ăbādêkā]* to whom *you* swore by *your own self [nišba'tā lāhem bāk]*. (v. 13)

At least one apparent purpose of Moses' prayer is to remind God that these people are indeed God's responsibility, not Moses'. If the brief notice given in verse 14 is a clue, Moses does persuade God to reclaim these wayward people: "And the LORD repented of the evil that the LORD thought to do to *his* people *[lĕ'ammô]*."

PRAYER AS A VEHICLE OF THEODICY

I now turn to probe how such prayers for divine justice relate to the larger and important issue of theodicy. Here my comments are only introductory in character; the full discussion must incorporate the contributions of the prayers in the lament tradition, which are the focus in the following chapter. Nevertheless these prose prayers constitute a major resource in the Hebrew Bible's inventory of responses to the concerns of theodicy, and one will profit from considering their contributions in their own right. To begin I focus on prayer's function as a means of maintaining a dialogical relationship between God and humanity. In this respect the sociological observations of P. Berger provide a helpful supplement to the preceding exegetical focus.

"All socially constructed worlds are inherently precarious," P. Berger observes.[33] They are precarious because the socially managed consensus concerning right and wrong, good and evil, actions and abilities that are acceptable and those that exceed tolerable limits, is constantly threatened by chaos. Suffering, evil, and especially death—all conditions endemic to the human situation—

---

33. P. Berger, *The Sacred Canopy: Elements of a Sociological Theory of Religion* (Garden City, N.Y.: Doubleday, 1969), 29.

represent the most serious forms of this chaos. If not adequately explained, any one of these will weaken and ultimately destroy the sense of order necessary for the maintenance of society. In sociological terms these threats to the consensus may be understood as "anomic phenomena" that one must not only live through but also explain in terms of the nomos established by society.[34] Efforts at explanation, or to use Berger's term, legitimation, occur on a variety of levels, but the most widespread and the most effective have historically been the efforts mounted by religion.[35] Religion typically seeks to legitimate or to explain the precarious nature of life in this world by locating anomy, disorder, and chaos within a sacred and cosmic frame of reference.[36] Scholars have traditionally defined these attempts at religious legitimation as theodicy. Efforts at theodicy surface repeatedly in the Hebrew Bible in a variety of genres and theological traditions. In chapter 7 I survey the major views and examine the various perspectives they offer concerning Israel's struggle to maintain faith in situations of pain and suffering. Here I restrict my comments to the particular contribution of prose prayers for divine justice.

To enter the discussion of theodicy in the Hebrew Bible I join with several others who have noticed that one fundamental characteristic is common to most all perspectives. Berger calls it the "surrender of self"; Crenshaw describes it as "self-abnegation."[37] Both descriptions focus on the same fact, namely, that most theodicies intend to explain disorder while defending God's integrity and innocence at the expense of human integrity and innocence. As Crenshaw summarizes it, theodicy is an attempt primarily to pronounce God "Not Guilty."[38] Berger maintains that all such efforts are rooted in a masochistic attitude that finds meaning in suffering through self-abasement, self-surrender, and ultimately self-absorption into a higher order or a transcendent power.[39] Those with a religious orientation sanction masochism as submission to a sovereign God whose ways are beyond human comprehension, whose justice one can ultimately neither question nor challenge. Such a

34. Ibid., 53.
35. Ibid., 32.
36. Ibid., 33.
37. Ibid., 54. J. Crenshaw, "Introduction: The Shift from Theodicy to Anthropodicy," *Theodicy in the Old Testament,* ed. J. Crenshaw (IRT; Philadelphia: Fortress, 1983), 6.
38. Crenshaw, "Introduction," 1.
39. Berger, *Sacred Canopy,* 54–58.

perspective encourages an understanding of God as one who is "above the fray,"[40] not completely indifferent to the pain of those "in the fray," but ultimately inaccessible to them as a source of real comfort. From this perspective suffering forces questions not about God's justice but about humanity's sinfulness. As both Berger and Crenshaw have noted, the issue is no longer theodicy but anthropodicy.[41]

Theodicies in the Hebrew Bible clearly embrace the notion of human sinfulness as explanation of and legitimation for pain and suffering. It is the controlling idea, for example, in the Deuteronomistic tradition.[42] It also undergirds the arguments of Job's friends (see chap. 7). Further, prose prayers of penitence espouse the same response by promoting confession, rather than protest, as the only legitimate posture before a just and merciful God (see chap. 5). Yet this view, though prominent in the Hebrew Bible, does not meet with uniform acceptance, as the prayers presented here make clear.

Some of these prayers do function as little more than opportunities for affirming the traditional view linking suffering and sin. For example, when Joshua questions why God should give the Israelites into the hands of the Canaanites, the narrator has God respond with the standard explanation: "Israel has sinned; they have transgressed my covenant" (Josh 7:11, NRSV). The remainder of God's response specifies instructions for removing the sin and the sinner from Israel's midst, and it is ultimately in response to the fulfillment of these instructions that God then turns away from divine anger (v. 26). Thus even though the prayer itself raises questions about God's behavior, it functions as little more than an introduction to an extended speech in support of divine justice.[43]

In other cases, however, these prayers do raise questions that challenge the traditional view—and even change it. The people falling down in worship before a golden calf clearly deserve judgment. The covenant calls for it; God would be entirely justified in executing it. But somehow God decides to depart from the plan. The narrative suggests that the "somehow" is linked to Moses'

40. The phrase is Brueggemann's to describe the part of the Hebrew Bible's witness that emphasizes the orderliness of life secured by a sovereign God who is beyond the reach of historical circumstance. Such a witness promotes an interest in "structure legitimation," and in this respect represents a theological motif basic to the "common theology" of the ancient Near East ("A Shape for Old Testament Theology, I: Structure Legitimation," *CBQ* 47 [1985]: 30).

41. Berger, *Sacred Canopy,* 74; Crenshaw, "Introduction," 5–12.

42. See, e.g., Crenshaw, "Introduction," 7.

43. This is not unlike the typical question-answer schema prominent in the Deuteronomistic tradition. See n. 20.

intercession. The sin of Sodom is great; the system of retribution sanctioned by God clearly warrants punishment in this instance. Yet Abraham raises questions that turn God's focus steadily from the wicked to the righteous, and to new notions of what it should mean for the Judge of all the earth to do justice. Although Sodom is still judged, Abraham has had his say.

It is just here, in people having their say before God, that these prayers for divine justice contribute an important dissenting voice to orthodox dogma concerning the acceptable boundaries of divine-human engagement. It is hard to imagine a higher role for humanity than that which is portrayed by Moses, Abraham, and Joshua. Where else in the Hebrew Bible does one find such bold presentations of individuals standing head-to-head with God, challenging, interrogating, petitioning, and being taken seriously? They not only assault God; at times they even prevail.

Prayers of this sort do not require that one emphasize any less the legitimate linkage between suffering and sin. But they do suggest that one of the operating perspectives concerning the struggle to retain faith in the midst of inexplicable misfortune is to promote the understanding that the maintenance of justice is the product of joint divine-human deliberations. Such a perspective does not result in self-surrender or self-abnegation. Rather, in a tradition where prayer is advocated as both effective and meaningful, humanity's status is lifted to a new level: to pray is to become a partner with God. To return once again to the language of Heschel, to pray is to participate with God in a "relationship of reciprocity."[44]

One may focus the theological importance of prayer as a vehicle of theodicy with a question: What would be the loss if prayer were not possible or effective and if the concerns of theodicy could not be addressed in prayer?[45] Berger argues on sociological grounds that individuals and their worlds must have a healthy dialectical relationship in which individuals participate as coproducers with the forces and powers that shape them. Without this dialectical relationship, actors become only the acted upon, the producer is apprehended only as the product.[46] The result is what Berger calls

---

44. See Heschel, *The Prophets.* (2 vols. New York: Harper and Row, 1962), 2.9. See above, pp. 37–38.

45. Brueggemann asks the same question with respect to the broader issue of lament in "The Costly Loss of Lament," *JSOT* 36 (1986): 59–60. I adapt it here in a slightly more specific context, although as I will attempt to make clear in chap. 7, I agree with Brueggemann's emphasis on the relevance of the question for the whole lament tradition.

46. Berger, *Sacred Canopy,* 6.

alienation—one loses all sense of mutuality and reciprocity with the shaping powers of the world.[47] All activity is replaced by notions of destiny and fate. The loss of this dialectical relationship entails an "imposition of a fictitious inexorability upon the humanly constructed world."[48]

Berger observes that religion may indeed be an agent of alienation or de-alienation.[49] On the one hand it may further the rupture of the dialectic by stressing the mysteries of the sacred order of the cosmos that guard against the penetration of any and all human wisdom. Men and women simply live in a world they do not control, a world created and governed by a God they can never fully know or even partially influence. They are fated to receive whatever comes their way. For example, such is the religious perspective of Zophar, who counsels Job to remember that he has challenged the conduct of a God whose wisdom he is in no position to evaluate: "Can you find out the deep things of God? Can you find out the limit of the Almighty? It is higher than heaven—what can you do? Deeper than Sheol—what can you know?" (Job 11:7-8, NRSV; cf. Job 28). On the other hand religion may serve as an agent of de-alienation by withdrawing the status of the sacred from some institution or theory, thereby relativizing it as ordinary and accessible for routine inspection.[50]

---

47. Ibid, 80–101.

48. Ibid., 95.

49. Ibid., 80–101.

50. For Berger it is alienation, not de-alienation, that marks religion's essential function in society. In this respect he concedes that alienation is not only positive but also "anthropologically necessary" (ibid., 85) for the creation and maintenance of social equilibrium. In other words, without religion's sacred legitimation of social reality, humanity would not possess the necessary compulsion to continue participating in societal processes. But as G. Baum has commented, such a position entails anthropological assumptions that may skew both sociological and theological observations concerning religion's role in society. For example, Baum rejects the idea of alienation as anthropologically necessary, preferring instead to stress that it is humanity's freedom (not burden) to participate in social responsibilities. Baum is also critical of Berger's analysis of religion's role as an agent of de-alienation. In Baum's view, to the extent that religion is critical and de-alienating, withdrawing sacred legitimation from social structures, then it at the same time paves the way for secular symbols of legitimation to replace sacred norms. A world without sacred norms is thus secularized, and religion's function as an agent of de-alienation has thereby contributed ironically to its own demise. For Baum's critique of Berger, see G. Baum, *Religion and Alienation: A Theological Reading of Sociology* (New York: Paulist, 1975), 108–11; idem, "Peter Berger's Unfinished Symphony," *Sociology and Human Destiny: Essays on Sociology, Religion, and Society,* ed. G. Baum (New York: Seabury, 1980), 110–29. Baum's criticisms, though cogent, do not seriously change the essential truth of what I most want to capitalize on in Berger's argument. That is, religion may

These sociological observations aid one to think of prayer as an important means of maintaining a dialectical relationship with God and the world. The kind of prayer modeled in the five texts I have examined here recommends a dialogic relationship between God and humanity: God speaks, people respond; people address God, God listens and responds, and the topic of the conversation is shaped and molded in the process. To put it simply, prayer implies and encourages dialogue, not monologue; the mutual participation of two partners in the deliberative process, not the domination of one over the other. In this sense, as Brueggemann has observed, prayer becomes a means of maintaining a balance of power in the divine-human relationship and, if necessary, a means of redistributing power so that the human partner is not squeezed out of the process.[51]

Each of the prayers I have examined portrays such a dialogic role for the human partner in the faith enterprise. What is particularly striking is the way in which some of these narratives appear to have been *edited into* a literary context that, without these prayers, would have suggested a very different portrayal of both God and humanity. For example, a majority of commentators assign Exodus 32 in the main to one literary source, J. If one excerpts the story line of this one source, usually reckoned to be present in verses 1-6, 15-20, 35,[52] then the narrative reports that Moses returned from Sinai to find the calf, grew angry at the people's disobedience and subjected them to a trial by ordeal, and, finally, the LORD sent a plague upon the people. In this form the narrative simply reports disobedience and judgment. God has very little involvement in the story, other than to add divine reprisals to those Moses has already initiated. The intrusion of verses 7-14 into this context changes the complexion of the narrative considerably. Now, between the announcement of the sin and the judgment it warrants, the narrative permits a glimpse of the deliberative process that precedes the judgment, and relates how it comes about. An automatic verdict of "Guilty" is not simply handed down from on high. The people are represented, and represented well, by Moses before the Judge.

---

either contribute toward or hinder a vital dialectic between sacred order and humanity. To the extent that religion promotes this dialectic, as in maintaining a role for humanity in prayer, then God and God's order become the subject not only of praise and wonder but also of scrutiny and challenge.

51. Brueggemann, "Costly Loss," 59.

52. E.g. Childs, *Exodus,* 538.

Genesis 18 portrays a similar scenario, though even more drama-tically. The present arrangement of Genesis 18–19 has a literary hiatus between the announcement of the visit to Sodom (18:16-21) and the execution of this visit (19:1-20). In theological terms a break occurs between the announcement of God's word and its fulfillment. Execution of the divine intention is not automatic. The narrator could have reported the fate of Sodom more directly by stating simply that Sodom was a sinful city that God punished. Indeed, from a strictly textual standpoint it seems highly likely that the original report was more matter-of-fact. But the structure of the received, composite narrative suggests a different understanding. Here God speaks, Abraham prays, and *then* God's word is executed. Abraham is portrayed as having participated with God at a crucial point, between proclamation and fulfillment. God is portrayed as sharing divine intentions with a human partner. Human response is portrayed as the conduit for divine fulfillment. The apparently de-liberate intrusion of these verses into this strategic position prompts the reader to consider the narrative from another perspective. What if Abraham had not prayed? What if he had not initiated this conversation with the Judge of all the world?

If he had not, and if Moses, Joshua, and all the others who dared follow their lead had not so engaged God in what G. Coats has referred to as "loyal opposition," or if having these testimonies of divine-human engagement the final editors of the text had con-sidered them inappropriate for inclusion with the other records of faith, then the existing Hebrew Bible would be quite different and, I believe, a different faith perspective would have been derived from it. Just how different both the text and the appropriation of its message would be has yet to be fully realized. But prayers such as these summon our attention, for in them a resource is yet untapped for the "embrace of pain" in the life of faith that Brueggemann has pressed to be incorporated into the theology of the Hebrew Bible. If such an embrace is and must remain only a minority voice, as Brueggemann has suggested, it is nevertheless a crucial voice.[53] Without these prayers and the model they encourage for engaging God authentically in the struggle for meaning in the midst of chaos, one would confront an intolerable inexorability that imposes mono-logue without dialogue, revelation without response, destiny and fate without hope.

---

53. Brueggemann, "A Shape for Old Testament Theology, II: Embrace of Pain," *CBQ* 47 (1985): 399.

CHAPTER 7

The Lament Tradition:
Holding to God
against God

In the final scene of *King Lear* the king comes center stage holding his dead daughter Cordelia in his arms. By play's end the once proud and sovereign monarch is broken and despondent, his kingdom torn asunder by his own foolishness, his family shattered by his own scheming. Holding the limp body of his beloved Cordelia, Lear moans,

> Why should a dog, a horse, a rat have life,
> And thou no breath at all? Thou shalt come no more,
> Never, never, never, never, never![1]

With this the king collapses and dies. Witnessing this misery-filled moment, the duke of Albany offers a final summation:

> The weight of this sad time we must obey;
> Speak what we feel, not what we ought to say.[2]

Such are the occasions that recognize lamentation as an inescapable ingredient of life. For the duke of Albany, and for all who like him have been confronted with experiences of hurt and loss, brokenness and grief, lamentation is no stranger. Some life experiences are simply too much, their disruption of one's stability too extensive, the pain that follows in their wake too overwhelming, their assault on what is precious too threatening. One cannot go on with life as usual.

When expectations are threatened or nullified by experiences, dare one speak what one feels, even if to do so transgresses some

1. *King Lear,* act 5, sc. 3, lines 305–7.
2. Ibid., lines 322–23.

stated or perceived canon of what one ought to say? For those whose expectations are linked by faith to the Genesis confession—"In the beginning God"—and all that such a confession implies about God's relationship with humanity and the world, negating experiences quite often leave one floundering in disillusionment, anger, and guilt. On the one hand one cannot be complacent concerning the clear biblical assessment of humanity's sinful nature and of the consequent divine judgment to which such a nature inevitably leads. A major voice in the Hebrew Bible, perhaps the majority voice, clearly espouses a type of contractual theology that equates suffering with sinfulness, prosperity with righteousness, in an unambiguous, quid pro quo distribution.[3] What the sinner ought to do in the face of suffering is confess and repent. This is the first step toward forgiveness and restoration. In chapter 5 I suggested that prayers of penitence (Daniel 9, Ezra 9, Nehemiah 9) reflect this view and model a piety that embraces its truth. Under the weight of these convictions one's sense of guilt is, and ought to be, deep and persistent. One is not easily, if ever, disengaged from the influence of these teachings, for in biblical faith to consider seriously alternatives to human culpability threatens to "change the calculus" in the relationship with God.[4]

On the other hand, so inexplicable may be the chaos that sometimes befalls one that what one feels renders the oughtness of repentance meaningless and inappropriate. What one feels is not contrition but disillusionment, not penitence but protest, not submission but revolt. But dare one express such feelings? The risk in doing so is indeed great,[5] because once one denies one's own guilt, one must fix the cause of suffering elsewhere. "In the beginning *God,*" which means that from the beginning God stands as sovereign Creator in relation to all that is. How does God respond to those who risk a faith that challenges divine prerogatives?

The testimony of Israel's lament tradition is that God not only receives the dangerous act of lamentation but also heeds it. I have already looked at examples of this bold confrontation with God in the prayers of Abraham, Moses, and Joshua surveyed in chapter 6. But these are by no means the only witnesses. The confessions of

---

3. Cf. Brueggemann "A Shape for Old Testament Theology, I: Structure Legitimation," *CBQ* 47 (1985): 32, 36-41.

4. Brueggemann, "A Shape for Old Testament Theology, II: Embrace of Pain," *CBQ* 47 (1985): 398.

5. Cf. ibid., 400–401.

Jeremiah, Job, Habakkuk, Lamentations, and the laments of the Psalter are a virtual reservoir of protest literature.[6]

Brueggemann has described this lament literature as a "counter-tradition" within the Hebrew Bible. It stands over against a contractual theology, which insists on carefully prescribing what one ought to say to God in the midst of suffering.[7] This countertradition insists that God and God's order can be "addressed, assaulted, impinged upon, and transformed." It risks confrontation with God in a way that permits a newness, both in the complainant and in God.[8] This countertradition is not the only voice of the Hebrew Bible, but it is an important one. This "voice of pain" relentlessly disturbs the status quo, giving "vitality and openness to the entire enterprise."[9] To return to the duke of Albany's observation, it is here in the lament tradition that Israel dares to speak what is felt at the deepest level, even at the risk of contradicting the strictures of established convictions.

This rich tradition of lament prayer is the focus of this chapter. I restrict discussion to Jeremiah, Job, and Habakkuk, omitting the psalms of lament only because others have so often covered this ground. It will become clear in the course of the discussion that the spirit of the lament psalms is very much alive in these other texts. Each of these exemplars in its own way embraces a like commitment to the possibility of radical dialogue with God. Indeed, the relentless insistence on addressing God from the midst of pain places these prayers, along with those discussed in chapter 6, in the forefront of the Hebrew Bible's recommendations for dealing with the issue of theodicy.[10] In the last section of this chapter I return to the theodicy question in an effort to locate the particular contributions of prayer within a number of additional Hebrew Bible perspectives.

One further word by way of introduction to these texts is appropriate. The fundamental starting point for understanding lament prayer is Westermann's analysis of the primary structural com-

---

6. Cf. J. L. Crenshaw, "The Human Dilemma and Literature of Dissent," *Tradition and Theology in the Old Testament,* ed. D. A. Knight (Philadelphia: Fortress, 1977), 235–58.

7. Brueggemann, "Embrace of Pain," 405–6.

8. Ibid., 402.

9. Ibid., 414.

10. As Brueggemann has noted, "Where the lament is absent, the normal mode of the theodicy question is forfeited" ("The Costly Loss of Lament," *JSOT* 36 [1986]: 63).

ponents of lament: invocation, lament, petition.[11] Each of these parts is integral to the process of lamentation. The *invocation* of God marks these addresses as prayer and signals that all that is spoken subsequently, however harsh or accusing, is directed explicitly and intentionally to God. These are not person-to-person interchanges, neither are they soliloquies or meditations. What is spoken is intended for God's ear and seeks a response. This address or invocation establishes the pray-er's intense quest for dialogue with God, the equally stubborn refusal to remain a mute partner in the divine-human enterprise. Especially in the midst of hurt and pain, one abandons monotonic passivity. These lamenters seek to engage God at all costs; they must have their say. On more than one occasion of having had their say, they still receive no word from God. In these cases the Hebrew Bible candidly recognizes that often the dialogue of prayer is painfully "one-sided."[12] Even so, stubborn pray-ers like Jeremiah and Job are not silenced; in effect they "hold to God against God."[13]

The *lament* proper serves to articulate the problem that has arisen for the pray-er. Characteristic in this articulation are hard and accusing questions (e.g., "Why?") mediating complaints that something terribly wrong has occurred in the life of the suppliant. These are complaints in the fullest sense, as Gerstenberger has stressed: statements of protest *(Anklagen),* not of resignation or submission *(Klagen).*[14] What is wrong is not acceptable, and the lament is an act meant not only to call God's attention to the problem but to secure its correction.

This intent is made more apparent in the accompanying *petition.* For Westermann the inclusion of petition is all-important, for it shows that the lament always functions as an appeal. Lament's concern is not primarily with the portrayal of suffering but with its removal or alleviation: "Lamentation has no meaning in and of itself."[15] Thus the typical structure of lament prayers—invocation,

11. C. Westermann, "The Structure and History of the Lament in the Old Testament," *Praise and Lament in the Psalms* (Atlanta: John Knox, 1981), 165–213; idem, *The Psalms: Structure, Content and Message* (Minneapolis: Augsburg, 1980); idem, *Elements of Old Testament Theology* (Atlanta: John Knox, 1982), 167–74.

12. Cf. R. Alter, *The Art of Biblical Narrative* (New York: Basic Books, 1981), 84.

13. Cf. Westermann, *Elements,* 172.

14. E. Gerstenberger, "Jeremiah's Complaints: Observations on Jer. 15:10-21," *JBL* 82 (1963): 393–408.

15. Westermann, *Praise and Lament,* 266; cf. idem, *Elements,* 169.

lament, petition—suggests an incline or a transition beyond lamentation into petition, and ultimately, through this process, to confession of trust or even to a vow of praise as the promise of God's response is realized.

These formal elements are standard in the lament genre, embellished with formulaic and stereotypical language. Westermann cautions, however, against mistaking their employment as merely the product of a poet's imagination: "The lament is not a construct of thought; it is a living reality. It arises in a cry of pain. It is a cry that has become an utterance."[16] Despite the use of traditional and well-established motifs, lament prayers are not primarily *reflections* on suffering. They do not offer thoughtful meditations on the problem of suffering. Rather, they express the *reality* of suffering. In this sense, as I have already suggested, lament expresses what one actually feels in the throes of suffering, not what tradition or the canons of orthodoxy propose that one ought to say.

JEREMIAH'S CONFESSIONS

Embedded within Jeremiah 11–20 are a number of texts that have come to be known traditionally as the "confessions" of Jeremiah. Although the delineation of these texts varies and depends on questions of exegesis and interpretation, the conventional boundaries are usually recognized as follows: 11:18-23; 12:1-6; 15:10-21; 17:14-18; 18:18-23; 20:7-13, 14-18.

The understanding of these texts as "confessional" has been exceedingly influential in both the academy and the church since the 1920s. In large measure one can trace such influence to the compelling presentation of J. Skinner, who saw in these texts the key to "the inner life of Jeremiah."

> They lay bare the inmost secrets of the prophet's life, his fightings without and fears within, his mental conflict with adversity and doubt and temptation, and the reaction of his whole nature on a world that threatened to crush him and a task whose difficulty overwhelmed him. There is nothing quite like them in the range of devotional literature.[17]

Skinner's presentation launched both a scholarly and a pastoral interest in the *life* of Jeremiah that R. Carroll has likened to A.

16. C. Westermann, *The Structure of the Book of Job: A Form-Critical Analysis* (Philadelphia: Fortress, 1981), 33.
17. J. Skinner, *Prophecy and Religion: Studies in the Life of Jeremiah* (Cambridge: Cambridge Univ. Press, 1922), 202.

Schweitzer's famous "quest of the historical Jesus," that is, a quest for the historical Jeremiah.[18] Not surprisingly this quest for the historical Jeremiah has been challenged.[19]

My interest is not in Jeremiah the pray-er per se, but in the prayers recorded in the book that bears his name.[20] To the extent that one can tie these prayers with confidence to specific historical occasions in the life of the prophet, it is clearly advantageous to do so. But I am increasingly skeptical about the measure of certainty that such an enterprise can enjoy. I am persuaded that the stereotypical nature of the language in these prayers, as in the Psalms, makes it unlikely that one can posit any single location to the absolute exclusion of all others.[21] It is more important to recognize

---

18. R. Carroll, *From Chaos to Covenant: Uses of Prophecy in the Book of Jeremiah* (London: SCM, 1981), 25–29.

19. Two primary alternative theories have won a place in the present state of the discussion. First, one may argue that the confessions witness to Jeremiah's function in the cultic office of prophetic mediator. In this view, particularly as advocated by Reventlow, the "I" of these laments is not a personal reference to Jeremiah. Rather, it is a *"prophetisches Ich,"* a "prophetic," or "communal I," as Jeremiah speaks on behalf of the corporate community in a liturgical setting (H. G. Reventlow, *Liturgie und prophetisches Ich bei Jeremiah* [Gütersloh: Gerd Mohn, 1963], 205–57). A second alternative emphasizes the stylistic character of the language in these texts, its traditional patterns and formulaic expressions, and therefore argues that what is represented here are typical prayers, analogous to those found in the Psalms. In this sense the pray-er(s) in these texts is (are) anonymous, and apart from the final redaction of the Book of Jeremiah, the speaker is not clearly identified as Jeremiah. In this view, esp. as argued by Carroll, these are not the personal statements of the historical prophet, but edited statements placed on the lips of the prophet, designed to produce an ideal portrait of a prophet at prayer (cf. Carroll, *Chaos;* idem, *Jeremiah* [OTL; Philadelphia: Westminster, 1986]). For a convenient summary of the issues, see L. Perdue, "Jeremiah in Modern Research: Approaches and Issues," *A Prophet to the Nations: Essays in Jeremiah Studies,* ed. L. Perdue and B. Kovacs (Winona Lake, Ind.: Eisenbrauns, 1984), 25–28; cf. P. Ackroyd, "The Book of Jeremiah—Some Recent Studies," *JSOT* 28 (1984): 47–59; J. Crenshaw, "A Living Tradition: The Book of Jeremiah in Current Research," *Int* 37 (1983): 117–29.

20. One may work with a model such as that proposed by Brueggemann: one may understand these texts as contributing to a "portrait" of Jeremiah ("The Book of Jeremiah: Portrait of a Prophet," *Int* 37 [1983]: 130–45). It is a portrait certainly shaped by literary imagination, but this shaping does not make it any less important or theologically instructive. Here Brueggemann joins others who would recognize in Jeremiah a model or paradigmatic pray-er; e.g., S. Blank, "The Prophet as Paradigm," *Essays in Old Testament Ethics,* ed. J. Crenshaw and J. T. Willis (New York: KTAV, 1974), 111–30; J. Crenshaw, "Seduction and Rape: The Confessions of Jeremiah," *A Whirlpool of Torment: Israelite Traditions of God as an Oppressive Presence* (OBT; Philadelphia: Fortress, 1984), 31–56; R. Davidson, *The Courage to Doubt: Exploring an Old Testament Theme* (London: SCM, 1983), 121–39; T. Polk, *The Prophetic Persona: Jeremiah and the Language of Self* (Sheffield: JSOT Press, 1984), 167–74.

21. The recent influx of commentaries on Jeremiah indicates that the debate

the connection of these prayers to the broad tradition of Hebraic lament and thus to place them among the witnesses to this form of dialogue with God that includes Job and the Psalms.[22]

In the following discussion of these texts I shall focus on just this "dramatic dialogue" between Jeremiah and God.[23] Although each of the texts in question presents an array of often complicated exegetical and redactional problems, one may nevertheless discern in their present arrangement what might be described as the essence of lament and the essence of divine response. To illustrate the importance of this basic structural framework of prayer-response I examine first 11:18—12:6 and 15:15-21, which anticipate a number of themes that appear in subsequent texts.

JEREMIAH'S LAMENT (11:18—12:6)

As the text now stands, 11:18—12:6 exhibits the following structure: lament (11:18-20), divine response (11:21-23), lament (12:1-4), divine response (12:5-6). This structure has likely been achieved only secondarily, yet a number of shared motifs and themes contribute to its rhetorical unity.[24]

The essence of Jeremiah's prayer is lament or complaint. Thus here, as throughout these texts, the traditional label "confession" is a misnomer, suggesting a measure of pious acquiescence more appropriate for an Augustine than for the deeply distraught speaker portrayed here. In both 11:18-20 and 12:1-4, the lament is couched in the language of the *rîb,* the legal case or cause (11:20; 12:1). In prophetic parlance the *rîb* is a common rhetorical form for the announcement of divine judgment. Thus in its typical employment, the prophet, speaking on behalf of God, summons Israel into court, as it were, to answer divine charges of misconduct. Within such a rhetorical scenario God is portrayed as both prosecuting attorney

---

concerning the historical location of these prayers is far from settled. For example, compare Carroll (*Jeremiah,* e.g. 55–58, 277–79), who rejects the effort to read the confessions in any biographical sense, with W. L. Holladay, who continues to interpret them as emerging out of specific historical circumstances in the life of the prophet (*Jeremiah,* vol. 1: *A Commentary on the Book of the Prophet Jeremiah, Chapters 1–25* [Hermeneia; Philadelphia: Fortress, 1986], 6–9, 358–61; *Jeremiah,* vol. 2: *A Commentary on the Book of the Prophet Jeremiah, Chapters 26–52* [Hermeneia; Minneapolis: Augsburg Fortress, 1989], 20–21, 30–33).

22. For this connection W. Baumgartner's analysis remains the fundamental starting point (*Jeremiah's Poems of Lament* [Sheffield: Almond, 1988] [= *Die Klagegedichte des Jeremia* (BZAW 32; Giessen: Töpelmann, 1917)]).

23. Cf. A. R. Diamond, *The Confessions of Jeremiah in Context: Scenes of Prophetic Drama* (Sheffield: JSOT Press, 1987), 19ff., et passim.

24. See, e.g., K. M. O'Connor, *The Confessions of Jeremiah: Their Interpretation and Role in Chapters 1–25* (Atlanta: Scholars Press, 1988), 16–26.

and judge, reading the charges against the accused and, failing their adequate defense, finally announcing the verdict "Guilty."[25] The drama of Jeremiah's *rîb* is that this conventional scenario is turned topsy-turvy. In this lament Jeremiah takes on the role of prosecutor and God is summoned and charged as defendant. W. Holladay has stressed the law-court imagery implied here with his translation of 12:1:

> You will be innocent, Yahweh,
> when I dispute *['ārîb]* with you;
> nevertheless I will speak judgments upon you.[26]

The phrase "speak judgments upon" *(dibbēr + mišpāṭîm 'et)* occurs only in Jeremiah, always with the connotation of specific accusations in a lament.[27] In 1:16 and 4:12, for example, the same language refers to God speaking judgments against a recalcitrant Israel. In 12:1, however, God stands accused, and Jeremiah insists on his right to hold God accountable to the same standards of conduct that apply to Israel.

Furthermore, Jeremiah's *rîb* or complaint focuses on the question of justice, more specifically, on the justice of God's judgments. On two occasions Jeremiah addresses God as "just": first as "righteous judge" (11:20: *šōpēṭ ṣedeq*), then simply as "righteous" or "innocent" (12:1: *ṣaddîq 'attāh*). In both instances God's justness is affirmed specifically in the process of "testing the mind and the heart" of humanity (11:20; 12:3). That is, it is God's special attribute to be able to discern the deepest thoughts and intentions of those who profess loyalty to divine standards. For Abraham God's discerning powers as "Judge of all the world" mandate a distinction in the judgment of the righteous *(ṣaddîq)* and the wicked *(rāšā')* at Sodom (cf. Gen 18:25). Jeremiah's lament expresses the same assumption of divine justice and fair play. Jeremiah frames the central concern as the timeless question about the prosperity of the wicked: "Why does the way of the wicked *[rĕšā'îm]* prosper *[ṣālēḥāh]*?" (12:1). The question in this context represents a challenge to a fundamental assumption about justice in God's ordered world. As canonized in Psalm 1 this assumption is stated in simple and unambiguous terms:

---

25. See, e.g., Isa 1:2-3; Jer 2:10-13; Mic 6:1-8.
26. Holladay, *Jeremiah* 1.364; cf. idem, *Jeremiah, Spokesman out of Time* (New York: Pilgrim, 1974), 92–94.
27. Holladay, *Jeremiah* 1.40, 376; cf. idem, "Jeremiah's Lawsuit with God," *Int* 17 (1963): 280–87.

Happy are those
who do not follow the advice of the wicked *[rĕšā'îm]*
or take the path that sinners tread. . . .
In all that they do, they prosper *[yaṣlîaḥ].*
The wicked *[hārĕšā'îm]* are not so. . .
but the way of the wicked *[rĕšā'îm]* will perish. (vv. 1, 3, 4, 6; NRSV)

So stated, the choices in life between good and evil are clear and distinguishable, the consequences of either are predictable and consistent. Yet Jeremiah's experience denies this assumption. Why do the wicked prosper?[28]

Still more problematic from Jeremiah's perspective is the question this reality raises about God. *"You* plant them, and they take root" (12:2, NRSV). They grow and bear fruit because of *your* initiative. Why? *You* do know and test the mind and the heart (11:18; 12:3). Why then do you not recognize the sincerity of my heart (cf. 12:3); that I am like a helpless lamb before those who plot my demise (cf. 11:19); that those who seek to cut me off from the land of the living (11:19) are those whose commitment to you is "near in their mouths, but far from their inward convictions" (12:2)? "You are righteous"; those engaged in treachery against me are wicked (12:1). Why?

For Jeremiah these questions raise doubts about God's justice. As disconcerting as are the plots against him by the "people of Anathoth" (cf. 11:21, 23), even perhaps by the members of his own family (cf. 12:6), his primary concern is God's intentions toward him. Is God reliable? Can God be trusted? Can God be trusted as a "righteous judge," as a tester and knower of people's deepest loyalties? If God's fundamental commitment to justice and fair play does not mean that the innocent are protected and the guilty are punished, what does it mean?

The essence of God's response to Jeremiah's prayer is provided at two junctures in the present arrangement of the text. Taken together these responses offer simultaneously both hope and threat. To Jeremiah's plea for vengeance against his opponents, the divine response comes in the form of a typical oracle of judgment announcing the annihilation of his foes (11:21-23). Such a response clearly places God on the side of Jeremiah, on the side of justice, and against those "people of Anathoth" who place themselves in oppo-

---

28. Cf. Holladay, who has suggested that Jer 12:1b-2 is authentic to Jeremiah and as such represents a deliberate variation of Psalm 1, which is designed to call into question its central affirmation about divine justice (*Jeremiah* 1.376-77; 2.31, 65).

sition to the "Lord of hosts, who is a righteous judge" (11:20). As A. R. Diamond observes, at this level "the prophet's 'cause' is set within a framework which at no point leaves its beneficial outcome in doubt."[29]

As the lament continues in 12:1-4, however, a second divine response places the outcome of Jeremiah's case in question. Jeremiah has raised hard questions relating to the seeming free hand of the wicked: "Why?" and "How long?" (12:1, 4). He has petitioned God to drag away these violators of divine ethics and to set them apart for the day of retribution (12:3). Yet the response provided in 12:5-6 takes no heed of either his questions or his petition. In the place of an expected oracle of assurance God asks a threatening counterquestion:

> If you have raced with those running on foot,
>   and they have wearied you,
>   how will you compete with horses?
> And if in a safe land you fall down,
>   how will you do in the thicket of the Jordan?

The images here are strange and their referents much debated, but their general sense is clear. Carroll suggests a paraphrase that captures the central thrust: "If you think this is a difficult situation, just wait and see what is going to happen next!"[30]

Even allowing for a variety of explanations that seek to relate this response to the preceding prayer by positing it as a secondary and ambiguous addition, one is hard-pressed to find much encouragement for Jeremiah. At one point God seems to be assuring the prophet that he can trust the divine promise of justice to manifest itself in the reality of his situation at the appropriate time (11:23). At another point the issue of divine justice is skirted altogether. What is, is what will be, only it will be worse, the expectation of justice notwithstanding. W. McKane suggests that such a response leaves Jeremiah no other option than to "hammer out a new theology."[31]

At the very least one may recognize that the present text has raised hard and accusing questions of God that receive no adequate response. As one may see in other texts in Jeremiah and also in Job

---

29. Diamond, *Confessions,* 35.

30. Carroll, *Jeremiah,* 287.

31. W. McKane, "The Interpretation of Jeremiah VII 1-5," *Transactions of the Glasgow University Oriental Society* 20 (1965): 48.

and Habakkuk that I will discuss subsequently, God's unsatisfactory response is rather typical. Like Moses and Abraham before him, Jeremiah's quest for justice threatens to swallow him up in the silence of one-sided dialogue. This particular sequence of prayer-response begins to suggest that such is the conundrum of theodicy.[32]

JEREMIAH'S PRAYER AND THE DIVINE RESPONSE (15:10-21)

The two poles of prayer and divine response are also at work in the confession found in 15:10-21. The material contained within these verses is arguably the most complicated and ambiguous of all the confessions. While a rather clear break is visible between verses 10-14 and verses 15-21, the relation of the two units to each other and especially the internal coherence of verses 10-14 continue to pose major and as yet unresolved problems.[33] For my purposes here I leave these questions aside and focus attention instead on verses 15-21, where exegesis can proceed with less difficulty. These verses divide clearly between prayer (vv. 15-18) and divine response (vv. 19-21). Thus the structure of this confession, like that of 11:18—12:6, suggests a dialogic encounter between Jeremiah and God.

The prayer of verses 15-18 contains the essential elements of a typical lament: invocation (v. 15a), petition (v. 15b), protestation of innocence (vv. 16-17), lament (v. 18). Within this structure the complaint begins in relation to the prophet's enemies: "remember me . . . and obtain satisfaction[34] for me from *my persecutors"* (v. 15). But the focus of concern shifts gradually to God and to the trouble that falls to the prophet precisely because of his relation to God:[35]

> On *your* account I suffer insult. (v. 15)
> *Your* words were found . . .

---

32. Cf. Holladay, *Jeremiah* 1.382. See further Diamond (*Confessions,* 50–51, 156–57), who suggests that not only here but throughout the confessions theodicy is the "central, controlling principle in the composition" (182).

33. The major problems concern vv. 13-14, which appear to be a doublet of 17:3-4. On the redactional questions see Gerstenberger, "Jeremiah's Complaints," 402; A. H. J. Gunneweg, "Konfession oder Interpretation im Jeremiabuch," *ZTK* 67 (1970): 404–05; F. D. Hubmann, *Untersuchungen zu den Konfessionen: Jer 11,18—12,6 und Jer 15,10-21* (Würzburg: Echter, 1978), 255–57; J. Vermeylen, "Essai de Redaktionsgeschichte des 'Confessions de Jérémie,'" *Le Livre de Jérémie,* ed. P. M. Bogaert (Leuven: Leuven Univ. Press, 1981), 266; Diamond, *Confessions,* 55–58.

34. On the significance of *nqm,* "obtain satisfaction," in this passage, see G. Mendenhall, *The Tenth Generation: The Origins of the Biblical Tradition* (Baltimore: Johns Hopkins Univ. Press, 1973), 97.

35. Cf. Diamond, *Confessions,* 69.

> *your* words became to me a joy . . .
> for I am called by *your* name. (v. 16)
> Under the weight of *your* hand I sat alone,
> for *you* had filled me with indignation. (v. 17, NRSV)

This growing preoccupation with God's role in his present dilemma attains its sharpest articulation in Jeremiah's lament of verse 18. Here, as in 12:1 (NRSV), the prophet hurls at God the thunderous question "Why?":

> Why *[lāmmāh]* is my pain unceasing,
>   my wound incurable,
> refusing to be healed?

The question "Why?" is the most common question in lament prayers. As I have commented previously on several encounters with its usage in other prayers (e.g., Num 11:11; Exod 32:11), it almost always carries a note of protest and accusation. Implicit in the question here is that (1) Jeremiah is suffering, and he should not be; and (2) Jeremiah's suffering seems endless, eliciting no response from God, no move toward comfort or healing, and this too from Jeremiah's perspective is wrong. His pursuit of the prophetic mission holds out the prospects of "joy" and "delight" (v. 16: *śāśôn, śimḥat),* the thrill of relationship associated elsewhere with the intimate bonds between bride and bridegroom.[36] Yet the result for him has been opposite and painful: not joy but hurt, not delight but perpetual misery.

This contradiction between expectation and experience raises for Jeremiah the specter of deception, divine deception; and harsh as it is, he does not muffle the charge.

> You really are to me like a lie *['akzāb],*
>   waters that are not true *[ne'ĕmānû].* (v. 18)

Although some translations set this sentence as a question (e.g., RSV: "Wilt thou be to me . . .?"), the text renders it clearly as an affirmation of the strongest sort.[37] The use of the infinitive absolute

---

36. Cf. Holladay, *Jeremiah* 1.458–59.

37. Newer translations more appropriately render the statement as an assertion, e.g., NRSV: "Truly, you are to me like a deceitful brook"; REB: "You are to me like a brook that fails"; NJPS: "You have been to me like a spring that fails." On the question whether *'akzāb* should be translated in a general way as "lie" or "deception," or more specifically with reference to an unreliable spring, see W. McKane, *A Critical and Exegetical Commentary on Jeremiah* (ICC; 2 vols.; Edinburgh: T. and T. Clark, 1986–), 1.355–56. In either sense, the imagery of divine deception is clear.

as emphatic supplement to the finite verb *(hāyô tihyeh)* serves in effect to sharpen the charge: "You *really [surely]* are to me. . . ." The imagery of divine deception is carried by the metaphor of water. God is like waters that lie, like waters that are not true; both images suggest the wadi that runs dry in the summer heat. From a distance it promises water to the parched and needy traveler, but it is a mirage, a deception. Upon closer inspection the streambed is cracked and dry and empty.[38]

The force of the imagery is strengthened still further when placed alongside similar language elsewhere in the book. In 2:13 (NRSV) Jeremiah charges that the community has rejected God, "the fountain of living water *[mayim ḥayyîm]*," for broken cisterns. Now Jeremiah accuses God of becoming for him no more than a lying, disappointing source of refreshment, no more reliable than the leaky cisterns that the people are condemned for relying on.[39] In 2:31 God asks rhetorically: "Have I become a wilderness to Israel?" The assumed answer is clearly no. For Jeremiah the question has now become no longer so rhetorical, the expected answer not so certainly accepted.[40] In 5:1 (NRSV) Jeremiah is instructed to run to and fro through the streets of Jerusalem in search of just one person who "seeks truth *['ĕmûnāh].'"* Now he charges that were the search extended to the heavens it would still come up empty! As horrifying as this charge of divine deception is, it is not the last time it appears in Jeremiah's prayers. In 20:7-14, which I will also discuss, the accusation resurfaces, this time with language so condemnatory of God that all that has preceded pales by comparison.

Verses 19-21 contain God's response to these charges. Whether

---

38. C. Westermann has noted that similar imagery is found in Job's lament about his friends who have proven untrue. They are as "treacherous as a torrent-bed" (Job 6:15), pretending consolation when in reality they assail him like enemies. For Job the reference is to human deception. Jeremiah takes the charge one dangerous step further to point the finger of accusation at God (Westermann, *Structure of Job,* 43-44). See further the suggestion of J. J. M. Roberts that divine deception here and elsewhere in Jeremiah can be interpreted as the occasion of divinely initiated false prophecy ("Does God Lie? Divine Deceit As a Theological Problem in Israelite Prophetic Literature," *VTS* 40 [1988], 217-18).

39. Cf. Holladay, *Jeremiah* 1.461; Carroll, *Jeremiah,* 331-32; Hubmann, *Untersuchungen,* 284; F. Ahuis, *Der Klagende Gerichtsprophet: Studien zur Klage in der Überlieferung von der alttestamentlichen Gerichtspropheten* (Stuttgart: Calwer, 1982), 93; N. Ittmann, *Die Konfessionen Jeremias: Ihre Bedeutung für die Verkündigung des Propheten* (Neukirchen: Neukirchener Verlag, 1981), 166. Note further Diamond (*Confessions,* 75), who suggests that Jeremiah's accusation essentially reduces God to the status of Israel's idols.

40. Cf. Holladay, *Jeremiah* 1.461.

one restricts the original form of this response to verse 19, or to portions of verses 19 and 20, with the remainder as secondary,[41] deciphering the relation of God's answer to what has preceded is difficult indeed—perhaps intentionally so. Carroll has stressed that divine responses to laments are typically no less formal than laments themselves, hence one should not expect specific complaints to be answered.[42] In this case specific answers are certainly not found in the divine reply. But this fact, whether occasioned by the canons of tradition or not, raises profound difficulties for interpreting the received text, not only from an exegetical perspective but also from a theological point of view.

If one restricts the focus to verse 19, *perhaps* the original element in the response, then the text portrays God responding, as in 11:21-23 and 12:5-6, with a mixture of rebuke and promise.[43]

> If you return and [if?][44] I will restore you,
> then before me you will stand.
> If you bring forth the precious rather than the worthless,
> then like my mouth you will be.

The syntax clearly links this response to what has preceded. Thus the introduction—"Therefore *[lākēn]* thus says the LORD"—recalls the positioning of oracles of assurance after lamentation, especially in prophetic liturgies. Such words of assurance or promise typically afford the supplicant a measure of confidence in God's ultimate response to and resolution of situations of announced distress.

Although verse 19 shares the *position* of such an oracle, its *content* is quite different. Here God responds with conditional promises at best, the conditions themselves serving apparently to rebuke the prophet for having transgressed the mysterious boundaries of divine sovereignty. *If* you return, and *if* you utter what is precious rather than what is worthless, *then* you may continue to stand before me as a prophet, your mouth my chosen vehicle of revelation. In sum and substance it is a summons to repentance, a repentance like that which Jeremiah himself has urged upon the sinful Israelites (e.g., 3:1—4:4). As Holladay remarks, "This is a

41. On v. 19 as original, see Hubmann, *Untersuchungen,* 289–99; Holladay, *Jeremiah* 1.450; Vermeylen, "Essai de Redaktionsgeschichte," 266. Cf. Ahuis, *Klagende Gerichtsprophet,* 101.
42. Carroll, *Jeremiah,* 334.
43. Cf. Diamond, *Confessions,* 78.
44. Cf. Holladay, *Jeremiah* 1.462–63.

surprise: whoever heard of a prophet of Yahweh who needs to repent?"[45]

The response is a surprise, if not also theologically quite disturbing, from another perspective as well. W. Baumgartner summarizes God's intent with an interpretation that other commentators echo:

> So to begin with Yahweh promises him nothing, except that he may continue to exercise his prophetic office. This service, which brings him so much pain, he "may" continue with! His profession, with all its sorrows, is still his most cherished privilege! There is one condition, it is true: the mouth that proclaims the divine words must not, alongside what is "precious," also utter the "worthless," human laments and petitions![46]

J. Bright's interpretation is not substantially different; he too sees here a divine rebuke of Jeremiah's accusations as not only unjustified but also impermissible. If Jeremiah is to continue in his role as prophet, "he will have to do a complete about-face, purge himself of such talk, and utter the word that is given him, and that alone, or he cannot continue."[47] In Bright's view such a rebuke encourages one to think that at some point in Jeremiah's life he becomes aware that he has very nearly forfeited his prophetic office, but just at that point he undergoes a second experience of call. Bright imagines that subsequent to this experience one may think of Jeremiah saying,

> In my weakness I spoke so; but I know that I sinned in doing so, for God rebuked me. And when he rebuked me, I repented, for as you can see from my book, I continued in the prophetic office till the end.[48]

From an exegetical standpoint it is difficult to dispute the interpretation that sees in this divine reply a rebuke for uttering what God deems "worthless." Jeremiah is admonished to turn from such speech, in Bright's words, to "purge himself of such talk." Such a rebuke is nevertheless difficult to assimilate theologically. What kind of God would place such restrictions of muted speech on faithful followers? A God before whom lament is inappropriate, questioning and complaint not allowed? A God who tolerates only silent cooperation, only the "Yes" of acceptance but not the "Why?"

45. Ibid., 464.
46. Baumgartner, *Jeremiah's Poems,* 50; cf. Diamond, *Confessions,* 77–78.
47. J. Bright, "A Prophet's Lament and Its Answer: Jeremiah 15:10-21," *Int* 28 (1974): 73.
48. Ibid., 74.

or the "No" of complaint and refusal? These questions tie themselves inextricably to the divine response offered in verse 19, and no
amount of clever exegesis can easily dislodge them.[49]

Yet Bright's imaginative reconstruction suggesting Jeremiah's
confession of sin and his chastened speech fails to reflect accurately
the tenor of the whole of these confession prayers. The essential
message of these prayers is that despite God's rebuke Jeremiah
refuses to acquiesce to silent suffering. In subsequent prayers the
prophet continues to lament and protest, to question and to petition
God, in the hope of securing relief. One ought to be cautious about
suggesting definite lines of progression or chronological sequencing
in successive complaints; nevertheless, they are in a sequence of
steadily increasing intensity.[50]

If Jeremiah ever heeded the admonition to muzzle his festering
complaints, at any point in his life, these prayers offer no evidence
of it. Rather, the cumulative witness of these prayers is that while
the speaker may stand to forfeit the prophetic mantle, he is not
prepared to give up his voice in the divine-human dialogue. Perhaps Jeremiah's persistence, even in the face of divine rebuke,
invites one to see the small ledge to which lamenters cling in this
assault of the heavens. The approach to God is dangerous—one
false step and they may slip from the precipice into the cavern that
awaits transgressors. Yet risk the climb they must, for they cannot
remain where they are and live. Such is the risky business of lament.

In these initial prayers of Jeremiah I have suggested that Jeremiah pursues a stubborn dialogue with God. Both 11:18—12:6 and
15:15-21 are structured in the basic form of lament-divine response.
Within this framework Jeremiah complains about his treatment at
the hands of wicked oppressors *and* at the hand of a seemingly
dispassionate God before whom the pleas for justice appear to have
little effect. These basic complaints are sustained and intensified in
succeeding prayers, but with one notable change. What previously
transpired within the discourse of dialogue—lament and response—now becomes decidedly one-sided. Jeremiah continues to
address God, but no divine responses are recorded. To these con-

---

49. Cf. Diamond, who interprets the divine response as a rebuke of Jeremiah's
misunderstanding of the prophetic mission. There is no other way for Jeremiah
than the present one, i.e., the way of suffering. Jeremiah must realize this and
repent from asking God to change it (*Confessions,* 74–78). This is a plausible
interpretation, but it gives no attention at all to the question of divine justice.

50. Cf. G. von Rad, *Old Testament Theology* (2 vols.; New York: Harper and
Row, 1962–65), 2.203.

tinuing laments and to the silence with which they are received I now turn.

JEREMIAH'S CONTINUING LAMENTS

In the present configuration of Jeremiah's prayers, 15:19-21 marks the last recorded response from God. In succeeding prayers Jeremiah continues to lament and protest and petition, but his pleas evoke only divine silence. The more God is silent, however. the more intense successive prayers become. Even if such an impression has been achieved only in the course of the text's redaction, the final context provides an important hermeneutical clue for appropriating Jeremiah as a theological model.

In the face of a silent God Jeremiah continues to pray. He does not retreat into silence. He does not abandon God for more responsive dialogue partners. His decision to continue addressing God seems little affected by his failure to secure divine response. As despair increases so too does the intensity, the urgency, the passion of prayer. Such a portrait promotes prayer as a desirable, functional, at times unavoidable, practice in the midst of hurt, even when the heavens seem so completely impenetrable "that no prayer can pass through" (Lam 3:44; cf. v. 8). As R. Ellison's Mary says to the invisible man, "Everybody has to be trouble to *some*body."[51] Jeremiah's stubborn prayers suggest that in the midst of hurt and pain that "somebody" must be God.

In Jeremiah's continuing laments the focus of concern rests on two opponents, one divine, the other human.[52] I may illustrate this focus by collecting various examples from the remaining prayers.

Against God Jeremiah continues to complain about (a) divine injustice and (b) divine deception. In the first case, I noted in 11:20 and 12:1 that Jeremiah raises questions with God, the "righteous Judge," about the justice of divine judgment. Thus in 12:1 the question is "Why does the way of the wicked prosper?" In subsequent prayers this issue of justice continues to be a central concern.

In 18:18-23 a similar question underlies Jeremiah's lament. The prose introduction in verse 18 suggests that the setting for this complaint is similar to that described in 11:18—12:6: opposition to Jeremiah and to his preaching. Given this thematic link to oppo-

---

51. R. Ellison, *Invisible Man* (New York: Vintage, 1972), 248.
52. Westermann (*Praise and Lament,* 169) has shown that laments typically concern three subjects: God, the one who laments, and the enemy.

sition against Jeremiah, the chapter as a whole creates a picture of a rejected message and messenger.[53] Thus the chapter coordinates a pattern of prophetic address (vv. 1-11), response of the people (v. 12), a second prophetic address (vv. 13-17) and a second response of the people (v. 18). This is the context for Jeremiah's lament in verse 19–23.

> Pay attention to me LORD
> and listen to the voice of my complaint *[rîbî]*.[54]
> Is evil the reward *[šlm:* lit. "completion"] of good?

The complaint is typical of that which is associated with the conflict between the righteous and the wicked in lament psalms (cf. Pss 35:11-12; 38:20 [MT v. 21]; 109:5). In Jeremiah's case the concern centers on the fact that he has "stood before you [God] to speak good *[ṭôbāh]* for them [the people]" (18:20), a reference to his interceding on their behalf in the hope of protecting them from God's anger (cf. 15:11).[55] Yet his efforts to do good for them are rewarded with their attempts to do evil *(rā'āh)* to him, here described metaphorically as digging pits to capture him (vv. 20, 22) and as refusing to heed his words (v. 18). Thus he asks, "Is evil the completion of doing good?" This question strikes at the root of fundamental assumptions about the correlation between deeds and their consequences. Is there no reward for doing good, no punishment for doing evil? Is it not the case that good deeds may be expected to secure good outcomes, or at least that they do not ordinarily boomerang on the well-intentioned by instigating their demise?

The remainder of the prayer is Jeremiah's appeal to the divine standards of justice that he presumes will vindicate him and condemn without mercy his opponents (vv. 21-23). Yet his petition for vengeance is so stringent and appalling that one may understand it to betray a veiled complaint: the system of rewards and punishment

---

53. Diamond, *Confessions,* 91. On the redactional seams, see F. Hubmann, "Jer 18, 18-23 im Zusammenhang der Konfessionen," *Le Livre de Jérémie,* ed. P. M. Bogaert (Leuven: Leuven Univ. Press, 1981), 280–93.

54. With LXX: *tou dikaiōmatos mou.* Cf. P. Volz, *Der Prophet Jeremia* (Leipzig: Deichert, 1928), 197; W. Rudolph, *Jeremia* (3d ed.; Tübingen: J. C. B. Mohr, 1968), 112. Holladay (*Jeremiah* 1.528) follows Hubmann ("Jer. 18, 18-23," 284) in reading MT (*yārîb,* "my adversaries") against LXX. For further discussion see Diamond, *Confessions,* 96–100.

55. For this and comparable language attesting prophetic intercession, see S. Balentine, "The Prophet as Intercessor: A Reassessment," *JBL* 103 (1984): 162–68.

is slow, too slow, to take effect.[56] Perhaps the system is inoperative or in need of repair. In any case Jeremiah's petition that God "forgive not their iniquity" (v. 23) reflects the fear that perhaps God has inexplicably chosen to forgive them.

Further, Jeremiah continues to charge God with deception, divine fraud. The charge is first raised in 15:18, where Jeremiah protests, "You really are to me like a lie, waters that are not true." Succeeding prayers amplify this complaint both generally and specifically. First, in a general sense, one may observe the contrasting and conflicting divine epithets in 17:14-18. One may also include 17:12-13 here, even though most reckon these verses as formally constituting a separate unit. Taken together these verses (in NRSV) address God respectively as "hope of Israel" (v. 13),[57] "fountain of living water" (v. 13; cf. 2:13 but also 15:18), "my praise" (v. 14), and "my refuge" (v. 17). On the surface each of these represents a positive attribution, affirmations of confidence not unfamiliar in psalms bespeaking trust in God's benevolent goodness.[58] These positive epithets are, however, put in a different perspective by the prophet's petition in verse 17 that God not be for him a "terror" or a source of "panic" *(limḥittāh)*. This same word in verbal form occurs in verse 18, where Jeremiah pleads: "Let my persecutors be shamed, but do not let me be shamed; let them be *terrorized,* but do not let me be *terrorized.*" In this specific case, as in the case of the more general ascriptions, epithets in this confession reveal some of the prophet's conflicting perceptions about who God is. Will God be for him a place of refuge from terror, or the cause of his terror (cf. 20:11)? "Fountain of living waters" or "waters that fail"? The tension implicit in these conflicting perceptions poses questions about the constancy or predictability of divine behavior, questions to which the silence following Jeremiah's prayer offers no reassurance.

In a far more specific way the issue of divine deception is raised in embarassingly strong terms in 20:7a:

---

56. Cf. Diamond, *Confessions,* 95.

57. The same word *(miqwēh)* is used elsewhere in verbal form to describe Israel's "disappointed hope" (Jer 8:15; cf. 13:16; 14:19). See further W. Rast, "Disappointed Expectation in the Old Testament," *Perspective* 12 (1971): 135–53. Cf. Holladay *(Jeremiah* 1.433, 502), who reads *miqwēh* as meaning "pool" here; thus "O pool of Israel, O Yahweh." He sees this as an example of double entendre particularly appropriate in the context of drought, which provides the background for Jeremiah's address to God in 17:12-13 (cf. 14:8).

58. See, e.g., Pss 39:7 (MT v. 8) ("hope"); 46:1 (MT v. 2) ("refuge"); 71:6; 109:1 ("praise"). Cf. Holladay, *Jeremiah* 1.504, 506; Baumgartner, *Jeremiah's Poems,* 54.

You have deceived me *[pittîtanî]*, LORD,
and I was deceived *[wā'eppāt];*
You are stronger than I,
and you have prevailed.

The language here is strong, even blasphemous, and beyond any conventional norm; yet to catch something of the anguish that lies behind such words, one must resist the temptation to soften them. The verb translated here as "deceive" *(pātāh)* connotes the imagery of power, brute force, more specifically the power associated elsewhere in the Hebrew Bible with sexual seduction (cf. Exod 22:15; Judg 14:15; 16:5; Job 31:9). Further, the verb translated "you are stronger" *(hāzāq)* may also refer to forcing a woman in an act of sexual violence (cf. Deut 22:25; 2 Sam 13:14). To put the issue bluntly, Jeremiah accuses God of the most grotesque form of sexual assault, of overpowering him, crushing his resistance, using him to satisfy divine whims, and then casting him aside.[59] The consequence as described in verse 7b is that Jeremiah has become the object of cruel fun, a "laughingstock" *(śĕhôq).* Jeremiah responds with the Hebraic version of an expletive: "Violence!" "Destruction!"[60]

The scenario envisioned suggests a struggle between two unequal powers, and hence recalls a similar encounter in Jeremiah 1. This opening scene of the book also presents Jeremiah as standing before God, overmatched and overruled. In this earlier confrontation Jeremiah submits, rather passively, accepting and playing out the role assigned to him as the inferior power. In the encounter reported in Jeremiah 20, Jeremiah rebels, refusing to accept his role without a struggle, and refusing to acknowledge his defeat without complaint.

The two scenes together raise grave and troublesome theological issues. If the relationship with God is based on power, when does, or

59. The verb *pātāh* also occurs without sexual overtones, e.g., in 1 Kgs 22:20-21, 22, where the context concerns God's deceiving a prophet. D. J. A. Clines and D. M. Gunn ("'You Tried to Persuade Me' and 'Violence! Outrage!' in Jeremiah XX 7-8," *VT* 28 [1978]: 20–27) have argued from this use that the meaning in Jer 20:7 is better grasped as "try to persuade." Such a connotation certainly softens the imagery here, but as Holladay has noted, the goal of such divine persuasion is still clearly destructive (*Jeremiah* 1.552). See further Diamond (*Confessions*, 110–11), who follows the suggestion of Clines and Gunn but notes that the neutral translation "persuade" does little to capture the tone of reproach and criticism represented in this portrayal of the prophet's victimization.

60. For this implication of "Violence!" "Destruction," see Holladay, *Jeremiah* 1.554; J. Berridge, *Prophet, People, and the Word of Yahweh: An Examination of Form and Content in the Proclamation of the Prophet Jeremiah* (Zurich: EVZ, 1970), 153–54.

can, the one controlled cease to submit and refuse to cooperate? When does divine power become oppressive, forcing the unequal partner to take that dangerous step from submission and obedience to protest and revolt? If such a step is taken, what then becomes of the divine-human relationship? Is it ruptured irreparably, or can the relationship accommodate challenge to the conventional distribution of power? I have yet to address what is perhaps the Hebrew Bible's most celebrated power struggle between God and humanity, that portrayed in the Book of Job. Yet even before I turn to this example, at least one thing seems clear from the witness of Jeremiah and his compatriots Abraham, Moses, and Joshua: God's acknowledged sovereignty and power does not always elicit mute collaboration.

Alongside Jeremiah's continuing complaints against God are his equally persistent laments concerning his human opponents. These too may be understood as escalating in their intensity through successive prayers. From the calls for vengeance mentioned but briefly in 11:20; 15:15; and in 17:18, his prayers turn increasingly to vehement curses in 18:21-23 and finally in 20:14-18.

This last passage rounds off the confessions with what is perhaps the most despairing language of all. Formally these verses belong clearly to the curse genre, although here the object of scorn is no longer Jeremiah's enemies per se but his own life. In this sense a close parallel occurs in Job 3:3-26, where, as Westermann has suggested, Job's cursing his day of birth (vv. 3-9) represents a thematic substitute for the lament about enemies.[61] In both Jer 20:14-18 and Job 3:3-26 self-lament dominates the prayer. Westermann argues that such an emphasis reflects the "primordial individual lament," combining self-lament and malediction with a boldness considered subsequently "too untamed to allow for incorporation into the prayer book of the community [i.e., the Psalter]."[62]

---

61. Westermann, *Structure of Job,* 37.
62. Ibid., 61 n. 14. D. J. A. Clines and D. M. Gunn have argued that the original setting behind Jeremiah 20 is the "conventional description of dismay at the hearing of bad news." As such they understand Jeremiah's response not as a personal reaction but as a conventional prophetic reaction to the mandate to preach judgment ("Form, Occasion and Redaction in Jeremiah 20," *ZAW* 88 [1976]: 390–409; cf. D. R. Hillers, "A Convention in Hebrew Literature: The Reaction to Bad News," *ZAW* 77 [1965]: 86–90). See Diamond (*Confessions,* 120), however, who notes that despite the likelihood of such an original setting, the close literary association of 20:14-18 with the preceding confession, 20:7-13, and with the preceding narrative of 20:1-6 "strongly suggests that editorial constraints have been placed upon our passage so that now it is meant to be read so personally."

In its present position this prayer brings to a climax Jeremiah's steady march into despair. He does not explicitly invoke God. He identifies the targets of his anger as only the day of his birth and the messenger who brought the news of his birth. But life itself is damned in Jeremiah's eyes. Although God is not expressly addressed, the context of the prayer, especially its close literary association with the preceding prayer in verses 7-13, suggests that this prayer is linked with the prophet's reaction to his treatment at the hands of the Creator of life. He has been so victimized that prayer now trails off into near soliloquy. The final question of verse 18 sounds the anguished response of one born to a meaningless existence.

> Why did I come forth from the womb
> to see trouble and torment
> and spend my days in shame?

Again the question elicits only silence from God. Like the stubborn pray-er of Psalm 88 whose persistent questions are also occasioned by a misery likened to a living death, Jeremiah concludes his prayer as one who is unanswered, unvindicated, undone. Some find a response in the redactional framework of the book as chapters 21ff. continue the report of the prophet's ministry under divine supervision. In this sense one may argue that the question about life's futility does not ultimately go unanswered, and self-lament is therefore not the final word.[63] From a rhetorical perspective this interpretation is attractive if only because it affords a more positive appraisal of the prophet's troubling experiences. Yet one ought not shade over too quickly what the prayers themselves seem determined to emphasize, namely, the plight of one who is abandoned, betrayed, and victimized in the course of a divinely mandated mission.

Perhaps one should leave the matter where 20:14-20 appears to leave it, with questions raised and answers still pending. From a theological perspective this text forces one to linger in the aftershock of the collision between faith commitments and their negation. Neither achieves ascendancy over the other. Such a view may threaten to "unravel" the confessions,[64] indeed to jeopardize, if not contradict, any parenetic purpose that one may derive from them concerning the practice of prayer. But in the Hebrew Bible such

63. Cf. Polk, *Prophetic Persona,* 162.
64. Cf. Carroll, *Jeremiah,* 403.

painful situations often shape the practice of prayer. Prayer is an exercise in dialogue with the deity that holds simultaneously great hope and immeasurable risks.

JOB

J. Hempel has described Job's dramatic encounter with God as a "personal struggle for the last truth about God."[65] In the present discussion I intend to show that Job's struggle to discover the "last truth" about God involves him—in a radical way—in the practice of prayer. This book's tracking of the truth about God is multi-faceted, and prayer is only one of the themes gathered up in the wake of its efforts. I do not wish to isolate prayer unfairly from the larger complex of issues into which it has been woven, nor to stress disproportionately its contribution to the overall Joban drama. If one follows Westermann's proposals concerning the structure of Job, however, then prayer, specifically lament prayer, does play a crucial role in shaping the entire presentation of the book.

In Westermann's view lament is both the literary genre that describes the Book of Job and the structural form that gives it its final shape.[66] At the level of genre, lament has its origin in the existential experience of suffering. It is not a "construct of thought" about suffering—it is the "living reality" of suffering, the cry of pain that has become an utterance (e.g., "Why must I suffer?"). In this sense it is a reaction to a previous action, a cry in response to hurt. The Book of Job is about "experienced suffering"; it is about the "existential process of lament."[67] At a second level Westermann has shown that this lament process has a structure, a fixed form of articulation, that can be traced throughout the Hebrew Bible. The structure consists typically of three components: the one who laments, God, and others.[68] In situations of distress the cry of pain is directed toward God (as accusation or complaint), toward others (as complaint against an enemy), and toward self (as self-lament).

---

65. J. Hempel, "The Contents of the Literature," *Record and Revelation,* ed. H. W. Robinson (Oxford: Clarendon, 1938), 73. From a different perspective, but using the same imagery, J. Miles suggests that the Book of Job returns to a forgotten truth about God, namely, "that Good is not always victorious and that God and the harshness of nature, though they may not be One, are not inseparable" ("Gagging on Job, or the Comedy of Religious Exhaustion," *Semeia* 7 [1977], 110).

66. Westermann, *Structure of Job,* 1–15.

67. Ibid., 3.

68. Westermann, *Praise and Lament,* 169; cf. 267–68; *Elements,* 170.

Precisely these components are brought together in the Book of Job to give it the form of a "dramatized lament."[69]

The drama begins with Job's lament, both self-directed and God-directed (chap. 3), then moves to a lengthy dialogue section (chaps. 4-27), before returning to Job's lament, once again against both self and God (chaps. 29-31). Within the dialogue section the friends respond to Job's suffering with consolation, yet their address quickly assumes the form of altercation and disputation. On his part Job responds with lament, against the friends but also against God, who throughout these dialogues remains the silent third partner in the conversation. When the dialogue ends Job returns to lament. Westermann stresses that this structure confirms that the dialogue stands *within* the lament: "The lament is there both before and after the dialogue with the friends; it has both the first and last word."[70] Out of this futile dialogue with the friends a new dialogue emerges as Job turns from the friends to summon God directly, assuming the position of both a suppliant and an initiator of a legal case against the deity (31:35-37).[71] God's response to Job (chaps. 38-41) is, like the friends' response to Job, in the form of disputation. But it is also an answer to Job's lament. Thus from beginning to end the structure of the book reinforces the linkage to the genre of lament, here dramatized in the roles of the three participating characters—Job, the friends, and God.

Given the controlling influence of lament in Job, which I think Westermann has persuasively demonstrated, one could look to nearly any of his many addresses to God for examples of prayers that place him in the company of Jeremiah. For my purposes here I take a slightly different approach than I have adopted in previous chapters. Before examining samples of Job's prayers, I first look at what the friends have to say about prayer in general and about how Job should pray in particular.

As D. Patrick has noted, Job's three friends never address God.[72] They come to talk *about* God; in their theologizing and pontificating, they occasionally discuss the *topic* of prayer. Such occasions afford virtually the only witness in the Hebrew Bible to a reflection on prayer.[73] It will come as no surprise that Job does not

69. Westermann, *Structure of Job,* 11-12.

70. Ibid., 4.

71. Ibid., 39.

72. D. Patrick, "Job's Address to God," *ZAW* 91 (1979): 269.

73. Cf. E. Gerstenberger, *Der bittende Mensch* (Neukirchen: Neukirchener Verlag, 1980), 157.

follow their recommendations in this regard. His way of praying is diametrically opposed to what they would deem appropriate and permissible. To the extent that one is to understand the friends as upholding traditional beliefs and practices, Job is portrayed as a rebel. This conflict between tradition and rebellion, between accepted boundaries in the relationship with God and disregard for these boundaries, invites one to understand Job as pushing against traditional ways of praying and redefining them.

How should Job respond to his suffering? On this question the friends are agreed. Eliphaz is the first to suggest the proper response; the others quick to confirm his advice: "As for me, I would seek *[drš]* God, and to God I would commit my cause" (5:8; cf. 8:5; 11:13; 22:23; 33:26). On this point Job and the friends are in accord. In the midst of misfortune one is to turn to God. But what should Job say when he turns to address God? From the friends' perspective Job's response is also carefully prescribed.

To secure God's intervention the righteous person must fulfill two essential conditions.[74] First, the address to God must constitute a return to God, that is, a turning back to God and away from a course of conduct that has opposed God's intentions:

> *If* you will seek God and make supplication to the Almighty. . . . (8:5, NRSV)

> *If* you set your heart and stretch out your hands to him. . . . (11:13)

> *If* you return to the Almighty. . . . (22:23a)

Second, this turning back to God must be accompanied by a confession and renunciation of sin:

> *if* you are pure and upright,
>   surely then he will rouse himself for you. (8:6, NRSV)

> *If* iniquity is in your hand, put it far away
>   and do not let wickedness reside in your tents.
> Surely then you will lift up your face without blemish. (11:14-15, NRSV)

> *if* you remove unrighteousness from your tents . . .
> then you will delight yourself in the Almighty,
>   and lift up your face to God.
> You will pray to him and he will hear you. . . . (22:23b, 26-27, NRSV)

The prescribed course of action that the friends urge on Job has

---

74. Cf. Westermann, *Structure of Job,* 91.

the weight of tradition behind it.[75] It is a standard and accepted response to suffering promoted not just in the Hebrew Bible but also apparently widely in the ancient Near East.[76] Such a view promotes prayer as a first-level response of the faithful sufferer. Especially for the friends of Job, such prayer is characterized by contrition and humility. Penitence, not protest, secures the "lifting of the head"; God will hear confession of sin, not accusations and charges. For these friends and for the theological perspective they represent, anything less than submission before the unassailable God is "babble" and "mockery" (11:3), serving to nullify consideration before God (15:4) and to condemn the one from whose mouth it escapes (15:6).

Job disagrees vehemently. First he insists resolutely on his innocence (e.g., 6:28-30; 9:21; 10:7; 16:17; 23:10, 12; 27:2-6). He is not guilty, hence there is no warrant for contrition or confession on his part. In this assessment of his character Job is only reiterating an evaluation that God has already confirmed (cf. 1:8; 2:3). From the beginning of the drama Job's blamelessness, his righteousness, and his faithfulness are upheld; indeed, it is his innocence that has caused him to be singled out for attack.

Further, Job argues against the friends' linkage of righteousness with prosperity and wickedness with punishment. His own suffering is proof enough of the fallacy in the first premise. As for the presumption that wickedness does not pay, Job suggests one needs only to observe the reality of human experience. "How often is the lamp of the wicked put out?" (21:17), Job asks. More often than not calamity bypasses the wicked altogether. They prosper in their un-

---

75. So similar are the conditions stipulated by the friends and so uniform are they in both content and form (e.g., "if you . . . then") that Westermann proposes they must reflect a specific cultic ritual. He identifies this rite with the seeking of an "assurance of blessing." Judging from the speeches of the friends, as well as from other texts that appear to address the same motifs (e.g., Psalms 91; 128; Deut 28:3-6; 30:5-9), Westermann describes this ritual as typically including the following elements: (1) a turning toward God with (2) an act of renunciation, followed by (3) a "lifting up of the head" (Job 11:15; 22:26), and (4) a recitation by friends of an assurance of blessing (ibid., 90–91).

76. For example, L. Perdue finds in both Sumerian and Akkadian texts evidence for what he describes as a "lament-thanksgiving ritual" that encourages those in the throes of misfortune to offer a prayer of penitence in the hopes of prompting the deity's favorable intervention. Thus prayers of contrition are promoted as the cultic channel for securing alleviation and blessing. Although he does not elaborate on how or if such a ritual may have passed over into Hebraic worship, Perdue suggests that Job's friends advocate a similar practice, perhaps most clearly discernible in Elihu's counsel in Job 33:18-33 (L. Perdue, *Wisdom and Cult* [Missoula, Mont.: Scholars Press, 1977], 96–119, 172).

godliness with such self-assurance (21:7-13) that any relationship to God based on the promise of reward is completely negated. They can and do secure prosperity on their own terms, and in the process dismiss God without a thought.

> They say to God, "Leave us alone!
>   We do not desire to know your ways.
> What is the Almighty, that we should serve him?
> And what profit do we get if we pray to him?" (21:14-15, NRSV)

In the end they die not only rich but satisfied (21:23-26), leaving the questions of justice for other poor fools to fret over. This is the way life is in reality, Job argues. The friends have whitewashed the painful truth of it all in order to protect God from the charge of presiding over a blatant miscarriage of justice (13:4, 7-8).

Job will pray, but he will not submit. As previously noted, his speech is dominated throughout by lament. His laments are directed toward the friends, who, in confronting him with criticism rather than consolation, have become his enemies (cf. 6:13-20; 19:13-19).[77] His laments also express his own sense of helplessness in the face of unbearable suffering (e.g., 3:11-26; 7:3-10; 30:27-31), a fate he fears is the common lot of frail humanity to share (cf. 7:1-2; 14:1-5).[78]

But it is in his laments to God that Job most brazenly defies the practice of prayer advocated by his friends. He does not accept his misery passively; he questions God about its rightness. He does not confess his sin and return contritely to God; he attacks God with accusations that shake the very foundations of faith commitments. In doing so he takes his life in his hands, as he himself seems to recognize (cf. 7:11; 10:1; 13:14-15); but without taking such a risk life itself seems to have little meaning and not much advantage over death (cf. 3:11-13, 21-22; 6:8-10; 7:15).[79] Job's horrendous suffering has pushed him beyond the limits of silent acceptance.

In this move his decision is echoed in Dostoyevsky's Ivan, who, in a similar effort to integrate untold misery and devotion to God, concludes,

> I refuse to accept this world of God's. . . . Please understand, it is not

---

77. Cf. Westermann, *Structure of Job,* 43–46.

78. Ibid., 46–50.

79. Westermann notes that Job's "wish to die" constitutes a major petition in his laments (*Structure of Job,* 67).

God that I do not accept, but the world he has created. I do not accept God's world and I refuse to accept it.[80]

A few scenes later Ivan takes his resolution a step further. If extreme and inexplicable misfortune is the cost of accommodating oneself to divine-human relationship, then Ivan concludes the price for admission to such an arrangement is too high.

> We cannot afford to pay so much for admission. And therefore I hasten to return my ticket of admission. . . . It's not God that I do not accept, Alyosha. I merely most respectfully return him the ticket.[81]

That Job at times is driven by despair to contemplate "returning his ticket" for life in relation to God is a measure of his pain. Yet he has another option to the either/or alternatives (either submit or be condemned) promoted by the friends. He opts instead to challenge the God whom he holds responsible and to seek a reversal of an unjust verdict.

His challenge to God takes the dual form of both interrogation and accusation.[82] As interrogator Job insists that such is the pain of life in relation to God that sometimes one can neither ignore nor silence questions. On such occasions they constitute an inevitable and legitimate part of the discourse that must pass from the sufferer to God. Job's questions begin almost immediately in the opening lament of chapter 3. They are initially shaped rather generally as mournful reflections on the futility of life itself:

> Why *[lāmmāh]* did I not die at birth,
> come forth from the womb and expire? (3:11; cf. v. 20, NRSV)

The questions gradually intensify and sharpen as Job fixes his sights more and more on God, whom he holds ultimately responsible for life's misery. Why should God set upon him with the same overpowering might that God has displayed in subduing the primordial creatures of the sea?

> Am I the Sea, or the Dragon,
> that you set a guard over me? (7:12, NRSV)

Turning praise for the Creator into lament against the relentless

---

80. F. Dostoyevsky, *The Brothers Karamozov* (Harmondsworth: Penguin, 1958), 275.
81. Ibid., 287.
82. Westermann, *Structure of Job,* 51; cf. idem, *Praise and Lament,* 176–77.

divine assailant, Job asks why humanity's favored status in the created order should become the opportunity for endless testing.

> What are human beings, that you make so much of them,
>   that you set your mind on them,
> visit them every morning,
>   test them every moment? (7:17-18; cf. Ps 8:4, NRSV)

Why should the relationship with God deteriorate into a contest of raw strength? Why should the quest for justice become a display of power that only God can control?

> If it is a contest of strength, he is the strong one!
> If it is a matter of justice, who can summon him? (9:19, NRSV)

Why should God fashion humanity according to divine intentions, only to scoff at the results and destroy the product?

> Does it seem good to you to oppress,
>   to despise the work of your hands. . . .
> Remember that you fashioned me like clay;
>   and will you turn me to dust again? (10:3, 9, NRSV)

The original question about the meaninglessness of life slowly and painfully reformulates itself, but it is no longer so general. Now it is put directly to the Creator of life:

> Why *[lāmmāh]* did you bring me forth from the womb? (10:18, NRSV)

Such is the route by which Job comes to his most pointed question, which summarizes the entire drama that the Book of Job is concerned to present.

> Why *[lāmmāh]* do you hide your face,
>   and count me as your enemy *['ôyēb]?* (13:24, NRSV)

Here Job's questioning most daringly spills over into accusation. On the one hand he charges God (in the strongest language the Hebrew Bible knows) with being absent from him at his moment of greatest need.[83] He moves forward and backward, first in one direction then in another, but God is nowhere to be found (cf. 23:8-9). He cries out for relief, but God does not answer (cf. 19:7; 30:20). God passes by, leaving him with only a dim perception of a presence come and gone (cf. 9:11). All Job can do is grope about in the

---

83. Cf. S. E. Balentine, *The Hidden God: The Hiding of the Face of God in the Old Testament* (Oxford: Oxford Univ. Press, 1983), 1–21.

darkness that trails in the wake of a vanished God (cf. 19:8), and call out in lament, "Oh, that I knew where I might find him, that I might come even to his dwelling!" (23:3, NRSV). On the other hand God's presence for Job is all too real, for this absent, silent God has marked him for an "enemy" (*'ōyēb;* cf. 19:11: *ṣar,* "adversary"). With language that has no equal in Hebraic prayer, Job lashes out at God for crushing him with hurricane-force winds (9:17; cf. 38:1 and 40:6, which describe the divine speeches with similar imagery), stalking him like a lion (10:16), tearing him limb from limb like a warrior (16:12-14), hemming him in so that he cannot escape (19:8). In the end even Job's hope is ripped from him like a tree torn from its roots (19:10). Such imagery is sustained through each of the three cycles of the dialogue section (chaps. 4–14, 15–22, 22–28). Job's final speech (chaps. 29–31) portrays him as still assailing a savage God who will not hear (30:19-23).

It is a measure of Job's relentless pursuit of dialogue with God that in the midst of his most stringent attacks he nevertheless maintains his trust in God's ultimate attention to his plight (cf. 16:19; 19:25-27).[84] The most urgent of all his petitions is the plea for encounter with God.[85] Three key texts sustain this concern and press the argument that God must respond to it. First, in 13:22-23 Job insists that whatever his guilt, God must make it known to him. Either God must speak and Job will answer, or Job must initiate the discussion and God must respond. In either event there must be discourse, mutual involvement of both parties to the dilemma, not merely an opponent and a victim. In the second text, 23:3-12, Job insists on (a) presenting his case (v. 4: *mišpāṭ*) before God and receiving God's answer (v. 5); and (b) believing that God is indeed open to such discussion, even with inferior plaintiffs, and will not quash the process by reverting to a self-serving display of power (v. 6).

The legal imagery that lies behind both 13:22-23 and 23:3-12 becomes more explicit in a third text, 31:35-37. These verses, as well as the larger context of chapter 31 for which they provide the climax, suggest that Job has increasingly come to view the court of law as the primary context for securing his vindication.[86] With a

84. Cf. Westermann, *Structure of Job,* 45–46.

85. Ibid., 69.

86. On Job 31 see G. Fohrer, "The Righteous Man in Job 31," *Essays in Old Testament Ethics,* ed. J. Crenshaw and J. T. Willis (New York: KTAV, 1979), 3–21; N. Habel, *Job* (OTL; Philadelphia: Westminster, 1985), 427–40; R. Gordis,

series of oaths (vv. 5-34, 38-40) Job swears his innocence. Following this declaration he asks for a "hearing" (v. 35; *šōmēaʿ*, lit. "one hearing," i.e., perhaps one to conduct a hearing), demanding not only an impartial judge but also an official statement (*sēper;* NRSV, REB: "indictment") testifying to the charges of his adversary. In verse 35 Job clearly identifies this adversary as God: "Let Shaddai [NRSV, REB: 'the Almighty'] answer me." Given the nature of his oaths, Job's petition demands that either he be proven guilty or the charges be dropped and he be acquitted.

Westermann has noted that in 31:35-37 Job stands before God as both a suppliant and an initiator of a legal proceeding. "That is the impossible but nonetheless actual 'standpoint' of Job; he stands there and awaits God's answer."[87] Here Job joins Jeremiah in the bold move of calling God to court. One can hardly overstate the tension of such a petition. Job summons God to court to answer Job's questions. Job himself frames the questions and thus as plaintiff seeks to define the perspective from which the answers must come. In so doing Job insists on fulfilling his role as an equal, at least potentially equal, dialogue partner with God. He would know what God will answer him; if God does not respond as Job has insisted, then from Job's perspective of the legal liabilities, God will be judged accordingly. It is a risky move on Job's part, defining justice as the primary quality that informs the relationship with God.[88] Job insists on dialogue with the Almighty, without which he deems the relationship neither just nor acceptable. But come what may, Job has pressed his case before the ultimate tribunal. He has had his say. With his final speech in chaps. 29–31 the case for the plaintiff rests. Now the drama of the book turns toward the defendant, God. Will God respond to Job? Perhaps more crucial is the question, *Can* God respond to Job, as Job has demanded, and still remain God?

After three rounds of dialogue plus a lengthy speech by Elihu (chaps. 32–37), the laments of Job remain unresolved. In his final address Job challenges God to a "verbal duel."[89] Given this challenge God must respond, for continued silence would decide the

---

The Book of Job: Commentary, New Translation, and Special Studies (New York: Jewish Theological Seminary of America, 1978), 344–56, 542–46.

87. Westermann, *Structure of Job,* 39.

88. Cf. W. Lee Humphreys, *The Tragic Vision and the Hebrew Tradition* (OBT; Philadelphia: Fortress, 1985), 106–11. On the rhetorical and theological importance of the legal metaphor in Job, see Habel, *Job,* 54–57.

89. Cf. L. A. Schökel, "Toward a Dramatic Reading of the Book of Job," *Semeia* 7 (1977), 50.

case in Job's favor. The friends are certain that God will respond and that the response will vindicate God and impose the ultimate penalty on Job for his brazen attacks. In their view, such a response will be justice. Bildad is the first to raise the question that for him can only be rhetorical:

> Does God pervert justice?
> Or does the Almighty pervert the right? (8:3, NRSV)

Throughout each of their disputes with Job the friends' confidence in the ultimate resolution of this question remains unshaken. Elihu provides a final summation that speaks for them all:

> far be it from God that he should do wickedness,
>   and from the Almighty that he should do wrong.
> For according to their deeds he will repay them,
>   and according to their ways he will make it befall them.
> Of a truth, God will not do wickedly,
>   and the Almighty will not pervert justice. (34:10-12, NRSV)

In the friends' view God's justice is beyond question; those who dare to challenge it will find that they have taken their place with the rebels whose future is not in doubt. Job has taken just such a position. He has demanded a lawsuit with God, staking his life on the belief that God cannot justly deny his petition. Thus the stage is set for God's response, a response that is meant to decide for the friends' or for Job's view of how God stands in relation to those who would encounter the Almighty Judge of the world.

God's response comes in two lengthy speeches (38:1—40:2; 40:6—41:34 [MT 40:6—41:26]), each of which elicits a brief response from Job (40:3-5; 42:1-6). Although both divine speeches are introduced as God's "answer" ('ānāh: 38:1; 40:6) to Job, it is clear from both their length and their content that they function more as disputation. In the end they do little to answer Job's concerns.[90] In these speeches God comes asking the questions, not answering them. The overall effect is to silence Job.

In the first speech God's opening salvo provides the framework for all that follows:

> Who is this that darkens counsel by words without knowledge?
> Gird up your loins like a man,
>   I will question you, and you shall declare to me (38:2-3, NRSV).

90. For a review of the variety of interpretations proposed for the divine speeches, see D. Gowan, "God's Answer to Job: How Is It an Answer?" *HBT* 8 (1986): 85–102.

The questions that follow are cast in the form of a disputation speech; that is, they are questions designed to dispute the challenges presented by Job.[91] Thus the answer to a question like "Who hemmed in the sea behind doors?" (38:8) is not "Who knows?" but "You, LORD, you alone." The answer to questions like "Can you send forth lightnings?" (38:35, NRSV), "Can you number the clouds?" (38:37), "Can you hunt prey for the lion?" (38:39) is not intended to be "Yes, I can," but rather "No, of course, only you can, LORD." Such questions do not seek information, as if the answer were in doubt; instead they challenge the one to whom they are directed to acknowledge and to accept a given truth. By these many questions God takes Job on a journey through the cosmos that is meant to be an enlightening and humbling experience. At the journey's end, God puts to Job a further question.

> Shall a faultfinder contend with the Almighty?
> The one who argues with God must answer. (40:2)

Having failed to answer even one of God's questions, does Job dare now to speak? God has become for him "the friends writ large,"[92] overwhelming him with a force of interrogation designed to insure submission. This is precisely the kind of God Job had feared he would meet. Such a God one cannot answer, not "once in a thousand times" (cf. 9:3). As Crenshaw has observed, "In the face of such a blustering deity, who would not be speechless?"[93]

Job's initial reply is indeed simple: "Behold, I am small *[qallōtî]*" (40:4). Before this all-powerful Creator of the cosmos Job acknowledges that he is of trifling account. Thus he claps his hand to his mouth and concedes his position (40:4-5). He will speak no further. Against such a formidable opponent he cannot continue to press his case. Although Job is silenced, he is not repentant. He does not confess "I am wrong" or "I have sinned," as the friends would have him do—only "I am small." God is the greater force; this point is indisputable. But Job has never disputed God's power. It is God's

---

91. Such questions may be understood, with J. Crenshaw, to be "impossible questions," i.e., questions designed to call attention to the limitations of human intellectual capacities ("Impossible Questions, Sayings, and Tasks," *Semeia* 17 [1980], 19–34). For a different view, see J. Janzen, who suggests these questions are to be taken ironically, as presenting Job with genuine existential questions about who he will be in relation to God (*Job* [Interpretation; Atlanta: John Knox, 1985], 19–22, 225–59).

92. D. Robertson, "The Book of Job: A Literary Study," *Soundings* 56 (1973): 467; cf. J. G. Williams, "'You Have Not spoken Truth of Me.' Mystery and Irony in Job," *ZAW* 83 (1971): 247.

93. J. Crenshaw, *Old Testament Wisdom: An Introduction* (Atlanta: John Knox, 1981), 111.

justice that Job has challenged. To this challenge God has thus far not responded, but the second divine speech now turns to it. The second speech is equally disputational in its intent. Once again God sets the questions and summons Job to respond (40:7). Here the question of divine justice is finally broached, yet from a divine perspective that once again leaves Job speechless.

> Will you really annul my justice *[mišpāṭî]?*
> Will you condemn me *[taršî'ēnî]* in order
> that you may be innocent *[tiṣdāq]?* (40:8)

Job is challenged to take the principles of justice that he argues must apply in his relationship with God and administer them in a cosmic context. If he is to be successful Job must (1) unleash his anger in appropriate measure (v. 11) and (2) bring down the proud and the wicked wherever he finds them (vv. 11-12). If he can do this then he will exhibit the capacities of God, and God will recognize him for the magnificence and the glory (cf. v. 10) that his victory requires (v. 14). But Job falls silent once again. God then proceeds without interruption to describe the contours of divine justice, here specifically identified with the subjugation of Behemoth (40:15-24) and Leviathan (41:1-34). On this cosmic scale of justice where the forces of primordial chaos threaten the order of creation, Job is no match for the controlling "arm of God" (cf. 40:9).

Job's final response (42:1-6) represents both a concession and a reversal. First Job concedes God's ability to "do all things" (42:2). God's interrogation has persuaded him that he has chanced to speak of matters far beyond his comprehension and knowledge (42:3).

As for his reversal, Job's response in verse 6 has occasioned a range of interpretations. The more traditional understanding, which draws support from a translation such as NRSV—"therefore I despise myself, and repent in dust and ashes"—finds here at last the confession of sin that thus far Job's lament has lacked. Yet such a reading flies in the face of everything that has transpired to this point in the Joban drama, including God's own assessment of this sufferer as an exemplary model of piety: in God's words, "there is no one like him on the earth, a blameless and upright man who fears God and turns away from evil" (1:8; 2:3, NRSV).

The syntax of verse 6 in Hebrew permits, if not requires, a different interpretation. The crucial verb is *mā'as,* "reject" or "despise," which is never used in the Hebrew Bible in a genuinely reflexive sense (e.g., "despise myself"). Following this lead a number of commentators have sought the required, but here lacking, object of the verb.

Two proposals merit serious consideration. On the one hand *God* may be the object of Job's rejection. Thus J. Curtis has suggested translating verse 6: "Therefore I feel loathing contempt and revulsion [toward you, O God]."[94] Less radical perhaps is N. Habel's suggestion that the implied object should be understood as *"case" (mišpāṭ)*.[95] The clue for such a suggestion may occur in 31:13 (NRSV), where the same verb is used for Job's assertion that he has not "rejected the cause *[mišpaṭ]"* of his servants. On this analogy Habel proposes that verse 6 be translated, "Therefore I retract [my case against Yahweh]," a translation that may then be expanded by the following clause, "and repent of [i.e., change my mind about] dust and ashes." Such a view understands Job's reversal in terms of a decision to give up his role as a litigant in the case against God.[96]

Both of these interpretations constitute valid and substantial arguments against understanding Job's final response in terms of simple repentance. Job clearly concedes God's sovereignty and power (40:3; 42:3), and decides to press his case no further. But Job makes no clear admission of guilt or wrongdoing, no capitulation to the friends' assessment of his sin. Instead, to the very end, Job is portrayed as standing his ground, insisting on his integrity as one who, perhaps naively, would enter into discussion with the Almighty.

But where does that portrayal leave the readers and the extended audience of this drama in understanding the weighty issues that have been presented here? The friends have steadfastly insisted that a doctrine of divine retribution, which is beyond question, requires the sufferer to pray in confession and petition for forgiveness. Prayer is a means of submitting oneself to the inestimable sovereignty of God, thereby securing one's reward or restoring one's good fortune. Job has insisted that for the innocent sufferer prayer is no occasion for submission. It is rather the one means of challenging doctrines that do not fairly address the reality of the human condition, and calling into radical review the assumptions about God that such doctrines are intent to promote and to protect. Just at the point where these contrasting arguments come to a standoff, God

---

94. J. Curtis, "On Job's Response to Yahweh," *JBL* 98 (1979): 505.

95. Habel, *Job,* 576, 582–83.

96. Cf. Patrick, "Job's Address to God," 280–81; idem, "The Translation of Job XLII, 6," *VT* 26 (1976): 369–71. See further Janzen, who interprets Job's decision to give up his case against God as a confession of his agreement with God (*Job,* 248–59).

speaks. As a result Job is silenced, submitting to divine power, yet unrepentant. How is one to judge the final outcome?

On the one hand, is one to understand Job's submission as the friends' vindication? Cannot one pursue prayers for justice, alleviation of pain, understanding of the mysteries of God's dealings with humanity? Must one simply bow before the sovereignty of God, even if it means being satisfied with something even more dark and threatening than physical pain?[97] Such a view finds in the theophany of Job 38–41 God's response to the problem of theodicy. As one advocate of this understanding, von Rad sees the purpose of the divine speeches as being to glorify God's justice: "Of course this justice of God cannot be comprehended by man; it can only be adored."[98] The only fitting response for Job, then, is to praise God. This is also the argument of the friends.

On the other hand, is one to understand Job's stubborn refusal to own any responsibility for his suffering as a vindication of his charge that when it comes to the question of divine justice, God cannot be expected to answer (cf. 9:16, 19)? Justice is determined solely by divine prerogative, which will be meted out in terms of power if need be. In this world God is both judge and jury, and there is no umpire to protect against foul play (cf. 9:33). In the divine speeches God does not deign to answer one of Job's questions about the cause of all that has befallen him. But if the divine speeches are interpreted as some form of vindication of Job's position, they scarcely promise any consolation. They leave Job, and any who dare follow his lead, facing a God whose contradictions in character threaten to dissolve relationship into meaninglessness. God is both present and hidden, impartial and capricious, sustainer of the world's order and architect of its chaos. As M. Tsevat puts it: "He who speaks to man in the Book of Job is neither a just nor an unjust god but God."[99]

Perhaps the final verdict on the Joban drama must be left in suspension. Perhaps it must be that those who ask "Why?" seldom receive satisfactory answers. So it is rather routinely in the Hebrew Bible, especially when one dares address such questions to God.[100]

---

97. Cf. the remarks of G. K. Chesterton in *The Dimensions of Job: A Study and Selected Readings,* ed. N. Glatzer (New York: Schocken, 1969), 234.

98. Von Rad, *Theology* 1.417.

99. M. Tsevat, "The Meaning of the Book of Job," *HUCA* 37 (1965): 105; repr. in *Studies in Ancient Israelite Wisdom,* ed. J. Crenshaw (New York: KTAV, 1976), 373.

100. Cf. Williams, "You Have Not Spoken Truth of Me," 248–50.

Yet in terms of the Book of Job's contribution to these issues, one further episode must claim some attention.

In the prose epilogue (42:7-14) that concludes the book, God is recorded as speaking one further word, directed to Eliphaz:

> My wrath is kindled against you and against your two friends; for you have not spoken truth *[nĕkônāh]* of me as my servant Job has. Now therefore take seven bulls and seven rams, and go to my servant Job, and offer up for yourselves a burnt offering; and my servant Job will pray for you *[yitpallēl 'ălêkem],* for I will accept his prayer [lit. "lift up the face"] not to do folly with you;[101] for you have not spoken truth *[nĕkônāh]* of me as my servant Job has." So Eliphaz the Temanite and Bildad the Shuhite and Zophar the Naamathite went and did what the LORD had told them; and the LORD accepted Job's prayer [lit. "lifted up the face"]. (42:7-9)

Even if one allows for the obvious redactional nature of these verses, their affirmation of Job as one who has spoken truth and one whose prayers God will accept constitutes a formidable finalizing of the portrait of Job the pray-er. One could argue that the movement of the entire book has been toward this end.[102] Job has requested justice; he has been granted communion (cf. 42:5 [NRSV]: "now my eye sees you").

Only here does the Hebraic vision give such an unqualified account of intimate, face-to-face encounter with God. It is important to recognize that such an experience in the presence of God takes place in the struggle with human pain and suffering.[103] This one who dares to speak what he feels in the presence of God, who risks pressing the outermost boundaries of what tradition labels as the acceptable response to God, is now invited into intimacy with the Almighty. It is this one, the epilogue now confirms, who can expect a hearing from God, not the friends, who know only how to parrot answers without understanding the questions. Job has complained his way to silence, but now his silence itself gives way to further speech. On the other side of Job's silence, his words are transformed and transforming. His friends have not spoken truth about God; Job, by God's own assessment, has spoken the truth. In the end his prayers, not theirs, penetrate the heavens.

---

101. For this translation of *'ăśôt 'immākem nĕbālāh,* "not to do folly with you," see Janzen, *Job,* 263–67.

102. Cf. Williams, "You Have Not Spoken Truth of Me," 250; idem, "Comedy, Irony, Intercession: A Few Notes in Response," *Semeia* 7 (1977), 138–41.

103. Cf. Humphreys, *Tragic Vision,* 116.

HABAKKUK

The historical circumstances underlying Habakkuk are located generally in the second half of the seventh century B.C.E., in the tumultuous period surrounding Judah's treatment at the hands of first the Assyrians and then the Babylonians. In its present form the book divides into three major structural units: (1) 1:1—2:4, an extended dialogue between Habakkuk and God consisting of two prayers of lament (1:2-4, 12-17), each followed by divine response (1:5-11; 2:2-4); (2) 2:5-20, five woe oracles of judgment; and (3) 3:1-19, a concluding psalm of thanksgiving. At this level the book reflects a basic thematic movement from lament to thanksgiving, hence a structural "incline" that is typical of the lament genre.[104] Within this framework the movement toward resolution of the crisis signaled by lament is represented as having been achieved, at least in part, by the prophet's dialogue with God.[105] In this sense Habakkuk's prayers place him in the company of Jeremiah and Job as an additional witness to the practice of lament.

The prayer in 1:2-4 follows the typical form of a lament, although it has no petition. Instead, following an opening invocation, two questions addressed to God dominate the prayer: verse 2, "How long?" *('ad 'ānāh);* verse 3, "Why?" *(lāmmāh).* These questions introduce descriptions of distress:

> How long, LORD, shall I cry out,
>   and you will not hear?
> Cry to you "Violence!"
>   and you will not deliver?
> Why do you make me see trouble
>   and look upon sorrow?
> Destruction and violence are before me;
>   and strife and contention go on and on.

Within this lament is the protest that (1) God is both responsible for

---

104. Cf. B. Childs, *Introduction to the Old Testament as Scripture* (Philadelphia: Fortress, 1979), 447–56.

105. The book's final form is obviously the product of multiple redactional efforts carried out over an extended period of time. On redaction history and the history of the critical discussion of Habakkuk, see esp. P. Jöcken, *Das Buch Habakuk: Darstellung der Geschichte seiner kritischen Erforschung mit einer eigenen Beurteilung* (Bonn: Hanstein, 1977). It is likely, however, that the dialogic structure of lament-response to which I have pointed remains intact at the earliest level of the book's history, specifically in the juxtaposing of 1:2-4, 12ff. with 2:1-4. See further E. Otto, "Die Theologie des Buches Habakuk," *VT* 35 (1985), 277–79, 283.

("*you* make me see"; "*you* cause me to look on") and unresponsive
to the present misery ("*you* will not hear"; "*you* will not deliver");
(2) already the crisis has gone on too long ("How long?"); and (3) the
situation is inexplicable to the pray-er ("Why?"). The precise nature
of the address remains to this point obscured by the general references to trouble and sorrow, violence and destruction, and strife
and contention. Verse 4 sharpens the focus by alluding to the suffering of the righteous at the hands of the wicked, linking this
suffering specifically with the complaint that such oppression represents a perversion of justice: "justice *[mišpāṭ]* never goes forth . . .
justice *[mišpāṭ]* goes forth perverted."
   To this quite general complaint about innocent suffering,[106] the
first clause of verse 4 adds an important new element.

   Therefore torah is numbed [weak] *[tāpûg]*.

The verb here, *pwg,* is rare in the Hebrew Bible, but its meaning is
consistent: "grow numb, weak, helpless." It conveys the idea of
being unable to function. The key point in the occurrence of the
verb in verse 4 is that its form is intransitive, not transitive. The
suggestion is that torah is ineffective—"paralysed," as M. D. Johnson has proposed,[107] —and that this paralysis has resulted not from
its mishandling or abuse by others but from an inherent failure or
weakness in the torah itself. Habakkuk's complaint then is that
violence and suffering abound, justice is perverted, the torah with
its promises of reward for faithfulness is a failure, and God, who is
both the origin of torah and its defender, is silent. Why? and for how
long?
   The present arrangement of the book positions 1:5-11 as a divine
reply to Habakkuk's lament. These verses announce the coming of

106. The identity of the "wicked" who "surround" and "swallow up" the
righteous (1:4; cf. v. 13) continues to elicit debate. A wide range of candidates has
been proposed, in the main identified either with internal opposition to the
prophet, e.g., from the Jerusalem aristocracy, or with various foreign aggressors,
the two most probable opponents usually identified as the Assyrians and the
Babylonians. In view of the text's long development and the fact that its intent has
been shaped by various hands in accordance with changing circumstances, it is
difficult to decide with full confidence for any particular historical referent. For a
survey of the various options, see Childs, *Introduction,* 448–50; A. Weiser, *The
Old Testament: Its Formation and Development* (New York: Association, 1961),
260–62; O. Eissfeldt, *The Old Testament: An Introduction* (New York: Harper and
Row, 1965), 417–20.
107. M. D. Johnson, "The Paralysis of Torah in Habakkuk I 4," *VT* 35 (1985):
259–60; cf. J. Janzen, "Eschatological Symbol and Existence in Habakkuk," *CBQ*
44 (1982): 396–97.

the Chaldeans who are to serve as God's instrument for ending the oppression about which Habakkuk has complained, thus rectifying the situation of injustice. Yet on close inspection these verses hardly describe the Chaldean solution in positive terms.[108] The Chaldeans are a "fierce and impetuous nation" (v. 6, NRSV), "dreadful and terrible" (v. 7). They are "swifter than leopards, more menacing than wolves at dusk," and they come "to devour" (v. 8, NRSV) and wreak "violence" (v. 9, NRSV: *ḥāmās;* cf. 1:2-3). The justice *(mišpāṭ)* they offer is their own, not God's (v. 7), for power is their god (v. 11).

This portrait presents difficulties for interpreting the Chaldeans' arrival as a positive response to Habakkuk's pleas.[109] Indeed, in their present position these verses heighten Habakkuk's lament rather than resolve it.[110] He has complained about violence and injustice only to be told that the violence will increase. The justice that is requested will be meted out by terror mongers who laugh at and mock those whom they seize and destroy. Given this scenario, the opening words of God's announcement—"Look . . . and see; wonder and be astounded; for I am doing a work . . . that you would not believe" (v. 5)—elicit a response seemingly opposite to that which God intended.

The response that does follow is a second lament (1:12-17), which continues the initial complaint. If God's response to the earlier lament is intended as an answer or a rebuttal to Habakkuk's charges, it has not yet secured his submission. Again Habakkuk addresses God, here invoked as "my Holy One" and "O Rock" (v. 12). His opening words consist of a rhetorical question accompanied by six successive declarations that in any other context might serve as reasons for praise. Here, however, they constitute fundamental assumptions about God's activities and God's character that Habakkuk's subsequent lament will call into question.

> 1. Is it not so that you are from of old?

---

108. Cf. Johnson, "Paralysis of Torah," 261.

109. These difficulties are linked to the redactional process by which this book has achieved its final form. Perhaps these verses are more logically positioned after 2:1-3; see, e.g., K. Budde, "Habakuk," *ZDMG* 84 (1930): 139–47; idem, "Zum Text von Habakuk, Kap. 1 und 2," *OLZ* 34 (1931): 409–11. Perhaps they are secondary, placed here at a subsequent time by a different author for whom the Babylonian intervention seemed at first a more positive experience (e.g., Otto, "Theologie," 289–90). These and other solutions proposed recognize that it is difficult to find here any positive response on God's part to Habakkuk's prayer.

110. Cf. Johnson, "Paralysis of Torah," 263.

2. My Holy One, you shall not die.[111]
3. LORD, you appointed them [i.e., the Babylonians] as justice [mišpāṭ].
4. You established them to execute judgment [lehôkîaḥ].
5. Too pure are your eyes to look on evil.
6. To look on trouble you are not able.

Habakkuk's lament in verse 13 places in doubt these affirmations; once again he returns to the painful question "Why?"

> Why *[lāmmāh]* do you look on treacherous ones
> and keep silent when the wicked swallow up those more righteous than they?

The following verses sharpen the complaint as Habakkuk charges that God has made humanity like the fish of the sea, victims of plunder for the fisherman's nets. They are no more than the objects of his gluttony and self-satisfaction, and upon the fulfilling of his cravings he rejoices in his skills as a self-provider (vv. 14-16). Given the reality of this suffering, Habakkuk can only ask "Why?" "Why do you make me see trouble and look upon sorrow?" (v. 3). "Why do you look on . . . and keep silent?" (v. 13). The question is not only "Why?" but also "How long?" "How long, LORD, shall I cry out, and you will not hear?" (v. 2). How long will the fisherman continue to enjoy his merciless plunder—forever? (cf. v. 17). With the conclusion of this second lament the dialogue with God returns to the point where it began—to the plaintive cries "Why?" and "How long?"[112]

At this juncture the dialogue is suspended momentarily as the text reports that Habakkuk takes his position to await God's response to his complaint. Like Job, Habakkuk has had his say before God and will stake out his ground until the divine word comes. The response does come and, again as in Job, it is specifically introduced as God's answer.

As answer, God's response in 2:2-4 serves immediately to shift the focus of attention away from the implicit charges of divine culpability for suffering to Habakkuk's own responsibility for faithfulness in such a situation. Like Isaiah before him (cf. Isa. 30:8), Habakkuk is to write the answer on tablets, making it suitably clear for public consumption. The answer is that the answer is coming. If

---

111. Reading original MT *tāmût,* rather than the *Tiqqun nāmût,* "we shall not die."

112. Janzen, "Eschatological Symbol," 402–3.

it seems slow, as Habakkuk's "How long?" has charged, this is only because the appointed time for its manifestation has not yet arrived. But it will come; it does not "lie," neither will it be judged "crooked" or "perverted" (cf. 1:4). Meanwhile Habakkuk and those on behalf of whom he has spoken in lament must conduct themselves as the *ṣaddîq,* the righteous, that they have claimed to be (cf. 1:4, 13).[113] As righteous people they are to commit themselves essentially to two activities. They are to "wait" (2:3) for the divine intervention that has been promised, and having received the promise they are to "run" (2:2) in accordance with their assurance of its fulfillment.

This combination of waiting and running is what it means for the righteous to "live." As the oft-quoted text of 2:4 puts it: "the righteous shall live by *its* faithfulness." The crucial word here is *be'ĕmûnātô,* commonly translated (e.g., RSV) "by *his* faithfulness." The suggestion implicit in this traditional rendering is that the righteous are to live faithfully. This sense is clearly part of God's admonition to Habakkuk. But the pronominal suffix for "his" is perhaps better understood as referring to God: the righteous shall live by *God's* faithfulness, or, perhaps more indirectly, by the faithfulness or the reliability of God's promised intervention. It is this latter sense that is suggested in the translation: "by *its* faithfulness."[114] Implicit in this rendering is the idea that faithfulness in the midst of suffering is not self-generated. It is God's loyalty, God's reliability, that summons a simultaneously patient faith and an active, expectant living.

Following a series of five woe oracles against the Chaldeans (2:5-20), the Book of Habakkuk concludes with a "prayer of Habakkuk," which recounts in hymnic form a cultic epiphany (3:1-19). Similarities in form and language between Habakkuk 3 and other epiphany texts (e.g., Deuteronomy 33; Judges 5; Psalm 68) have sustained a widely shared judgment that subsequent redactors appropriated this poetry as a set piece.[115] Even so, the rhetoric of this psalm is well suited to the present context. The psalm speaks of the defeat of the wicked by Yahweh the warrior God, who comes to the

---

113. On the suffering of the righteous in Habakkuk, see A. H. J. Gunneweg, "Habakuk und das Problem des leidenden *ṣaddîq,"* *ZAW* 98 (1986): 400–415.

114. For the argument in support of this translation, see J. Janzen, "Habakkuk 2:4 in the Light of Recent Philological Advances," *HTR* 73 (1980): 53–78, esp. 61.

115. Cf. T. W. Mann, *Divine Presence and Guidance in Israelite Traditions: The Typology of Exaltation* (Baltimore: Johns Hopkins Univ. Press, 1977), 176–77.

defense of the poor and the downcast (cf. vv. 12-14). The one who has been privileged to learn of this coming salvation is described as "waiting quietly" (v. 16) for its ultimate realization.

These and other rhetorical links between the psalm and the rest of the book suggest that 3:1-19 provides the final dramatic resolution of Habakkuk's quest for meaningful existence in the midst of suffering.[116] Habakkuk had asked of God "Why?" and "How long?" To the first question God makes no direct response. But to the second the divine response is "wait" expectantly and "run" confidently with the assurance that ultimate deliverance is certain. Habakkuk 3 portrays the prophet as actualizing this admonition. The whole scenario is now framed within a cultic setting of formalized worship. In this way Habakkuk's actions assume more than merely personal relevance; now they become paradigmatic for the wider congregation. The prophet's "waiting" is filled with remembering, remembering the record of the God who comes with a terrible wrath and a delivering mercy (vv. 3-15). In the midst of his remembering he comes finally to hear the truth in his reflections (v. 16) and to derive new strength from that truth. Such strength makes his feet "like the deer's," ready to run, "to tread upon the heights" (v. 19) that mark the path from experience to expectation.

J. Janzen suggests that Habakkuk is the model of "eschatological existence." His is an "existence in time towards an appointed time."[117] Janzen explains:

> Faithfulness is the moral and spiritual character of such existence, and patience is its exercise. Patience exercises itself in two modes: in action and in passion. The interrelation of these two modes . . . arises from the character of reality as a radically temporal field of power originating in the aboriginal life of God ("I will be who I will be") and in which all are given a share.[118]

I suggest that for Habakkuk and those who stand alongside him in the struggle of eschatological existence, prayers of lament constitute an inevitable and necessary part of the action and passion of faithfulness. Such praying is inevitable because of the mystery of who God is—at times unquestionably present, on other occasions inexplicably aloof. Such praying is also necessary. Without it, waiting for relief would threaten to stagnate and leave one in despair. With-

---

116. Janzen, "Eschatological Symbol," 408–12.
117. Ibid., 412.
118. Ibid.

out it, one's feet could not begin to traverse the path that Habakkuk describes as the way of faith.

PERSPECTIVES ON THEODICY IN THE HEBREW BIBLE

At both the beginning and the ending of Jeremiah's confessions the thunderous question "Why?" erupts with a force that assaults the inequities of life and the God who allows them or tolerates them—or causes them.

> Why does the way of the wicked prosper? (12:1)
> Why did I come forth from the womb? (20:18)

Similar questions propel the complaints of Job and Habakkuk as well as those of their forebears Abraham, Moses, and Joshua.

What functions do such questions serve? For Jeremiah and his costrugglers, what is the importance of prayers that raise these questions with God? For members of the extended community of faith for whom their witness has been preserved? To put the question the other way around, what would the Hebraic tradition of lament and contemporary piety lose if they had no such prayers? How would the life of faith—or life in general—be different without these kinds of questions and complaints? What difference does it make to have a faith that permits or requires this kind of address to God?

In chapter 6 I have suggested that one important gain of practicing such prayer is the maintenance of the divine-human dialogue, which is at all times important for faith and in times of suffering especially crucial. At this juncture of the discussion I return to this observation and press further its theological and sociological implications. But first I must make clear that prayers of lament are by no means the only response to suffering promoted in the Hebrew Bible. Nor does the experience of disruption and dislocation always provoke challenges to God's sovereignty and justice. As I have already had occasion to comment, one may best describe such prayers as a countertradition to other, more dominant responses, a minority wonderment about the embrace of pain that probes and challenges central and widely accepted theological maxims.[119]

To illustrate this last point I have categorized the major perspectives on pain and suffering and the justice of God in the Hebrew Bible. I have grouped these perspectives under three headings, each category representing an interpretation of suffering (or other more

119. Cf. Brueggemann, "Embrace of Pain," 405–14.

generalized situations of unrest) that elicits a specific response from the sufferer and (b) presupposes a particular understanding of the justice (or at least the character) of God. Neither the categories I propose nor the texts I offer as illustrative of them are intended to be comprehensive. Other perspectives could be included: additional texts could be cited. But this outline seems responsibly representative of the major views and hence may serve adequately to facilitate the discussion of prayer's particular contribution to the issue of theodicy as expressed in the Hebrew Bible.

Suffering as . . .	*Response of Sufferer*	*Divine Justice*
1. Justified/ warranted deserved, i.e., just punishment	Acceptance; repentance	God is just

Examples:

 a. Wilderness wandering narratives—Num 11–21
  (e.g., Num 11:1-3; 12:1-16; 20:1-13; 21:4-9)[120]
 b. Deuteronomy/Deuteronomistic History[121]
  (e.g., Deut 28; Judg 2:11-23; cf. Jer 5:18-19; 16:10-13; 22:8-9)
 c. Prophets[122]
  (e.g., Mic 3:9-12; Amos 4:1-4, 6-13; Isa 12:1-2; 59:2ff; Jer 3:12-14; 4:1-2; Ezek 18)
 d. Wisdom[123]
  (e.g., Prov 12:7-21; Psalm 1, 73; Job 5:8; 8:5-6; 11:13-15; 22:21-30; 33:18-23)
 e. Ezra 9; Nehemiah 9; Daniel 9

---

120. Childs has noted that in the two major groups of wilderness wandering texts—Exodus 15–18 and Numbers 10–21—complaints by the people are portrayed differently. In the pre-Sinaitic material God responds to the complaints with a positive and miraculous demonstration of divine presence. The post-Sinaitic texts, however, suggest that complaints provoked God's anger, are understood as evidence of faithlessness, disobedience, and rebellion, are met therefore with divine punishment (*Exodus,* 258–74). See further Balentine, "Prayer in the Wilderness Traditions," 53–74.

121. Cf. M. Weinfeld, *Deuteronomy and the Deuteronomic School* (Oxford: Clarendon, 1972), 307–19.

122. Cf. P. D. Miller, Jr., *Sin and Judgment in the Prophets* (Chico, Calif.: Scholars Press, 1982).

123. Cf. Crenshaw, "Popular Questioning of the Justice of God in Ancient Israel," *ZAW* 82 (1970): 386–90; idem, "The Problem of Theodicy in Sirach," *JBL* 94 (1975): 47–64.

2. Not justified warranted/deserved, i.e., innocent suffering	Lament-Protest	God is unjust capricious, unresponsive

Examples:

    a. Gen 18:22-33; Exod 32:7-14; Num 11:4-34; 14:11-23; Josh 7:7-9
    b. Jeremiah's confessions
    c. Lament Psalms
    d. Job
    e. Hab 1:2-4, 12-17
    f. Lamentations (e.g., 3:43-45, 55-59; 5:20-22)

3. Redemptive/ vicarious, i.e,., God-ordained and positive	Obedience; acceptance as vocation of the faithful	God is sovereign and mysterious

Examples:

    a. Job (e.g., 1:21-22; 2:10; 5:17; 33:12-18, 29-30)
    b. Isaiah's Suffering Servant Songs (e.g., 50:4-11; 52:13—53:12)

This outline of perspectives should make clear that the experience of suffering or distress in the Hebrew Bible is met with a variety of responses. Perhaps the majority view is the one championed by the prophets and the Deuteronomistic theologians. Here the perceived link between good deeds and their rewards, evil deeds and their punishment, is the basis for arguing that all misfortune is but the working out of divine punishment. Such a view is indeed promoted by the three most clearly distinguished segments within Israel's official leadership—prophets, priests, and the wise—and as such can be described as a central tenet of the "common theology" whose roots can be traced to Mesopotamia and Egyptian religion.[124] As articulated by Job's friends, for example, such a conviction promotes submission to suffering and a turning back to God, whose justice is characterized not only by wrath but also by mercy. The prayers of contrition that the friends try in vain to press on Job are given eloquent exposition in Ezra, Nehemiah, and Daniel, where penitent sinners beseech "the great and awesome

---

124. Brueggemann, "Structure Legitimation," 31–36.

God who keeps covenant and steadfast love to those who love you and keep your commandments" (Neh 9:32; Dan 9:4).

The Hebrew Bible also encourages the view, though much less vigorously, that suffering is to some degree the vocation of God's elect. The God who mysteriously hides in order to save (cf. Isa 45:15) is capable of wounding in order to heal (cf. Isa 53:5). To bear such affliction on behalf of others is the task of the servant of God whose life, rather than words, is mandated to be an "intercession for transgressors" (Isa 53:12).

In neither of these perspectives does suffering call into question the justice of God. Pain is understood as punishment, justly decreed in accordance with covenantal expectations; affliction that transcends punishment is sometimes the way of the God who in sovereign mystery chooses to be known as "I am who I am." Yet as the outline should also make clear, and as I have tried to show in the texts examined here and in chapter 6, neither of these perspectives is able to silence the "rumblings of discontent"[125] that surface when suffering strikes unexpectedly and inexplicably. For the victims of such pain neither punishment nor vocational calling is a viable answer to the questions "Why?" and "How long?" Hebraic faith has both a place and a legitimate practice for questioning sufferers. Their place is before God, whose promise of presence is never withdrawn from those in pain; their practice is prayer to the God who promises always to hear.

Prayers of lament concern issues that theologians call theodicy.[126] That is, they focus on the problems of God (Gk. *theos*) and justice (Gk. *dike*) that suffering almost inevitably raises. But pray-ers are not usually concerned to offer a theodicy in any formal sense. In the grip of pain one does not theologize—one simply hurts and cries out for help. Theodicies come from those who, like Job's friends, have the luxury of looking on from a distance and abstracting from someone else's grief rational theories and propositions. Perhaps it is inevitable therefore that most theories of suffering tend to fall far short of genuine appreciation for the truly tragic, the evil, dimen-

---

125. Cf. Crenshaw, "Popular Questioning," 382.

126. The major contributions to the study of theodicy in Hebrew Bible scholarship are conveniently collected in *Theodicy in the Old Testament,* ed. J. Crenshaw (IRT; Philadelphia: Fortress, 1983). See also J. Crenshaw, "Theodicy," *IDBS,* 895–96; idem, "Human Dilemma," 235–58; W. Brueggemann, *The Message of the Psalms* (Minneapolis: Augsburg, 1984), 168–76; idem, "Theodicy in a Social Dimension," *JSOT* 33 (1985): 3–25.

sion of a broken life.[127] Jeremiah, Job, and Habakkuk, and the supporting host of lament pray-ers who surround them do not offer theodicies. They simply offer prayers whose content may become the subject of those who scrutinize them from a safe distance. They offer a first level of discourse, a practice of praying in the midst of hurt.[128] If one attends to these prayers carefully, they may rupture shallow theological propositions. More importantly, they may arm one for the day when pain presses one to speak what one feels, not what one ought to say.

From the philosopher's perspective theodicy has to do with reconciling the existence of evil with the existence of a sovereign and righteous God. The issue is generally traced to the discussion between Leibniz and Voltaire concerning the Lisbon earthquake of 1775: Where is God to be found in such horrific calamity? The dilemma receives its most succinct formulation in the words of David Hume (1711–1776):

> Is he [God] willing to prevent evil, but not able? then he is impotent. Is he able, but not willing? then he is malevolent. Is he both able and willing? whence then is evil?[129]

From a theological perspective the problem of evil threatens to unhinge faith commitments to a good and loving God. In the wake of the horrendous suffering manifest in human existence, in the nightmares of Auschwitz and Hiroshima, in the tragedy of disease and death, deprivation and disappointment, theodicy is equated with the effort to pronounce God "Not Guilty."[130]

But such perspectives on the problem and the prosposals they engender as solutions almost invariably are articulated from the standpoint of the outsider looking on—by the philosophers who observe suffering from within the comfort of their studies; by the theologians, be they prophets, priests, or sages, who view suffering

---

127. On the problem of theodicists' abstract conception of evil, see K. Surrin, *Theology and the Problem of Evil* (Oxford: Basil Blackwell, 1986), 46–52. From another perspective D. Hall has written perceptively of biblical faith's persistent denial of the reality of suffering (*Lighten Our Darkness: Toward an Indigenous Theology of the Cross* [Philadelphia: Westminster, 1976], 73–109; *God and Human Suffering: An Exercise in the Theology of the Cross* [Minneapolis: Augsburg, 1986], 31–48).

128. Cf. Surrin, *Theology*, 149.

129. D. Hume, *Dialogues Concerning Natural Religion*, ed. H. D. Aiken (New York: Harper, 1948), part 10, 66 (as cited in Surrin, *Theology*, 2).

130. Crenshaw, "Introduction," *Theodicy in the Old Testament*, 6.

as a problem to be solved in the interest of protecting the religious structure that defines their status. From the victim's standpoint suffering raises much more existential questions. For the victim the issue of theodicy is forced by pain, not by discomfiting philosophical or theological non sequiturs. As Rabbi Kushner has put it, for these ones theodicy is forced as an issue "when bad things happen to good people."[131] When bad things happen to good people, what do good people do? How do they respond? How *can* they respond and still cling to those faith commitments that define their world order and their understanding of their God-given position within it?

In the Hebraic tradition the prayer of lament represents one of the major responses available to the victims of suffering. As modeled in the texts I have examined, especially in Jeremiah and Job, lament conceives the relationship with God in terms of *power*. From the call narrative in Jeremiah 1 to the accusation of divine assault in Jeremiah 20, the prophet knows himself to be an unequal partner with a God who does not refrain from imperative force. Simply put, God is the powerful one, Jeremiah the overpowered. Similarly Abraham (cf. Gen 18:27, 30-31, 32) and Job recognize the risks of standing head-to-head with God. As Job realizes, how can a mere human be just before God (9:2), for when one understands the issue in terms of power, the human's inferiority is an insurmountable handicap.

> If it is a contest of strength, he is the strong one!
> If it is a matter of justice, who can summon him? (Job 9:19, NRSV)

From the victim's standpoint then, theodicy, the question about God and justice, is in many ways experienced as the pain of powerlessness. Brueggemann has pointed out that such powerlessness is manifest not only in the religious realm of experience but also in social and political ways.[132] In terms of social power, theodicy is linked to the regnant social structure's arrangement concerning one's access to goods and their benefits. On the one hand, who has the material goods that make for a prosperous and healthy life? Who controls them and who administers their distribution? On the other hand, who has access to these goods and on what terms? As long as those who have and those who need reach a consensus on these issues, then society's equilibrium is maintained and the jus-

---

131. L. Kushner, *When Bad Things Happen to Good People* (New York: Schocken, 1981).

132. Brueggemann, "Theodicy in a Social Dimension."

tice of social structures is not questioned. But when the needy's access to social goods does not square with their expectations then questions of unfairness, and abuse disrupt the consensus, and the inequality of society's power relationships becomes a problem.

Social inequality is a question of political power as well. Those who have political power—the Republicans, the rich, the men, the whites, and so forth—exercise control over those they represent. So long as those who make the decisions and those for whom they are made understand and accept one another, then the political system may function without serious dissent. But if the consensus breaks down, then the political arena becomes a battleground, and political structures must either be modified in accordance with public demand or reinforced against it. At this point the war for agreement or accommodation can become painful indeed, and victory for either side is likely to be bittersweet, as any daily newspaper can confirm.

The same is true for religion, where the relationship between God and people involves power, which is necessarily distributed unevenly. When no crises or traumas upset the partner's trust in the sovereign power of God, then the issue of justice is moot. But when the realities of life force hard questions, then the issue of divine justice cannot remain dormant. In the Hebrew Bible, challenges to injustice usually take one of two forms.[133] First, if one perceives the political and social structures as corrupt and contrary to *God's* justice, then one can appeal to God against the system. The classic example of such an occasion is the Israelites' cry for relief from Egyptian oppression (Exod 2:23-24). Here the Israelites presume that God is reliable and capable of restoring a proper balance of power. The exodus experience becomes the linchpin of faith in God's abiding commitment to rescue the victims of oppression and injustice.

Second, sometimes it is not the system that is perceived as unjust but rather the God who appears to sanction or at least tolerate the system. On these occasions one can appeal *to* God *against* God. Here too one presumes that God is reliable and committed to justice, but from the victim's perspective God needs to correct or to adjust the way justice is meted out, to have a more equitable distribution of divine power.

Jeremiah, Job, Abraham, and Moses represent this second type of challenge. For them lament is a means of appealing for a shift in the balance of power between God and God's human partners. One

---

133. Brueggemann, *Message of the Psalms,* 168–76.

may recall Jeremiah's complaint in 12:1: "You will be innocent, Yahweh, when I dispute with you; nevertheless, I will speak judgments on you." Here, in 11:20, and in 18:19 Jeremiah presents God with a *rîb,* language suggesting a claim filed in court in order to insure that a complaint is formally articulated. Charged with the responsibility of instructing the people of Israel in the ways of righteousness and justice (Gen 18:19), Abraham similarly dares to hold God to the same requirements: "Shall not the Judge of all the world do justice?" (Gen 18:25). Job too demands a court appearance from God. He lays his cause before God (cf. Job 13:3, 18; 23:4; 30:35), risking his life on the hope that God will not be indifferent to the appeal of the innocent (Job 13:16). These faithful ones hold on to God against God, convinced that they can file their complaints in the ultimate court of appeal. Although they cannot determine the outcome or manipulate the verdict—God is still the judge—they can and do argue their case.

What does it mean for the community of faith to be able to file a complaint against God? To be able to address the "Judge of all the world" with concerns about justice and fairplay? On the positive side I suggest that this approach to God confirms that the complainant has a legitimate role to play in God's court. It is not the complainant's responsibility only to *receive* divine decrees, without response. Prayer as lament insists that two parties must be involved in the decision-making process. The lesser of the two parties, though an unequal partner, is taken seriously. One can question the power of the greater party. God is available to the petitioner, and divine decisions can be reviewed.

On the negative side one may return to an earlier question: What is lost if such an approach to God is forfeited? Following Westermann and others, Brueggemann has suggested that the loss of lament is costly in two important respects.[134] First, the loss of such prayer distorts the dialogue between God and humanity, sacrificing honest covenant interaction to a monopoly of divine power. Such a monologue, where God is the only speaker/actor, promotes either passive silence on behalf of the human partner or pious, but often hollow, words of praise or thanksgiving. Such a relationship cannot

---

134. Brueggemann, "Costly Loss," 60–64; cf. Westermann, *Praise and Lament,* 259–80; H. G. Reventlow, *Gebet im Alten Testament* (Stuttgart: Kohlhammer, 1986), 312–13; Balentine, *Hidden God,* 164–76; M. Limbeck, "Die Klage—eine verschwundene Gebetsgattung," *TQ* 157 (1977): 3–16.

survive the traumas of life, where hurt and pain will not permit a simple "Yes" or a manufactured "Hallelujah." As Brueggemann makes the point, "covenant minus lament is finally a practice of denial, cover-up, and pretense."[135]

The "cover-up" signaled by the loss of lament has far-reaching effects, disturbing not only spiritual equilibrium but also the cause of social justice. Again Brueggemann raises the critical issue: the absence of lament represents the "stifling of the question of theodicy."[136] When the right to raise legitimate questions about justice is denied or is not appropriated, then the reality of suffering is denied. For those who encounter suffering only as an idea, only in the abstract, such a denial may not seem crucial. But for those whose plights land them in the company of Job, such a denial encourages a silence that rends the soul already victimized. It is a denial that serves only to reinforce the hurt of the hurting, the powerlessness of the powerless. It is a denial that negates hope and sanctions misery. It is a denial of God, of the God whose own embrace of pain is measured in the Hebrew Bible by "unending love" *(ḥesed),* in the New Testament by a son on a cross.[137] In the suffering God and in the suffering Christ, God declares that God is on the side of the victim, on the side of those for whom lament is the only sound that misery can make.[138]

Nor is the denial of suffering only a spiritual loss. When questions of divine justice are forfeited, Brueggemann has suggested that questions of social and political justice will also likely be silenced.[139] If one can take the prophets as a guide, then the community of faith must know itself charged with the responsibility for seeing to it that confessions pronounced within the confines of the holy temple are matched with deeds of justice in society (e.g., Jer 7:3-15; Mic 3:9-

---

135. Brueggemann, "Costly Loss," 60.

136. Ibid., 61.

137. Note esp. J. Moltmann, *The Crucified God* (New York: Harper and Row, 1974).

138. The suffering or pathos of God has been addressed from a variety of perspectives. See, e.g., D. Soelle, *Suffering* (Philadelphia: Fortress, 1975); E. Wiesel, esp. in *Night* (London: Fontana/Collins, 1972) and *Ani Maamin: A Song Lost and Found Again* (New York: Random House, 1973); K. Kitamori, *Theology of the Pain of God* (Richmond: John Knox, 1965); S. Endo, *Silence* (New York: Taplinger Publishing Company, 1980). But the theme has only gradually begun to find a place in Hebrew Bible scholarship. Note esp. A. Heschel, *Prophets;* T. Fretheim, *The Suffering of God: An Old Testament Perspective* (OBT; Philadelphia: Fortrress, 1984); Brueggemann, "Embrace of Pain."

139. Brueggemann, "Costly Loss," 64.

12; Amos 5:21-24). Anything less is an abomination to God and a denial of life as God intends it to be. If questions are not raised in the temple, they threaten eventually to become invisible outside the temple as well. What is, is affirmed as what will be—in religion, in society, in the political and economic structures of life. In such acquiescence the sufferers are damned, and the God of righteousness and justice is lost.

CHAPTER 8

Praise
That Makes Sense

Thus far I have described Hebraic prayer primarily in terms of its function as petition. When one acknowledges sin as the major obstruction in one's relationship with God, then petition for forgiveness prepares the way for reconciliation with a God perceived as unassailably sovereign yet compassionate (chap. 5). When suffering, particularly undeserved or inexplicable suffering, or some other form of injustice threatens the divine-human relationship, then lament dominates one's approach to God (chap. 6–7). On such occasions one directs petition for relief or redress to a God who, though sovereign, is judged nonetheless accountable and responsive. Yet prayer is clearly more than petition that presents to God either submission or protest. Prayer is also praise, and to this important dimension of Israel's dialogue with God I now turn.

In a brief article P. Miller has called attention to two important characteristics of Hebraic praise: it is (1) "devotion that tells about God"; and (2) "a making glad that makes sense."[1] Praise that acts as devotion testifies that not only sin and suffering compel one to address God. The very nature of God, God's majesty and goodness, also evoke adoration and gratitude. Such a response serves to honor God while proclaiming to all who hear that this Yahweh God is worthy of one's love and fidelity. Hence praise is not only devotion but also testimony, both an exalting of God and a proclamation that seeks to draw others into the worship of God.

That praise functions as both devotion and proclamation requires little argumentation. But Miller has ventured beyond this point to make a far more important claim for Israel's praise: it is

---

1. P. Miller, "'Enthroned on the Praises of Israel': The Praise of God in Old Testament Theology," *Int* 39 (1985): 9, 11.

also "a making glad that makes sense." He supports this claim by
observing that a typical hymn of praise follows a two-part structure:
(1) a declaration of praise or a call to praise; and (2) a reason for
praise that sets forth why such a response is appropriate under the
circumstances. That is, given who God is and how God has demonstrated divine care for the one (or ones) who now addresses God,
praise makes sense. It is the natural and understandable response to
make. This response may be accompanied by feelings of great joy
and delight, perhaps even ecstasy, but it is never irrational, never a
response abstracted from human experience.[2]

In this chapter I address especially this second characteristic of
praise—its sensibility. If contemporary religious jargon is any
guide, one would have to admit that praise which attains the right
balance between exultant adoration and good sense is often in short
supply. But a number of studies, mostly focused on the Psalms,
have pointed out that the difficulty in engaging in such praise is not
only a contemporary one. Israel also struggled to insure that praise
did not deteriorate into empty, meaningless rhetoric. Especially
worthy of mention are the contributions of C. Westermann in
Praise and Lament and W. Brueggemann in *Israel's Praise.*[3]

Westermann has argued that while praise is rightly perceived as a
response that moves beyond self-interested petition, one should be
careful not to assume that such praise severs all connection with
petition. It is more accurate to understand praise and petition, or to
use Westermann's broader categories, praise and lament, as standing in polar relationship. Just as joy and suffering constitute polar
reactions that encompass the totality of human experience, so
praise and lament serve as the prayer responses appropriate for such
occasions. In Westermann's estimation, all prayer in Israel, whether
offered in cultic ritual or private address, moves between the two
poles of plea and praise (pp. 152–54).

For Westermann and for most who have followed his lead, the
recognition of this polar relationship between praise and lament has
functioned primarily as a perspective for reassessing the theological
importance of lament.[4] For his part Westermann has shown that in

2. Ibid., 11.

3. Westermann, *Praise and Lament in the Psalms* (Atlanta: John Knox, 1981),
15–162; W. Brueggemann, *Israel's Praise: Doxology against Idolatry and Ideology*
(Philadelphia: Fortress, 1988).

4. See, e.g., the works listed previously in chap. 7, n. 134, to which may be added
P. Miller, "Trouble and Woe: Interpreting the Biblical Laments," *Int* 37 (1983):
32–45; repr. in *Interpreting the Psalms* (Philadelphia: Fortress, 1986), 48–63; and

the Psalms the logic of Israel's prayers moves *from lament to praise*. Especially significant for Westermann is the structural shift from complaint to petition for divine intervention that is typical of psalms of lament. Such a shift signals that in lament one fundamentally desires not just the articulation of some grievance but the removal of its cause. In Westermann's opinion, "Lamentation has no meaning in and of itself" (p. 266). The point of theological importance is that lamentation always flows into petition. In this sense lament is always "on the road to praise" (p. 154).

Less fully appreciated, however, have been Westermann's complementary observations concerning the movement of *praise to lament*. For Westermann the polarity between these two basic modes of approach to God involves not opposition but interchange. It is not just lament that achieves structural and theological clarity in the transition to praise. Praise also attains its clearest and most meaningful expression when the joy of the moment is identified as the response to God's intervention in a former time of anguish or suffering. Just as all petition is "on the road to praise," so "praise can retain its *authenticity* and *naturalness* only in polarity with lamentation" (p. 267; emphasis added).

This "vital, tension-filled polarity of plea and praise" (p. 154) is for Westermann most clearly on display in psalms that on formal grounds may be categorized as "declarative" or "confessional" praise. In these psalms one comes to the "center of the praise of God in Israel" (p. 154). Here the structural link between praise and the reason for it (God has acted) suggests that a grievous situation has been overcome but still echoes in the background. Praise is offered because God has acted. The joy that is expressed is the response to God's intervention in a time of suffering.

Praise gradually lets go of this linkage with lament, however, in Westermann's opinion promoting a summons to praise unrelated to concrete memories of divine activity (pp. 135–42). What results takes the formal shape that Westermann calls "descriptive praise." Especially in later examples of this form, a one-sided emphasis on God's majesty tends to obscure if not altogether displace the specific reasons upon which such an acknowledgment is grounded. Without this vital polar link to lamentation, praise loses both its *naturalness*

---

esp. a number of studies by W. Brueggemann: "From Hurt to Joy, From Death to Life," *Int* 28 (1974): 3–19; "The Formfulness of Grief," *Int* 31 (1977): 263–75; "Psalms and the Life of Faith: A Suggested Typology of Function," *JSOT* 17 (1980): 3–32; *The Message of the Psalms* (Minneapolis: Augsburg, 1984), 51–122.

and its *authenticity,* leaving in its place little more than "mere stereotyped liturgy" (p. 154).

Despite Westermann's conceptualization of the praise-lament relationship, scholars have been slow to capitalize on its importance for understanding Hebraic prayer. One notable exception is the contribution of W. Brueggemann, *Israel's Praise: Doxology against Idolatry and Ideology.*

Brueggemann has also focused on the structure of Israel's hymnic praises, although he has pursued the theological and sociological implications of this structure in a much more intentional way than Westermann. For Brueggemann both the summons and the reason for praise must inform the practice of praise if it is to be authentic and credible. The summons is vital as a generative agent in world-making. That is, praise may be a constitutive and transforming act. The summons to "Praise the LORD" serves a social function of calling forth people to participate in new worlds where Yahweh, not some other god, evokes adoration and fidelity (pp. 29–53).

Yet, it is also important that the summons not preempt reason, for then praise serves no longer to summon forth new worlds but only to defend a world already made (pp. 89–121). Brueggemann identifies three ways the shift from reason to summons may take place in Israel's praise (pp. 90–104): (1) The reason for praise may be minimized or eliminated altogether and the summons extended (e.g., in Psalm 150). (2) The reason for praise may be generalized or stereotyped so as to mask any reference to specific occasions of God's actions. Such a move regularly occurs in the transition from declarative to descriptive praise. (3) The reason for praise may be silenced by an uncritical preoccupation with creation theology that allows the goodness of the present order to camouflage the hurt and brokenness, which require that one first petition, then praise, God as transformer.

With Miller and Westermann, Brueggemann argues that it is specifically in the reason for praise that the hymn "lives closest to the real ground and substance of praise" (p. 84). While the Psalms are "sung down" from summons to reason, Brueggemann suggests they must be "experienced up" from reason to summons (p. 78). For doxology to be authentic it must be sung "back down to pain, where hope lives; to hurt, where newness surfaces; to death, where life is strangely given" (p. xi). When this movement back down to lament does not occur, when the reason for praise is sacrificed, muted, or abstracted, when to the summons "Praise the LORD" one cannot give an answer to the question "Why?" then praise is on the way to being co-opted by self-interested officiants for ideological, and ultimately idolatrous, purposes.

In this chapter I (a) extend the search for "praise that makes sense" beyond the current focus on the Psalms to those examples occurring within narrative contexts; and (b) suggest that such exemplars of praise embedded in narrative provide a clue to the Hebraic effort to preserve the link between praise and human story, and furthermore to the interpretive move that the community of faith is invited to make when participating in meaningful adoration of God.

I offer two specific probes. First, I examine *bārûk* sentences, which offer one of the earliest attestations of praise. These sentences explicitly ground praise in concrete reasons by the use of the relative pronoun *'ăšer* (i.e., "Blessed be the LORD *who . . . ";* e.g., Gen 24:20; Exod 18:10; 1 Sam 25:39; 1 Kgs 1:48; Ezra 7:27). Second, I look at several extended hymnic pieces that have been inserted into narrative contexts (e.g., Exod 15:1-18; Judg 5:1-31; 1 Sam 2:1-10; Jonah 2:1-9; Isa 38:9-20). I give special attention to 1 Samuel 2 and Judges 5 as texts illustrative of the effort to retain the linkage between praise and narrative and historical context.

Finally, I submit that in these two areas of "embedded praise"— the *bārûk*-sentences and the inserted hymnic pieces—the Hebraic effort to promote a praise that makes sense moves in opposite yet mutually supportive directions. Whereas the history of *bārûk*-praise suggests a movement from an original narrative and historical context to a cultic context, in hymnic praise such as 1 Samuel 2 and Judges 5 the interpretive move has been in the opposite direction, from cultic to narrative and historical context. Such an understanding of praise as response to God that (potentially) moves from life situations to liturgical recitation and vice versa provides an important witness concerning *how* authentic praise occurs.

THE *BĀRÛK* SENTENCES

As just noted, Westermann locates the center of Hebraic praise in declarative or confessional praise. Although his focus is primarily on the Psalms, he observes that in their simplest form declarative psalms of praise have the same structure (praise plus reason for praise) as the *bārûk* sentences embedded in narrative contexts (p. 87). The basic similarity is apparent in a comparison of two texts:[5]

---

5. Westermann (*Praise and Lament,* 88 n. 36) cites the following as additional

	Praise	Reason for Praise
Ps 124:6	Blessed be the LORD	who[6] has not given us as prey to their teeth
Exod 18:10	Blessed be the LORD	who has delivered you from the Egyptians

Westermann concludes that Exod 18:10 and other similar narrative occurrences of the *bārûk* sentence preserve "the most original and immediate form of the praise of God, the simple and joyous response to a definite act of God which has just been experienced" (p. 88).

One can isolate eighteen narrative occurrences of the *bārûk* sentence.[7] These texts raise two important issues for the present discussion. First, the formal structure of *bārûk* sentences is generally consistent. Second, the setting for most of these occurrences is noncultic. In a few instances the formula functions in a liturgical or cultic context, and in these cases one may detect the first signs of what Westermann calls the shift from "simple and joyous praise" to the "solemn language" of "timeless liturgy" (p. 89).

The form of these *bārûk* sentences shows little variation. The basic pattern consists of three parts: (1) the *qal* passive participle *bārûk,* "Blessed (be)"; (2) an ascription identifying God as the subject (i.e., recipient of the praise); and (3) a grounding clause, usually introduced by the relative pronoun *'ăšer,* "who," followed by a verb in the perfect. This basic form—"Blessed be the LORD who . . ."— occurs fourteen times.[8]

The third element in these *bārûk* sentences is of particular interest. The grounding clause (*'ăšer* plus perfect verb) establishes this earliest form of praise as a response to a definite act of God. For example, God may be praised as the one who has "not abandoned" (*'āzab*) steadfast love and faithfulness (Gen 24:27); who has "delivered" (*nāṣal, hiphil)* from the Egyptians (Exod 18:10); who has "defended the case" (*řab'et rîb*) of a chosen servant (1 Sam 25:39); who has set *(nātan)* upon the throne the chosen king of succession (1 Kgs 1:48).

Psalms texts that share the same structure: 68:19; 28:6; 66:20; 18:46; 144:1.

6. The relative pronoun here is *še,* though the longer form *'ăšer* is more common.

7. Gen 14:20; 24:27; Exod 18:10; 1 Sam 25:32, 39; 2 Sam 18:28; 1 Kgs 1:48; 5:7 (MT v. 21); 8:15, 56 (= 2 Chr 6:4); 10:9; Ruth 4:14; Ezra 7:27; 1 Chr 29:10; 2 Chr 2:12 (MT v. 11); 6:4; Dan 3:28; Zech 11:5.

8. Gen 24:27; Exod 18:10; 1 Sam 25:32, 39; 2 Sam 18:28; 1 Kgs 1:48; 5:7 (MT v. 21); 8:15, 56 ([= 2 Chr 6:4); Ruth 4:14; Ezra 7:27; 2 Chr 2:11; Ps 66:20; cf. Ps 124:6 with *še* instead of *'ăšer*). On this basic form of *bārûk* praise see further C. A. Keller and G. Wehmeier, *"brk," THAT* 1.374.

In the majority of these cases some concrete experience of God's intervention evokes praise, which thus represents a spontaneous response of gratitude for a particular divine favor. Given what God has done, such praise is the natural and sensible response for an individual to offer. Texts such as these have no indication that individuals require a cultic setting or the assistance of cultic personnel to mediate their gratitude. Praise is not an act to engage in separate from life's everyday experiences, not some ritual to practice in a formal setting where words relate to life's experiences with God only as reflection or meditation. As Westermann describes it, "This praise of God accompanies God's great deeds as their necessary echo. . . . There was no need here for any intermediate step, any arrangement, any particular representation" (p. 88).

In at least three instances, however, both the form and the setting of *bārûk* sentences suggest that praise gradually evolves into a more liturgical response. Two of these occurrences are in Solomon's dedication prayer at the temple (1 Kgs 8:15, 56). In chapter 4, I suggested that the core of this prayer, especially verses 22-53, serves primarily to characterize the temple as a house of prayer.[9] Here I may add the observation that Solomon's prayer is both introduced and concluded with the rhetoric of blessing (vv. 14-21, 54-61). Both of these framing pieces use the *bārûk* sentence:

> Blessed be the LORD, God of Israel, who spoke by mouth with my father David. (v. 15)

> Blessed be the LORD, who has given rest to his people Israel according to all that he promised. (v. 56)

From these examples it is apparent that the form of Solomon's praise does not differ from that which occurs in the earlier stage of *bārûk* sentences. The same three elements that are generally determinative for these sentences are present here also. Thus praise takes the usual form "Blessed be the LORD who. . . ." On closer inspection, however, the setting for this prayer, as well as certain slightly nuanced variations in its rhetoric, points to a more liturgical function. Two particular observations are pertinent: (1) Although cast as Solomon's prayer, this praise is more a *proclamation* addressed to "all the assembly of Israel" (cf. vv. 14, 55) than a personal response of gratitude. In this sense the prayer is only indirectly addressed to God. It is primarily a statement *about* God intended for the hearing of those assembled on this ceremonial occasion of temple dedi-

---

9. See pp. 80–88.

cation. (2) In keeping with its function primarily as formal address rather than personal response, this prayer offers reasons for praise that are not as singular or concrete as earlier instances. God is praised for the fulfillment of promises given to David (vv. 14-21) and to Moses (vv. 54-61), in the latter case particularly the promise of "rest" (v. 56: *měnûḥāh*). Although ostensibly related to specific acts of God, this praise is in fact focused on God's continuing fidelity to "all that he had promised" (v. 56) over a long period of time.

Westermann notes that such a blurring of historical specifics constitutes a step in the direction toward the liturgical doxologies that conclude the books of the Psalter (Pss 41:13; 72:18-19; 89:52; 106:48).[10] Here too the rhetoric of blessing dominates—"Blessed be the LORD"—but concrete reasons are completely lacking. Instead God's blessedness is linked to timeless qualities. God is praised as the God who is "from everlasting to everlasting" (Pss 41:13; 72:19; 106:48; cf. 89:52) or as the one who alone is worthy of recognition as a "doer of wondrous deeds" (Ps 72:18). In Westermann's judgment, *bārûk* praise such as this has moved a considerable distance from the simple and concrete expressions of an earlier stage. If praise formerly accompanied God's great deeds like a simple and joyous "necessary echo," in Solomon's address, and even more in the Psalter's doxologies, praise that is "liturgically full" and "solemn" has become "like the heavy, golden implements of an altar" (p. 89).

In addition to the two examples from Solomon's prayer, a third narrative occurrence of the *bārûk* sentence provides further evidence of the formula's development as liturgical praise. In 1 Chr 29:10 blessing rhetoric serves as the introduction to David's prayer on the occasion of the dedication of the gifts brought to the temple: "Blessed are you, O LORD, God of our ancestor Israel, forever and ever." The setting is clearly cultic, a formal and ceremonial gathering in the holy place of "all the assembly" (vv. 1, 10, 20). Two of the three determinative formal elements of the *bārûk* sentence are present here—the *bārûk* participle and the ascription to God.

But, as was true in Solomon's prayer, the connection between the praise due God and the reasons for it is noticeably loosened. In

10. Westermann, *Praise and Lament,* 88–89. See further W. S. Towner, "'Blessed be Yahweh' and 'Blessed are Thou, YHWH': The Modulation of a Biblical Formula," *CBQ* 30 (1968): 388–90; J. Scharbert, "Die Geschichte der *bārûk*-Formel," *BZ* 17 (1973): 23–24; C. W. Mitchell, *The Meaning of BRK "To Bless" in the Old Testament* (Atlanta: Scholars Press, 1987), 146–60.

place of the grounding clause with *'ăšer*, David's blessing of God is followed by a hymn of praise (vv. 10-12) designed rhetorically, as I suggested in chapter 5, to highlight the sovereignty of God.[11] It is God's "greatness" *(haggĕdullāh)*, "power" *(haggĕbûrāh)*, "glory" *(hattip'eret)*, "eminence" *(hannēṣaḥ)*, and "majesty" *(hahôd)*, that elicit this praise. There is no remembrance here of one specific, recognizable incident of divine intervention. In this regard 1 Chr 29:10 is similar to the doxological use of the formula that Westermann has noticed in 1 Kings 8 and especially in the Psalter.

Beyond these observations, W. S. Towner has proposed that the Chronicles text points in the direction of yet another stage in the liturgical use of the *bārûk* formula.[12] He calls attention specifically to the insertion of the personal pronoun *'attāh*, "you," as the subject of the participle *bārûk*. In place of the customary "Blessed be the LORD" one now encounters the form "Blessed are *you*, O LORD." Towner sees here a shift to direct address which in effect reclaims the role of prayer as a personal response to God, even when set within a cultic context.

Towner suggests that this shift represents more than a chance variation. He observes that the formula of direct address in cultic blessings from late biblical texts (in addition to 1 Chr 29:10 he cites also Ps 119:12) mirrors a common practice in the liturgical tradition of the synagogue, particularly as reflected in the repetition of *bārûk 'attāh Yhwh* in the *ḥătîmôt* (epilogues, seals) of the Eighteen Benedictions.[13] He notes further that in the Benedictions the formula *bārûk 'attāh Yhwh* is not accompanied by a grounding *'ăšer* or *kî* clause, but instead by a participial clause or a simple appositive (e.g., "Blessed are you, O LORD, who revivest the dead").[14] In this respect synagogue practice and that suggested in late biblical texts like 1 Chr 29:10 seem to agree. Towner postulates, therefore, that both the liturgical practice of the synagogue and the formula of direct blessing of God in late biblical texts reflect the liturgical standardization of the *bārûk* sentence that was prevalent in Jewish worship of the Persian and Hellenistic periods.[15]

To summarize, the search for "praise that makes sense" has led

---

11. See pp. 100–102.
12. Towner, "Blessed be Yahweh," 386–99; cf. J. Scharbert, *"brk," TDOT* 2.285–86.
13. Towner, "Blessed be Yahweh," 394–99.
14. Ibid., 394.
15. Ibid., 397–99.

me to examine the *bārûk* sentence, which Westermann judges to be
"the most original and immediate form of the praise of God"
(p. 88). A survey of the narrative occurrences of the *bārûk* sentence
supports two general conclusions. First, three constitutive elements
are present in the majority of these occurrences: the *bārûk* participle, the ascription to God, and an accompanying clause, usually
introduced by *'ăšer,* which ties the expression of praise to some
specific and relatively concrete reason. The inclusion of the reason
for praise most clearly identifies these expressions as responses of
joy to some definite act of God. Second, the setting for the majority
of these occurrences is noncultic. One can discern a ritual context in
only a few texts, which are primarily from later periods of biblical
history. In these instances the link between praise and reason for
praise seems to have increasingly blurred as specificity and spontaneity gave way to liturgical standardization.

To these conclusions I may now add one further observation.
Taking the *bārûk* sentence as his guide, Westermann proposes that
the basic character and the simplest structure of Hebraic praise
could have been expressed originally in one sentence. Indeed, in his
view, "The nearer this praise is to God's deed, the shorter and
simpler it will be."[16] To illustrate Westermann points to Exod
15:21, perhaps the earliest recorded example of Israel's praise:

> Sing to the LORD because he has risen up proudly;
> the horse and the rider he has thrown into the sea.

Here Westermann finds a typical declarative psalm of praise, with a
cry of praise followed by the reason for it.[17] All three constitutive
elements of praise are in place: an imperative summons ("Sing"),
the identification of the recipient ("LORD"), and a *kî* clause, which
supplies the reason for the praise, here specified as God's victory
over the enemy at the sea ("because he has risen up proudly").

What is striking about this earliest exemplar of praise is that its
basic structure parallels so clearly the simplest form of lament
prayers. In a form-critical investigation of lament prayers, A.
Aejmelaeus has identified essentially the same three features: im-

---

16. Westermann, *Praise and Lament,* 88.

17. Ibid., 89–90. See further F. Crüsemann who also regards Exod 15:21 as the
beginning point for the Israelite hymn. But Crüsemann understands the *kî* clause
not so much as a reason for praise but as a statement signaling "execution" or
"fulfillment" *(Durchführung)* *(Studien zur Formgeschichte von Hymnus und Dan-
klied in Israel* [Neukirchen: Neukirchener Verlag, 1969], 32–35).

perative petition, address, and "motivation clause," usually introduced by *kî*.[18] She finds the best illustration of this pattern in prose
prayer in Gen 32:11 (MT v. 12): the prayer of Jacob at the river
Jabbok:[19]

Imperative petition	*Motivation clause*
(+ implied address)	
Deliver me now [LORD] I pray,	. . . because *[kî]* I fear him
from the hand of my brother	

In this example Jacob's prayer for deliverance is occasioned by the
particularities of his immediate situation, specifically by his "fear"
of the impending encounter with Esau. The narrative itself introduces into the drama the mention of Jacob's "fear" (cf. v. 7), thus
the prayer's motivation is clearly and inextricably linked to the
situation of the moment.[20] It is petition anchored in a specific
situation of need.

Aejmelaeus uses and builds on the work of Gerstenberger to show
that this basic pattern—petition, address, motivation clause—is
the natural way of persons making everyday requests of one
another.[21] It represents in essence "one of the basic modes of speech
in Hebrew,"[22] and thus one should not be surprised to find that it
serves equally well for both ordinary petitions and those occurring
within the framework of prayer. When such petitions do occur in
prayer they appear both in the simple prose form illustrated by Gen
32:11 (MT v. 12) and in the poetic form of the Psalms, where
repetition and parallelism elaborate on the basic features and make
the occasion for the prayer's use more generally applicable. Still,
both prose and poetic examples remain tied to the basic pattern of
the "traditional prayer."

Aejmelaeus concludes that this basic pattern should cause one to
reconsider theories that posit the priority of cultic models of prayer.
"These models were originally not an invention that the people had
to adjust themselves to, but more probably an elaborated and at the
same time canonized form of what was known and practiced by

18. A. Aejmelaeus, *Traditional Prayer in the Psalms* (BZAW 167; Berlin and New
York: de Gruyter, 1986), 88–89.
19. Ibid., 89–90.
20. For the previous discussion of this passage, see pp. 68–69.
21. Cf. E. Gerstenberger, *Der bittende Mensch* (Neukirchen: Neukirchener Verlag,
1980), 40–42.
22. Aejmelaeus, *Traditional Prayer,* 88.

them earlier."[23] To make the point more specifically, Aejmelaeus submits, "It is particularly the appearance of the pattern of traditional prayer which renders it more plausible that the cultic form grew out of living practice than the reverse."[24]

What emerges from these form-critical investigations is an understanding of both praise and lament as expressions inextricably tied, at least in their primary (original) forms, to concrete reasons anchored in real-life experiences. This linkage of praise and lament with reasons may be illustrated as follows:

Imperative petition/praise	*Motivation*
Lament: Deliver me	. . . because *[kî]* . . . (Gen 32:12)
[haṣṣîlēnî] now [LORD]	
Praise: Sing *[šîrû]* to the LORD	because *[kî]* . . . (Exod 15:21)

This understanding is consonant with Westermann's proposal concerning the historical development of prayer in the Hebrew Bible.[25] He finds that in the earliest stage biblical literature employs no special term for prayer as such. Instead one encounters only short cries or calls to God that appear as inseparable parts of a narrated course of events. Such prayers are presented as the normal and natural product of the situation in which they are spoken. They do not require a cultic or liturgical framework. On the contrary, Westermann suggests that in the oldest strata of the Hebrew Bible, prayer is "not yet a process separate from the rest of existence."[26] Hebraic prayer does subsequently become more liturgical in character, particularly in the Psalms, as these short calls to God come together in standarized compositions suitable for formal services of worship. Traditional speech forms continue to provide the nucleus for address to God, yet both praise and lament have less emphasis on the reasons for such speech. In the place of specificity one finds poetized formulations that generalize prayer's referents, thus extending its applicability to a wide range of situations.

For Westermann and Aejmelaeus these observations concerning prayer's development are determined primarily by form-critical considerations; others have reached similar conclusions by different

---

23. Ibid., 90.
24. Ibid., 90–91.
25. C. Westermann, "Gebet im Alten Testament," *BHH* 1.519–22; cf. idem, *Elements of Old Testament Theology* (Atlanta: John Knox, 1982), 154–56.
26. Westermann, *Elements,* 153.

means. For example, H. Guthrie has argued on sociological grounds that declarative praise *(tôdāh)* was the norm for the praise of God in Israel.[27] He supports this assertion by linking the preference for concrete expressions of gratitude to the Hebrews' origins among the Hapiru of the ancient Near East.[28] The Hebrews emerged first as one of those fringe classes of people whose fight for survival had to be waged outside the social-political-cultural orders of society. Their home was *midbār,* "desert, wilderness," not the city. They had originally to carve out an existence, where desolation and chaos were the regnant powers, not the security and order enjoyed by those residing in the city-kingdoms.[29] Given their status as marginalized and powerless, and their experience of God as deliverer, particularly shaped by the Exodus from Egypt, Guthrie suggests that Israel's natural response to God took the form of thanksgiving for specific acts of divine rescue.

The work of E. Gerstenberger and R. Albertz has further clarified the social settings of prayer, particularly as reflected in the Psalms. Gerstenberger has postulated two principal social settings as the matrix for prayer: (1) The small social units of family, neighborhood, or community in which individuals attain their sense of personal orientation, interdependence, and support; and (2) the larger, superregional organizations, such as temple or academy, where membership is mostly anonymous and the emphasis is on the administration of power and wealth to the benefit of bureaucratic leaders.[30]

Albertz has accepted these two principal settings and has attempted to delineate the characteristics of "personal piety" and

27. H. Guthrie, *Theology as Thanksgiving: From Israel's Psalms to the Church's Eucharist* (New York: Seabury, 1981), 1–30.

28. Ibid., 20–21.

29. Ibid., 18–19. Guthrie's discussion of Israel's transition from *midbār* community to statehood is not pursued on rigorous sociological grounds. His interest is primarily theological; only secondarily is he concerned with social-cultural backgrounds. Others, however, have given considerable attention to clarifying the sociopolitical shifts in early Israel from tribal organization to monarchy, rural population to urban, the "little" traditions of the peasantry to the "great" traditions of the ruling elite. See, e.g., R. Coote and K. Whitelam, *The Emergence of Early Israel in Historical Perspective* (Sheffield: Almond, 1987); R. Coote and D. Ord, *The Bible's First History* (Philadelphia: Fortress, 1989), esp. 1–7, 18–23; R. Coote, *Early Israel: A New Horizon* (Minneapolis: Augsburg Fortress, 1990), esp. 71–93, 113–39.

30. E. Gerstenberger, *Psalms, Part 1; with an Introduction to Cultic Poetry* (FOTL; Grand Rapids: Eerdmans, 1988), 33; see further idem, *Der bittende Mensch,* 139–46.

"official religion" that he understands to derive from them.[31] Like Gerstenberger his focus has been primarily on lament psalms. He notes that individual and community laments reflect deep differences in what is expected and experienced from God. For example, offered within the context of the *Kleinkult* (i.e., the small social units to which Gerstenberger has called attention), individual laments most often petition God as Creator of humanity *(Menschenschöpfer)*. By contrast, as institutionalized expressions of piety reflecting the concerns of official religion, communal laments are more likely to appeal to God as Creator of the world *(Weltschöpfer)*, particularly with reference to power over primeval forces of chaos.[32]

Neither Gerstenberger nor Albertz addresses the issue of Hebraic praise per se. Nevertheless, their observations, coupled with Guthrie's, suggest a plausible theory of the social settings of praise that does not contradict Westermann's form-critical distinctions. One may postulate that both praise and lament originate in concrete experiences of divine activity, both most likely articulated in simplest form as responses of personal piety such as typically occur in everyday life situations. As society becomes more centralized, one may suppose that worship experiences, and along with them the responses of praise and lament, become more and more formalized.

For both praise and lament the shift toward liturgical standardization represents a weakening of the relationship between worship rhetoric and life experiences. As Albertz has suggested, when lament begins to lose contact with specific and personal crises (e.g., as in communal lamentation), the focus of the rhetoric shifts from personal issues to national and political ones, from private concerns to official necessities.[33] At stake for the suppliant is not so much the personal relationship with God as the political existence of the national entity.

As Brueggemann has shown, a similar set of consequences accompanies the practice of praise isolated from the experience of lament that occasioned it. When praise begins to lose contact with the reasons that sustain it, then the natural response of gratitude is overshadowed by the official summons to express it. The joy of the occasion is supplanted by standardized rhetoric that is not compelling. At worst, praise that originates as direct and immediate re-

---

31. R. Albertz, *Personliche Frömmigkeit und offizielle Religion* (Stuttgart: Calwer, 1978), 23–96.

32. Ibid., 37–38.

33. Ibid., 36–37.

sponse to God may be co-opted by public managers for idolatrous purposes.[34]

One must take seriously Gerstenberger's caution against compartmentalizing these social settings too neatly. In his view smaller social groups and larger institutional structures must have coexisted from the beginning in Israel. Thus "rituals and prayers in both social realms have obviously been in contact all along, each exercising influence over the other."[35]

Yet Guthrie is surely correct to suggest that once Israel ceased being a *midbār* community and became a temple community, it was much more difficult to maintain *tôdāh* as the norm for praise.[36] At least from the time of the monarchy, when worship came to be more specifically defined by holy times and holy places, the mixing of personal piety with institutionalized rhetoric must have been common. Westermann suggests that such occasions of formal worship were ideally characterized by a "double movement of those who go from their own homes into the 'House of God,' and then from the worship service back into their own homes and work."[37]

The difficulty (no less ours than Israel's) is in realizing such an ideal worship that values equally both personal and ritual dimensions of the divine-human relationship. Biblical literature does promote the understanding that praise is to be both anchored in human story and sustained through ritual practice. This concern is illustrated in the *bārûk* sentences, which, as I have tried to show, reflect a movement from personal response to liturgical standardization. This concern is also evident in liturgical rhetoric, such as that preserved in 1 Samuel 2 and Judges 5, employed in narrative contexts of particularized human experiences. To this rhetoric I now turn my attention.

EXTENDED HYMNIC PIECES IN NARRATIVE CONTEXTS

Thus far I have been suggesting that the *bārûk* sentences are one of the earliest examples of Hebraic praise that makes sense. These

---

34. Brueggemann, *Israel's Praise*, 105–13.

35. Gerstenberger, *Psalms*, 33. Note further Reventlow's charge that a good deal of the scholarly debate seeking to distinguish between the "sacred" and the "profane" in ancient Israel is prompted by little more than modern presumption (*Gebet im Alten Testament* [Stuttgart: Kohlhammer, 1986], 299–301).

36. H. Guthrie, *Israel's Sacred Songs: A Study of Dominant Themes* (New York: Seabury, 1966), 74; cf. idem, *Theology as Thanksgiving*, 14–30, 45–59.

37. Westermann, *Elements*, 155.

sentences, typically structured in the form "Blessed be the LORD who . . . ," articulate a joyful and immediate response of gratitude for a specific experience of divine intervention. In the majority of cases these sentences appear to have originated and functioned in noncultic contexts, although they are eventually employed as ritualized doxologies in liturgical worship. From a hermeneutical perspective I have proposed that the shift in the context of these *bārûk* sentences suggests that the practice of praise in Israel had the potential to move from private and personal devotion to God to formalized liturgical adoration.

Such a movement is, of course, not a negative one. The praise of God certainly belongs to the ritual of worship. Without it worship tends too easily to focus inward rather than upward, and private preoccupations tend to replace acknowledgment of the cosmic lordship of God. Yet the move toward liturgical praise also carries inherent risks. By definition ritual tends to generalize the reasons for praise and thus risks promoting responses to God that no longer compel enthusiasm or engender passion. If the movement in the practice of praise is not a double one in the sense that Westermann has proposed (i.e., from home to House of God and from worship service back to home and work), then praise ceases to function as a living, vital, sensible ingredient in the divine-human relationship.

If the *bārûk* sentences reflect the simplest stage of Hebraic praise as it is occasioned by concrete historical circumstances, then the songs of thanksgiving and the hymns of praise in the Psalter attest the development of praise into "timeless liturgy."[38] Here one catches a glimpse of praise that has moved from a myriad of daily life circumstances to the formalized assembly of liturgical prayer. My concern in this investigation is to explore how Hebraic praise, once made a part of the cult, makes the return movement from worship service to daily life that Westermann has described. In other words, once praise attains formality as standardized liturgical rhetoric, does it—can it—continue to function naturally and simply outside the cult as well?

Perhaps the question as I have stated it cannot be answered with any significant degree of confidence. Biblical texts that record or

---

38. Westermann, *Praise and Lament,* 89. See the similar observation of N. Gottwald that once Israel's exodus-conquest paradigms are taken up in cultic recitations, concrete memories of specific historical events tend to recede into "timeless" ideas (*The Tribes of Yahweh: A Sociology of the Religion of Liberated Israel, 1250–1050 B.C.E.* [Maryknoll, N.Y.: Orbis, 1979], 698, 705).

allude to prayers of praise seldom provide information about the actual practice of such activity. This is patently the case for the poeticized prayers of the Psalter, but it is also true of prose prayers embedded in narrative contexts. As I have tried to show in preceding chapters, prayer serves quite frequently in such contexts as a literary vehicle that editors or redactors employ for theological and ideological reasons. At best, narrative contexts permit one to hypothesize about the historical practice of prayer, or at least what the narrator has portrayed the practice to have been.

When one asks, therefore, about the potential interchange between the cultic practice of praise reflected in the Psalms and the everyday response of gratitude modeled in prose narrative, one's answers must be tentative. Nevertheless, the biblical text affords at least one promising avenue of exploration: the several poetic pieces of praise that in the final form of the text are embedded within narrative contexts, specifically Exod 15:1-18; Judg 5:1-31; 1 Sam 2:1-10; 2 Sam 22:2-31; Deut 32:1-43; Isa 38:9-20; and Jon 2:1-9. Here I limit my comments to two of these examples: the Song of Hannah (1 Sam 2:1-10) and the Song of Deborah (Judg 5:1-31).

THE SONG OF HANNAH (1 SAM 2:1-10)

A general consensus has long held that the Song of Hannah is secondary in its present context. Two arguments are consistently cited in support of this judgment.[39] First, the poetic form of the song contrasts sharply with the prose of the immediate literary context. One encounters here lyrical and metaphorical statements that appear to have little or no relevance to the particular circumstances of the Hannah narrative. For example, it is not clear how references to the bows of the mighty being broken or the feeble being girded with armor (v. 4) bear directly on the life of barren and plaintive Hannah. Even the stereotypical language that does connect with Hannah's situation cannot be taken simply as a literal representation of the facts. For example, the song refers to the "barren woman" who "has borne seven" (v. 5), but according to the narrative Hannah had only six children, five in addition to Samuel (2:21). Second, the

---

39. These arguments are common in a wide range of works from both early and modern interpreters, e.g., K. Budde, *Die Bücher Samuel* (Tübingen: J. C. B. Mohr, 1902), 13–14; H. Gressmann, *Die Bücher Samuel* (Göttingen: Vandenhoeck und Ruprecht, 1910), 2; G. B. Caird, "I and II Samuel," *The Interpreter's Bible,* ed. G. A. Buttrick (12 vols.; Nashville: Abingdon, 1952–57), 2.862, 882–85; H. W. Hertzberg, *I and II Samuel* (OTL; Philadelphia: Westminster, 1963), 29; P. K. McCarter, *I Samuel* (AB; Garden City, N.Y.: Doubleday, 1980), 75.

reference in verse 10 to God's "king" or "anointed one" has been interpreted as a strong indication that the song's original setting is in the monarchical period, perhaps as early as the tenth or ninth century, but in any case a time not consonant with the age of Hannah.

Scholars have challenged or in some cases simply bypassed this consensus view as their attention has shifted away from preoccupation with the song's historical setting to focus instead on its narrative function. B. Childs has led the way in recognizing that important structural links between 1 Samuel 2 and David's prayer in 2 Samuel 22 provide the hermeneutical key for the entire Samuel literature.[40] Other readings of 1 Samuel, such as those by L. Eslinger and P. Miscall, have called further attention to numerous syntactic and thematic connections that function rhetorically to link Hannah's prayer to this particular literary context.[41]

My own interest here is not so much to offer additional exegetical information about this text, or even to develop its rhetorical connections in this narrative setting. In the latter regard I am persuaded with Eslinger and others that Hannah's prayer of thanksgiving functions rhetorically and sensibly within the present narrative as the appropriate response to God's granting of her previous petition (cf. 1:10-11, 26-27). Instead, I am interested in probing the hermeneutical move suggested by this narrative's embrace of poetic praise.

In pursuing this line of thought I have been particularly grateful for an observation by P. Miller. In an article on the biblical laments, Miller suggests that the interpreter's difficulty in finding referents for the figurative and metaphorical language common to these prayers can be somewhat resolved by focusing on those laments

40. B. Childs, *Introduction to the Old Testament as Scripture* (Philadelphia: Fortress, 1979), 272–73; Reventlow, *Gebet,* 287–90; W. Brueggemann, "II Samuel 21–24: An Appendix of Deconstruction?" *CBQ* 50 (1988): 383–97; idem, "I Samuel 1: A Sense of a Beginning," *ZAW* 102 (1990): 33–48, esp. 43–48; idem, *First and Second Samuel* (Interpretation; Louisville: John Knox, 1990), 15–21, 339–45; R. Polzin, *Samuel and the Deuteronomist: A Literary Study of the Deuteronomic History,* Part 2: *1 Samuel* (San Francisco: Harper and Row, 1989), 30–39.

41. L. Eslinger, *Kingship of God in Crisis: A Close Reading of I Samuel 1–12* (Sheffield: Almond, 1985), 99–112; P. Miscall, *I Samuel: A Literary Reading* (Bloomington: Indiana Univ. Press, 1986), 15–16. Although Miscall regards the poems in 1 Samuel generally to function as integral parts of the overall narrative (p. xii), he concludes, rather curiously it seems to me, that in the case of 1 Samuel 2 "the Song as a whole is a lure; it offers much but produces little" (p. 16).

embedded in historical and narrative contexts.[42] To illustrate he shows how the stereotypical language of Jeremiah's laments is literalized or particularized by having been set within the narrative context of Jeremiah's experience.[43] For Miller such embedded lament constitutes a witness to the Hebraic desire to sustain the "resonance between lament and human story."[44] If interpreters would but attend to these examples of lament in narrative, Miller submits, they would find important clues not only about the actualization of such prayer in Israel but also about contemporary appropriation of lament prayer in the concrete experiences of faith and practice.[45]

Although Miller's focus is on lament prayers, his observations are equally instructive when applied to prayers of praise. Form criticism helps one to realize that both lament and praise employ highly metaphorical language. For both forms of address, locating particular persons or circumstances to fit the generalized expressions of the address nearly always confounds the best efforts of interpreters. With reference to the subject at hand this point can be clarified by excerpting 1 Samuel 2 from its present narrative context and reading it as a typical song of thanks from an anonymous pray-er. Then it becomes obvious that both the form and the content of verses 2-10 place it among numerous other thanksgiving songs in the Psalter that on any given occasion could have been appropriated by a number of different persons for different reasons. The psalm with which it is most often compared is Psalm 113.[46]

Yet, just as certainly as the stereotypical laments in Jeremiah are particularized by their narrative association with the prophet from Anathoth, so is this general song of thanks particularized when identified specifically with the circumstances of Hannah. No longer is it the prayer of just anyone; in this context it is specifically the prayer of Hannah, wife of Elkanah of Ephraim, of the city of Ramathaim. Now it is not a prayer of thanksgiving unattached to the

---

42. Miller, "Trouble and Woe," 32–45.
43. Ibid., 44.
44. Ibid., 45.
45. Ibid., 36.
46. See, e.g., J. T. Willis, "The Song of Hannah and Psalms 113," *CBQ* 35 (1973): 139–54. See further Polzin's analysis of the similarities to Psalm 18 (= 2 Samuel 22). In his view, Hannah's song is an artful abbreviation of David's final hymn of praise, the two poems forming a poetic inclusio for the Deuteronomist's history of kingship (*Samuel and the Deuteronomist*, 31–36).

specifics that call it forth; it is a prayer of gratitude offered on the specific occasion of once-barren Hannah's conception of the child for which she has petitioned. Now the otherwise general references in verses 4-10 to the reversal of fortunes experienced by the feeble and the hungry, the barren and the poor, become focused on the particular change in Hannah's status occasioned by the birth of Samuel.[47]

In effect, the narrative context of Hannah's prayer promotes childlessness as the concrete occasion of grief from which praise is born. Hannah's response of joy and exultation is not merely descriptive or disinterested. Rather it is a praise offered *because* God has delivered from the anguish of life that *first* summoned one to lament and petition. This linkage to lament defines Hannah's rejoicing as the natural and sensible response in this situation: "praise God because. . . ."

One may pursue the function of such praise a step further. Miller has proposed that narrative contexts function to literalize poetic metaphor. With this observation I agree completely. I wish to extend the argument, however, by suggesting that in 1 Samuel 2 the literalization of poetic praise encourages two interpretive moves, both supportive of the Hebraic interest in maintaining the vital connection between praise and human story.

At one level 1 Samuel 1–2 has a personal focus. Hannah is portrayed as a pious individual whose relationship with God is lived out very much within the "claims of time and sorrow."[48] She prays out of pain, is delivered of grief, and gives thanks. Hers is in general a private world where personal decisions bear little influence beyond their immediate context. If scholars are correct in positing an original cultic setting for 2:1-10, then the present arrangement of the Samuel narratives encourages the reader to search for ways in

---

47. The movement toward the particularization of general poetic passages is at work elsewhere in the Hebrew Bible as well. My argument here is parallel with the work of B. Childs ("Psalm Titles and Midrashic Exegesis," *JSS* 16 [1971]: 137–50; *Introduction,* 520–22) and E. Slomovic ("Toward an Understanding of the Formation of Historical Titles in the Book of Psalms," *ZAW* 91 [1979]: 350–80). Both have suggested that historical notices in the psalm titles represent a movement toward the historicization of poetic songs with reference to events in the life of David. On this method of "inner-biblical interpretation" (Childs, "Psalm Titles," 148) as but one example of the considerable range of haggadic exegesis in the Hebrew Bible, see M. Fishbane, *Biblical Interpretation in Ancient Israel* (Oxford: Clarendon, 1985), esp. 403–7.

48. The phrase is from W. Berry, *A Place on Earth* (San Francisco: North Point, 1983), 94. For its appropriateness as a description of the importance of pain as the locus for Hebraic praise, see Brueggemann, *Israel's Praise,* 129–40.

which liturgical rhetoric may be anchored in human story. In Hannah's case the rhetoric of timeless liturgy is personalized in the concrete passion of fulfilled maternity. At this level of interpretation the literalization of praise has the effect of shifting its sphere of influence from the cultic arena of public testimony to that of private devotion.

But this text's literalization of poetic praise also encourages a second move. I have suggested that here cultic praise is personalized, that public adoration coincides with private piety. Even so, taking the Samuel narratives as a whole, one can plausibly argue that Hannah's prayer functions rhetorically on a much broader scale. As previously noted, several commentators have identified structural links between 1 Samuel 2 and 2 Samuel 22. For example, following Childs, Brueggemann interprets Hannah's and David's prayers as an inclusio for the Samuel narratives' emphasis on power and the transformation of power. In this regard Hannah models a submissive fidelity to the power of God that serves as an extreme counterpart to royal power. To the extent that David embodies Hannah's dependency on God, he becomes "a man after [God's] own heart" (cf. 1 Sam 13:24).[49]

Beyond this particular linkage between Hannah's piety and David's power, Eslinger has called attention to the way 1 Samuel 2 functions within the larger narrative. Hannah offers a concrete example of a standard assertion concerning the "proper relation between Israelite need and divine response to need."[50] The theological and political desirability of God's sovereignty over Israel as a *nation* is given validity and supported by the example of the deliverance of a pious *individual.* Thus, if in Hannah's Song cultic praise has been personalized, it has not been for the purpose of denying to praise its public witness. Rather, praise has been *personalized* in order to function rhetorically as a model for *communal* emulation.[51]

The observations of both Brueggemann and Eslinger suggest that this text permits a second hermeneutical move. On the one hand the

49. Brueggemann, "II Samuel 21–24," 397. See also Polzin's observations concerning the rhetorical merging of the maternal and the monarchic in the person of Hannah (*Samuel and the Deuteronomist,* 31–34).

50. Eslinger, *Kingship of God,* 107.

51. Ibid. Cf. Brueggemann, who suggests that Hannah's song requires a "double-focused singing" in which personal joy is linked to public destiny (*First and Second Samuel,* 17). See further R. Clements, *In Spirit and in Truth: Insights from Biblical Prayers* (Atlanta: John Knox, 1985), 60.

personalization of praise encourages the reader to search outside the public arena of worship for concrete occasions when the rhetoric of praise is not only desirable but also sensible. On the other hand personal devotion can and does make public witness, especially when individual piety becomes the model for communal fidelity. In the Samuel narratives Hannah both personalizes praise that is liturgical and exemplifies praise that, however personal and concrete, always has public influence, at least if, in the Hebraic perspective, it is to be praise that makes sense.

THE SONG OF DEBORAH (JUDGES 5)

A similar argument can be made for the Song of Deborah in Judges 5. Here too we find poetic praise embedded in narrative context. Here also it is plausible to understand that praise has moved from an original cultic locus to a secondary association with a specific historical event.[52]

Despite some important and as yet unresolved issues concerning the text's literary transmission, my concern here is to investigate the narrative meaning of Judges 4–5.[53] These two chapters have con-

---

52. The text's literary history is complex. Some have argued that the poem is a literary unity, artfully composed in paratactic style to celebrate God's cosmic power over and control of hostile, enemy forces. The emphasis on *literary* unity cautions against using the poem to reconstruct a particular historical scenario. See, e.g., A. Hauser, "Judges 5: Parataxis in Hebrew Poetry," *JBL* 99 (1980): 23–41; cf. A. Globe, "The Literary Structure and Unity of the Song of Deborah," *JBL* 93 (1974): 493–512; M. D. Coogan, "A Structural and Literary Analysis of the Song of Deborah," *CBQ* 40 (1978): 143–166. Others, however, have questioned the song's unity. For example, following J. Blenkinsopp and W. Richter, J. Soggin suggests that the "actual song of Deborah" consists of vv. 6-8 and vv. 12-30. This original form is then later supplemented by a "liturgical framework" (vv. 2-5, 9-11, 31a). This view understands the text to have moved from an original secular setting to a liturgical one before its incorporation in the present narative. See J. Soggin, *Judges* (OTL; Philadelphia: Westminster, 1981), 94–97; J. Blenkinsopp, "Ballad Style and Psalm Style in the Song of Deborah: A Discussion," *Biblica* 42 (1961): 61–76; W. Richter, *Traditionsgeschichtliche Untersuchungen zum Richterbuch* (Bonn: Hanstein, 1963), 91.

53. At issue is the historical relationship of Judges 4–5. Blenkinsopp proposes that Deborah's call to battle in 4:14 provides the grounds for a subsequent reviser "to fill out and transpose into a more religious key the accompanying ballad" ("Ballad Style," 64). In his view the prose version of Judges 4 generates the poetry of Judges 5. B. Halpern, however, argues the opposite position (*The First Historians: The Hebrew Bible and History* [San Francisco: Harper and Row, 1988], 76–77; cf. F. M. Cross, "The Epic Traditions of Early Israel: Epic Narrative and the Reconstruction of Early Israelite Institutions," *The Poet and the Historian: Essays in Historical Biblical Criticism*, ed. R. E. Friedman [Chico, Calif.: Scholars Press, 1983)], 21). According to Halpern the poetic version of Judges 5 provides the historian the resources for the prose reconstruction in Judges 4. By interrogating the poetic source, the historian is able to reconstruct in prose detail locations, numbers, and relationships lacking in the original version. While this

siderable duplication of basic data. Both portray Deborah and Barak as warring against Sisera; both attribute a primary role to Jael, wife of Heber the Kenite; both confirm that Sisera is killed and that with his death the Israelites are released from a stranglehold of Canaanite oppression. In view of such duplication the interpreter quite logically asks why it should be necessary or helpful to place two such similar accounts of this victory side by side?

Attention to narrative artistry has helped to address this question more sensitively than once was the case. My own understanding of the narrative coherence of Deborah's praise has been sharpened by the work of R. Alter, B. Webb, and L. Klein.[54] Here I wish to build on their insights to focus specifically on the rhetorical function of praise in this particular context. I submit that the final narrative sequence of Judges 4–5 characterizes praise that is appropriate and sensible, indeed, even necessary, not only for the individual Deborah but also for the nation as a whole.

On the one hand Judges 4–5 serves to particularize the metaphors of praise with reference to the person and circumstances of Deborah. This is not just any victory celebration—it is the joyful response occasioned "on that day" (cf. 4:23; 5:1, NRSV) of Sisera's defeat.[55] This is not a thanksgiving offered by an anonymous prayer—it is the song of Deborah, who, in the afterglow of a particular encounter with God, comes to praise as a natural response. In this regard Judges 4–5 represents a move similar to that in 1 Samuel 1–2 to concretize the rhetoric of praise in the life circumstances of a particular individual.

On the other hand Deborah's song functions in this context as more than a personal or private act of piety. Deborah invites a communal response to a deliverance with national consequences. It is significant that the summons to corporate praise departs from the paradigmatic characterization of Israel offered in Judg 2:11-15. There the community's relationship to God is spelled out within the framework of six elements: (1) Israel does what is evil in God's sight; (2) God gives them into the hand of oppressors; (3) Israel cries to God; (4) God raises up a deliverer; (5) the enemy is subdued; and

---

reconstruction is artful, it is not wholly fanciful. In Halpern's view Judges 4 should be evaluated as a "modestly ornamented" work of history, not a "historical romance" (ibid., 97).

54. R. Alter, *The Art of Biblical Poetry* (New York: Basic Books, 1985), 43–50; B. Webb, *The Book of the Judges—An Integrated Reading* (Sheffield: JSOT Press, 1987), 138–44; L. Klein, *The Triumph of Irony in the Book of Judges* (Sheffield: Almond, 1988), 44–46.

55. Cf. Webb, *Book of Judges,* 138–39.

(6) the land has rest. These six elements are common to the accounts of Othniel (3:7-11), Ehud (3:12-30), Gideon (6:1—8:35), Jephthah (10:6—12:7), and Samson (13:1—16:31). They are also present in the Deborah story. But in this instance the paradigm varies in order to include the response of praise, which is inserted after the defeat of the oppressor.[56]

Without Judges 5 the narrative sequence reduces to crisis → deliverance. In this form the account is consonant with other judges episodes, except that on this occasion a woman secures the victory.[57] But with Judges 5 the sequence enlarges to crisis → deliverance → praise.[58] In this sequence the narrative focus shifts from the woman Jael, who put her hand to the fatal tent-peg blow, to God, who comes forth in battle with terrible majesty as Israel's true champion. Such a coming, conquering God necessarily turns the focus away from acts of individual heroism. Before this God the whole community is summoned by their deliverance experience to make the appropriate response of praise (cf. 5:2, 9).

Among the accounts of the judges, only in this episode is praise or thanksgiving offered in response to divine deliverance. The relative constancy of the sixfold pattern throughout the judges' accounts (Judges 3–21) makes clear that thanksgiving or praise is not portrayed as a regular part of Israel's interchange with God during the judges' era.[59] In this respect Deborah's summons to praise stands out in the narrative as an exceptional moment of corporate gratitude that was short-lived. Taken as a piece of the larger picture, such brief and infrequent bursts of piety are symptomatic of the progressively deteriorating fidelity of Israel outlined in Judg 2:19:

> Whenever the judge died, they would relapse and behave worse than their ancestors, following other gods, worshiping them and bowing down to them. They would not drop any of their practices or their stubborn ways. (NRSV)

---

56. Cf. D. M. Gunn's observations that it is particularly the departures from, variations upon, and development of the ideal paradigm in 2:11-19 that helps the reader chart the contours of the book ("Joshua and Judges," *The Literary Guide to the Bible,* ed. R. Alter and F. Kermode [Cambridge: Belknap, 1987], 113).

57. Webb, *Book of Judges,* 138–39; cf. Klein, *Triumph of Irony,* 44–46.

58. Webb (*Book of Judges,* 138–39) recognizes that the prose narrative is not properly concluded until the song is completed and the expected report is given that "the land had rest forty years" (5:31b; cf. 3:11, 30, NRSV). In its present context, then, the song serves to conclude the Barak episode with a hymn of praise.

59. In fact, only with Hannah and Deborah is there *any* praise in the canonical presentation of Israel's history between settlement and kingship!

In this chapter I have attempted to demonstrate that not only lament and petition but also praise and thanksgiving constitute part of the repertoire of responses offered to God in Hebraic prayer. Indeed, these two fundamental responses—lament and praise—are vitally connected in the Hebrew Bible's portrayal of Israelite piety. Lament is born of situations shaped by grief and anguish, situations that compel petition for help and relief. The hope that God will hear, the belief that God can effect change, undergirds both the lament and the expectation of divine intervention that it embodies. Once God has intervened, lament moves naturally and sensibly to praise. But in its most concrete expression such praise reverberates with echoes of the lament that first shapes the address to God.

I submit that this sequence is relatively constant in the Hebrew Bible as in life itself. The cry for help first brings one into relationship with God, then (and almost always in this order) the address of praise and thanksgiving marks the response of one whom God has encountered. The sequence is important, if much neglected, for it reminds one that lament is not only an authentic and desirable response to offer God but also the first step toward adoration and gratitude that is both passionate and sensible.[60] This movement between lament and praise seems to support Westermann's claim that lamentation in the Hebrew Bible is never an end in itself.[61] It is always in transition to petition, and petition that has been heard is "no longer mere lament, but lament that has been turned to praise."[62]

I have argued in this chapter that the polarity between lament and praise is necessarily genuinely reciprocal. Just as all petition is "on the road to praise," so, with Westermann, I have contended that praise can retain its authenticity only in polarity with lamentation. This "vital tension-filled polarity of plea and praise" is on display in the declarative psalms of praise on which Westermann and others have focused. But I have maintained that it is also evident in narrative contexts, particularly in the *bārûk* sentences and in extended hymnic pieces like 1 Samuel 2 and Judges 5 that are integrated into narrative contexts. In the *bārûk* sentences the Hebrew Bible invites

---

60. On the importance of the cry to God as the agent of initiation in securing God's deliverance, see E. K. Kim, "Outcry: Its Context in Biblical Theology," *Int* 42 (1988): 229–39; R. N. Boyce, *Cry to God in the Old Testament* (Atlanta: Scholars Press, 1988), esp. 1, 71–79; Miller, "Enthroned on the Praises," 8–9.

61. Westermann, *Praise and Lament,* 266.

62. Ibid., 80.

one to see that private moments of gratitude and devotion occasioned by specific experiences with God can and should find their way into the public arena of liturgical doxology. Such a transition from ordinary life to cultic life necessarily weakens the linkage between praise and the experience that calls it forth. Specifics give way to generalities, immediacy to formal recitation, as the summons to praise extends beyond private worlds into the corporate witness of the community gathered in worship.

Cultic praise is necessary but risky, as both Westermann and Brueggemann have seen. For Westermann praise removed from concrete reasons is neither authentic nor natural. To the extent that cultic praise reduces to "timeless liturgy," the joyful response of gratitude to God is replaced by a solemnity that Westermann compares to the heavy-laden golden ornaments adorning the altar. For Brueggemann such heavy, passionless praise is dangerous because it falls potentially into the hands of liturgical managers. These managers of religion—often identified with royal powers—have a vested interest in subordinating praise for concrete reversals of fortune to praise that affirms fortunes anchored in concrete.

And yet the Hebrew Bible also encourages one to see that cultic praise can and should find a natural outlet in private practice. In extended hymnic pieces like 1 Samuel 2 and Judges 5, liturgical rhetoric has been personalized by the specifics of surrounding narratives. In both instances the metaphors of public piety have been literalized with reference to named and known individuals (Hannah and Deborah). Generalities revert to specifics, formal recitation is replaced by immediate address, and the summons to praise is understood to be issued by the concrete experiences of life itself, not by worship leaders whose investment in the establishment may hinder rather than enhance one's encounter with God. In both cases, however, the move to particularize praise serves larger narrative interests. In Hannah, a mother's gratitude becomes the model for royal and communal fidelity. In Deborah, a leader's modeling of praise as an essential ingredient of life serves to highlight the lack of praise in the nation's steadily deteriorating devotion to God.

I submit that in both these areas—*bārûk* sentences and hymnic praise within narrative contexts—the interpreter is encouraged to hear and embrace a praise that makes sense. In Hebraic perspective, participating in such praise means that in both private and public settings, one does not lose sight of the fundamental reasons that evoke general gratitude and sustain it with passionate witness.

CHAPTER 9

Prayer in
the Theology of the
Hebrew Bible

In chapter 1 I acknowledged dual commitments that I recognize as influential in this presentation of the prayers of the Hebrew Bible: my commitments to the church and to the academy. Now that a substantial number of prayers have been examined, it is appropriate to reflect on the theological gains relative to both these commitments. That is, what do these Hebraic prayers contribute to the church's understanding of God? How is faith and its practice instructed by these prayers, not only in the church's worship but also in its ministry to the world? How is the academy's understanding of God informed by these prayers? Specifically, what role do they play in the academy's ongoing interest in and responsibility for the development of the theology of the Hebrew Bible?

In the final three chapters I address these issues in reverse order. In chapters 9 and 10 I focus specifically on the theology of prayer and its contribution to the theology of the Hebrew Bible. If the academy can discern the principal theological claims of ancient prayers and can present them clearly and persuasively to a wider audience, then the church should be better served in its effort to embody and promote prayer both *in* ministry and *as* ministry. This issue is the subject of the concluding chapter.

THE NEGLECT OF THE SUBJECT OF "PRAYER"
IN THE THEOLOGY OF THE HEBREW BIBLE

In chapters 1 and 2 I noted the neglect of the subject "prayer" within the general field of biblical studies. Publications by Greenberg, Clements, and Reventlow, and the dissertations by Corvin and Staudt, both confirm the general disinterest in this subject and seek to redress the situation with their own critical analyses.[1] Here I focus more specifically on the enterprise called Hebrew Bible theology. I begin with a negative observation that I seek to explicate in the following discussion: from at least the middle of the nineteenth century to the present, with few exceptions, prayer has not been a major subject in the development of Hebrew Bible theology. Although I do not propose to survey this field comprehensively, I believe highlighting the following general developments will verify this observation.

THE HISTORY-OF-RELIGION APPROACH

The history-of-religion approach dominated Hebrew Bible theology for roughly fifty years, between the last half of the nineteenth century and the early decades of the twentieth. Beginning with the historical-critical investigations of K. H. Graf (1815–69), A. Kuenen (1828–91), and J. Wellhausen (1844–1918), and continuing through the emergence of the *religionsgeschichtliche Schule* represented principally by H. Gunkel (1862–1906), J. G. Eichorn (1856–1926), W. Bousset (1865–1920), and W. Wrede (1859–1906), the search for religious teachings and theological truths in the Hebrew Bible was supplanted by a strictly historical description of the religion and religious practices of ancient Israel. "Theologies" of the Hebrew Bible gave way to "histories" of religion. This emphasis dominated the academy until the 1920s when, under the influence of R. Kittel and especially W. Eichrodt, the summons went out for a return to a more theologically oriented study of the Hebrew Bible.[2]

A full discussion of the characteristics of the history-of-religion approach can be found in the standard literature on the subject and need not be repeated here.[3] I wish instead to call attention to several

---

1. M. Greenberg, *Biblical Prose Prayer As a Window to the Popular Religion of Ancient Israel* (Berkeley: Univ. of California Press, 1983), 7–9; R. Clements, *In Spirit and Truth: Insights from Biblical Prayers* (Atlanta: John Knox, 1985), 3–4; H. G. Reventlow, *Gebet im Alten Testament* (Stuttgart: Kohlhammer, 1986), 9–80; J. Corvin, "Stylistic and Functional Study of the Prose Prayers in the Historical Narratives of the Old Testament" (Ph.D. diss., Emory University, 1972), 1–3; E. Staudt, "Prayer and the People in the Deuteronomist" (Ph.D. diss., Vanderbilt University, 1980), 30–52.

2. R. Kittel, "Die Zukunft der alttestamentlichen Wissenschaft," *ZAW* 39 (1921): 84–99; W. Eichrodt, "Hat die alttestamentliche Theologie noch selbständige Bedeutung innerhalb der alttestamentlichen Wissenschaft," *ZAW* 47 (1929): 83–91. See further the discussion on pp. 230–37.

3. See, e.g., G. Hasel, *Old Testament Theology: Basic Issues in the Current Debate* (Grand Rapids: Eerdmans, 1982), 23–31; J. Hayes and F. Prussner, *Old Testament Theology: Its History and Development* (Atlanta: John Knox, 1985),

general traits of this approach that are particularly relevant for understanding its treatment of prayer.

I begin by noting that a primary objective of this approach was to trace the *origin* and *development* of Israelite religion.[4] A general consensus emerged in the works of this genre that Israelite religion had its origin in the customs and practices of the ancient Near East (e.g., the practice of sacrifice). It was also commonly stressed, however, that Israelite religion had developed beyond these primitive customs to more mature expressions of faith. Evidence for this development from earlier, more primitive religions to later, more advanced forms was found in at least three areas: (1) the move beyond the worship of many gods to a more mature expression of monotheism; (2) the move beyond mythical and magical connotations of religion as a means of inducing, imitating, or otherwise controlling the deity's relationship with the world to a more advanced understanding of religious obedience to a sovereign God; and (3) the move beyond institutionalized expressions of religion to more personal and spiritualized ones. In this third area the prophetic period in Israel's history came to be regarded as most representative of authentic religion in Israel.[5]

Within this broad area of general understandings one may make a number of observations about how prayer is treated in this approach to Hebrew Bible theology. First, most histories of Israelite religion give little or no attention to the subject of prayer.[6] A survey of the indices of some of the more influential publications from this period shows that if the term prayer is cited at all, it usually receives little more than a brief comment.[7] For substantive discussion of prayer during this era, one must go outside the realm of histories of Israelite religion, strictly conceived, to studies more limited in

126–42; H. G. Reventlow, *Problems of Old Testament Theology in the Twentieth Century* (Philadelphia: Fortress, 1985), 6–13.

4. Cf. Hayes and Prussner, *Old Testament Theology,* 133–34.

5. For a summary statement on these and other characteristics, see ibid., 136–42.

6. See, e.g., B. Duhm, *Die Theologie der Propheten als Grundlage für die innere Entwicklungsgeschichte der israelitischen Religion* (Bonn: Adolph Marcus, 1875); W. O. E. Oesterley and T. H. Robinson, *Hebrew Religion: Its Origin and Development* (London: SPCK, 1930), 330–33, 403; W. R. Smith, *Lectures on the Religion of the Semites* (London: A. and C. Black, 1899).

7. Typical is the treatment by R. Smend (*Lehrbuch der alttestamentlichen Religionsgeschichte* [Freiburg: J. C. B. Mohr, 1899]). In a brief paragraph within a section on "Sacrifice and Offering," he suggests that the oldest form of prayer is that represented by "calling on the name of God" (*qārā' bĕšēm Yhwh*) to accept the sacrifice that a worshiper brings (140). The remainder of Smend's discussion focuses on the various kinds of sacrifices employed in Israel's religion.

focus. I cite the following two discussions of prayer as representative of how general history-of-religion concerns may influence the presentation.

In a lecture presented to the Hohensteiner Conference in 1921 titled "Aus dem Gebetsleben des Alten Testaments," J. Hempel laments the neglect of critical research on prayer in Protestant theology.[8] He attributes this neglect to the post-Enlightenment preference in Protestant theology for the examination of doctrine and theory *(Lehr)* over piety. Hempel seeks to revive both academic and religious interest in the prayers of the Hebrew Bible by showing that they constitute a unique repository of the "pulsating life" characteristic of Israel's religion (p. 3). For this task he takes as his starting point a history-of-religion approach.

He begins by asserting that prayer is a fundamental response deeply embedded within human nature. It is witness to the "soul seeking to draw near to God" (p. 4). He argues that prayer customs and prayer forms survive through history, despite political and religious upheavals. In this sense prayers afford an important witness to the origin and development of religion in ancient societies. Hempel then proceeds to trace both the dependency of Israel's prayers on ancient Near Eastern customs and their advance beyond these customs. His particular concern is to show that the prayers of the Hebrew Bible indicate that Israel overcame the "mythical and magical connotations" of the prayers of its neighbors (p. 4).

Similar concerns shape the presentation in H. Schmidt's "Gebet und Gebetssitten in Israel und in nachexilischen Judentum," published a few years later.[9] Schmidt begins with a discussion of the "speciality" *(Besonderheit)* of Israelite prayer. He observes first the strong influence of practical monotheism on Israelite religion (col. 875). From this starting point, he then addresses a further distinctive informing Israel's prayers. In other religions one finds frequent reference to prayers and prayer rituals whereby a suppliant seeks to force or compel a deity to act. Schmidt acknowledges that such an understanding of prayer's function is not completely unknown in the Hebrew Bible. In general, however, he concludes that Israelite prayer is far removed from the practice of magic *(Zauber)* and incantation *(Beschwörung)* (col. 876). From this perspective of the

---

8. Hempel, *Gebet und Frömmigkeit im Alten Testament* (Göttingen: Vandenhoeck und Ruprecht, 1922), 3. See further the discussion of Hempel in chap. 1.

9. H. Schmidt, "Gebet II. Gebet und Gebetssitten in Israel und in nachexilischen Judentum," *RGG* (2d ed.), 2.875–79.

uniqueness of Israelite prayer, he turns to trace its development in the Hebrew Bible through three major periods: the popular religion of the cult; the spiritualization of prayer in the prophets; and finally, prayer's emergence in postexilic Judaism as the principal form of confession.

The presentations by Hempel and Schmidt help bring into focus three tendencies in the academy's valuation of prayer that emerge at an early stage in the development of Hebrew Bible theology.

(1)   It is worth reiterating that prayer is not a principal subject in the history-of-religion approach to theology. Most histories give it only passing mention. It is typically subsumed in larger discussions of Israel's various worship practices.

(2)   One of the underlying objectives of the history-of-religion approach is to establish, by way of comparison with other ancient religions, Israel's more developed status.[10] This objective is especially evident in the emphasis on Israel's advance to a monotheistic faith. Israel's disdain for prayers designed to manipulate or coerce divine action is understood to be one corollary of this overriding commitment to the sovereign God Yahweh. This view regards prayer that attempts to secure from the deity something not freely offered as an unacceptable infringement on divine prerogative.

(3)   Finally, this approach prefers the individual expressions of religion over the prescribed, the spiritual over the technical. Prescribed or ritualized forms of worship that subsume the individual into corporate or national anonymity represent only deteriorations from what is authentic and genuine. Religion that has devolved into cultic ritual on institutionally prescribed occasions produces mindless rhetoric that is sterile and lifeless. The generally low valuation that historians of religion give the Priestly tradition reflects this judgment. Authentic religion, especially as modeled by the prophets, is spontaneous and alive to the immediacy of the moment; it is unfettered by ritual or format.[11]

---

10. On this and other evaluative and apologetic tendencies in the nineteenth-century German tradition of historiography, see R. Oden, *The Bible Without Theology: The Theological Tradition and Alternatives to It* (San Francisco: Harper and Row, 1987), 1–39.

11. No one articulated such an opinion with more eloquence or appeal than J. Wellhausen. He described the loss occasioned by Josiah's centralization policies, when prayer and sacrifice were transferred from the natural exegencies of life to temple ritual:

As the following discussion indicates, each of these tendencies is still represented today.

THE GOLDEN AGE OF HEBREW BIBLE THEOLOGY: 1930–60.

The 1930s ushered in a period that G. Hasel has described as the "golden age" of Hebrew Bible theology. He lists no less than thirteen contributions to Hebrew Bible theology that appeared between 1930 and 1960 alone.[12] Of these none were more influential than those of W. Eichrodt and G. von Rad, whose Hebrew Bible theologies effectively marked the beginning and the climax (respectively) of this great age of the discipline.[13] Indeed, following von Rad the publication of Hebrew Bible theologies had a discernible lull until the early 1970s, when a number of new works began to appear. At least for a while after Eichrodt and von Rad, scholars seemed to think that little more could be said on the matter.[14]

It is instructive to examine how the theologies of Eichrodt and von Rad treat the subject of prayer. A review of the indices of the texts cited by Hasel suggests that little would be added by widening the focus to include other publications from this period. In this golden age of theology, prayer does not occupy a position of prime importance. Eichrodt and von Rad are not only the two most influential contributors to the field but also virtually the only source for any substantive discussion of prayer in Hebrew Bible theology during this era.

Others have extensively analyzed and evaluated the factors leading up to and informing the methodologies and objectives of the

---

> If formerly the sacrifice had taken its complexion from the quality of the occasion which led to it, it now had essentially but one uniform purpose—to be a medium of worship. The warm pulse of life no longer throbbed in it to animate it; it was no longer the blossom and the fruit of every branch of life; it had its own meaning all to itself. It symbolized worship, and that was enough. The soul was fled; the shell remained, upon the shaping out of which every energy was now concentrated. A manifoldness of rites took the place of individualising occasions; technique was the main thing, and strict fidelity to rubric.

(J. Wellhausen, *Prolegomena to the History of Ancient Israel* [Gloucester, Mass.: Peter Smith, 1973], 78).

12. Hasel, *Old Testament Theology,* 23.

13. W. Eichrodt, *Theologie des Alten Testaments* (3 vols.; Leipzig, 1933–39), translated as *Theology of the Old Testament* (OTL; 2 vols.; Philadelphia: Westminster, 1961–67); G. von Rad, *Theologie des Alten Testaments* (2 vols.; Munich: Chr. Kaiser, 1957–60), translated as *Old Testament Theology* (2 vols.; New York: Harper and Row, 1962–65).

14. Cf. J. Barr, "Biblical Theology," *IDBS,* 109.

theologies by Eichrodt and von Rad. That discussion need not be repeated here.[15] It is enough to note that in the 1920s a move began in Germany to redirect the focus of Hebrew Bible theology toward a more theological orientation. In an important 1929 article, Eichrodt himself argued that the historian of Israel's religion must push beyond a mere descriptive account of religious practices.[16] What is required is a systematic presentation of the recurring and binding truths that constitute the inner meaning of Israel's religion. This insistence on attending to the inner meaning of Israel's religion, what Kittel calls its "truth content and its abiding value,"[17] is a primary emphasis for both Eichrodt and von Rad, although the means by which they seek to derive it differ considerably.

(1) Eichrodt begins his *Theology* by stating that the principal concern is "to construct *a complete picture of the OT realm of belief*" (p. 25). He presents this "picture" in three principal relational categories: "God and the People," "God and the World," and "God and Man." The key to God's relationships in each of these areas is the covenant. The nature of Israel's covenant God is to be in relationship particularly with the people of Israel, and at the same time also with the larger universe and with humanity as such. The nature of this covenant relationship, particularly as it is embodied in God's union with Israel, is bilateral and reciprocal in character (p. 36). God chooses to be bound to Israel in both sovereign and personal ways. The people must respond to the covenant God with love and obedience. Relationship is thus essentially two-sided, with both partners promising and requiring fidelity, "even though the burden is most unequally distributed between the two contracting parties" (p. 37).

The discussion of these three relational categories takes up well over one thousand pages spread over two volumes in English translation. The only sustained discussion of prayer is in a section of a chapter dealing with "The Cultus" (pp. 172–76).

Eichrodt understands Israel's life under the "authority of the covenant God" to require obedience to the covenant statutes (p. 70). This obedience means adherence not only to the secular law contained in the Decalogue but also to the sacred laws of the cultic ordinances. Whereas obedience in the first area commits Israel to a

15. See the works cited in n. 3; in addition, see R. C. Dentan, *Preface to Old Testament Theology* (New Haven: Yale Univ. Press, 1950), 37–39, 61–65; D. G. Spriggs, *Two Old Testament Theologies* (SBT 2/30; London: SCM, 1974).
16. Eichrodt, "Alttestamentliche Theologie," 83–91.
17. Kittel, "Zukunft," 97.

life of morality and justice, obedience in the second entails the exclusive worship of God, who is the source and sustainer of all that is good. Such worship takes place supremely in the cult and is defined in terms of sacred sites, sacred objects, sacred seasons, and sacred actions (pp. 102–76). In all these ways the cult provides a medium for the "straitening of man's intercourse with God" in accordance with two fundamental spiritual realities: (1) the requirement to bring the human spirit "into subjection to divinely ordered reality," and (2) the requirement that one's piety remain bounded by a "deep sense of . . . creatureliness" (p. 100).

Within this general framework, Eichrodt includes prayer as one of the important "sacred actions" of the cult (pp. 172–76). The primary objective of this discussion seems to be to show how the practice of prayer in Israel gradually came to discard all "irreligious ideas" (p. 175) or "primitive elements" (p. 172) that may have carried over from ancient customs. Although some of the terms in Israel's vocabulary of prayer may recall primitive nuances of imitative magic,[18] "this proves nothing as to whether these particular meanings of the words were still present to the consciousness of Yahweh worshippers in their prayers" (p. 172). Some types of invocation, such as blessings and curses, may be closely related to witchcraft, but in Israel one can clearly see that "Yahweh became Lord over the blessing and the curse and stripped them of their original character" (p. 173). For Eichrodt this advance beyond primitive understandings is witness to Israel's "strong sense of the exalted Lordship of God" (p. 175).

One cannot fail to notice here a similarity to the history-of-religion approach to prayer that I have already mentioned in the discussions of Hempel and Schmidt. Like them, Eichrodt's concern is to compare and contrast Israel's practice with other religions. The final judgment is clear: the practice of prayer in Israel reflects a more mature understanding of faith.

How Eichrodt supports this assessment is particularly interesting. In his view, Israel's commitment to the exclusive sovereignty of God translates into prayer, which functions principally as an act of obedience and submission. He suggests the analogy of the pray-er as a vassal:

> The acts of kneeling and raising the hands, followed by the bowing of the face to the ground, correspond to the behaviour of the vassal in the presence of his king, and symbolize the submission of the supplicant to a will higher than his own. (p. 175)

18. For example, *hitpallēl,* e.g., "to pray," is lit. "to make cuts in oneself."

Such an analogy fits well with Eichrodt's understanding of the cult as the medium for the "straitening" of the human response to God, the "subjection" of the human spirit to divine reality, and the deep sense of "creatureliness" that must inform the prayers of all who approach the sovereign God.

One does well to remember that Eichrodt's discussion of prayer is relatively brief and is certainly not intended to be a full statement of the matter. The immediate context of the presentation suggests that his concern is to distance Israel's practice of prayer from the magical and mystical practices common in so-called primitive prayers of incantation. Perhaps this is his only concern. But the vassal analogy of prayer, supported with the emphasis on "submission," "subjection," and "creatureliness," raises the question whether prayers of lamentation, protest, or accusation, which I have suggested were important in Hebraic life, would find a place in Eichrodt's theology.[19]

(2) G. von Rad shares with Eichrodt the concern that Hebrew Bible theology should recover its proper theological focus. In von Rad's view, one cannot achieve this recovery by a purely "rational" and "objective" historical reconstruction of Israel's religious development. Such an approach is ill equipped to discern or explain the theology embedded in historical traditions. Nor can one accomplish it by a systematic presentation of key religious ideas and concepts, for such a presentation does not give sufficient attention to the history of which Israel itself speaks. Despite the gains of Eichrodt's attempt to present a unified picture of a covenant theology, such a systematic approach to Hebraic faith is foreign to both the form and the content of the Hebrew Bible itself. The true subject matter for the Hebrew Bible theologian lies neither in a history separated from faith understandings nor in theology abstracted from historical traditions. It lies instead, von Rad insists, in "Israel's own explicit assertions about Jahweh" (1.105). It is this confessed history to which the theologian must attend. Israel's own testimony concerning God yields not merely *one* theology (e.g., a covenant theology), but multiple theolog*ies,* widely divergent in their assertions, in keeping with Israel's changing political and cultic history (2.414–15).

Although von Rad resists efforts to unify these theologies into central concepts or basic tendencies,[20] he does understand that they

---

19. Eichrodt himself did not understand this "straitening" in terms of "suppression" (*Theology,* 1.100). His overall presentation, however, seems to suggest otherwise.

20. On the quest for the "center" of Hebrew Bible theology, see Hasel, *Old*

embody two fundamental assertions: (1) God's continuing activity in history on Israel's behalf; and (2) Israel's response or "answer" to God's saving acts. For von Rad, both these assertions represent areas of appropriate and fruitful theological investigation. The former affords him the opportunity to unfold the theology of Israel's historical traditions, especially what he terms the "salvation history" represented in the Hexateuch and in the works of the Deuteronomist and the Chronicler. The latter invites attention to Israel's conversation with God in which one finds basic features of a "theological doctrine of man" (1.356). Von Rad discovers this doctrine primarily in the Psalter. It is just here that one also encounters von Rad's most sustained discussion of prayer (pp. 356–70).

Von Rad asserts that in Israel's "late period," the Psalter is representative of "the totality of what Israel said by way of prayer" (p. 356). From hymns and thanksgivings to lamentations and didactic meditations, the answer that Israel offers up to God sounds forth as a "single polyphony of praise." It is praise for God's acts of deliverance, praise for God's righteous judgments, praise for God's actions in nature, praise for God's creation and preservation of the world, praise for God's rule of the world, praise for the "reality of the Beautiful" (pp. 356–64). It is praise that is essentially "ceaseless" (p. 356), until death itself renders it mute. In a curious way even death underscores that praise is the fundamental "token of being alive," because in death praise is no longer possible (p. 370). Here the Psalter provides insight into the basic features of a "theological doctrine of man" that goes beyond understandings common to the ancient world (p. 356). In the Hebraic view humanity is created to praise: "Praise is man's most characteristic mode of existence: praising and not praising stand over against one another like life and death" (p. 370).[21]

Von Rad continues this discussion by acknowledging that trials and sufferings at times tempered Israel's response to God (pp. 383–418). The vicissitudes of life inevitably pushed Israel to lamentation and to addressing God with the question "Why?" For the most part, however, at least until the seventh and sixth centuries, these questions did not threaten the foundations of faith. Ideas

---

Testament Theology, 117–43; Reventlow, *Problems of Old Testament Theology*, 125–33; R. Smend, *Die Mitte des Alten Testaments* (Zurich: EVZ, 1970).

21. Cf. Westermann (*Praise and Lament in the Psalms* [Atlanta: John Knox, 1981], 159), who makes the same point without isolating praise from its necessary complement, the prayer of lamentation.

about divine justice or the prosperity of the godless were not typically the subject of theoretical consideration. They did not necessarily call into question the meaning of life. Israel generally lived with these ideas "uncritically" (p. 384). "Looking at it as a whole, we must credit the older ages of Jahwism with a far greater ability to acquiesce even in vicissitudes it did not understand" (p. 387). The key to this acquiesence is the deeply ingrained Hebraic sense of corporate solidarity. In the face of threat or affliction, both individual and community found consolation in corporate worship (e.g., p. 389). Here too the Psalter provides for Israel's prayer, with psalms of lamentation that embolden the sufferer to "'hope in Jahweh' and await his fate-averting intervention" (p. 387; see also pp. 398–407).

At the beginning of the sixth century, however, a genuine crisis did emerge that initiated "an age of dangerous disintergration for the faith" (p. 391). The crisis was the collapse of the nation in 587. With the loss of the sense of corporate belonging, the individual Israelite was cast adrift in a sea of questions. "Why?" questions led to "monstrous observations" about divine justice and compassion (p. 391), in the face of which God seemed to withdraw into an "impenetrable and unbearable hiddenness" (p. 398). Von Rad is clear that it is not God but the people who have changed (p. 391). With Jeremiah and Ezekiel a generation begins to emerge who have lost contact with the saving history. The search for God is transferred from the cult to secular life. A "vapid" mental climate and a "hollow" piety develop that forsake foundational concepts of Jahwism (p. 391). The final result is the skepticism embodied in Ecclesiastes. Here at the "farthest frontier of Jahwism" (p. 458), faith is subjected to its gravest danger (p. 453).

To summarize, I offer the following observations about the treatment of prayer in this golden age of Hebrew Bible theology.

(1) In the major theologies of this era, prayer is not a subject for substantive discussion. It does receive attention in the two most influential works of this period, those of Eichrodt and von Rad, but neither intends to present a full theology of prayer. Instead, prayer is part of larger concerns (e.g., the cult or psalmody), and is introduced only generally.

(2) Where prayer does become a topic for even general discussion, it is the formalized cultic prayer represented in the Psalms that is understood to provide the primary biblical witness. As such, prayer is presented as a sacred action, offered in re-

sponse to God's saving acts of deliverance. Its principal form is praise. Its sustaining disposition is gratitude, humility, and submission before the exalted Yahweh God. Von Rad acknowledges responses other than praise, but generally he assigns these to a later stage in Israel's history when faith had begun to deteriorate.

(3)   A corollary of (2) is that little or no discussion is devoted to prayers outside the Psalter. Even von Rad, who gives pride of place to the theology of Israel's historical traditions, does not focus centrally on the prose prayers embedded within these narratives. Instead, he understands the theological focus of these traditions to be their witness to God's saving acts. Von Rad does not overlook humanity's response to God, but he relegates it to a position of secondary importance. For von Rad, the paradigmatic response of Israel is not found in historical narratives but in the Psalter and in the cultic worship that it serves.

(4)   One final observation is more difficult than the preceding ones to articulate clearly. Both Eichrodt and von Rad value the cult as the indispensable medium for "straitening" the discourse of individual piety into a liturgically authorized blend of passion and reverence. Conversely, they suggest that without the liturgical formalization of religion, private prayer becomes potentially disruptive. It may drift toward "a purely self-determined piety"[22] that claims too much freedom from the divine order. Or it may degenerate into a life of detachment where, like Ecclesiastes, skepticism about God's intervention in the world leaves one vulnerable to despair on all sides.[23]

Two things strike me as interesting about this understanding of cult in relation to prayer. First, it stands at some distance from the devaluation of cultic religion that characterized the history-of-religion approach. For example, Wellhausen considered the move from individualized forms of spontaneous worship to ritually prescribed ones to be a move away from authentic religion.[24] For Eichrodt and von Rad, the ritualization of worship does not represent the loss of authenticity. Instead, it represents something more like the preser-

---

22. Eichrodt, *Theology,* 1.100.
23. Von Rad, *Theology,* 1.456.
24. See n. 11.

vation or protection of religion from that which threatens to redirect it from its primary goal, the praise of God.

Second, Eichrodt and von Rad differ radically from the preceding generation in their understandings of individual religion. For Eichrodt and von Rad, one needs to guard against individual piety, lest it develop into destabilizing forms of religion. For earlier scholars it is the goal toward which authentic religion naturally moves, provided that its progress is not hindered by the imposition of ritual and prescription.

Both views seem to assume that religion and religious practices like prayer move in a linear development from one stage to another. It is also evident that these views disagree concerning the direction of this development. Is it from the individual and spontaneous to the official and prescribed, or vice versa? As I have already indicated in chapters 1 and 2, contemporary scholarship continues to debate this question, thus far without resolution. This discussion of Hebrew Bible theology's development between 1930 and 1960 makes clear that when one draws a dichotomy between the prayers represented by the Psalter and those occurring elsewhere, the Psalms garner most of the attention.

THE CONTEMPORARY DISCUSSION:
A DIALECTICAL SHAPE FOR OLD TESTAMENT THEOLOGY

In 1984 W. Brueggemann introduced a discussion of the "Futures in Old Testament Theology" with two observations: (1) the approaches of Eichrodt and von Rad are no longer adequate; and (2) the academy does not agree about what to do next.[25] Brueggemann suggests that scholars are therefore in a period of experimentation. They will try many approaches, and they will be criticized, but perhaps not too strongly, because, as Brueggemann notes, "no one is sure."[26] A measure of the truth of Brueggemann's analysis is the tremendous amount of activity in the area since 1970. Seven major Hebrew Bible theologies were published in English from 1978 to 1982.[27] From 1978 to 1988 numerous articles and monographs

---

25. W. Brueggemann, "Futures in Old Testament Theology," *HBT* 6 (1984): 1.
26. Ibid.
27. W. Zimmerli, *Old Testament Theology in Outline* (Atlanta: John Knox, 1978); R. E. Clements, *Old Testament Theology: A Fresh Approach* (Atlanta: John Knox, 1978); C. Westermann, *Elements of Old Testament Theology* (Atlanta: John Knox,

appeared that continue the exploration of new proposals for doing Hebrew Bible theology.[28] In this era of experimentation, the discipline of Hebrew Bible theology struggles to this day both to *embrace* and to *overcome* its indebtedness to Eichrodt and von Rad. On the one hand, one clearly cannot ignore either the multiplicity of the theologies in the Hebrew Bible or their diversity. On this point von Rad still speaks with great authority. The Herew Bible reflects theologies, not one theology, and the diversity of these theologies presents an ever-present caution against proposals that any one of them can adequately represent the whole.[29] Indeed, as R. Knierim has observed, the task for the future is largely defined by this most crucial problem: the coexistence within the Hebrew Bible of a plurality of theologies.[30] This fact increases significantly the difficulty of doing Hebrew Bible theology in the modern era. While the Hebrew Bible itself is the origin of the problem and its demand, it "offers no direct approach and answer to it."[31]

On the other hand, the quest for some unity in this recognized diversity, some central focus through which one can evaluate and appropriate essential theological claims, remains quite strong.[32] In this regard Eichrodt's attempt to find a central theme that provides structural unity for the Hebrew Bible message continues to have appeal. The current discussion of this matter, however, has shifted away from the pursuit of single themes, ideas, or concepts, such as covenant, as the organizing principle of Hebrew Bible theology. Now the general consensus is that no single motif is adequate foundation for a comprehensive theology. Instead, an effort has emerged to find dual concepts or polarities that, when held in dialectical tension, may serve a central, unifying purpose.

This dialectical approach produced a convergence of argument in recent Hebrew Bible theologies. W. Brueggemann has described such a convergence in the works by C. Westermann, S. Terrien, and

---

1982); E. A. Martens, *God's Design: A Focus on Old Testament Theology* (Grand Rapids: Baker, 1978); W. C. Kaiser, *Toward an Old Testament Theology* (Grand Rapids: Zondervan, 1978); S. Terrien, *The Elusive Presence: Toward a New Biblical Theology* (San Francisco: Harper and Row, 1978); W. A. Dyrness, *Themes in Old Testament Theology* (Downers Grove: InterVarsity, 1979).

28. For a survey see G. Hasel, *Old Testament Theology.*

29. Cf. J. Goldingay, *Theological Diversity and the Authority of the Old Testament* (Grand Rapids: Eerdmans, 1987).

30. R. Knierim, "The Task of Old Testament Theology," *HBT* 6 (1984): 25.

31. Ibid.

32. See n. 2.

P. Hanson.[33] Each of these authors uses a bipolar approach in order to place in necessary tension the theological claims of the historical-covenantal traditions on the one hand and the psalmic-sapiential traditions on the other. Brueggemann suggests that these bipolar proposals serve as a corrective to Eichrodt and von Rad by insisting that the historical-covenantal traditions alone are too narrow a basis for the theology of the Hebrew Bible.[34]

I focus here on this emerging interest in a dialectical approach, because it seems to provide the most fruitful context to date for a substantive inclusion of prayer in the theology of the Hebrew Bible. It is a simple but true observation that presentations constructed around a single center have produced theology with a decidedly *theo*centric perspective.[35] By contrast, theologies with a bipolar approach have sought to retain the necessary focus on God while according a complementary focus on humanity. In short, the foundation for theology in the one approach is *God,* in the other *God and humanity.*

One can discern the beginning of how such emphases develop by recalling a variety of the single and bipolar centers that scholars have proposed. Single concepts or motifs such as "covenant," "election," "promise," the "holiness of God," the "rulership of God," and the "kingdom of God" have as their common focus God, God's nature, and God's acts and deeds.[36] Dual centers like "the rule of God and the communion between God and man," "Yahweh the God of Israel, Israel the people of Yahweh," "I am Yahweh your God" (Exod 20:2) and (in response) "You Yahweh . . ." (Deut 26:10), propose that theology involves an interchange between God and people.[37] Without God, of course, one cannot have *theo*logy in

---

33. Brueggemann, "A Convergence in Recent Old Testament Theologies," *JSOT* 18 (1980): 2–18.

34. Ibid., 8.

35. Cf. Hasel, *Old Testament Theology,* 139–40.

36. See respectively Eichrodt, *Theology;* H. Wildberger, "Auf dem Wege zu einer biblischen Theologie," *EvT* 19 (1959): 70–90; W. C. Kaiser, "The Center of OT Theology: The Promise," *Themelios* 10 (1974): 1–10; E. Sellin, *Theologie des Alten Testaments* (Leipzig: A. Deichert, 1933), 19; H. Seebass, "Der Beitrag des AT zum Entwurf einer biblischen Theologie," *Wort und Dienst* 8 (1965): 34–42; G. Klein, "'Reich Gottes' als biblischer Zentralbegriff," *EvT* 30 (1970): 642–70. For other "centers" and further discussion, see Hasel, *Old Testament Theology,* 138–43.

37. See respectively G. Fohrer, *Theologische Grundstrukturen des Alten Testaments* (Berlin: de Gruyter, 1972), 95–112; Smend, *Mitte,* 49, 55; W. Zimmerli, "Alttestamentliche Traditionsgeschichte und Theologie," *Probleme biblischer Theologie: Gerhard von Rad zum 70. Geburtstag,* ed. H. W. Wolff (Munich: Chr. Kaiser, 1971), 632–47. See further idem, *Outline,* 13–15.

the strictest sense of that word. The dialectical approach to theology suggests, however, that another perspective is necessary: without proper attention to humanity's response to God, one loses essential elements of who and how God is in relationship with people.

No one has perceived this point more clearly or developed it more fully than C. Westermann in *Elements of Old Testament Theology*. Westermann understands that the theology of the Hebrew Bible is necessarily determined by the ongoing dialogue between God and humanity (p. 153). From God's side the relationship is initiated by saving acts and blessing words. The former entails specific historical acts of divine deliverance, principally recorded in the exodus-Sinai materials. The latter consists of God's continual blessing bestowed on all of humanity, especially as manifest in the context of creation. Both God's words and deeds are directed toward eliciting a response and in a real sense remain unfulfilled without this response (pp. 27, 153). What humanity offers then is the desired complement to God's initiative.

In Westermann's presentation humanity brings to the dialogue with God its own responding words and actions. The words are brought as prayers, particularly prayers of praise and lament. The actions are defined by obedience to commandment and law and by worship. Within this framework Westermann assigns a significant role to prayer in shaping the divine-human interchange (pp. 153–74). Although some may question whether prayer is a necessary and integral part of theology,[38] Westermann is certain that it is: "Decisive elements of what the Old Testament says about God can only be found in this response, so that it is indispensable for a theology of the Old Testament" (p. 154).

As preparation for his discussion of praise and lament, Westermann begins by tracing the historical development of prayer in the Hebrew Bible (pp. 154–57).[39] I have already summarized this presentation, and will only recapitulate the major points here.[40] Westermann traces three stages in prayer's development. In the earliest stage he identifies brief appeals to God that arise directly and natur-

---

38. Westermann notes that Western theology has tended to separate prayer from theology "in the real sense." One often finds it treated as a subordinate subject in the area of "liturgy" or "ethics" (*Elements,* 27). See further Zimmerli's affirmation of the role of the human "response" in Hebrew Bible theology (*Outline,* 141).

39. See further Westermann's presentation in "Gebet im Alten Testament," *BHH* 1.519–22; and more recently, *The Living Psalms* (Grand Rapids: Eerdmans, 1989), 13–16.

40. See pp. 28, 115–16, 210.

ally from situations in daily life. Such prayers occur typically within a narrative context and are presented as integral parts of the recounted course of events (e.g., Exod 18:10; Judg 15:18; 2 Sam 15:31). The occasion for the prayer requires no cultic framework, the pray-er no liturgical assistance.

In the second or middle stage these short calls to God come together in the formal structures of the Psalms. Units of once independent, brief prayers are fused into poetic compositions, which then become vehicles for worship. The monarchy and the state provide the undergirding societal structure that makes such prayer possible.

With the dissolution of the monarchy and the end of worship in the temple, prayer enters the third stage. In the long prose prayers of 1 Kings 8, Ezra 9, and Nehemiah 9, prayer undergoes a transformation with respect to both style and content. The style shifts from poetry to prose. The content shifts from lament to confession of sin. In Westermann's view this shift from protest to penitence is commensurate with the historical trauma of the exile, in the aftermath of which any protest of innocence would seem to have lost its foundations.

This historical overview of prayer's development enables Westermann to evaluate the Psalms as the highest level of prayer in the Hebrew Bible. The first stage provides the compositional units, which are then transformed into poetic creations, thus serving successive generations of the community of faith in ever-fresh worship experiences. In *Elements* he describes the third stage of prayer as a "post-history" (p. 154). When spontaneous and responsive prayers "retreat into the background," prayers that are "performed" offer a piety that is "weaker and more restrained."[41]

In this high valuation of liturgical prayer, Westermann follows von Rad and others in looking primarily to the Psalter for Israel's response. Like von Rad, Westermann finds in the Psalms that praise of God is an essential part of Israel's life. Unlike von Rad, however, Westermann insists that Israel's response was never confined to praise alone. In the Psalter Westermann finds the clearest witness in the Hebrew Bible to the continual polarity between praise and lament. Von Rad spoke only of praise, Westermann suggests, because of his "one-sided conception of salvation history" (p. 28). Westermann makes it clear that in his estimation lament is no less an essential part of what Israel offers to God than praise. "Praise of

---

41. Westermann, *Living Psalms,* 15.

God is the joy of life directed to God, while human suffering which turns to God comes to expression in the lament" (p. 28). Here are the two basic modes of prayer in Israel—praise and lament. In Westermann's opinion, "In Israel all speaking to God moved between these two poles."[42]

Westermann's form-critical work on praise and lament psalms began in the 1950s.[43] Through a number of important studies Westermann has helped clarify the distinctions between "narrative" and "descriptive" praise as well as the structure of lament and its three-dimensional frame of reference.[44] I have already summarized Westermann's contributions in these areas, and my reliance upon them, in chapters 7 and 8. Here I focus specifically on Westermann's decision to attribute to both praise and lament a substantive role in the formation of the theology of the Hebrew Bible.

In *Elements of Old Testament Theology* one can see the goal toward which Westermann's long work on the Psalms has been directed: the incorporation of lament and praise as integral and necessary parts of human existence before God. Both praise and lament reflect in important ways who God is; hence both are indispensable for the theological enterprise. The saving acts of God elicit "narrative praise" as the appropriate response to specific divine initiatives toward humanity. The ongoing, continual blessings of God become the subject of "descriptive praise" when who God is, rather than what God has done, summons the worship of praise. In these two modes of the praise response, Israel's prayers proclaim the encounter with God from the human perspective. The saving and blessing God is at work in the lives of people, who cannot help but respond accordingly.

---

42. Westermann, *Praise and Lament,* 154; cf. idem, *Elements,* 156; *Living Psalms,* 1.

43. C. Westermann, *Das Loben Gottes in den Psalmen* (Göttingen: Vandenhoeck und Ruprecht, 1954), translated as *The Praise of God in the Psalms* (Atlanta: John Knox, 1965).

44. On praise see Westermann, *Praise and Lament,* 81–135; *The Psalms: Structure, Content and Message* (Minneapolis: Augsburg, 1980), 24–27; *Living Psalms,* 168–69, 202–3. Concerning lament, Westermann has demonstrated on form-critical grounds that the lament is characterized by three determinative elements: God, the one who laments, and the enemy. Cf. "Struktur und Geschichte der Klage im Alten Testament," *ZAW* 66 (1954): 44–80 (translated as "The Structure and History of the Lament in the Old Testament," *Praise and Lament,* 165–213); "The Role of the Lament in the Theology of the Old Testament," *Int* 28 (1974): 20–38 (repr. in *Praise and Lament,* 259–80); *The Structure of the Book of Job: A Form-Critical Analysis* (Philadelphia: Fortress, 1981), 11–13; *Living Psalms,* 21–23, 65–68.

The response of lament is not different. This too proclaims with equal authenticity the encounter with God from the human perspective. Lament's perception of God is of course different from that of praise. Although no less affirmed, the saving and blessing God is encountered as not as much at work in the lives of people as they expect or desire or need. Here too the people can only respond accordingly with lament and protest and petition for renewed divine initiatives.

While the response of praise has regularly been accorded a role in Hebrew Bible theology, one cannot say the same for lament (p. 168). No one has worked harder to redress the neglect of the theological significance of lament than Westermann. In *Elements* he presents his various proposals in this regard in a fuller theological context. The human response of lament is "an inevitable part of what happens between God and man."[45] A theology that does not attend to this fact does not report the full picture. Indeed, such a theology stands to diminish the Hebraic understanding of both God and humanity.

Westermann has made the only effort to date to treat prayer as a major contributing element in the theology of the Hebrew Bible. But at least one other proposal has emerged that in many ways builds on Westermann's central ideas and suggests that they be extended in new directions. I refer to two programmatic essays by Brueggemann outlining a new dialectical shape for the theology of the Hebrew Bible.

Brueggemann proposes that in the Hebrew Bible faith serves both to "legitimate structure" and to "embrace pain."[46] In his first essay he contends that it legitimates structure by partaking fully in the "common theology" of the ancient Near Eastern world.[47] This commonly held theology affirms, among other things, that a sovereign god secures and maintains an orderliness to the world. One addresses this high god in flattering prayer and praise, and, if the order of the world should seem disrupted, also in prayers of confession and submission. The divine-human relationship is understood to be "contractual" and nonnegotiable. That is, a strict principle of retribution applies: the good are rewarded; the evil, punished. The sys-

---

45. Westermann, *Praise and Lament,* 261; cf. *Elements,* 169.

46. Brueggemann, "A Shape for Old Testament Theology, I: Structure Legitimation," *CBQ* 47 (1985): 28–46; "A Shape for Old Testament Theology, II: Embrace of Pain," *CBQ* 47 (1985): 395–415.

47. Here Brueggemann follows the argument of M. Smith, "The Common Theology of the Ancient Near East," *JBL* 71 (1952): 35–47.

tem is always in effect, its reliability never in question. Such contractual theology serves to legitimate order and the current social, economic, and political structures that are (divinely) designated to implement this order (pp. 32–36).

Brueggemann finds affirmations of this common theology throughout the Hebrew Bible, from the sanctions in the Sinaitic covenant traditions promising rewards and punishments, to the prophets and the sages who repeatedly endorse the linkage between deed and consequence. Indeed, one may say that this common theology is the primary theological perspective in the Hebrew Bible (pp. 40–41).[48] Brueggemann is intent on pursuing both the positive and the negative theological consequences of this common theology.

Common theology must always be subjected to "sharp critique," Brueggemann suggests, and in the Hebrew Bible it is (p. 42). The Hebrew Bible is not just a reaffirmation of common theological maxims. Instead it witnesses candidly to the inevitable crisis that emerges when the reality of life does not square with the affirmations of faith. In his second essay Brueggemann argues that the primary challenge to a "contractual theology" has to do with justice issues, especially those issues usually framed by the term "theodicy" (pp. 397–98). Here Brueggemann observes that the key element in Israel's critique is the practice of lament (p. 400). Lament insists that pain and suffering must be embraced, not only by the social-political-economic structures, or by the individuals within these structures, but also by God (p. 398).

Israel's practice of lament represents for Brueggemann a distinctive departure from "common theology" affirmations. Although it is in one sense a "rhetorical form of civil (sometimes uncivil) disobedience" (p. 402), it is at the same time a daring act of obedience that forces a recalculation of the divine-human relationship for both God and Israel.

Like Westermann, Brueggemann recognizes that lament is not a marginal act in Hebraic faith. Brueggemann moves beyond Westermann's rather singular focus on the Psalms, however, to trace what he calls a "countertradition" of lament throughout the Hebrew Bible (p. 405). He cites as major witnesses to this countertradition the protests of Moses (e.g., Exod 32:31-32; Num 11:10-15), the lament psalms (esp. Psalm 88), the laments of Jeremiah (e.g., Jer 20:7-12), and the protests of Job (e.g., Job 9:19-24) (pp. 402–6).

---

48. See further "Embrace of Pain," 414.

This countertradition remains only a minority voice in the Hebrew Bible—the primary voice bespeaks structure legitimation—but it is nevertheless a crucial voice, for the embrace of pain forces a new connection between theological affirmations and the troublesome reality of life (p. 399). From this perspective Brueggemann raises the possibility that this lament tradition, with its radical approach to God, may be "the primary material for Old Testament theology" (p. 407).

In the preceding survey I have described the general neglect of the subject "prayer" in Hebrew Bible theology. The presentation has admittedly not treated many important aspects of the discussion.[49] Nevertheless, I have noted certain developments and emphases that help shape a general understanding of how prayer has been considered within the theological enterprise. I summarize these as follows:

(1) By and large, from the middle of the nineteenth century to the present, prayer has not been a major subject in the discipline of Hebrew Bible theology. To date, the only substantive treatment of the subject within this context has come from C. Westermann.

(2) In those who accord some peripheral discussion to prayer, one may discern particular one-dimensional emphases: (a) attention focuses usually on the Psalms as the preeminent witness to Hebraic prayer; (b) the Psalter, then, is usually treated as witness to Israel's formal practice of worship in the temple

---

49. One of the more glaring omissions is the whole matter of the biblical theology movement. For the major elements of consensus in this approach, see B. Childs, *Biblical Theology in Crisis* (Philadelphia: Westminster, 1970), 32–50; Barr, "Biblical Theology," 105; Hayes and Prussner, *Old Testament Theology,* 209–18. For a more comprehensive presentation of the historical developments leading up to and influencing this approach, see H.-J. Kraus, *Die Biblische Theologie: Ihre Geschichte und Problematik* (Neukirchen: Neukirchener Verlag, 1970); H. G. Reventlow, *Problems of Biblical Theology in the Twentieth Century* (Philadelphia: Fortress, 1986).

In general this movement showed little interest in including "prayer" as a subject for theological reflection. One may note in this regard the work of B. Childs, who has continued to pursue these matters with respect to the "canonical context" of Hebrew Bible theology (*Old Testament Theology in a Canonical Context* [Philadelphia: Fortress, 1986]). Childs includes a chapter on "The Shape of the Obedient Life" in which he focuses on Israel's "response" to the activity of God. Here he refers to the prayers of the Psalter, which, from a canonical perspective, have undergone a hermeneutical shift. In its final form the Psalter provides the means for the community of faith to continue to hear God's word through the voice of the psalmist's prayer: "these prayers now function as the divine word itself" (207).

that, along with the practice of sacrifice, constitutes Israel's offerings to God; (c) prayer as perceived in the Psalter and understood in association with sacrifice comes to be defined as a sacred act of obedience to the sovereign God; and (d) prayer as obedience expresses itself principally as praise and submission to the sovereign will of God. Indeed, the avoidance of primitive conceptions of prayer as a means of manipulating or coercing divine favor helps establish the spiritual maturity of Hebraic faith.

(3)   Most Hebrew Bible theologies have been decidedly theocentric in orientation. The major theological truths of the Hebrew Bible have consequently been understood to derive from who God is and what God has done. Humanity's contribution to the divine-human relationship has usually received comparatively little attention even from those who include some theological reflection on it.

(4)   Proposals advocating a dialectical or bipolar center for Hebrew Bible theology have given a fuller discussion of prayer. Especially Westermann and Brueggemann have considered humanity's response to God an integral part of the nucleus of theology. This response is understood to include both praise and lament. The one is an authentic witness to God's specific and continual presence; the other is an equally authentic expression of human need and quest for divine presence. The polarity of praise and lament is for Westermann indispensable in the theological evaluation of the divine human relationship. For Brueggemann the "restless probes" of Hebraic lament "may be the *primary* material for OT theology" (emphasis added).[50]

RETROSPECT AND PROSPECT:
THE NEED FOR A STUDY OF THE STUDY

In the preceding survey I have limited myself to a merely descriptive account of the major developments in Hebrew Bible theology with respect to the subject of prayer. Such a survey enables one to document the academy's consistent neglect of this particular subject throughout most of the history of the discipline. It does not, however, address one question that I believe should also be important to the guild: *Why?* Why does biblical scholarship pursue the

---

50. Brueggemann, "Embrace of Pain," 407.

topics it does, when it does, as it does? To focus the question more specifically, Why was prayer not a central concern in the historical approach to religion that dominated the end of the nineteenth century? What was the setting for biblical scholarship during this period that pushed scholars toward preoccupation with history as the key for interpreting the Bible and away from other concerns? Why was prayer relegated to a position of relative unimportance in the work of Eichrodt and von Rad precisely during a period when theological emphases within the Hebrew Bible were becoming the center of attention? What were the cultural, political, and historical contexts that gave to that generation of scholars their particular questions and concerns? Why now, in the last decades of the twentieth century, is a hermeneutic emerging in biblical studies that permits, if not requires, a focus on prayer as an important topic in theological reflection?

Such questions point to the need for what J. Rogerson calls a "study of the study."[51] Responding to Wellhausen's suggestion that "philosophy does not precede, but follows [biblical criticism]," Rogerson counters that a study of the history of biblical scholarship does not support such a claim. Instead, a "study of the study" shows that seemingly neutral discoveries have been made in and affected by philosophical, cultural, and political contexts.[52] Rogerson himself has analyzed discerningly the different philosophical presuppositions that provide the context for biblical scholarship in England and Germany in the nineteenth century.[53]

Others have made important, yet partial, probes into the history of biblical scholarship from several different perspectives.[54] Each of

51. J. Rogerson, "Philosophy and the Rise of Biblical Criticism: England and Germany," *England and Germany: Studies in Theological Diplomacy,* ed. S. W. Sykes (Frankfurt: Peter Lang, 1982), 63–79.

52. Ibid., 75.

53. See Rogerson's subsequent, more comprehensive, treatment of these matters in *Old Testament Criticism in the Nineteenth Century: England and Germany* (Philadelphia: Fortress, 1985).

54. For example, T. K. Cheyne's classic survey, *Founders of Old Testament Criticism: Biographical, Descriptive, and Critical Studies* (New York: Charles Scribner's Sons, 1893), represents an early effort to place Hebrew Bible scholars and their work in their historical setting. Unfortunately, as Rogerson has noted (*Criticism,* 2), Cheyne's work is an extreme example of analysis in which the criterion for the judgment of others is the opinion of the one doing the judging. R. Oden represents another approach *(Bible Without Theology).* He seeks to clarify the broad intellectual context in which biblical scholarship has operated for much of the nineteenth and twentieth centuries. He points specifically to the influence of the nineteenth-century German tradition of "theological historiography," which produces a biblical scholarship characterized by "radically contextualized value

these efforts to engage the history of biblical scholarship has helped clarify some of the contexts that have led to particular questions and answers. The picture is still far from complete. In many cases one does not have access to the biographical material that would make it possible to interpret a scholar's work against his or her life setting.[55] In other cases one may possess the data but lack the sophisticated skills of the historian or the sociologist to interpret it. Indeed, one may wonder whether a guild of biblical scholars is fully capable of an in-house, critical assessment of its own scholarship.[56] To put the question more directly, is a study of the study too important to be left to biblical scholars alone?[57] Perhaps a new mode of investigation is required, one characterized by collegiality and interdependence among several fields of study and expertise.[58]

Within the context of these limitations I risk the following provisional observations concerning the cultural setting of scholarship

---

judgments" (155). J. Hayes and F. Prussner *(Old Testament Theology)* represent a third approach. They have included philosophical, cultural, and historical issues in their comprehensive analysis of Hebrew Bible theology. For a similar approach, though restricted to the "biblical theology movement," see Childs, *Biblical Theology in Crisis,* 17–27.

55. Cf. R. Smend, *Deutsche Alttestamentler in drei Jahrhunderten* (Göttingen: Vandenhoeck and Ruprecht, 1989). In a series of short biographical essays Smend traces the relationship between the thoughts and the lives of some of the most important German Hebrew Bible scholars of the last three centuries. Smend himself does not pursue sociological questions as such, but he has certainly provided the kind of biographical material that should inform interpretations of the life work of given scholars.

56. It is increasingly clear that one's own particular religious prejudices play no small role in one's biblical interpretation. I noted in chap. 1 that a number of scholars from Hempel to Reventlow have criticized the Protestant bias that too often has influenced objective scholarly assessments (see pp. 10–12). A more embarrassing and unsettling critique of the confessional tilt in the academy has come from Jewish scholars. They insist, quite correctly, that Christian scholars must wake up to the anti-Semitic prejudices that dog our theological methods and skew our interpretation of the Hebrew Bible. See, e.g., J. Levenson, "Why Jews Are Not Interested in Biblical Theology," *Judaic Perspectives in Ancient Israel,* ed. J. Neusner and B. Levine (Philadelphia: Fortress, 1987), 281–307; idem, "Theological Consensus or Historicist Evasion? Jews and Christians in Biblical Studies," *Hebrew Bible or Old Testament?* ed. R. Brooks and J. Collins (Notre Dame: Univ. of Notre Dame Press, 1990), 109–45; M. H. Goshen-Gottstein, "Tanakh Theology," *Ancient Israelite Religion: Essays in Honor of Frank Moore Cross,* ed. P. Miller, et al. (Philadelphia: Fortress, 1987), 617–44; M. Tsevat, "Theology of the Old Testament—A Jewish View," *HBT* 8 (1987): 33–50.

57. Cf. Rogerson, "Philosophy and the Rise of Biblical Criticism," 76.

58. Cf. the comments of S. McFague concerning the necessity of a paradigm shift toward more collegiality in the construction of a theological agenda for the twenty-first century ("An Earthly Theological Agenda," *Christian Century* 108, no. 1 [Jan. 2–9, 1991]: 12–15).

and why scholars have or have not taken up the subject of prayer. I offer these thoughts not as a final word on these matters but as a first word, as an invitation to other words that may correct, deepen, clarify, and advance our common understanding.

One may begin by locating the three major periods in Hebrew Bible theology that I have identified within the matrix of their respective historical settings. As Hempel suggested, one may view the history-of-religion approach to the Hebrew Bible as originating in the eighteenth-century Enlightenment.[59] The Enlightenment's emphasis on rational, objective inquiry informs a period of biblical scholarship that accents the autonomy of both the Bible and the scholar. The Bible is no longer exclusively the sacred text of the church. It is also, perhaps even primarily, one text among many texts that invites and requires critical, historical investigation. The scholar does not look first to the dogmas of the church before turning to the text for scriptural support. Rather, the scholar looks first objectively to the text, frequently as a means of countering directives of the church that skew biblical interpretation in support of self-sustaining doctrines.

Given this context, one can speculate on the linkage between the Enlightenment ideology of autonomy and the neglect of the subject "prayer" in biblical scholarship. In the history-of-religion approach, the emphases on *history* and *religion* both derive from and critique a particular cultural context. The emphasis on history derives from the Enlightenment commitment to empirical research. With this commitment it is likely that biblical scholarship in the nineteenth century did not find prayer to be a productive subject for investigation. Scholarship might document that particular prayer rituals existed in Israelite history or that specific prayer texts could be dated to general periods; but beyond such particulars, the theological issues of the phenomenon of prayer itself—what it says about God and God's relation to humanity—fall outside the possibility of empirical verification. Such issues are best left to the discipline of dogmatic theology, where philosophical speculation and confessional prejudice have a more determinative influence.

It is also likely, however, that the subject of prayer is undervalued for more than only the lack of empirical data. One may understand the emphases in biblical scholarship on religion and religious practices as both a critique of and a means of escape from the normative

---

59. See pp. 10, 228. For further discussion see Hayes and Prussner, *Old Testament Theology*, 35–71.

interpretation of *Theologie* that dominated in Germany during this period. With the breakdown of scholastic orthodoxy in the eighteenth century, Pietism and Rationalism emerged as the two principal contenders for authority in religious life. Pietism expressed itself primarily in terms of subjective experience and personal religion. From an institutional perspective it tended to operate within the Lutheran Church, hence generally to support, either through acquiescence or silence, the tacit alliance between crown and altar. Rationalism was far broader in its outreach, penetrating not only the field of religion but also economic, political, and social fields. In all these fields Rationalism promoted a critique of the current landscape that called for reevaluation of the operative norms. One of the clearest statements of the matter comes from Kant:

> Our age is the age of criticism, to which everything must be subjected. The sacredness of religion, and the authority of legislation, are by many regarded as grounds of exemption from the examination of this tribunal. But, if they are exempted, they become the subjects of just suspicion, and cannot lay claim to sincere respect, which reason accords only to that which has stood the test of a free and public examination. (*Critique of Pure Reason*, p. 15)[60]

It is in the spirit of this critique that the history-of-religion school focuses on the function of religion in society. No doubt prayer and other expressions of religious piety that could be understood to support uncritically the authority of the church in society become the "subjects of just suspicion."

If the setting for much of biblical scholarship in the nineteenth century is the Enlightenment's confident accent on the autonomy of human reason, the setting in the first half of the twentieth century is quite different indeed. It is estimated that from 1915 to 1945 (i.e., from the start of World War I to the end of World War II) some seventy million people died in Europe and Russia as the result of various acts of human barbarism. It is a period so defined by the horrors of death, destruction, and inhumanity that one may describe it with G. Steiner as "a season in hell."[61] In the midst of such brutality and brokenness the business of rational analysis becomes increasingly bankrupt. Traditional historiography proves inadequate precisely because the reality of the evil far exceeds any calculable causality. Biblical scholarship, no less than any other disci-

---

60. Quoted in Hayes and Prussner, *Old Testament Theology,* 53.
61. G. Steiner, *In Bluebeard's Castle: Some Notes towards the Redefinition of Culture* (New Haven: Yale Univ. Press, 1971), 29–56.

pline of inquiry into truth and knowledge, must create a new language if it is to speak meaningfully to a humanity so destroyed and self-destroying.

The new language of biblical scholarship during this season in hell is enunciated most clearly in the work of K. Barth (1886–1968). Barth rejects the anthropocentrism of the nineteenth century, which insists that the starting point for truth and knowledge is the autonomy of human reason. He maintains that the starting point is not humanity but God, not reason but revelation. Thus begins a new *theo*logical language with a focus on the transcendent God, who is independent of human thinking, feeling, or willing. This emphasis on God corresponds with both human need and human helplessness. Apart from divine initiative, humans cannot, through natural faculties, comprehend the transcendent God. Likewise, the transcendent God can never be identified as equal to the sum total of human reason.

In Barth's neo-orthodoxy, prayer becomes a subject of central importance for theological reflection.[62] Although I cannot review here his full discussion of the matter,[63] it is worth reflecting on how certain salient characteristics of his presentation contribute to the new context for the golden age of Hebrew Bible theology.

For Barth, prayer is first and foremost a matter of obedience to God.[64] One prays not out of power or powerlessness, not out of desire or disposition, but rather in obedience to God's order and command. In this sense, prayer is turning toward God and away from self. It is a preoccupation with God and God's initiative in the world that testifies to the human willingness to conform to God's inscrutable providence. It is a *listening to* God rather than a *speaking about* God. It is a response to who God is and what God has done in God's world, not a declaration of humanity's potential or initiative. In short, for Barth authentic prayer necessarily begins and ends in the worship of God through praise and thanksgiving. The emphasis is clearly on theology, not anthropology, on God's

---

62. Note esp. Barth's discussion of prayer in *Church Dogmatics,* III/3 (Edinburgh: T. & T. Clark, 1960), 239–88; III/4 (1961), 97–102; IV/2 (1958), 699–708; IV/3.2 (1962), 865–901; *Evangelical Theology: An Introduction* (New York: Holt, Rinehart and Winston, 1963), 159–70; *Prayer,* ed. D. Saliers (2d ed.; Philadelphia: Westminster, 1985).

63. For further discussion see P. LeFevre, *Understandings of Prayer* (Philadelphia: Westminster, 1981), 28–45; K. Schmidt, "Karl Barth's Theology of Prayer" (Ph.D. diss., Princeton University, 1980).

64. Barth, *Church Dogmatics* III/4, 92ff.

sovereignty and humanity's response of self-surrender and glad obedience.[65]

Barth is also clear that prayer is not only an act of worship directed to God but also a means of ministry in the world.[66] Authentic prayer has a necessary movement from praise and adoration to petition and intercession. The ordering of this movement is important, for God hears only those prayers that conform to God's initiatives for the world. Barth illustrates this point with reference to the Lord's Prayer.[67] He notes that the first three petitions in this model prayer focus on God's glory: "Hallowed be *thy* name," *"Thy* kingdom come," *"Thy* will be done." When one prays for these ends one confesses a willingness to participate with God in the accomplishment of God's will for the world. The last three petitions— "Give *us . . . ,"* "Forgive *us . . . ,"* "Lead *us . . ."*—move directly into the world of human need. Together, these petitions affirm two important truths about biblical prayer: (1) God does not will to accomplish the divine plan for the world *without* human participation. That is, God's cause in the world is also humanity's cause. (2) God does not will that the needs of the world be the object of human concern alone. That is, humanity's cause in the world is also God's cause.[68] When petitions and intercessions for human need are ordered under God's design for the world, the biblical witness is that God hears the prayers of God's own.

Barth's emphasis on prayer as obedience in ordered praise and petition marks a confessional response to a world falling apart. In a time of crisis Barth accents *theo*logy rather than *anthropo*logy, the sovereignty of God over the autonomy of human reason, praise and petition that conform to God's will in place of human initiatives that are self-concerned and self-promoting. It is reasonable to suggest that the theological emphases of Eichrodt and von Rad are part of this same confessional endeavor to respond to the crisis of the times.

For both Eichrodt and von Rad it is a matter of urgent impor-

---

65. Cf. Reventlow, who suggests that the emphasis in Western theology on divine transcendence and human surrender is the product of an Aristotelian metaphysics that effectively "depersonalizes" the God of the Hebrew Bible (*Gebet,* 9–80). Although Reventlow discusses a wide range of theologians whose presentations on prayer he judges to reflect this philosophical orientation, he does not discuss Barth in any substantive way.

66. Barth, *Church Dogmatics,* IV/3.2, 865–901. See further Barth's discussion of prayer as "theological work" (*Evangelical Theology,* 159–70).

67. Cf. Barth, *Prayer,* 47–86.

68. Cf. Schmidt, "Karl Barth's Theology of Prayer," 183–211.

tance to affirm the sovereign, covenanting God who works in the history of Israel—and in *all* history—to secure the salvation of the faithful. The need is to be able to look beyond the foibles and fearful designs of humanity to the God who transcends the horrors of the moment with the promise of hope and deliverance. For Eichrodt, who was Barth's colleague at Basel, this understanding is reflected in the interpretation of prayer as obedient and willing submission to the "authority of the covenant God."[69] In relationship with this covenant God, piety is necessarily bounded by a deep sense of creatureliness.[70] For von Rad prayer as praise is the normative response of the faithful to the God who is so powerfully at work in history.[71] With Barth, Eichrodt and von Rad find in the biblical text an important, effective, and credible theological response to the crisis that shapes their world.

Despite the undisputed theological contributions of Eichrodt and von Rad, one notices a curious non sequitur between their response to the crises of the twentieth century and the responses to the crises of the sixth century B.C.E. in Israel preserved in the Bible. With the destruction of Jerusalem in 586 B.C.E., Israel enters a period defined both geographically and theologically as exile. It is a time of displacement and alienation not only from the land but seemingly from God as well. Although many responses emerge from Israel's experience in exile, as I have suggested in chapter 7, one response is clearly the practice of lamentation and mourning, protest and challenge. In Israel, praise and trustful submission to divine providence are legitimate confessional responses to a world full of violence and despair. But these are by no means the limits of faithful response.

The first half of the twentieth century, punctuated by the rise to power in 1933 of the National Socialists in Germany, presented that generation of biblical scholarship with an experience in exile no less demanding than that of their biblical ancestors. Indeed, Jewish thought identifies two events in history as equally horrifying experiences of God's hiddenness: the destruction of Jerusalem by Nebuchadnezzar, and the systematic annhilation of six million Jews by Hitler.[72] It is interesting that in such a world Eichrodt and von Rad

---

69. Eichrodt, *Theology,* 1.70.

70. Ibid., 100.

71. Von Rad, *Theology,* 2.369–70.

72. On the discussion of God's presence in the aftermath of the radical evil of the Jewish holocaust, see E. Fackenheim, *God's Presence in History: Jewish Affirmations and Philosophical Reflections* (New York: Harper and Row, 1970). The

are drawn primarily to *one* of the confessional responses modeled in the biblical texts: praise and confident yielding to the sovereign dominion of God. For von Rad especially, Israel's other, more dissenting responses are evidence of a "hollow" and skeptical piety that forsakes foundational beliefs in God.[73] The theological message would seem to be: God is at work in the world, and whether in Babylon or in Europe, God's people should remain focused with "a single polyphony of praise"[74] on the inscrutable sovereignty of God.

It is not my intention to be critical or suspicious of the influences informing the theological judgments of Eichrodt and von Rad. I do want, however, to invite reflection on several questions based on the preceding observations. In the midst of crisis, does a religious community typically feel itself compelled by internal uncertainty and external threat to survival to reaffirm trust in God's ultimate dominion? Perhaps to allow questions and doubt a free hand in the midst of crisis is to risk severing the already tenuous grip of faith and hope. Does the community of faith tilt toward praise and submission as necessary mechanisms for survival especially when alternative responses are too fearful to sustain community identity and support? Is the community of faith inevitably drawn to reaffirm God's sovereignty in the midst of human barbarity, because otherwise it can affirm nothing, expect nothing, hope for nothing beyond the cruel reality of the present? These questions are clearly not only theological but also sociological. What are the social constituents of exile and what are the behavioral as well as theological responses typically generated by religious groups in the midst of crisis?[75] From a sociological or anthropological point of view, one wonders whether crisis situations for religious communities generate theological affirmations rather than analytical reflections.

The biblical literature portrays lamentation as not only a *post-crisis* reflection but also an *in-crisis* response that speaks to the pain of the moment.[76] In the biblical scholarship that produces the golden age of Hebrew Bible theology, however, the recognition of

---

literature on this subject is growing significantly. In my own thinking I have especially appreciated the work by A. Cohen, *The Tremendum: A Theological Interpretation of the Holocaust* (New York: Crossroad, 1988).

73. Von Rad, *Theology,* 1.391, 458.

74. Ibid., 356.

75. On this question see esp. D. Smith, *The Religion of the Landless: The Social Context of the Babylonian Exile* (Bloomington, Ind.: Meyer Stone, 1989), 49–90.

76. Cf. Smith (ibid., 52–53, 204), whose sociological approach confirms that in times of great stress religious communities commonly produce lament and mourning literature as an important mechanism for surviving the crisis.

lamentation as an in-crisis response for the community of faith is not demonstrably present. Rather, in its "season of hell" biblical scholarship promotes a confessional response marked by an overriding commitment to *theo*logy, not *anthropo*logy, to divine sovereignty that transcends human failure. In one sense it is a scholarship of theodicy. Its theological emphases affirm God's providential guidance in history and summon the community to survive the crisis of the times through praise and ordered petition.

Before moving to an analysis of postwar theologies, I will summarize the presentation thus far. I have suggested that biblical scholarship in the nineteenth century operates out of an Enlightenment context where confidence in human reason informs decidedly anthropocentric emphases. But, two world wars and unparalleled acts of human savagery so silence this confident anthropocentrism that biblical scholarship in the first half of the twentieth century must find a new voice. It speaks no longer primarily of humanity, but of God. Its principal agenda is theology, not history. In the former setting, prayer is a subject of little importance, because it defies rational inquiry and yields too easily to confessional and institutional prejudice. In the latter, prayer is a more urgent concern, because it is a principal means for a beleaguered faith community to refocus on a transcendent and still sovereign God. In this setting historical calamity reshapes biblical scholarship by insisting that the history of God's people cannot be *told* or *lived* without reference to God. Hence, in its golden age of Hebrew Bible theology, biblical scholarship is markedly *theo*centric, not *anthropo*centric, in its orientation.

In the aftermath of World War II, a different landscape defines the theological task of biblical scholarship. Just as in a previous generation confidence in humanity's capacity to reason and to direct the goal of history is undone by incalculable human barbarity, so in the wake of this seemingly unrestrained barbarity, confessional accents on divine dominion in history may seem to have only a "lacquered depth."[77] I have suggested that the theologies that emerge from this postwar context share a common commitment to explore the Hebrew Bible for a credible balance between divine sovereignty and human responsibility. In this dialectical approach, especially as represented by Westermann and Brueggemann, prayer becomes an indispensable subject in the development of the theology of the Hebrew Bible.

---

77. This suggestive phrase I take from Steiner (*In Bluebeard's Castle,* 60) for whom it describes the claims of Western civilization in the wake of two world wars.

My task here is to probe for the reasons that scholars in the last decades of the twentieth century are open to theological constructs that attempt to balance *theocentric and anthropocentric* perspectives. In a general way one may certainly understand contemporary scholarship to be both a product of and a response to the paradigmatic shifts in hermeneutical models with which scholars work. Biblical scholarship is in the midst of a methodological shift, moving from traditional diachronic forms of exegesis to synchronic approaches, in which mostly ahistorical, literary concerns increasingly shape biblical interpretation. It is not yet clear how or if scholars will finally work out these shifting emphases. Meanwhile, it is reasonable to suspect that the new-found pluralism and openness to a variety of reading perspectives will continue to invite new subjects, like prayer, into the arena of critical, theological discussion.

It is also likely that this openness to new methodologies is linked to a shift in the institutional setting that provides the context for much of contemporary biblical scholarship. Brueggemann has suggested that the contemporary emphasis on a dialectical approach can be related to the current ease between confessing community and academy.[78] Scholars today are not confronted as much with a normative *Theologie* or an imposing political co-option of religion as were previous generations of biblical scholars—at least not blatantly so. The contemporary cultural context of relative stability affords scholars the luxury of pluralism and scholarly balance. As Brueggemann puts it, "the maintainers of such a neat dialectic are not likely to be the ones who defy Pharaoh for the sake of freedom."[79]

R. Oden has made a similar point about the institutional setting of contemporary biblical scholarship. He notes that the setting throughout most of the nineteenth and twentieth centuries has been the Christian seminary or universities expressly committed to training ministers for the church.[80] In such a setting it is understandable that historical judgments about the Bible have been influenced by the decidedly apologetic context in which they have arisen. This context of theological historiography exists clearly, according to Oden, in the confession-laden value judgments informing the theologies of both Eichrodt and von Rad.[81]

78. Brueggemann, "Convergence," 13. See further the discussion in chap. 1, pp. 6–7.
79. Brueggemann, "Convergence," 13.
80. Oden, *Bible Without Theology,* 4.
81. Ibid., 155–57.

Contemporary biblical scholarship takes place in a different intellectual and institutional setting. The seminary no longer provides the only, or primary, context for biblical study. Now, more than ever before, the setting is the modern university, and in this context theologically prompted autonomy is no longer necessary or appropriate.[82] This new context requires that traditional biblical study be replaced by something more like comparative religion or the anthropology of religion. In short, Oden argues that the new institutional setting for biblical study requires a "systematic shunning of theological argumentation,"[83] failing which the study of religion cannot survive in modern academia.

Both the methodological paradigms and the institutional settings for biblical scholarship have clearly changed for the post–world war generation. How to evaluate these changes requires more and different critical analyses than is currently available to scholars. At this preliminary juncture in the study of the study one must be content with tentative observations and partial conclusions. My own assessment at this stage is that the majority of those who have taken up the contemporary challenge of writing Hebrew Bible theologies do not share Oden's sense of the need for biblical study that is theologically neutral. This is patently true of Westermann and Brueggemann, both of whom have consciously worked to hold in dynamic tension the focus on the biblical text by both the academy and the confessing community.

Westermann himself has offered a brief glimpse into the world that shaped his own theological thinking.[84] His career began at the church seminary *(Kirchliche Hochschule)* in Berlin a few years after World War II. He describes it as a time defined by "intense suffering" and "the collapse of everything."[85] For a teacher of theology it was a time marked by the need for "a strong coalescence of 'academic' theology (determined by disciplined study) and 'pastoral' theology (determined by practical requirements)."[86] In the aftermath of war biblical scholarship could ignore neither the pain nor the politics that confronted a divided nation. Likewise, in Westermann's view, the confessing community could no longer

---

82. Ibid., 160.

83. Ibid.

84. C. Westermann, "Experience in the Church and the Work of Theology," *Word and World* 10 (1990): 7–13.

85. Ibid., 7.

86. Ibid.

remain preoccupied only with internal religious issues. Piety stood desperately in need of a disciplined rediscovery of the Hebrew Bible. Westermann summarizes the situation as follows:

> The individualistic pietism, concerned only for the religious self and personal salvation, that continued to be maintained by our parents and grandparents was no longer comprehensible to us. We were much too burdened by the question why we as Christians had not been able to resist more firmly the rise of National Socialism. Shouldn't we have been able to stand up against it, in the name of God, at the outset? A church and a theology which desired only to remain private was no longer possible for us.[87]

For Westermann, the work of theology in a world shaped by suffering and collapse leads to a rediscovery of the "elementary speech" of lament and praise in the Hebrew Bible.[88] The movement of lament to praise, representative of humanity's journey between suffering and joy, is no less constant or necessary than the rhythm of breathing itself. In Westermann's development of this idea, prayers of lament and praise emerge as indispensable elements of what the Hebrew Bible says about God.[89] For Westermann, the work of Hebrew Bible theology is to rediscover and to promote the dialogue between heaven and earth that binds humanity to God in a life that is meaningful through the depths of distress as well as in the heights of joy. Westermann's commitment to restoring the human response of suffering to the theological vocabulary of both the church and the academy is undoubtedly forged in the historical experience of post-war pain and despair.[90]

When the discipline of Hebrew Bible theology is tracked through its various historical settings, even in such a superficial way as I have done, it becomes clear that scholars' interests are indeed products of and responses to the worlds in which they live. At this point in time, in the world that shapes contemporary biblical scholarship, I suggest that efforts to articulate the theology of the Hebrew Bible are shaped by at least two culturally related learning

87. Ibid., 8.
88. Ibid., 11.
89. See pp. 242–43.
90. It may be noted in this connection that Westermann's highly influential dissertation, "Das Loben Gottes in den Psalmen," published in 1954, was begun in a prison camp during World War II. This work appeared in English as *The Praise of God in the Psalms* (Richmond: John Knox, 1965); repr. in *Praise and Lament*, 15–162.

experiences. First, scholars have learned that one cannot satisfactorily reconstruct the history of Israel's religion without reference to Israel's God, Yahweh. That is, the temptation to reduce argumentation to political, social, and historical factors does not address adequately the reality of evil that exceeds rational analyses. But historical experience has also taught scholars that a narrowly focused piety is no better option for living responsibly in a world of power. Perhaps in the midst of crises one can do little more than strive to retain traditional confessions that reaffirm God's sovereignty. But as Westermann notes, the church's temptation to speak *only* of God, too often apart from humanity's sufferings and joys, offers no critique of or resistance to the evils of this world that are done in the name of religion. Perhaps it is only in a relatively stable, post-crisis world that biblical scholarship is afforded the luxury of probing the boundaries of divine-human responsibilities. If so, then I suggest scholars are well advised to seize the moment, because what one may be able to construct now in relative calm will no doubt be put to the test by some yet unforeseen season in hell.

CHAPTER 10

The Theology
in Hebraic Prayer

I shall now move beyond the preceding evaluation concerning the neglect of prayer in Hebrew Bible theology to address the issue in a more positive manner. If prayer is included more substantively in future presentations, how will they differ from previous construals? Simply put, what is the theology in Hebraic prayer and what does it contribute to the discipline of Hebrew Bible theology?

At numerous places in this study I have offered observations about the role of prayer as a means of conveying theological perspective. Here I want to gather up the repeating emphases I have uncovered in order to delineate some basic theological principles that inform and sustain Hebraic prayer. But first, a brief caveat is in order.

This study has focused on prose prayer in Hebrew Scripture. Although I have examined a broad range of prayers in this context, I have left to the side an even greater number of prayers outside this category: the poetic prayers represented in the Psalter and elsewhere. This emphasis has enabled me to concentrate on an important dimension of Hebraic prayer that heretofore has gone largely without notice. But it also means that the foundation upon which this study has been built is incomplete. A full theology of prayer in the Hebrew Bible needs to incorporate the witness of both prose and poetic prayer formulations.

I suggest, however, that prose and poetic prayers do not represent different activities or contradicting forms of discourse with God. Rather, prayers offered in the prose of everyday life are genetically connected with those lifted to the poetry of liturgical worship.[1]

---

1. Cf. A. Aejmelaeus, *Traditional Prayer in the Psalms* (BZAW 167; Berlin: de Gruyter, 1986), 90–91; E. Gerstenberger, *Der bittende Mensch* (Neukirchen: Neukirchener Verlag, 1980), 119–27; M. Greenberg, *Biblical Prose Prayer As a*

Liturgical prayers grow out of living practice. They are not pure inventions of discourse that people have to adjust to using. They are instead only elaborations on what is already known.[2] Furthermore, as Westermann has recognized, liturgical worship is itself characterized by a "double movement" between the poetry of cultic gathering and the prose of real experience: "spontaneous calls to God from daily life come together with the members of the cultic assembly in the liturgical Psalm-prayer, and this prayer then returns with them to daily life."[3]

In view of this vital linkage between prose and poetic prayer, I do not envision that the theological principles derived from the one will conflict with those informing the other. I suggest that prose prayer and the relative specificity of the narrative context that provides its setting allow one to discern more clearly the theological dynamics of Hebraic prayer that are inherent, but ambiguous, in poetic address.

What then are the theological affirmations made especially available in the prayers of the Hebrew Bible? Prayer may contribute important theological perspectives in four areas. At this juncture I present these matters with little discussion. The textual evidence in support of each point will, I trust, be readily discernible in the discussion of specific prayers in chapters 4–8. Here I only recapitulate major emphases. Further, I leave these theological emphases in rather abstract form. Of course, theology has little effect when abstracted from the life and ministry of the church, and in chapter 11, I address more concretely how these issues lay claim on contemporary faith and piety. Here, however, my primary objective is more restricted. I want to delineate fundamental theological affirmations of Hebraic prayer that in my judgment the academy would do well to explore in the development of future Hebrew Bible theologies.

THE DIVINE-HUMAN RELATIONSHIP
IS FUNDAMENTALLY DIALOGICAL

I began this study by noting that the God who summons forth and enables prayer is a God who chooses to engage humanity, and the

---

Window to the Popular Religion of Ancient Israel (Berkeley: Univ. of California Press, 1983), 20–37.

2. Aejmelaeus, *Traditional Prayer,* 90–91.

3. C. Westermann, *Elements of Old Testament Theology* (Atlanta: John Knox, 1982), 29; cf. 155.

world, in a relationship of reciprocity. With respect to divine-human relationships specifically, this reciprocity is nowhere more evident than in the dialogue of prayer. The texts I have examined repeatedly present God with reality-depicting metaphors as speaking and acting toward humanity, *and* as listening for, hence inviting, human response. As Westermann has noted, on the one hand God's words and deeds are directed toward eliciting a response and in important ways are unfulfilled without this response.[4] On the other hand from humanity's perspective the dialogue with God is never self-generated. It is truly response, reaction to God's initiating actions.[5] In other words, prayer is enabled and summoned forth by the confession "In the beginning God. . . ." From the beginning this present God, sometimes also this absent God, desires not only to speak and act but also to listen and respond. In Hebrew Scripture this is a consistent description of the divine-human relationship. Wherever God is being God and humanity is acting in full accord with its nature, God and people are in dialogue.

This dialogue between God and humanity involves a genuine partnership. From a theological perspective the Hebrew Bible presents this partnership as a covenant relationship. God is committed to Israel and requires moral conduct befitting the divine will and intention for a holy people. The people of Israel are committed to the one God Yahweh and pledge obedience to divine prescriptions for life and worship. In return for their covenant faithfulness, the people expect reciprocal fidelity from the holy sovereign One. To be sure, this covenant partnership involves an unequal distribution of power and authority. God is the initiator of the covenant, not Israel. Even so, both parties have responsibility for the maintenance of the partnership. It cannot be sustained in its fullest form by either party alone.

The central point here is that covenant relationship is fundamentally dialogical. Two parties are mutually bound to one another in a relationship that is desirable and important for both. Both parties have a voice and a role to play; neither can disregard the appeals of the other and maintain the relationship as it is intended to be. If either God or Israel does not participate in the dialogue, then communication fails and the relationship is impoverished by silence.

To sharpen this point with respect to the discourse of prayer,

---

4. Ibid., 27, 153.
5. Ibid., 154.

covenant partnership means that God cannot and does not use the divine prerogatives of power to reduce Israel's response to monotones of praise, submission, or silence. Such limitations on human response effectively eviscerate genuine covenant relationship, substituting instead enforced obedience and passive devotion. Covenant partnership also means that Israel cannot and does not withhold from God the full range of human experience. Joy and suffering, prosperity and deprivation, success and failure, communion and confrontation—all characterize life in covenant relationship with God. Without the sharing of this full range of human experience, partnership becomes potentially only a veneer for tacit understandings that have no real claim on either party.

Most Hebrew Bible theologies have adopted a format that does not address adequately humanity's role in maintaining the dialogue with God. Although Eichrodt understands Israel's covenant with God to embody notions of reciprocal relationship, his brief presentation of Israel's practice of prayer suggests that in this form of discourse mutuality needs to be "straitened" in accordance with a "strong sense of the exalted Lordship of God."[6] Von Rad's position is not radically different, despite his important disagreements with Eichrodt concerning methodology. Von Rad understands that Hebraic prayer reveals Israel's unique "doctrine of man" and is therefore deserving of the "highest attention theologically."[7] In his development of this idea, however, he makes clear that in the praises of Israel one finds humanity's most characteristic mode of existence. Eichrodt and von Rad are representative in different ways of a prevailing tendency in Hebrew Bible theology that by and large portrays the divine-human relationship in terms of dichotomy rather than reciprocity. God is the principal focus in this view of theology. Humanity's role, if accorded theological significance at all, is primarily limited to obedience and praise.

One should derive theology from the biblical witness to God's words and deeds, and any theological assessment of the role of humanity before God should include Israel's response of praise and obedience. I do not disagree with either of these standard emphases in Hebrew Bible theology. I do suggest, however, that these foci alone do not adequately describe the full portrait of either God or humanity as embodied in the dialogue of prayer.

6. Eichrodt, *Theology of the Old Testament* (OTL; 2 vols.; Philadelphia: Westminster, 1961–67), 1.175; cf. 100.
7. G. von Rad, *Old Testament Theology* (2 vols.; New York: Harper and Row, 1962–65), 1.356.

Westermann has clearly seen that prayer—both praise and lament—contains decisive elements of what the Hebrew Bible says
about God that can be found nowhere else.[8] Because of its *portrait
of God,* prayer becomes indispensable for Hebrew Bible theology. I
shall affirm this insight and elaborate on it below. But I also want to
argue for the corollary of this statement: Prayer contains decisive
elements of what the Hebrew Bible says about humanity that can be
found nowhere else in quite the same way. Thus also because of its
portrait of humanity, prayer becomes indispensable for the theological enterprise.

PRAYER'S PORTRAIT OF GOD

Prayer is clearly a human response, a human activity. Nowhere is
the vocabulary of prayer used with God as the subject of the action.
That is, the Hebrew Bible nowhere suggests that God prays. In this
respect it is logical to look to prayer as an index of human character,
for one's words may reveal inner thoughts and intentions. But it is
less often recognized that humanity's words to God also reveal
divine character. Although God is not the one speaking in the act of
prayer, God is being addressed. In this sense, what one says *to* God
and *about* God in prayer provides insight into God's identity, *from
the pray-er's perspective.*[9]

In terms of responsibility for the theology of the Hebrew Bible, it
is important to recognize that these biblical records affirm a place
for humanity's portrait of God. God's identity is, of course, made
known through God's own actions and words, conveyed either directly by God or through spokespersons, like the prophets, who
become channels for divine revelation. This portrait of who God is
one may describe as given to humanity from above. It is, in a sense,
God's self-portrait, God's own account of who God is. Humanity's
perspective on God's identity may differ from this portrait. Although God may *intend* to be known in a particular way and may be
proclaimed by the mediums of divine communication *to be* a
particular way, the human experience from below of who God is

---

8. Westermann, *Elements,* 154.

9. Cf. Greenberg, *Prose Prayer,* 13. See further the comments of N. B. Johnson
concerning prayer in the Apocrypha and Pseudepigrapha: "there is no better index
of a man's understanding of God than his prayers" (*Prayer in the Apocrypha and
Pseudepigrapha* [*JBL* Monograph Series, vol. 2; Philadelphia: Society of Biblical
Literature and Exegesis, 1948], 3).

may not coincide with the divine will. For example, God may intend to be known as just and righteous, yet be experienced as capricious and criminal; God may be proclaimed as ever-present, even in the midst of suffering, yet be experienced as painfully, inexplicably absent.

Humanity's portrait of God is certainly not more important than God's portrait of God. Indeed, human perceptions must always be informed and corrected by God's self-revelation. Even so, the biblical text has preserved, not excised, the witness of these human perspectives, and scholars should include them among the multiple theologies of the Hebrew Bible. In short, the time has come to recognize that the pray-er's perspective of who God is down below, in the warp and woof of human experience, plays an important role in shaping the biblical portrait of God.

I have tried to illustrate in chapter 5 how prayer functions in Hebrew narrative as a means of portraying divine character. Several general theological affirmations about prayer's portrait of God derive from that discussion. First, the *address to God* plays an important role in these prayers. Invocation serves repeatedly as proclamation that God is perceived as *personal.* Thus God is portrayed as "Lord, God of Israel" (1 Kgs 19:15), "Lord our God" (2 Chr 14:11; cf. 2 Chr 20:6-7, 12; Dan 9:9-10, 13-14, 17), "Lord, God of our ancestor(s)" (1 Chr 29:10, 18). Such rhetoric is not neutral; it conveys more than simply a recognition of God's official title or status. This God is related to the ones who approach the throne, and because of this relationship they dare to speak, and God deigns to hear. Prayers embedded in narrative contexts serve further to affirm that God's work in the world does not proceed with an impersonal, mechanistic precision. God's will for the world is not simply articulated, then implemented without further ado. Rather, Hebrew narrative suggests that God's speaking and acting in the world may be and are regularly interrupted by the address of prayer. God is not only personal but also *accessible.*

Second, prayer's portraits of God affirm divine attributes. For example, Hezekiah emphasizes God's exclusive sovereignty (2 Kgs 9:15, 19); Asa and Jehoshaphat, God's power (2 Chr 14:11; 20:12); Daniel and Nehemiah, God's mercy and justice (Dan 9:4, 7, 9; Neh 9:8, 17, 19, 27-28, 31). These and other attributes of God (e.g., love, compassion) regularly constitute the rhetoric of Hebraic prayer. In this sense prayer functions to offer to God a litany of divine qualities as perceived and experienced and desired by humanity. Prayer thus offers a *theo*logy, statements about God, but in the form of subjective confession.

One may well ask at this point how prayer's portrait of God differs from the portrayals available in other sources. If prayer presents God as personal and accessible, is not this view also registered in other ways in the Hebrew Bible? If prayer functions to identify important features of God's character, would these divine characteristics be unknown if no prayers from the ancient community were preserved for scrutiny? I imagine that the most probable answer to this question would be no. Prayer's portrait of God is not so unique in its content. Prayer's affirmations of who God is can be discerned in other places. What is important is *how* these portrayals of God are presented in prayer.

Prayer's portrait of God is not abstract. It is directly shaped by concrete human experiences. For example, the texts discussed in chapter 5 indicate that the perception of God is shaped by the immediacy of the moment and by the hope for the future. In prayers for divine intervention modeled by Hezekiah, Asa, and Jehoshaphat, a military crisis provides the setting of the petition for deliverance. These prayers portray God as sovereign, as creator, as allpowerful, in association with the need for God to exercise these qualities in the immediate moment of crisis. Likewise, in the prayers of Daniel and Nehemiah, the recognized judgment of exile elicits the confession of sin and the plea for divine forgiveness. This particular setting and this special need for restoration undergird the repeated portrayals of God as merciful and forgiving.

In 1 Chr 29:10-19 David's prayer portraying God as sovereign is occasioned both by the circumstances of the moment and by the hope for the future. David does not petition God to exhibit mastery and control at the moment of the prayer, for these divine qualities are not presently in question. Rather, he asks that God's supervision and guidance, so clearly evident up to this moment, be extended to Solomon's future reign. The prayer itself is set in the temple ceremonies of the moment. But the theology it espouses is directed toward a future generation.

In each of these cases the *theology of prayer* is shaped by human need. People need God to be God in particular ways in different times and places. At least for the pray-er, God becomes the God portrayed in the prayer. Prayer's characterization of God is not objective or propositional. It is not organized or synthesized in accordance with theories or creeds, either ancient or modern. It is not learned in the academy or the worship center, at least not for the first time. It is instead the particular characterization of God wrought from the crucible of life where all theology meets its ultimate test.

PRAYER'S PORTRAIT OF HUMANITY

Hebraic prayer is an authentic source not only for the Hebrew Bible's theology but also for its anthropology. Von Rad notes in this regard that prayer provides a unique picture of a theological doctrine of man. Whereas biblical anthropology can be addressed through a study of rather abstract concepts like heart, and soul, and flesh, which present humanity as the measure of body parts and their function,[10] Hebrew narrative invites another approach. The prose of the Hebrew Bible prefers direct speech as the medium to present a character's motives, attitudes, and morality. This is true in interhuman speech situations, as a number of studies have stressed.[11] But it is also true of the speaking of humans to God in prayer. In this context as well, the words of prayer reflect and expose the character of the speaker,[12] not in abstract ways but as presented specifically in the dialogic relationship with God.

In chapter 4 I have examined a number of texts in which prayer serves as a literary means for portraying human character. I noted two dimensions of prayer's function in this regard: (1) prayer may serve to confirm or to emphasize qualities of faith and practice that are essential in assessing one's character; and (2) prayer that speaks a piety not confirmed in practice may function to call one's character into question. In both these areas prayer's portrait of humanity is worth theological reflection.

In the prayers assigned to Elijah, Solomon, and Hezekiah one may see how the biblical tradition judges words addressed to God to be authentic expressions of piety. Elijah is pronounced a "man of God," and this status is confirmed by both his miraculous deeds and his effective prayer. Solomon is confirmed as a wise king, Hezekiah a truly faithful one, because in moments of import and crisis they

---

10. See, e.g., H. W. Wolff, *Anthropology of the Old Testament* (Philadelphia: Fortress, 1974), 10–79.

11. See the discussion in chap. 4, and the works cited there.

12. Cf. S. Bar-Efrat, *Narrative Art in the Bible* (Sheffield: Almond, 1989), 64. See further Bar-Efrat's helpful distinction between character as "represented" in biblical narrative and the "real nature" of a person. One cannot judge how "accurate" a characterization is, i.e., whether a specific historical person was like the person represented in a narrative. One can say only that this is the character that "emerges" from the narrative (47–48).

turn in prayer to place themselves at God's disposal. In each case their prayers are presented as consonant with the behavior attributed to them in the immediate narrative. They pray as they act; their deeds do not contradict their words.

The prayers of Jacob and Jonah are judged quite differently. In Jacob's case, pious language cannot mask self-serving intentions. For him, prayer is but one of a number of strategies to turn a potentially volatile situation toward his own end. He schemes in human interactions to manipulate his brother. He schemes in prayer to manipulate God. For Jonah, prayer represents a "retreat into piety."[13] It is an opportunity to flee from God rather than to encounter God. In the end it is an effort to resist in spirit while feigning obedience in practice. For both Jacob and Jonah, then, the dialogue with God is defined not so much by the rhetoric of prayer as by the deeds of the pray-er.

The point at issue here is that prayer portrays humanity as embodying an indissoluble mix of word and deed. In a literal sense prayers offer only words to God, yet these words directed heavenward are laden with the lives of the speakers who utter them from below. Life may either confirm the prayer as authentic or nullify it. In any event words offered to God are linked to the life lived on earth. Prayer's portrait of humanity testifies that one's character will be defined ultimately by one's fidelity in both these areas.[14]

PRAYER AS A CONSTITUTIVE ACT OF FAITH

I have suggested that in the dialogue of prayer a relationship is struck between God and humanity that reveals the identity and character of both parties. I wish now to push beyond this observation to offer one additional judgment. In the act of prayer God and humanity are not only characterized but "recharacterized."[15] That is, prayer is a constitutive act of faith that creates the potential for newness in both God and humanity.[16] Neither partner remains

13. Cf. J. Magonet, *Form and Meaning: Studies in Literary Techniques in the Book of Jonah* (2d ed.; Sheffield: Almond, 1983), 179.

14. Cf. the comments of A. Heschel: "All of life must be a training to pray. We pray the way we live" (*The Insecurity of Freedom* [New York: Farrar, Straus, and Giroux, 1966], 260). I am indebted to P. LeFevre's discussion of Heschel's understanding of prayer for calling my attention to this quotation (*Understandings of Prayer* [Philadelphia: Westminster 1981], 185).

15. Cf. W. Brueggemann, "A Shape for Old Testament Theology, II: Embrace of Pain," *CBQ* 47 (1985): 402.

16. For the idea that prayer may function as a "constitutive" act, specifically with reference to praise, see Brueggemann, *Israel's Praise: Doxology against Idolatry*

unaffected or unchanged after the discourse of prayer. In both heaven and earth prayer is at work creating new possibilities for the implementation of the divine will.

From a theological perspective I suspect that most people have little difficulty understanding that the act of prayer can transform the human soul. Perhaps one most often expects this transformation in prayers of confession because prayers of penitence convey one's desire to become a more obedient follower of God. Hebraic prayer certainly affirms this understanding (e.g., Nehemiah 9, Daniel 9).

Some texts I have examined suggest that prayer may be a constitutive act for humanity in other important ways. For example, Jacob's prayer in Gen 32:9-12 is a prelude to an encounter that leaves him broken and blessed. On the other side of this encounter it is *Israel* who limps into the promised land, transformed in name and character for new opportunities as the scion of Hebraic faith. The dialogue of prayer is no less altering for Job. However one interprets the divine speeches and Job's responses, the final form of the book makes clear that Job and Job's status in relation to his friends has been transformed. For Nehemiah and Daniel, Jacob and Job, and a host of unnamed predecessors in the community of faith, to pray is to become a new and different self.

But prayer is an act of faith that creates new possibilities for God as well as for humanity. It is a daring probe into God's world that summons forth and enables new modes of divine fidelity. This aspect of prayer's function is less often recognized and is somewhat more difficult to assimilate theologically. To speak of prayer as a constitutive act that may recharacterize God is to recognize that in Hebraic understanding God is open and receptive to change. Such an understanding is principally derived from God's unrelenting commitment to be in relationship with humanity. As embodied in God's covenant with Israel and epitomized in the dialogue of prayer, this relationship is genuine. God does not choose to act in a unilateral fashion as the enforcer of a contractual fidelity.[17] Humanity has a voice and a participatory role in this relationship. Unless one construes the relationship as forever fixed and settled by divine fiat, God must reckon with the possibility that the ongoing conversation with the covenant partner may necessitate changes in divine plans.

To suggest that God changes in response to humanity's prayer is a

---

and Ideology (Philadelphia: Fortress, 1988), 6–28.

17. Cf. Brueggemann, "Embrace of Pain," 397.

delicate matter one must carefully explain in order to avoid misunderstanding.[18] I do not suggest that prayer and divine action have a simple quid pro quo relationship. The Hebrew Bible never promotes prayer as a means to manipulate or to control God. When God changes, God acts in ways that are consonant with the divine nature. God does not act *before* prayer out of character, then *after* prayer more in character. Instead God changes *as God,* not as the creatures,[19] hence God always acts in ways that are consistent with divine purposes.

Still one must recognize that Hebraic faith sees no contradiction between the affirmation of God's sovereign Lordship and God's openness to change.[20] In order to maintain the integrity of relationship, God chooses to respond to the concerns of humanity. This choice means necessarily that God will not exercise divine options mechanically but within the context of a living, dynamic relationship. Within this relationship humanity can know that on God's part, God's ultimate will and purpose for creation remain consistent.[21]

In the texts I have examined, one may understand particularly the prayers of lament to effect a recharacterization of God. I have suggested that in prayers for divine justice (chap. 6) and in the broader lament tradition represented by Jeremiah, Job, and Habakkuk (chap. 7), hard questions are put to God that not only challenge divine decisions but change them. This daring speech of Israel pushes covenant relationship to its farthest boundaries with assaults, protests, and accusations that call into question God's intentions and God's character. These prayers construe God as open to the pain of anguished believers whose fidelity is expressed with the passionate cry "Why Lord?" Such grief-filled questions are dangerous, because they portend change. They leave neither the questioner nor the questioned the same as before.

To summarize, I have tried to delineate the primary theological principles that I believe inform and sustain the practice of prayer in Israel.

---

18. T. Fretheim has addressed this matter most helpfully in a number of studies concerning divine repentance: *The Suffering of God: An Old Testament Perspective* (OBT; Philadelphia: Fortress, 1984), 49–53; "Prayer in the Old Testament: Creating Space in the World for God," *A Primer on Prayer,* ed. P. Sponheim (Philadelphia: Fortress, 1988), 59–62; "The Repentance of God: A Key to Evaluating Old Testament God-Talk," *HBT* 10 (1988): 59–66; "The Repentance of God: A Study of Jeremiah 18:7-10," *HAR* 11 (1987): 81–93.

19. Fretheim, "God-Talk," 63.

20. Cf. ibid., 64.

21. Ibid.

(1) Prayer is the quintessential dialogue of faith in which God and humanity work in partnership to maintain covenant relationship.

(2) Hebraic prayer contains essential elements of what the Hebrew Bible says about both God and humanity.

(3) Hebraic prayer is not a static activity that merely reflects a fixed world and a settled relationship with the Creator. Rather, it is a dynamic act of faith that brings into existence new possibilities for both divine and human fidelity.

I do not wish to leave these as a mere list of theological affirmations. Prayer is not simply a subject for analytical scrutiny. What it reveals about God and humanity is not only a repository for theology. Prayer is an act of faith, a practice of addressing God that makes a difference in heaven as well as on earth. To postulate that this is true of Hebraic prayer is, however, only half the challenge. I must now go on to ask how this legacy from our forebears in faith informs the life and ministry of the church. Toward this end I address myself in the final chapter to the task of thinking about prayer *in* ministry and *as* ministry.

CHAPTER 11

House of Prayer
or Den of Robbers?
A Summons to the Church

The church, no less than the academy, is summoned to attend to the theology of prayer. Such a summons is grounded in the recognition that prayer is of itself an act of ministry. It is not just a preparatory ritual antecedent to real ministry. It is one of the principal means by which the church participates concretely as a coworker with God in accomplishing the divine will for the world.[1] Indeed, I submit that the church has no higher calling than to realize its commission to become a house of prayer.

In his dedication speech for the newly finished temple in Jerusalem, Solomon announces that this temple, this central place of the presence of God, is to serve primarily as a place for prayer (1 Kgs 8:22-53). Years later, according to the final biblical presentation, the prophet of the exile known as Third Isaiah offers the same evaluation of the temple's role: "for my house shall be called a house of prayer [bêt tĕpillāh]" (Isa 56:7, NRSV). Yet when Jesus enters Jerusalem and surveys the worship of his contemporaries in this most holy, central place of the presence of God, he proclaims it null and void with this stinging observation: "My house shall be called a house of prayer, but you are making it a den of robbers" (Matt 21:13 and parallels, NRSV). Indeed, in this condemnation Jesus is only echoing the charge of his predecessor Jeremiah who also denounced such abuse of the holy place: "Has this house, which is called by my name, become a den of robbers in your sight?" (Jer 7:11, NRSV).

---

1. On prayer as one of the basic ministries of the church, see K. Barth, *Church Dogmatics,* IV/3.2, 865-901. On prayer as a means of exercising political responsibility for the world, see D. Soelle, *Politisches Nachtgebet in Köln* (Stuttgart and Mainz: Kreuz Verlag, 1970), 24-25. For further discussion of Soelle's political understanding of prayer, see H. G. Reventlow, *Gebet im Alten Testament* (Stuttgart: Kohlhammer, 1986), 57-61.

The temple is first dedicated as a house of prayer, but is later condemned as a den of robbers. Worshipers are summoned to be pray-ers, but are judged to be thieves. How did it happen? How *does* it happen? Perhaps more important for those in the church, how can we stand fast in the Hebraic tradition of prayer without deserving the judgment of both Jeremiah and Jesus?

In this final chapter I reflect on the role of the church as a house of prayer and on the role of the house of prayer in individual lives, in communities, and in the world at large. I address two primary responsibilities of the church at prayer that I believe derive from the Hebrew Bible and Jewish heritage: (1) The role of the church as a house of prayer is *to keep the community and the world in God;* and (2) the role of the church as a house of prayer is *to keep God in the community and in the world.*

KEEPING THE COMMUNITY IN GOD.

The Role of the Church as a House of Prayer

The biblical assessment of the sanctuary as a focal point of prayer may be traced to Solomon's address in 1 Kgs 8:22-53. The specifics of this text I have already discussed in chapter 4.[2] Here it is sufficient to recall the general tenor of Solomon's prayer.

Standing in the temple before the altar of the Lord, Solomon prays. His prayer is really a speech about prayer, more particularly, about the temple as the place in which or toward which people should pray. Specifically, Solomon's prayer lists seven occasions when the people should look to the temple as the principal forum for addressing God and securing a hearing. Whatever the circumstances, whether famine or pestilence, personal illness or corporate crisis, Solomon prays that the people will pray, and that God will hear and respond. Even in captivity, estranged from the temple and other material symbols of God's presence, the people are encouraged to believe that prayer toward the holy place will bind together heaven and earth (vv. 46-53).

I have noted that this emphasis on the temple as a place of prayer is rather striking in the Hebrew Bible.[3] The temple is typically, indeed almost exclusively, described as a place of sacrifice. Priestly instruction concerning temple worship usually treats prayer as a gesture of secondary importance. It is clearly otherwise in Solo-

---

2. See pp. 80–88.
3. See chaps. 3 and 4.

mon's speech. Here prayer is not a secondary but a primary means of addressing God. Indeed, it is the principal act of faith that ties together God and humanity.

This view of prayer as the principal act of worship likely began to emerge most clearly during the period of exile. When the temple was destroyed in 586 B.C.E., the holy place burned and desecrated, it was no longer possible to offer sacrifice. New means of sustaining a relationship with God were required. Generally within this context new gatherings for worship began to appear, and new mediums of communication with God began to take root. To oversimplify this situation greatly, one may suggest that the synagogue emerged in place of the temple, and in place of sacrifice prayer came to be regarded as the primary channel of divine-human communication.

By the time of the destruction of the second temple in 70 C.E. and the subsequent emergence of Rabbinic Judaism, prayer is clearly no longer regarded as merely an accompaniment of worship. It comes to be, in and of itself, virtually the entirety of worship.[4] Daily prayers were instituted to correspond to what used to be daily sacrifices. Worshipers were to be just as careful to recite these prayers at the appropriate time as they had formerly been in obeying the requirements of sacrifice. The rabbis developed prayers for the weekdays, prayers for the Sabbath, prayers for special occasions—in effect, prayers intended to orient and to sustain the whole of every day and all of life. In Rabbinic Judaism, and in large measure in contemporary Jewish faith and practice, prayer is the "service *['ăbôdāh]* of the heart," which constantly interrupts the routine and the mundane with an awareness of the sacred and the absolute.[5]

The transition in the orientation of Jewish worship from sacrifice to prayer is obviously far more complex than I have allowed. The point I wish to establish is that the Hebrew Bible and Jewish forebears have left a legacy of prayer that contemporary members of the community of faith should preserve and nurture.[6] They have bequeathed the understanding that prayer is a principal act of worship; that prayer is a primary reason for the gathering of the faithful, whether in synagogue or church; and hence that prayer is a primary means of ministry wherever the faithful are in communion with

4. Cf. J. Heinemann, *Prayer in the Talmud* (Berlin: de Gruyter, 1977), 14–17.
5. Ibid., 14–15.
6. On the legacy of fixed, statutory prayer that both Christianity and Islam inherit from Judaism, see ibid., 13–36.

God. In short, the Hebraic legacy affirms that prayer is a principal means of keeping the community bound to God in an ongoing dialogue of faith. I suggest that the church is summoned to a ministry that both promotes and enables this dialogue.

AFFIRMING THE PRAISES AND LAMENTS OF ISRAEL

What is gained if the church dares to pray and preach the prayers of Israel? Or if it proclaims from pulpits and lives out in communities the affirmations of Hebraic praise and lament? Conversely, what is lost if it does not?

I submit that when one prays and preaches the theology embodied in Hebraic praise and lament, one engages in the ministry of keeping the community in God. Specifically, this ministry of prayer proclaims that a transcendent reality pervades *all* of life's experiences. When one praises God one acknowledges that the joy of life is a gift from God. When one brings the pain and disappointment of life before God in lamentation, one affirms that even in these experiences one is not cut off from the God who is Creator of all. In both joy and suffering prayer is the act of faith, the *work* of faith,[7] that keeps one in God. The work of prayer turns one away from self—from one's best efforts and worst failures, from one's happiest moments and most grievous afflictions—and turns one toward God, who alone is worthy of worship.[8]

It is crucial that the church claim and reclaim this transcendent dimension for life's joys and its sorrows. When one praises God one proclaims that the joy of life is never finally self-generated. One cannot create of one's own resources the real joys of life. One cannot will them into existence either by faith or by technology. One cannot sustain them by the fervor of passions. Life and the joy that fills it are gifts from God. This gift is what one affirms when one prays and preaches doxology: "Praise God from whom all blessings flow." To put the matter in the terms of my previous discussion of Hebraic praise: "Blessed be the LORD *who . . .*" (e.g., Exod 18:10) and "Sing to

---

7. In Hebrew the word '*ăbōdāh*, "work, service" is used to describe temple worship, esp. the sacrificial practices of temple worship. In Rabbinic Judaism '*abōdāh* is the standard term for prayer. See further the comments of G. Wainwright on the Christian perspective concerning prayer as work (*Doxology: The Praise of God in Worship, Doctrine, and Life* [New York: Oxford Univ. Press, 1980], 25–26).

8. See esp. Barth's development of this idea under the premise that prayer is "the first and basic act of theological work" (*Evangelical Theology: An Introduction* [New York: Holt, Rinehart and Winston, 1963], 149–58). See further my discussion on pp. 251–52.

the LORD *because . . ."* (Exod 15:21). Both of these early exemplars of praise remind one that human experience ultimately *informs* but does not *define* the meaning of life. God and God alone is Lord of life. To praise God in the Hebraic sense is to affirm this transcendent reality.

To put the edge on this point, one might ask what would be the loss for the church, for the community of faith, for the world, if we do not promote the ministry of praise. What do we stand to lose if we do not preach and pray the Hallelujah of faith's affirmation? I suggest two costly losses should the church neglect the ministry of praise.

First, without the summons to doxology, the natural human bent toward narcissism will likely turn us inward rather than upward. We will languish in a stupor of self-intoxication. The realization of the transcendent God will fade.[9] In its place will be the gods we have made with our own hands, and they will look like us. Our lives and our institutions (including the church), our communities and our world, will be one step closer to yielding to the ultimate idolatry— self-deification. In this sense the summons to doxology is a summons to obey the first commandment, to be loyal to God and God alone. Hence it is a summons radically subversive of the idolatry of self-love or mindless allegiance to other persons or programs.[10]

Second, if the church does not practice the ministry of praise, it will forfeit its role in celebrating, hence promoting, the freedom and power of God to overturn the status quo. As I argued in chapter 8, praise that makes sense is praise that always echoes with the remembrance of the reversal of suffering. To participate in such praise is to remain ever mindful that in God's world human impossibilities always yield to the wonderful possibilities of divine reversal. It is to remember and to give thanks with Hannah that the lowly can be lifted up, the powerful can be brought down. Without doxology both the lowly and the powerful will be tempted to conclude that the *status* is *quo,* that possibilities unseen are inauthentic and unlikely, that the world's power to define reality is ultimate and unchallenged.[11]

---

9. Cf. M. Greenberg, *Biblical Prose Prayer As a Window to the Popular Religion of Ancient Israel* (Berkeley: Univ. of California Press, 1983), 51–52.

10. Cf. P. Miller, "In Praise and Thanksgiving," *Theology Today* 45 (1988): 187–88. He observes that "Any community that sings with conviction 'All people that on earth do dwell, sing to the Lord with cheerful voice; Him serve with fear, his praise forth tell' cannot give its ultimate allegiance to a Hitler or a Kennedy or a Reagan or a political party of any stripe" (188).

11. Cf. ibid., 186–87. On praise as a basic yet irrational trust in the endless power

Not only in life's joys and successes but also in its sorrows must the church practice the ministry of prayer. To pray and to preach the theology of lament is to proclaim that there is also a transcendent reality in suffering. In this regard the church must attend to two basic affirmations inherent in the Hebraic practice of lamentation: (1) suffering is real, not imaginary, and it is not always, if ever, containable, not even through pious machinations or technological expertise; and (2) suffering is not the last word. That is, suffering may be ultimate, but it is not final.[12] It may comprehend the totality of what one understands to be negative and destructive, but it is still not final. The last word, the final reality, is God, who is at the beginning and ending of all that is.

Hebraic faith struggles relentlessly to hold both these affirmations in tension. But if the tension becomes too great, if it becomes impossible to sustain both the acknowledgment of suffering and the sovereignty of God at the same time, the latter, not the former, is let go.[13] Such is the Hebraic commitment to the reality of suffering that not even loyalty to God can silence the cry of pain. This is the hard truth of the Book of Job.

It is first and foremost the practice of lament that enables the believer to live within the tension of these two faith commitments. Prayers of lamentation speak pain to God as an act of faith. Lamentation is an act of faith that persists in believing that God can be addressed with the hard questions that suffering always brings: "Why Lord?" "How long, Lord?" Lamentation persists in believing that God is not only open to such address but responds to it. Lamentation persists in believing that the future is not finally determined by either the past or the present; that it is open to new possibilities; that the cry of pain addressed to God is an important step toward the realization of these possibilities. Such is the ministry of lament in Hebraic faith.

How different much contemporary ministry seems by comparison. The indices of most church hymnals usually have no entry marked "lament." How many sermons or prayers or worship emphases provide vocabulary and opportunity for the articulation of

---

of God to surprise, see W. Brueggemann, "The Psalms as Prayer," *Reformed Liturgy and Music* 23 (1989): 19–20.

12. For this conceptualization, see D. J. Hall, *God and Human Suffering: An Exercise in the Theology of the Cross* (Minneapolis: Augsburg, 1986), 19–20. On the distinction regarding the "finality" and "ultimacy" of evil, see the powerful statement of A. Cohen in *The Tremendum: A Theological Interpretation of the Holocaust* (New York: Crossroad, 1988), 48–52.

13. Hall, *God and Human Suffering*, 27.

pain and grief? The church does not sing about these matters; the church does not often preach about them or pray about them (at least not in public worship), or even recite them from responsive readings. Rather, the Church typically encourages a cheerful, uncritical celebration of life.[14] The church prays and preaches praise but not lament, the truth of doxology but not the truth of despair. Brueggemann has cautioned that such muted speech in worship, such a ministry of praise without lament, is in the end "a practice of denial, cover-up, and pretense."[15]

I agree with this judgment, and those who are responsible for rightly handling the whole of the biblical witness should be duly chastised. The biblical affirmation is clear that east of Eden the practice of lament is a regular and necessary response of faith, because east of Eden life is not perfect: evil often triumphs over good, injustice over justice, sickness over health, doubt over faith, despair over hope. East of Eden humanity's language is necessarily punctuated with questions, questions about the "Why?" and the "How long?" of the struggle to which this mysterious "I AM" of a God has summoned us. Such questions are never completely silenced in this world outside Eden; the ever-widening gap between expectation and experience has seen to that. One cannot return to the world of perfection and paradise; the way back is forever blocked by God's appointed cherubim and the flame of the flickering sword.

Outside Eden, faith will always be forged by the grim dialectic of hope and despair: the hope extended by God to estranged humanity, and the despair returned by humanity to God.[16] When the church severs this dialectic into either of these separate tensions—either hope uninformed by despair, or despair that cannot hope—then it has covered up the reality of the life it brings before God, and it has denied the invitation of the biblical witness.[17]

Before God one need not engage in such pretense or cover-up.

---

14. On uncritical worship that serves to stifle "alienation" and "rage," see W. Brueggemann, *Finally Comes the Poet: Daring Speech for Proclamation* (Minneapolis: Fortress, 1989), 43–50.

15. Brueggemann, "The Costly Loss of Lament," *JSOT* 36 (1986): 60. See further my discussion on pp. 196–98.

16. See Cohen, *Tremendum,* 23.

17. Cf. the observations of R. Niebuhr: "Faith is always imperiled on the one side by despair and on the other side by optimism. Of these twin enemies of faith, optimism is the more dangerous" ("The Ultimate Trust," *Beyond Tragedy: Essays on the Christian Interpretation of History* [New York: Charles Scribner's Sons, 1937], 115).

Indeed, one must not. To do so is to deny the heritage of faith. The summons is to preach and to pray both lament and praise. When one does so one invites the community of faith to stay in God in both joy and suffering.

ACTS OF OBEDIENCE ON EARTH

I have been urging the church toward a practice of prayer that proclaims a transcendent reality in all of life's experiences. Now, however, I must extend this discussion to include another important matter. Faith focused on a transcendent God is never absolved from the demands of fidelity on earth. Put another way, to *stay in God* in prayer does not give one license to *stay out of God* in practice. The church is summoned by its Hebraic legacy to a ministry of prayer that keeps the community of faith focused on God in all its experiences. But it is also summoned by this same heritage to a ministry in which all words addressed to the heavens are matched with acts of obedience on earth.

I have addressed this matter in a rather general way in the previous discussions of prayer's portraiture of humanity.[18] I have suggested that in Hebraic understanding the dialogue with God is defined both by the rhetoric of prayer and by the life of the pray-er. When the words of piety addressed to God in heaven are congruent with a life of fidelity on earth, then both prayer and pray-er are judged positively (e.g., Elijah, Solomon, Hezekiah). Conversely, when prayer feigns a piety that is not confirmed by behavior, then one's integrity is called into question, and the dialogue between heaven and earth is weakened (e.g., Jacob, Jonah). Here I wish to go beyond these generalizations to address specifically the necessary linkage in Hebraic faith between prayer and justice. I illustrate briefly with two texts.

Jeremiah's Temple Sermon (Jer 7:1-15; cf. 26:1-24)

With this temple sermon one encounters one of the more significant prose texts in the Book of Jeremiah. Whether such texts are authentically Jeremianic or the product of editorial expansion (usually identified as Deuteronomistic) continues to be an unresolved issue.[19] For my purposes here I simply acknowledge the

18. See chap. 4 and pp. 267–68.
19. Among commentators, on the one hand E. Nicholson (*Preaching to the Exiles: A Story of the Prose Tradition in the Book of Jeremiah* [Oxford: Basil Blackwell, 1970], 68–70) and R. Carroll (*Jeremiah* [OTL; Philadelphia: Westminster, 1986], 206–12) interpret the sermon as Deuteronomistic. On the other hand, W. L.

limitations of scholarly understanding concerning the matters of date, authorship, and historical provenance of Jeremiah 7. Even so, the theological thrust of this text, taken as a whole, is clear. In its present context, this chapter follows on the heels of a sweeping condemnation of the idolatrous character of Judah's religion and society (chap. 2-6). In this setting Jeremiah preaches against the kind of faith that addresses pious affirmations to heaven but has no concern for moral behavior on earth.

The core of Jeremiah's sermon consists of proclamation (vv. 3-7), indictment (vv. 8-11), and announcement of judgment (vv. 12-15). The word proclaimed begins with an imperative that is absolute and unqualified: "Make good your ways and your deeds" (v. 3). This rather general exhortation to do good is further defined in verses 5-6 and again in verse 9 in terms of "doing justice" (v. 5: *'āśāh mišpāṭ*) in accordance with the commandments of torah. Jeremiah's address makes clear that worship in the presence of God must be accompanied by obedience to both the broad and the specific requirements of torah justice. That is, one must attend faithfully to the legal requirements prohibiting stealing, murder, adultery—in short, the commandments of covenant law. But one must also "do good" and "do justice" by exhibiting special compassion for the weak and the vulnerable (the widow and the orphan) and even for the "resident alien," whose legal rights are limited. The requirement is that one must do justice by observing both the letter and the spirit of torah.

If these justice requirements are not satisfied? Verses 5-7 explicate the "if-then" understanding of life in relationship with God: *"If* you do good . . . *then* I will let you dwell in this place." The "then" part of this clause (v. 7) repeats the language first encountered in verse 3. In both cases the MT vocalizes the verb *šākan,* "to dwell," in such a way that it should be translated "I [God] will cause [allow] you [the people] to dwell." The sense of this interpretation is that with obedience the people will be privileged to worship in the temple and to dwell in the land.

Holladay argues that the rhetoric of the sermon is Jeremianic and "reflects what Jrm said on that occasion, or at least what he himself recalls having said on that occasion" (*Jeremiah* [Hermeneia; 2 vols.; Philadelphia and Minneapolis: Augsburg Fortress, 1986–89], 1.240). W. McKane finds a corpus within the sermon that he attributes to Jeremiah (vv. 4, 9, 10, 11, 12, 14), although he acknowledges that it is impossible to say finally whether Jeremiah's own words have been preserved (*A Critical and Exegetical Commentary on Jeremiah* [ICC; 2 vols.; Edinburgh: T. and T. Clark, 1986–], 164–65).

It is interesting to note, however, that good versional evidence supports a different reading. Both the Vulgate and Aquila treat the verb *šākan* in verses 3 and 7 as a *qal* form, which, with the following expression, should be translated as "I will dwell with you."[20] According to this reading, what is at stake in this situation is not whether the people will be allowed to dwell in the temple, but whether God will be present there. In other words, the "house of the LORD" is only an ordinary place in and of itself. What makes it a sacred place is the presence of God.[21] And God is present only if the people obey justice requirements.

In either reading, a basic theme in Hebraic prophecy is clear.[22] The temple is to be a place of encounter with the righteous and compassionate God. The temple is to embody this encounter by engaging in a ministry that mirrors God's righteousness and unending compassion.[23] R. Carroll has focused the theological crux of this issue with his suggestion that the temple is supposed to define the character and the conduct of those who go out from it.[24] Jeremiah makes clear that this was not the case with those whom he addressed. They come mouthing words ("the temple of the LORD, the temple of the LORD . . .") inside the sanctuary, while their conduct outside the sanctuary is an "abomination" (v. 10). Hence God regards their words as a "lie" (*šeqer*, vv. 4, 8),[25] and their worship is in vain. Such conduct, Jeremiah charges, turns the "house of the LORD" into a "den of robbers" (v. 11, NRSV). The place of encounter with God becomes little more than a hideout from

20. JB and NRSV adopt this translation.

21. Note the suggestive interplay in the text between two phrases commonly used to refer to temple, *bêt Yhwh*, "house of the LORD" (vv. 2, 10, 11, 14) and *hêkal Yhwh*, "temple of the LORD" (v. 4), and the more ambiguous designation *māqôm* "place" (vv. 3, 6, 7, 12, 14). For further discussion see McKane, *Jeremiah*, 1.159–61; Holladay, *Jeremiah* 1.241–42; Carroll, *Jeremiah*, 207.

22. For the prophetic insistence on the linkage between worship and justice, see, e.g., Isa 1:10-17 (note esp. v. 15); Amos 2:6-8; 5:10-12; 8:4-6; Mic 3:9-12; 6:6-8.

23. Cf. P. Hanson's discussion of Israel's triadic notion of community—righteousness, compassion, worship—which is based on their own experience of God's righteous and compassionate acts (*The People Called: The Growth of Community in the Bible* [San Francisco: Harper and Row, 1986], e.g., 69–78).

24. Carroll, *From Chaos to Covenant: Uses of Prophecy in the Book of Jeremiah* (London: SCM, 1981), 88; cf. idem, *Jeremiah*, 210.

25. For a full discussion of *šeqer*, "lie, falsehood," in Jeremiah, see T. Overholt, *The Threat of Falsehood: A Study in the Theology of the Book of Jeremiah* (SBT 2/16; London: SCM, 1970). Overholt interprets the term in Jeremiah 7 as referring to a false sense of security that keeps the people from responding to God's call for repentance (1–23).

God for those who do violence under the cloak of empty piety. As the announcement of judgment (vv. 12-15) goes on to make clear, God will not tolerate either such behavior or such worship.

I suggest that these words of Jeremiah are a two-pronged condemnation. The *people* come with words of meaningless piety that give the lie to their worship by their lives of corruption. Such conduct is an abomination in the eyes of God. But the *priests* and the *religious leaders* provide these false worshipers with sanctuary.[26] This too is an abomination in God's eyes. The church as the house of God is to keep the community *in God* and *in God's purposes on earth*. In Hebraic perspective, the requirement of faithfulness in both these responsibilities is nonnegotiable.

Jesus' Cleansing of the Temple
(Matt 21:12-17; Mark 11:15-19; Luke 19:45-46; John 2:13-22)

The episode of the cleansing of the temple is found in each of the Gospels, although they have important differences in details and theological emphases.[27] What is common to all the accounts is the following: Jesus enters the temple area; he drives out the merchants; and he draws upon Hebraic tradition to protest the abuse of the "house of prayer."[28]

I am particularly concerned here with Jesus' application of Hebrew Scripture to his contemporary setting. The key text is found in Matthew, Mark, and Luke as follows: "My house shall be [called][29] a house of prayer [for all the nations],[30] but you have made it a den of robbers." Here Jesus quotes two scriptures that inform his judgment of temple practices. The reference to the temple as a "house of prayer" is from Isa 56:7; its evaluation as a "den of robbers" is dependent on Jeremiah's temple sermon, specifically Jer 7:11.

The context of the reference to the temple as a "den of robbers" should be clear from the preceding discussion. In its Jeremianic setting it is part of the prophet's attack on the reliance of ritual

---

26. Cf. Jer 5:30-31; 6:13; 8:10.

27. For a convenient summary see R. E. Brown, *The Gospel According to John I–XII* (AB; Garden City, N.Y.: Doubleday, 1966), 116–20; J. A. Fitzmyer, *The Gospel According to Luke X–XXIV* (AB; Garden City, N.Y.: Doubleday, 1985), 1262–65. For further discussion of the history of the tradition that appears in the four Gospels, see C. K. Barrett, "The House of Prayer and the Den of Robbers," *Jesus und Paulus: Festschrift für Werner Georg Kümmel zum 70. Geburtstag*, ed. E. E. Ellis and E. Grässer (Göttingen: Vandenhoeck und Ruprecht, 1974), 13–20.

28. John 2:16 refers to the temple only as "my Father's house."

29. Omitted in Luke.

30. Omitted in Matthew and Luke.

inside the sanctuary to coverup unethical behavior outside the holy place. For Jesus it is not so much conduct outside the temple that turns religion into a lie but the behavior he witnesses inside the temple. Inside the temple environs[31] Jesus finds that more attention is devoted to commercial transactions than to encountering God; so much attention to purchasing, exchanging, and acquiring that what is supposed to happen in the holy place has gotten lost in the jingling of the merchant's purses. Money changers and animal brokers turn the holy place into a "marketplace" (John 2:16), where misplaced preoccupations are no less abominable in God's sight than a den of robbers.[32]

The allusion to the temple as a "house of prayer" in the first part of Jesus' declaration brings into view a second way in which the house of God may be abused. The quotation is from part of Third Isaiah's post-restoration oracle (i.e., after 538 B.C.E.) in Isa 56:1-8. The substance of this oracle is a summons to those who have returned to a ruined Jerusalem to begin rebuilding their future by being good stewards of justice and righteousness (56:1). They are to demonstrate fidelity to the torah in two specific ways.

First, they are to keep the Sabbath (56:2). They are to observe faithfully the laws of cultic purity so as not to profane the holy day. Second, they are summoned to avoid exclusivism. Specifically mentioned are the eunuchs (vv. 4-5) and the foreigners (vv. 3, 6-7), who by law might be excluded from the community (cf. Deut 23:1-8) but by God's standards of justice and compassion ought not be. These outcasts of society—the one group without posterity, hence without a future, the other without a home, hence essentially strangers in the land—are to find a place in God's community. They are to be welcomed in God's "house of prayer" (Isa 56:2-8), and they are to have equal access to the heavenly throne.

In Isaiah this oracle is clearly polemical. It is directed against the Zadokite priestly hierarchy who view the temple as a principal means of reordering the structure of the postexilic community.[33] In their view, their own position at the head of the sacerdotal order is

31. In Greek *hiepos,* "temple precincts," i.e., the outer court of the temple, or the Court of the Gentiles.

32. Cf. Barrett's interpretation of the Markan text as a sign of the destruction of the temple because "it manifests not religion but commerce, and can no longer serve any purpose in the will of God" ("House of Prayer," 14).

33. See further E. Achtemeier, *The Community and Message of Isaiah 56–66* (Minneapolis: Augsburg, 1982), 23–26, 32–37; P. Hanson, *The Dawn of Apocalyptic: The Historical and Sociological Roots of Jewish Apocalyptic Eschatology* (Philadelphia: Fortress, 1975), 388–89; idem, *People Called,* 259–68, 287–89.

God's design for the well-being of the new community. Isaiah's oracle is a challenge to this view, and as such a call for both the temple leadership and the community it serves to return to more inclusive policies.

It is little wonder, given this Hebraic backdrop, that the chief priests and scribes of Jesus' day react strongly to his use of the Isaiah oracle. They must understand all too well that their leadership is being measured against standards not their own. It is also perhaps not too surprising that outside this inner circle the reaction to Jesus' words is quite different. In Matthew's account, immediately upon hearing the declaration of the temple as a house of prayer, those who had been excluded by religious tradition and practice—the blind and the crippled—come to Jesus for healing.[34]

In both the temple sermon and the account of the cleansing of the temple, the biblical witness affirms that it is the role of the house of prayer to keep the community in God. This mandate involves promoting faithful worship and ethical obedience. It is a mandate to the whole church for a ministry to the whole community. It is a summons to stay focused on God's transcendent glory, whatever life's joys and sorrows, and to stay committed with equal passion to the stewardship of God's earthly justice and compassion. A ministry of prayer in the Hebraic sense will work toward the realization of these goals both inside and outside the sanctuary.

KEEPING GOD IN THE COMMUNITY

In the ministry of prayer the church will keep the community in God. That is, it will keep the community mindful of the transcendent dimension in life. All of life is a gift from God, and those in the church are required therefore to live with a sense of deep gratitude, genuine honesty, and profound responsibility. The church, then, must be at work in the world *shaping the future of people and institutions* in accordance with this transcendent reality and its demands.

But the church at prayer has a second responsibility. I suggest that in the ministry of prayer the church will also be at work *shaping the future of God*. In essence, part of the church's task in the ministry of prayer is to keep God in the community and in the world. One may think of this task along the lines proposed by A. Heschel: "To pray

---

34. Cf. E. Schweizer, *The Good News According to Matthew* (Atlanta: John Knox, 1975), 408–9.

means to bring God back into the world . . . to expand His presence." Such a task is not only possible but necessary, because, as Heschel continues, "His being immanent in the world depends on us."[35]

In response to such an observation the church may well ask, How can this be? Surely God is always in the world. Surely God's presence in the world or God's action in the lives of people does not *depend* on the prayers of the church. These are legitimate and necessary questions, and I do not propose that simple or easy answers will satisfy them. But, I would argue that in considering its role as a house of prayer, the church should attend especially to the kinds of Hebraic prayers I presented in chapters 6 and 7. The task of keeping God in the world is perhaps nowhere more clearly illustrated than in these bold prayers of the lament tradition.

To recapitulate briefly, in chapter 6 I surveyed a selection of prayers that focused on the *work of intercession.* In each of these texts prayers of intercession result in God's changing announced intentions. Each text follows a basic pattern of crisis-prayer-resolution of crisis, which suggests a crucial role for prayer in determining the final outcome of the situation.[36] To recall but one example, in Exod 32:7-14 Moses responds to God's decision to destroy the calf-worshiping Israelites by petitioning God (1) to turn away from such wrath and (2) to repent concerning such evil. The text then reports rather matter-of-factly that God "repented of the evil," just as Moses had prayed.

In short, Moses' prayer is portrayed as having made a difference not only for the people but also for God. In this and other such reports of intercessory prayer, the text invites the question, What if Moses and the rest had not prayed? Would God have stayed in the world (in Moses' case, in covenant relationship with such disobedient followers) if no one had prayed for intercession? One may be inclined to rush quickly past these prayers to answer that God always intends to forgive and to relent. But several of the texts I examined make clear that these prayers have been *edited into* a narrative context, as if to force one to suspend evaluation of the reported outcome until one has read the dialogue between pray-er and God.[37]

---

35. A. Heschel, *The Insecurity of Freedom* (New York: Farrar, Straus, and Giroux, 1966), 258. On Heschel's understanding of prayer, see further, P. LeFevre, *Understandings of Prayer* (Philadelphia: Westminster, 1981), 172–91.

36. See pp. 120–39.

37. See pp. 144–45.

In chapter 7 I expanded this discussion to include a broader range of the lament tradition, represented specifically in Jeremiah, Job, and Habakkuk. Here I attempted to show how the standard structure of lamentation—invocation, lament, petition—serves to bring before God serious issues concerning suffering and injustice. With thundering "Why?" questions these pray-ers rail against the inequities of life and the God who allows them—or causes them. In this regard I noted that prayers of lament often focus on the problems of theodicy, of God and justice.[38] The task of lament is not simply to complain to God about injustice, but to *move God to be just.* These are prayers offered in the certain conviction that God must stay in the world as a God of justice. As Abraham's question puts it so sharply in Gen 18:25: "Shall not the Judge of all the earth do justice?"

In view of the Hebraic affirmation of lament as a proper and authentic act of faith, I want to issue a summons to the church. I appeal to the church to find a place both in its liturgy and in its ministries for lamentation that keeps God bound to this world of too much suffering and injustice. I do not suggest that lament is the only word to be addressed to God; the legacy of Hebraic praise ought to be sufficient caution against making this mistake. Nor do I suggest that lament is the only response to make to suffering; clearly it is not. I do submit, however, that alongside these other responses to God, lamentation also has a place in the vocabulary of faith. Indeed, I submit that lamentation *will* take place in the life of faith, with or without the church's encouragement or permission. The church then must resolve whether its place is on the sidelines, silent and passive in the face of a world crying out, or whether it will join with the afflicted, even if it means questioning the Judge of the whole world. D. Soelle states the matter bluntly: "In the face of suffering you are either with the victim or the executioner—there is no other option."[39]

I urge the church to side with the victims, with the blind and the crippled, the weak and the vulnerable, with all those who by divine decree must be welcome in the house of prayer. The church does this best when it joins with them in the practice of lamentation, for then the church is most effectively engaged in the ministry of keeping the God of compassion and justice in this world.

In the following pages I sketch out the major advantages and the

38. See pp. 192–98.
39. D. Soelle, *Suffering* (Philadelphia: Fortress, 1975), 32.

major risks of taking seriously the biblical mandate for the ministry of lament. I begin with the advantages.

To Lament is to Question Life and God

To engage in such a practice is to be true to the biblical portrait that defines both God and humanity. On the one hand the Bible acknowledges candidly that God is by definition both present and absent, both near and far away, both actively and discernibly concerned with the affairs of humanity and, on occasion, seemingly disengaged and unresponsive to the human plight. Wherever God is being God, God is this way. God's presence *is* witness to divine intention to reward faithful obedience, as the prophets proclaimed, but fidelity does not guarantee God's presence. This is the hard lesson of the Book of Job. God's hiddenness *does confirm* the indissoluble linkage between sin and punishment. On this truth the entire biblical witness is unequivocal. But the pain and hurt that sunders the soul claims as its victims the just as well as the unjust. This too is the hard lesson of the Book of Job. The present God is the hidden God, and the hidden God is still God. This is the truth of Isaiah's announcement to the exiles in Babylon: "Truly, you are a God who hides himself, O God of Israel, the Savior" (Isa 45:15, NRSV). It is a truth tied inherently to the nature of God, not primarily to the obedient or disobedient nature of humanity. This is the truth claimed for the mysterious "I AM WHO I AM." When the church participates in questioning God, it is simply honoring the biblical portrait of the One whose mysterious ways summon forth with equal passion both the affirmation *'āmēn,* "Amen, may it be so" (cf. Deut 27:15-26), and the anguished cry, *lāmmāh,* "Why?"

On the other hand, the biblical portrait of humanity's questioning spirit is a candid acknowledgment of a basic and persistent characteristic of human consciousness. The human drive to question is a basic tenet of almost every philosophical anthropology from Plato and Aristotle to Heidegger and Lonergan.[40] Wherever man and woman are being fully human, the drive to question and probe and explore and wonder about anything and everything—including God—is relentlessly at work. Like any other human drive, it may be stifled or blunted, evaded or suppressed, by external constraints or internal compulsions. But of itself the drive to question keeps work-

---

40. See, e.g., B. Lonergan, *Insight: A Study of Human Understanding* (New York: Philosophical Library, 1956); M. Heidegger, *Being and Time* (London: SCM, 1962). See further M. Novak, *The Experience of Nothingness* (New York: Harper and Row, 1970), 44–51.

ing toward its own liberation.[41] When the church joins this quest to ask about that which is, it is simply honoring the spirit of those human souls both inside and outside its walls to whom it is commissioned to minister.

RADICAL DIALOGUE

When the church encourages the practice of lament, it promotes an understanding of divine-human communion or partnership where radical dialogue is both normative and productive. True covenant relationship like that which is struck at Sinai involves the mutual participation of two partners. The partnership is clearly between persons of unequal power and authority. God is *the* creator, and God is *the* covenant maker. But in the Hebraic notion of covenant, God is not the only one with power, not the only one having a voice in what is to take place. The human partner also has a say. On occasion the human voice speaks with words of praise and thanksgiving, signaling not only consent to the divine will but also grateful submission. But on those occasions when the hurt and pain of life do not permit a simple "Yes" or a manufactured "Hallelujah," Israel does not retreat into passive silence. On these occasions the dialogue calls for lament and the covenant relationship permits it—indeed, even requires it.[42]

The point here is that covenant relationship, like human relationships, requires communication. The better the communication, the better the relationship, that is, the healthier it is and the more possibilities it has for growth and development. In the same way, restricted communication or, worse, silence reduces the possibilities within the relationship.[43] A divine-human relationship that exchanges praise but not lament is not the covenant partnership that God desires. A relationship of such limited discourse means essentially that God cannot be the God that God wants to be. Without lament *and* praise from the human partner, God's pos-

---

41. Novak, *Experience of Nothingness,* 48–49.

42. Cf. G. Steiner, who recognizes that in Hebraic faith God is capable of all speech acts except that of monologue. In his judgment, however, it is monologue that too often characterizes our own relationship with God (*Real Presences: Is There Anything in What We Say?* [London: Faber and Faber, 1986], 225).

43. For the idea of prayer as interpersonal communication that creates relational closeness or (negatively) relational distance, see T. Fretheim, "Prayer in the Old Testament: Creating Space in the World for God," *A Primer on Prayer,* ed. P. Sponheim (Philadelphia: Fortress, 1988) 51–52. See further idem, "The Color of God: Israel's God-Talk and Life Experience," *Word and World* 6 (1986): 256–65.

sibilities within the relationship are limited in important ways. Consider again the suggestive picture of God standing before Abraham in Genesis 18,[44] awaiting his response before deciding the fate of Sodom and Gomorrah. In short, the practice of lamentation, no less than praise, makes for a healthier relationship for both God and humanity, creating more possibilities for both to develop, for both to address and to resolve issues of mutual concern. As Fretheim has observed, "prayer gives God more room in which to work, makes God more welcome, creates more relational space (less distance) for God."[45]

A MINISTRY OF QUESTIONING

When the church practices the ministry of lament, it proclaims the biblical truth that life is finally open-ended, not settled or closed or bound. Even east of Eden, where limitations and impossibilities seem status quo, change, new beginnings, surprise are possible. Questions are harbingers of change. In the practice of lament the church engages most daringly in the *ministry of questioning.* Whatever the reality of the institutions, the cultural forms, or the sacred dogmas that define life in the present, accurately placed questions can shatter their claim on people.[46] Questions dare to imagine that things can change, that nothing, not even God, is locked into static, unalterable sacredness.[47] In this sense questions always call for recalculation, refiguring, rethinking, imagining that one has more than one way to comprehend and to cope. For the victims of grief and despair, the license to question is the key to hope that something different and better is still possible.

The nature of Hebraic lament is to resist resignation and to press

---

44. Most standard translations adopt a "corrected text" in Gen 18:22, thus "Abraham still stood before the LORD." But the original text, without the *Tiqqun,* is much more intriguing. "The LORD remained standing before Abraham." This uncorrected text allows for the possibility of understanding God as waiting on Abraham, perhaps even inviting discussion or response. In his suggestive commentary on this passage, J. Levenson understands Abraham to exemplify the radical "autonomy of humanity over against God" that Israel's covenant relationship legitimizes (*Creation and the Persistence of Evil: The Jewish Drama of Divine Omnipotence* [San Francisco: Harper and Row, 1988], 149).

45. Fretheim, "Prayer in the Old Testament," 52.

46. Cf. Novak, *Experience of Nothingness,* 14.

47. Cf. P. Berger's description of religion's function as a "sacred canopy" that protects God and God's world from such unsettling questions (*The Sacred Canopy: Elements of a Sociological Theory of Religion* [Garden City, N.Y.: Doubleday, 1969], 81–101). See further my discussion on pp. 139–43.

for change.[48] Where there is lament, there is life, and even in the midst of suffering this life is vital and expectant. When the lament ceases to function and all questions are silenced, then one accepts what is as what will be, in religion, in society, in the political and economic structures of life.

Here the church must recognize that the denial of suffering is not only a spiritual loss. When questions about oppression and suffering are forfeited, questions of social and political justice will also likely be silenced. With the prophets as guide, the church must know itself forever constrained to promote both piety and justice. Words addressed to the heavens in the sanctuary must be shored up with acts of justice on earth. Anything less renders spirituality a ruse and an abomination to God. As Brueggemann has suggested, if there is silence on justice issues in the sanctuary, eventually these issues are muffled outside the sanctuary as well.[49] When the church acquiesces in this silence, it ceases to minister to the suffering. Of greater consequence, when the church strips faith of lament, it proclaims suffering and injustice not only ultimate but final.

ADVOCACY FOR THE VICTIM

Finally, when the church takes seriously the practice of lament, it affirms that in a suffering world God is on the side of the victim. If any word from God is to be spoken in the face of suffering, it must be articulated from the standpoint of the victim, not the onlooker.

The Bible clearly endorses theodicies formulated by onlookers and theorists.[50] The church is right to promulgate these theodicies, right to proclaim that where there is suffering one dare not be complacent about sin and failure. Under the direction of this teaching, humanity's sense of guilt is, and ought to be, deep and persistent.

But the Bible just as clearly recognizes that theological affirmations stand always to be shaken by the primal screams of victims. For victims, lament is the only sound that misery can make. Such cries of anguish also belong in the sanctuary; to put the matter more

---

48. Cf. E. Gerstenberger, "Jeremiah's Complaints: Observations on Jer. 15:10-21," *JBL* 82 (1963): 405 n. 50. See further idem, "Der klagende Mensch," *Probleme biblischer Theologie: Gerhard von Rad zum 70. Geburtstag,* ed. H. W. Wolff (Munich: Chr. Kaiser, 1971), 68–72; idem, *Psalms, Part 1, with an Introduction to Cultic Poetry* (FOTL; Eerdmans, 1988), 11–14.

49. Brueggemann, "Costly Loss," 64.

50. See pp. 189–92.

directly, the church must be sanctuary in the midst of cries of anguish. The danger is that the church will provide sanctuary only for Job's friends, not for Job, and like them will address suffering only as a theodicist, with safely distanced explanations and imperatives. When the church speaks only as an onlooker, it becomes like the persons Joseph Conrad described who "talk with indignation and enthusiasm . . . about oppression, cruelty, crime, devotion, self-sacrifice, virtue, and . . . know nothing real beyond the words. Nobody knows what suffering or sacrifice means—except perhaps the victim."[51]

One may ask, however, if it is really possible for the church to side with the victim. After all, the church is a corporate institution. Perhaps it can respond to suffering humanity only indirectly and theoretically. Perhaps the church's institutional status explains in part why the church has so often assumed the theological high ground in response to the suffering of others. I submit, however, that the church has at its disposal a great reservoir of lament literature that will enable it to bear the scar of the victim without the wound, and to sustain the afflicted without direct experience of the pain.[52] Such ministry will always place the church at the side of Job, where to be faithful to God is to speak pain *with,* if not like, the victim.[53]

These then are some of the reasons why I believe it is important for the church to attend to the ministry of lament.

(1)   In the practice of lament the church makes its clearest affirmation of the biblical portrait of God and humanity. Here humanity's relentless drive to question collides most dramatically with the God who is present and available and at the same time hidden and unresponsive.

51. J. Conrad, "An Outpost of Progress," *Tales of Unrest* (Harmondsworth: Penguin, 1977), 100. Quoted and discussed in K. Surrin, *Theology and the Problem of Evil* (Oxford: Basil Blackwell, 1986), 51–52.

52. Cf. Cohen, *Tremendum,* 2.

53. J. Hick, a major contemporary theodicist, acknowledges the inevitable gap between theory and experience. After formulating his own proposal for an Irenaean type of theodicy, he sympathizes with those who will not find his work satisfactory. On the last page of his book *Evil and the God of Love* (rev. ed.; San Francisco: Harper and Row, 1977), he writes: If I had myself experienced some deep and engulfing personal tragedy, drawing me down into a black despair and a horrified rejection of life, I might well share this negative response. But we believe or disbelieve, ultimately, out of our own experience and must be faithful to the witness of that experience." Perhaps with Hick the church must recognize that even when it chooses to side with the victim, it may not be able to identify completely with the victim. Nobody knows what suffering means except the sufferer. Nevertheless, the church's mandate to stand with the sufferer is clear.

(2) In the practice of lament the divine-human partnership becomes most radically dialogic.

(3) In the ministry of lament the church arms faith with shattering questions that keep hope alive, even in the grips of despair.

(4) In the ministry of lament the church takes its place at the side of the victim, and hence in a suffering world most clearly embodies divine compassion.

RISKS OF QUESTIONING GOD

I do not issue this summons to the church lightly. I am certain that the rewards for attending to the truth of despair are significant and, I hope, compelling. But I do not believe they can be attained without cost. The practice of lament as modeled in Hebrew Scripture is dangerous and risky. Anyone who has ever stood on Job's side of the divine-human encounter will appreciate what is at stake here.

I mention but two of the risks involved that must be faced honestly if the church is to secure the practice of lament as a ministry.

Lament Is Unmanagable

It is the stuff of lament to address God with hard and accusing questions. The biblical witness is that God does not resist such speech; indeed, God takes it seriously, and it is effective. But the biblical record is equally clear that God seldom answers questions, at least not in the way they are asked. Often the dialogue between God and humanity is painfully one-sided. God is expected to hear, believed to be receptive, but when questions end, faith must bear the burden of the silence that follows.

It is just here in this dialogue framed by questions on one side and silence on the other that the practice of lament poses an enormous challenge to the modern church. In a pluralistic society, the church is competing for the allegiance of its parishioners with a variety of nonreligious rivals. Since the church no longer can claim a monopoly on defining the world, it must now market its product with consumer concerns in mind.[54] While scholarship may call for the incorporation of lament into the ministry of the church on historical and theological grounds, market economics may render it irrelevant, perhaps even damaging, for retail distribution. The dilemma that market economics poses for the honest practice of lament, or any other ministry the church might consider, is the ques-

---

54. Cf. Berger's sociological critique of religious traditions as "consumer commodities" (*Sacred Canopy*, 137–53).

tion, Will it sell? In a world where the church can no longer take for granted its authority, how will a product that promotes questions but cannot promise answers vie in the marketplace?

I fear that the church may have already decided this question. When institutional self-preservation becomes the fundamental criterion for selecting which ministries will be offered, the ministry of lament will probably be let go. My own experience suggests that the church feels tremendous pressure to give answers, not questions, and furthermore to market its answers stylishly and fashionably so that they outshine all rival answers. Such religion is engaged in the building of a world without mystery, where questions are either eliminated or painlessly dismissed by slick answers.[55]

I do not believe that market economics are attuned to the deepest yearnings of the human soul, and I do not believe they ought to determine the church's gospel. But lament *is* risky, because it is so unmanageable. Primal screams rarely bother with orthodoxy, and silence is so quiet and unpredictable. Will it lead to renewed speech and fresh faith, or will it be a step further into the black hole of doubt, despair, and cynicism? Through the character Elisha in his book *Dawn*, E. Wiesel asks: "Where does suffering lead? To purification or to bestiality?"[56] I do not consider these as rhetorical questions. The risks of lament are not illusory. Much is to be gained by accepting the risks, as I have tried to indicate, but the costs of such acceptance in terms of faith and trust will be great indeed.

Questioning Alters One's Faith

A second risk for the church inheres in the recognition that questioning is a dangerous act. Questions portend change in the scheme of things. Their tools are curiosity, anxiety, uncertainty, restlessness. With these tools the questioner brings the definitions of everything presented to her or him under review: the real, the true, the good, self, God. Everything can be scrutinized, and the process leaves neither the questioner nor the questioned the same as before.

This drive to question is both creative and destructive. It both builds new worlds and shatters old ones.[57] When questioning leads

---

55. D. J. Hall has offered a penetrating analysis of Christianity as an "answering" religion in an officially optimistic society (*Lighten Our Darkness: Toward an Indigenous Theology of the Cross* [Philadelphia: Westminster, 1976], 73–106). In his view such a society and such a religion collaborate in a joint effort "to build a world in which the tragic is obsolete" (*God and Human Suffering*, 40).

56. E. Wiesel, *Dawn* (New York: Avon, 1970), 24.

57. Cf. Novak, *Experience of Nothingness*, 50.

to changes that are liberating and joyful, it is welcomed as a positive experience, and whatever its cost the result is judged to have been worth the price. Perhaps the clearest illustration of both the power and the product of this dramatic act of questioning is what is happening in eastern Europe. People armed with questions are a force to be reckoned with. Walls fall, regimes are toppled, freedom replaces oppression. The Western world should note that the church provided and sustained the forum for the protest movement in East Germany.

Sustained questioning opens up new possibilities, creates new worlds. It is the principle of revolution and evolution. But questioning is also destructive, and its shattering effect on that which once was defined as necessary, solid, and permanent is not always welcome. When honest questioning leads one to see through the inadequacies of one's sources of stability, disappointment may replace confidence, insecurity certainty, and depression joy.[58]

To put the matter bluntly, it is one thing to applaud the fall of the Berlin Wall, quite another to celebrate the fall of one's convictions about God and self. Are we in the church prepared to risk questions that compel us to understand God differently from our ancestors, differently from the definitions secured in our confessional statements, differently from the affirmations that have provided our identity and sustained our values? Are we willing to rethink God's power, God's compassion, God's justice? Let us not stop short of ultimate questions—Are we willing to rethink the very reality of God?

Again, I do not believe such questions are rhetorical. I do not believe it is honest to pretend that we know already the answers, so that however painful the process of questioning, we may be confident of the ultimate outcome. We must admit that to engage in such questioning is to risk losing one's faith. When one loses faith, where can one turn?

Perhaps the greatest irony of the biblical witness, and perhaps also its most impenetrable legacy of prayer, is that when one loses faith in God, it is precisely to God that one turns. The lament tradition recognizes the risk of falling out of faith and accepts it. In the face of suffering our predecessors in faith risked standing side by side with the atheist, and discovered that they did not become

---

58. Ibid., 50–53.

atheists.[59] Their questions were the same, but their rebellion was different. As a living witness to this tradition, Wiesel writes:

> From inside his community [the Jew] may say anything. Let him step outside it, and he will be denied this right. The revolt of the believer is not that of the renegade; the two do not speak in the name of the same anguish.[60]

Dare we risk this anguish, the truth of this kind of despair? I summon the church to do so. The risk is great, but the cost of not doing so is greater. We must ask ourselves what kind of God and what kind of faith we will be promoting if we do not pray and preach the prayers of Israel.

What if we do not exercise our God-given responsibility as a community of faith? What if we do not pray to keep ourselves and our world in God? What if we do not pray and fight to keep God in the world? I submit that if we do not, either the church will become a den of robbers where thieves congregate to count their loot and hide out from God, or it will become a shining, splendid edifice, pointing to the heavens but counting for nothing on earth. In either case, God is anguished and the world is impoverished.

> I was ready to respond, but no one asked,
>   ready to be found, but no one sought me.
> I said, "Here I am, here I am,"
>   to a nation that did not call on my name. (Isa 65:1)

---

59. For this analogy see M. Marty, *A Cry of Absence: Reflections for the Winter of the Heart* (San Francisco: Harper and Row, 1983), 12.

60. E. Wiesel, *Souls on Fire* (New York: Vintage, 1973), 111.

Index of Modern Authors

Index of Scripture References